BY JOHN MCPHEE

COMING

INTO THE

COUNTRY

———

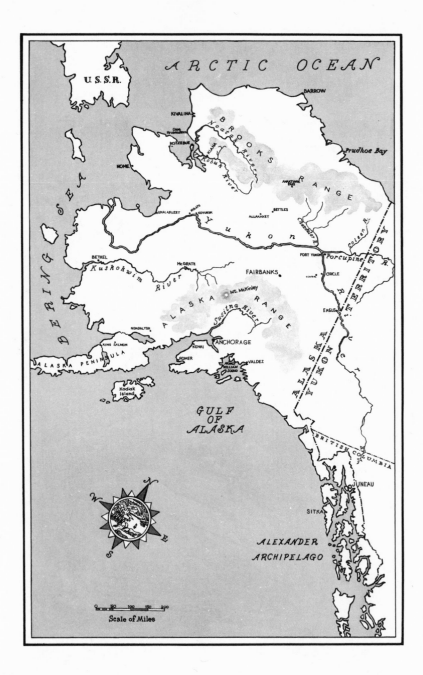

COMING INTO THE COUNTRY

JOHN McPHEE

Farrar, Straus and Giroux

NEW YORK

Library of Congress Cataloging in Publication Data

McPhee, John A.

Coming into the country.

1. Alaska

2. McPhee, John A. I. Title.

F910.M29 1977   917.98′04′50924   77–12249

Maps by Tom Funk

The text of this book originally appeared

in *The New Yorker*,

and was developed with

the editorial counsel of *William Shawn*

and *Robert Bingham*

For Martha

CONTENTS

THE

ENCIRCLED

RIVER

❨ My bandanna is rolled on the diagonal and retains water fairly well. I keep it knotted around my head, and now and again dip it into the river. The water is forty-six degrees. Against the temples, it is refrigerant and relieving. This has done away with the headaches that the sun caused in days before. The Arctic sun—penetrating, intense—seems not so much to shine as to strike. Even the trickles of water that run down my T-shirt feel good. Meanwhile, the river—the clearest, purest water I have ever seen flowing over rocks—breaks the light into flashes and sends them upward into the eyes. The headaches have reminded me of the kind that are sometimes caused by altitude, but, for all the fact that we have come down through mountains, we have not been higher than a few hundred feet above the level of the sea. Drifting now—a canoe, two kayaks—and thanking God it is not my turn in either of the kayaks, I lift my fish rod from the tines of a caribou rack (lashed there in mid-canoe to the duffel) and send a line flying toward a wall of bedrock by the edge of the stream. A grayling comes up and, after some hesitation, takes the lure and runs with it for a time. I disengage the lure and let the grayling go, being mindful not to wipe my hands on my shirt. Several days in use, the shirt is approaching filthy, but here among grizzly bears I would prefer to stink of humanity than of fish.

Paddling again, we move down long pools separated by short white pitches, looking to see whatever might appear in the low hills, in the cottonwood, in the white and black spruce—and in the river, too. Its bed is as distinct as if the water were not there. Everywhere, in fleets, are the oval shapes of salmon. They have moved the gravel and made redds, spawning craters, feet in diameter. They ignore the boats, but at times, and without apparent reason, they turn and shoot downriver, as if they have felt panic and have lost their resolve to get on with their loving and their dying. Some, already dead, lie whitening, grotesque, on the bottom, their bodies disassembling in the current. In a short time, not much will be left but the hooking jaws. Through the surface, meanwhile, the living salmon broach, freshen—make long, dolphinesque flights through the air—then fall to slap the water, to resume formation in the river, noses north, into the current. Looking over the side of the canoe is like staring down into a sky full of zeppelins.

A cloud, all black and silver, crosses the sun. I put on a wool shirt. In Alaska, where waters flow in many places without the questionable benefit of names, there are nineteen streams called Salmon—thirteen Salmon Creeks, six Salmon Rivers— of which this one, the Salmon River of the Brooks Range, is the most northern, its watershed wholly above the Arctic Circle. Rising in treeless alpine tundra, it falls south into the fringes of the boreal forest, the taiga, the upper limit of the Great North Woods. Tree lines tend to be digital here, fingering into protected valleys. Plants and animals are living on margin, in cycles that are always vulnerable to change. It is five o'clock in the afternoon. The cloud, moving on, reveals the sun again, and I take off the wool shirt. The sun has been up fourteen hours, and has hours to go before it sets. It seems to be rolling slowly down a slightly inclined plane. A tributary, the Kitlik, comes in from the northwest. It has formed with the

Salmon River a raised, flat sand-and-gravel mesopotamia—a good enough campsite, and, as a glance can tell, a fishing site to exaggerate the requirements of dinner.

There are five of us, four of whom are a state-federal study team. The subject of the study is the river. We pitch the tents side by side, two Alpine Draw-Tite tents, and gather and saw firewood: balsam poplar (more often called cottonwood); sticks of willow and alder; a whole young spruce, tip to root, dry now, torn free upriver by the ice of the breakup in spring. Tracks are numerous, coming, going, multidirectional, tracks wherever there is sand, and in gravel if it is fine enough to have taken an impression. Wolf tracks. The pointed pods of moose tracks. Tracks of the barren-ground grizzly. Some of the moose tracks are punctuated with dewclaws. The grizzlies' big toes are on the outside.

The Kitlik, narrow, and clear as the Salmon, rushes in white to the larger river, and at the confluence is a pool that could be measured in fathoms. Two, anyway. With that depth, the water is apple green, and no less transparent. Salmon and grayling, distinct and dark, move into, out of, around the pool. Many grayling rest at the bottom. There is a pair of intimate salmon, the male circling her, circling, an endless attention of rings. Leaning over, watching, we nearly fall in. The gravel is loose at the river's edge. In it is a large and recently gouged excavation, a fresh pit, close by the water. It was apparently made in a thrashing hurry. I imagine that a bear was watching the fish and got stirred up by the thought of grabbing one, but the water was too deep. Excited, lunging, the bear fell into the pool, and it flailed back at the soft gravel, gouging the pit while trying to get enough of a purchase to haul itself out. Who can say? Whatever the story may be, the pit is the sign that is trying to tell it.

It is our turn now to fish in the deep pool. We are having grayling for dinner—Arctic grayling of firm delicious flesh. On their skins are black flecks against a field of silvery iridescence.

Their dorsal fins fan up to such height that grayling are scale-model sailfish. In the cycles of the years, and the millennia, not many people have fished this river. Forest Eskimos have long seined at its mouth, but only to the third bend upstream. Eskimo hunters and woodcutters, traversing the Salmon valley, feed themselves, in part, with grayling. In all, perhaps a dozen outsiders, so far as is known, have travelled, as we have, in boats down the length of the river. Hence the grayling here have hardly been, in the vernacular of angling, fished out. Over the centuries, they have scarcely been fished. The fire is high now and is rapidly making coals. Nineteen inches is about as long as a grayling will grow in north Alaska, so we agree to return to the river anything much smaller than that. As we do routinely, we take a count of the number needed—see who will share and who can manage on his own the two or three pounds of an entire fish. Dinner from our supplies will come in hot plastic water bags and be some form of desiccated mail-order stew—Mountain House Freeze Dried Caribou Cud—followed by Mountain House Freeze Dried fruit. Everyone wants a whole fish.

Five, then. Three of us pick up rods and address the river —Bob Fedeler, Stell Newman, and I. Pat Pourchot, of the federal Bureau of Outdoor Recreation, has not yet cast a line during the trip. As he puts it, he is phasing himself out of fishing. In his work, he makes many river trips. There will always be people along who want to fish, he reasons, and by removing himself he reduces the number. He has wearied of take-and-put fishing, of molesting the fish, of shocking the ones that, for one reason or another, go back. He says he wonders what kind of day a fish will have after spending some time on a hook. John Kauffmann has largely ignored the fishing, too. A National Park Service planner who has been working for five years in Arctic Alaska, he is a New England mastertouch dry-fly fisherman, and up here his bamboo ballet is regarded as effete. Others taunt him. He will not rise. But neither will the grayling

to his Black Gnats, his Dark Cahills, his Quill Gordons. So—
tall, angular—he sits and observes, and his short gray beard
conceals his disgust. He does agree to time the event. He looks
at his watch. Invisible lines, glittering lures go spinning to the
river, sink in the pool. The rods bend. Grayling do not sulk, like
the salmon. They hit and go. In nine minutes, we have our five.
They are seventeen, eighteen inches long. We clean them in
the Kitlik, with care that all the waste is taken by the stream.
We have a grill with us, and our method with grayling is simply
to set them, unscaled, fins intact, over the fire and broil them
like steaks. In minutes, they are ready, and beneath their skins
is a brown-streaked white flesh that is in no way inferior to the
meat of trout. The sail, the dorsal fin, is an age-old remedy for
toothache. Chew the fin and the pain subsides. No one has a
toothache. The fins go into the fire.

When a lure falls into the water, it can become arrested at
the bottom, and you tug and haul at the line and walk in an
arc, whipping the rod, four-lettering the apparent snag that has
spoiled the cast and is stealing your equipment. Tug some
more. Possibly a small boulder or a sunken log has stopped the
lure. Possibly not, too. You may have a pensive salmon. He
contemplates. He is not yet ready to present his response. Not
long before this river trip, I was fishing in lake-and-stream
country northwest of Anchorage and the line became snagged
in a way that to me suggested big things below. When I
tugged, there was a slight movement at the other end, a gesture
in my direction, the signal—obviously—of an irritated salmon
getting ready to explode. I strained the line. It moved a bit
more in my direction. A couple of minutes later, I landed a
Safeway Stores Cragmont orange-soda can, full of silt and sand.

Over the fire now, I tell that story, and Bob Fedeler responds
that that country near Anchorage, where many people have
summer cottages, has long since been virtually fished out and
is now supplied with stocked rainbows from a state hatchery.
"That is the myth of Alaska," he says. "The myth is that in

Alaska there's a fish on every cast, a moose behind every tree.
But the fish and the moose aren't there. People go out with
high expectations, and they're disappointed. To get to the
headwaters of a river like this one takes a lot of money. The
state needs to look to the budgets and desires of people who
cannot afford to come to a place like this."

John Kauffmann, sitting on the ground and leaning against
his duffel, shifts his weight uncomfortably. "You can charter
a lot of aircraft time for the cost of summer cabins and Win-
nebagos," he says, and he bangs his pipe on a rock.

Fedeler shrugs. He scratches his cheek, which is under a mat
of russet beard. He is compact, sturdy, not particularly tall,
with a wide forehead and intelligent brown eyes. He would
resemble Sigmund Freud, if Sigmund Freud had been a prospector. Fedeler says that he and his wife, Lyn, almost left
Alaska during their first year, because they saw so little, and
could afford so little, of the outdoors, of the wild—let alone of
wildlife. In 1972, he took an advanced degree from South
Dakota State and straightaway headed for Alaska. To support
themselves, he and Lyn found jobs in Anchorage. He worked
at McMahan's Furniture. He is a wildlife biologist. The state
work he sought was given preferentially to people who had
been resident in Alaska for at least a year. Meanwhile, in
Anchorage—a city sealed away by water and mountains, a city
that would be right at home at the west end of the George
Washington Bridge—he had to go to the movies to see anything wild. He did not have the hundred dollars an hour
needed for air charter. He did not have a hundred dollars. He
knew the wilderness was out there—several hundred million
acres of it—but he lacked the means to get to it, and his soul
began to stale. Fortunately, he stuck out the wait, went on
shoving McMahan's furniture around. At last, he got the work
he wanted, his present job as a wildlife biologist with the Alaska
Department of Fish and Game, based in Fairbanks.

Pat Pourchot, of Anchorage, puts in that he finds plenty to

do near home. He climbs cliffs. He kayaks on fast white rivers.

Stories emerge about others like Fedeler—for example, a young man I know from Arkansas, who came to Alaska a year and a half ago specifically to fish and hunt. Where he could afford to go he found no fish and nothing much to hunt. He drove a cab in Anchorage until he couldn't stand it anymore. Taking a two-month vacation, he went home to Mountain Home. Then he came back to Alaska and his taxi. "It was the prettiest spring I've ever seen," he reported. "The dogwoods and redbuds blossomed and they just stayed and stayed. I got all the fishing I wanted, in Arkansas. You need the bucks for the good hunting and fishing up here. Fishing is supposed to be, you know, so out of sight here. It really *is* out of sight for me. I haven't made the bucks."

People from outside write and say to friends in Alaska that they want to come stay with them and fish. "Fine," says the return letter, "but you'll have to charter. Air charter." "No," says the next letter. "We just want to stay at your place and fish from there." Urban Alaskans shake their heads at such foolishness and say, typically, "These people in the Lower Forty-eight, they don't understand."

Something in the general drift now has John Kauffmann on his feet and off to the river. He assembles his trout rod, threads its eyes. Six feet three, spare, he walks, in his determination, tilted forward, ten degrees from vertical, jaws clamped. He seems to be seeking reassurance from the river. He seems not so much to want to catch what may become the last grayling in Arctic Alaska as to certify that it is there. With his bamboo rod, his lofted line, he now describes long drape folds in the air above the river. His shirt is old and red. There are holes in his felt hat and strips of spare rawhide around its crown. He agitates the settled fly. Nothing. Again he waves the line. He drops its passenger on the edge of fast water at the far side of the pool. There is a vacuum-implosive sound, a touch of violence at the surface of the river. We cheer. For two minutes, we wait it out while Kauffmann plays his fish. Adroitly, gingerly, he brings it in. With care, he picks it up. He then looks at us as if he is about to throw his tin star in the dust at our feet. Shame—for our triple-hooked lures, our nylon hawsers, our consequent stories of fished-out streams. He looks at his grayling. It is a twenty-five-ounce midget, but it will grow. He seems to feel reassured. He removes the fly, which has scarcely nicked the fish's lips. He slips the grayling back to the stream.

Grayling are particularly fast swimmers. In Arctic Alaska, where small rivers like this one for the most part freeze solid, grayling can move big distances rapidly to seek out safe deep holes for winter. They are veterans of runs for life. They are indices, too, of the qualities of a stream. They seek out fast, cold, clear water. So do trout, of course, but grayling have higher standards. Trout will settle for subperfect waters in which grayling will refuse to live.

The sun, which two hours ago was behind the apex of a spruce across the Kitlik, is now far to the right of that and somewhat closer to the ground. All day, while the sun describes a horseshoe around the margins of the sky, the light is of the rich kind that in more southern places comes at evening, heightening walls and shadowing eaves, bringing out of things the beauty of relief. It is ten-thirty, and about time for bed. Everything burnable—and more, too—has long since gone into the fire. We burn our plastic freeze-dry bags and we burn our Swiss Miss cocoa packets. If we have cans—devilled ham, Spam—we burn them, until all hint of their contents is gone. This is in part tidiness. Everything the fire does not consume is later put into bags that will go with us all the way through and out of these tens of thousands of square miles of wilderness. Nothing is buried. Also, the burning of the cans is an expression of regard for bears. The scent of the food is scorched away. It is not necessary for us to string up our meat high in the air. What meat we have is either dried or canned, and is presumably without odor. I can think of places where all these

foil-lined packets and plastic containers might be an affront to
the woods, but in Alaska their advantage is great. They are a
way to move through bear country without drawing bears.
More accurately, I should say "without in all likelihood drawing bears." Unopened cans of sardines have been found in the
scat of grizzlies.

Bear stories, for a time, traverse the campfire. John Kauffmann remembers when Ave Thayer, the refuge manager of the
Arctic National Wildlife Range, surprised a grizzly one day and
when the bear charged stood his ground. In a low voice, Thayer
said, "Shoo!" The grizzly stopped short. The two faced each
other ten feet apart, neither making a move. Thayer cautiously
stepped backward. The grizzly slowly advanced. Thayer said,
"Shoo!" The grizzly stopped. Thayer walked backward, with
no sudden starts. The grizzly followed. In such manner, Thayer
walked backward about two hundred yards. Then the grizzly
moved off a distance and walked parallel to him all the way—
a mile or so—to his camp, where it lost interest and turned
away.

Fedeler makes the point that grizzlies in general will avoid
people and people should avoid them, by not foolishly getting
in their way—by not, for example, pitching a tent on a bear
trail. Once, not long ago, a writer visiting Alaska pitched his
tent on a trail. A bear removed the writer from the tent,
ate him, and left nothing much but the pencil.

"All right, that's enough!" decrees Pat Pourchot, official
leader of the trip. "No more bear stories. It is never a good idea
to tell bear stories at night. I've known people to wake up
screaming in their sleeping bags."

As it happens, there is behind the tents a dry channel, a
braid of the river when the river is in flood, and now a kind
of corridor that comes through the woods and past the tents
to the river. Tracks suggest that it is something of a trail. I am
mildly nervous about that, but then I am mildly nervous about
a lot of things. We get into the tents and zip them up. Mos-

quitoes, while not overwhelming, are much around. We slap
a few inside, and prepare for sleep. In moments, nearly everyone else is snoring. I look up through the mesh of the tent
window past spruce boughs and into the sky. Twilight sky. The
sun is down. It is falling nine minutes earlier per day. In three
months, it will have ceased to rise. Now, though, in the dead
of night, the sky is too bright for stars. I cannot quite read by
the light at two.

⟨ 7 A.M., and the water temperature is forty-four, the air fifty-
six, the sky blue and clear—an Indian-summer morning, August 18, 1975. Pourchot, after breakfast, goes off to measure
the largest of the spruce near the campsite. He finds a tree
twenty-two inches in diameter, breast high. Most of the spruce
in this country look like pipe cleaners. The better ones look like
bottle washers. Tough they may be, but they are on the edge
of their world, and their trunks can grow fifty years and be
scarcely an inch through. Yet here is a stand of trees a foot
thick. A specimen nearly two. Pourchot says he will write in his
report that there is *one* tree of such girth. "Otherwise, the
Forest Service might think there's timber here."

Two of our boats—the kayaks—are German. They can be
taken apart and put back together. They were invented long
ago by someone known as the Mad Tailor of Rosenheim. The
Mad Tailor, at the turn of the century, was famous for his
mountain-climbing knickers and loden capes. It was in 1907
that he went into naval architecture on a diminutive scale.
Every major valley in Bavaria had a railroad running through
it. The forests were laced with small white rivers. It was all but
impossible to get boats to them, because boats were too bulky
to accompany travellers on trains. Wouldn't it be *phantastisch,*
thought the tailor, if a boat could fit into a handbag, if a

suitcase could turn into a kayak? His name was Johann Klepper. He designed a collapsible kayak with a canvas skin and a frame of separable hardwood parts. In subsequent manufacture, the boat became an international success. Klepper might have stopped there. Not long after the First World War, he designed a larger version, its spray cover apertured with two holes. Where the original boat had been made for a single paddler, this one was intended for a team. We have with us a single and a double Klepper. The smaller one is prompt, responsive, feathery on the stream. The double one is somewhat less maneuverable than a three-ton log. Stell Newman, of the National Park Service, began calling it Snake Eyes, and everyone has picked up the name. Snake Eyes is our *bateau noir,* our Charonian ferry, our *Höllenfahrt.* Throughout the day, we heap opprobrium on Snake Eyes.

Pourchot and I have the double Klepper this morning. The ratio of expended energy to developed momentum is seventy-five to one. This is in part because the bottom of Snake Eyes at times intersects the bottom of the river, which is shallow at many of the riffles. The hull has become so abraded in places that it has developed leaks. The Grumman canoe is wider, longer, more heavily loaded. It carries at least half of all our gear. Nonetheless, it rides higher, draws less water, than Snake Eyes. Fortunately, the pools are extensive here in the lower river, and are generally a little deeper than a paddle will reach. Pockets are much deeper than that. Miles slide behind us. A salmon, sensing the inferiority of Snake Eyes, leaps into the air beside it, leaps again, leaps again, ten pounds of fish jumping five times high into the air—a bravado demonstration, a territorial declaration. This is, after all, the salmon's eponymous river. The jumper moves on, among its kind, ignoring the dying. These—their spawning done—idly, sleepily yield to the current, their gestures slow and quiet, a peaceful drifting away.

We have moved completely out of the hills now, and beyond the riverine fringes of spruce and cottonwood are boggy flat-

lands and thaw lakes. We see spruce that have been chewed
by porcupines and cottonwood chewed by beavers. Moose tend
to congregate down here on the tundra plain. In late fall, some
of the caribou that migrate through the Salmon valley will stop
here and make this their winter range. We see a pair of loons,
and lesser Canada geese, and chick mergansers with their
mother. Mink, marten, muskrat, otter—creatures that live
here inhabit the North Woods across the world to Maine. We
pass a small waterfall under a patterned bluff—folded striations
of schist. In bends of the river now we come upon banks of
flood-eroded soil—of mud. They imply an earth mantle of
some depth going back who knows how far from the river.
Brown and glistening, they are virtually identical with rural
stream banks in the eastern half of the country, with the
difference that the water flowing past these is clear. In the
sixteenth century, the streams of eastern America ran clear
(except in flood), but after people began taking the vegetation
off the soil mantle and then leaving their fields fallow when
crops were not there, rain carried the soil into the streams. The
process continues, and when one looks at such streams today,
in their seasonal varieties of chocolate, their distant past is—
even to the imagination—completely lost. For this Alaskan
river, on the other hand, the sixteenth century has not yet
ended, nor the fifteenth, nor the fifth. The river flows, as it has
since immemorial time, in balance with itself. The river and
every rill that feeds it are in an unmodified natural state—
opaque in flood, ordinarily clear, with levels that change within
a closed cycle of the year and of the years. The river cycle is
only one of many hundreds of cycles—biological, meteorologi-
cal—that coincide and blend here in the absence of intruding
artifice. Past to present, present reflecting past, the cycles com-
pose this segment of the earth. It is not static, so it cannot be
styled "pristine," except in the special sense that while human
beings have hunted, fished, and gathered wild food in this
valley in small groups for centuries, they have not yet begun

to change it. Such a description will fit many rivers in Alaska. This one, though, with its considerable beauty and a geography that places it partly within and partly beyond the extreme reach of the boreal forest, has been thought of as sufficiently splendid to become a national wild river—to be set aside with its immediate environs as unalterable wild terrain. Kauffmann, Newman, Fedeler, and Pourchot are, in their various ways, studying that possibility. The wild-river proposal, which Congress is scheduled to act upon before the end of 1978, is something of a box within a box, for it is entirely incorporated within a proposed national monument that would include not only the entire Salmon River drainage but also a large segment of the valley of the Kobuk River, of which the Salmon is a tributary. (In the blue haze of Interior Department terminology, "national monument" often enough describes certain large bodies of preserved land that in all respects except name are national parks.) The Kobuk Valley National Monument proposal, which includes nearly two million acres, is, in area, relatively modest among ten other pieces of Alaska that are similarly projected for confirmation by Congress as new parks and monuments. In all, these lands constitute over thirty-two million acres, which is more than all the Yosemites, all the Yellowstones, all the Grand Canyons and Sequoias put together—a total that would more than double the present size of the National Park System. For cartographic perspective, thirty-two million acres slightly exceeds the area of the state of New York.

Impressive as that may seem, it is less than a tenth of Alaska, which consists of three hundred and seventy-five million acres. From the Alaska Purchase, in 1867, to the Alaska Statehood Act, of 1958, Alaskan land was almost wholly federal. It was open to homesteading and other forms of private acquisition, but—all communities included—less than half of one per cent actually passed to private hands. In the Statehood Act, the national government promised to transfer to state ownership a hundred and three million acres, or a little more than a quarter of Alaska. Such an area, size of California, was deemed sufficient for the needs of the population as it was then and as it might be throughout the guessable future. The generosity of this apportionment can be measured beside the fact that the 1958 population of Alaska—all natives included—was virtually the same as the population of Sacramento. Even now, after the influx of new people that followed statehood and has attended the building of the Trans-Alaska Pipeline and the supposed oil-based bonanza, there are fewer people in all Alaska than there are in San Jose. The central paradox of Alaska is that it is as small as it is large—an immense landscape with so few people in it that language is stretched to call it a frontier, let alone a state. There are four hundred thousand people in Alaska, roughly half of whom live in or around Anchorage. To the point of picayunity, the state's road system is limited. A sense of the contemporary appearance of Alaska virtually requires inspection, because the civilized imagination cannot cover such quantities of wild land. Imagine, anyway, going from New York to Chicago—or, more accurately, from the one position to the other—in the year 1500. Such journeys, no less wild, are possible, and then some, over mountains, through forests, down the streams of Alaska. Alaska is a fifth as large as the contiguous forty-eight states. The question now is, what is to be the fate of all this land? It is anything but a "frozen waste." It is green nearly half the year. As never before, it has caught the attention of conflicting interests (developers, preservers, others), and events of the nineteen-seventies are accelerating the arrival of the answer to that question.

For a time, in the nineteen-sixties, the natives of Alaska succeeded in paralyzing the matter altogether. Eskimos, Indians, and Aleuts, in coordination, pressed a claim that had been largely ignored when the Statehood Act was passed. Observing while a hundred and three million acres were legislatively prepared for a change of ownership, watching as exploration geologists came in and found the treasure of Arabia under the Arctic tundra, the natives proffered the point that their immemorial occupancy gave them special claim to Alaskan land. They engaged attorneys. They found sympathy in the federal courts and at the highest levels of the Department of the Interior. The result was that the government offered handsome compensations. Alaska has only about sixty thousand natives. They settled for a billion dollars and forty million acres of land.

The legislation that accomplished this (and a great deal more) was the Alaska Native Claims Settlement Act, of 1971. Among events of significance in the history of Alaska, this one probably stands even higher than the Statehood Act and the treaty of purchase, for it not only changed forever the status and much of the structure of native societies; it opened the way to the Trans-Alaska Pipeline, which is only the first of many big-scale projects envisioned by development-minded Alaskans, and, like a jewel cutter's chisel cleaving a rough diamond, it effected the wholesale division, subdivision, patenting, parcelling, and deeding out of physiographic Alaska.

Because conservationists were outraged by the prospective pipeline, Congress attempted to restore a balance by including in the Native Claims Settlement Act extensive conservation provisions. The most notable of these was a paragraph that instructed the Secretary of the Interior to choose land of sufficient interest to its national owners, the people of the United States, to be worthy of preservation not only as national parks and national wild rivers but also as national wildlife refuges and national forests—some eighty million acres in all. Choices would be difficult, since a high proportion of Alaska could answer the purpose. In the Department of the Interior, an Alaska Planning Group was formed, and various agencies began proposing the lands, lakes, and rivers they would like to have, everywhere—from the Malaspina Glacier to Cape Krusenstern, from the Porcupine drainage to the Aniakchak Caldera.

Congress gave the agencies—gave the Secretary of the Interior—up to seven years to study and to present the case for each selection among these national-interest lands. Personnel began moving north. Pat Pourchot, for example, just out of college, had taken the Civil Service examination and then had wandered around the Denver Federal Center looking for work. He had nothing much in mind and was ready for almost any kind of job that might be offered. He happened into the Bureau of Outdoor Recreation. Before long, he was descending Alaskan rivers. He had almost no experience with canoes or kayaks or with backpacking or camping, but he learned swiftly. John Kauffmann (a friend of mine of many years) had been planning new Park System components, such as the C.&O. Canal National Historical Park and the Cape Cod National Seashore. Transferring to Alaska, he built a house in Anchorage, and soon cornered as his special province eight and a third million acres of the central Brooks Range. When confirmed by Congress, the area will become Gates of the Arctic National Park. It is a couple of hundred miles wide, and is east of the Salmon River. For five years, he has walked it, flown it, canoed its rivers —camped in many weathers below its adze-like rising peaks. Before he came up here, he was much in the wild (he has been a ranger in various places and is the author of a book on eastern American rivers), but nonetheless he was a blue-blazer sort of man, who could blend into the tussocks at the Metropolitan Club. Unimaginable, looking at him now. If he were to take off his shirt and shake it, the dismembered corpses of vintage mosquitoes would fall to the ground. Tall and slim in the first place, he is now spare. After staring so long at the sharp, flinty peaks of the central Brooks Range, he has come to look much like them. His physiognomy, in sun and wind, has become, more or less, grizzly. Any bear that took a bite of John Kauffmann would be most unlikely to complete the meal.

Now, resting on a gravel island not far from the confluence of the Salmon and the Kobuk, he says he surely hopes

Congress will not forget its promises about the national-interest lands. Some conservationists, remaining bitter about the pipeline, tend to see the park and refuge proposals as a sop written into the Native Claims Settlement Act to hush the noisome ecomorphs. Those who would develop the state for its economic worth got something they much wanted with their eight hundred miles of pipe. In return, the environmentalists were given a hundred and thirty words on paper. All the paragraph provided, however, was that eighty million acres could be temporarily set aside and studied. There was no guarantee of preservation to follow. The Wilderness Society, Friends of the Earth, the Sierra Club, the National Audubon Society, and other conservation organizations have formed the Alaska Coalition to remind Congress of its promise, of its moral obligation, lest the proposed park and refuge boundaries slowly fade from the map.

The temperature is in the low seventies. Lunch is spread out on the ground. We have our usual Sailor Boy Pilot Bread (heavy biscuits, baked in Tacoma), peanut butter, jam, and a processed cheese that comes out of a tube—artifacts of the greater society, trekked above the Arctic Circle. Other, larger artifacts may be coming soon. The road that has been cut beside the Trans-Alaska Pipeline will eventually be opened to the public. Then, for the first time in human history, it will be possible to drive a Winnebago—or, for that matter, a Fleetwood Cadillac—from Miami Beach to the Arctic Ocean. Inevitably, the new north road will develop branches. One projected branch will run westward from the pipeline to Kotzebue and Kivalina, on the Chukchi Sea. The road alignment, which Congress could deflect in the name of the national-interest lands, happens to cross the Salmon River right here, where we are having lunch. We are two hundred and fifty miles from the pipeline. We are three hundred and fifty miles from the nearest highway. Yet here in the tundra plain, and embedded in this transparent river, will stand perhaps, before long, the piers of a considerable bridge. I squeeze out the last of the cheese. It emerges from the tube like fluted icing.

There is little left of the river, and we cover it quickly—the canoe and the single kayak bobbing lightly, Snake Eyes riding low, its deck almost at water level. The meanders expand and the country begins to open. At the wide mouth of the Salmon, the gravel bottom is so shallow that we get out and drag Snake Eyes. We have come down through mountains, and we have more recently been immured between incised stream banks in the lower plain, and now we walk out onto a wide pebble beach on the edge of a tremendous river. Gulfs of space reach to horizon mountains. We can now see, far to the northeast, the higher, more central Brooks Range, blurred and blue and soft brown under white compiled flat-bottomed clouds. There are mountains south of us, mountains, of course, behind us. The river, running two full miles to the nearest upstream bend, appears to be a lake. Mergansers are cruising it. The Kobuk is, in places, wide, like the Yukon, but its current is slower and has nothing of the Yukon's impelling, sucking rush. The Yukon, like any number of Alaskan rivers, is opaque with pulverized rock, glacial powder. In a canoe in such a river, you can hear the grains of mountains like sandpaper on the hull. Glaciers are where the precipitation is sufficient to feed them. Two hundred inches will fall in parts of southern Alaska, and that is where the big Alaskan glaciers are. Up here, annual precipitation can be as low as fifteen inches. Many deserts get more water from the sky. The Arctic ground conserves its precipitation, however—holds it frozen half the year. So this is not a desert. Bob Fedeler, whose work with Alaska Fish and Game has taken him to rivers in much of the state, is surprised by the appearance of the Kobuk. "It is amazing to see so much clear water," he says. "In a system as vast as this one, there is usually a glacial tributary or two, and that mucks up the river."

Standing on the shore, Fedeler snaps his wrist and sends a

big enamelled spoon lure, striped like a barber pole, flying over the water. Not long after it splashes, he becomes involved in a struggle with something more than a grayling. The fish sulks a little. For the most part, though, it moves. It makes runs upriver, downriver. It dashes suddenly in the direction of the tension on the line. His arms now oscillating, now steady, Fedeler keeps the line taut, keeps an equilibrium between himself and the fish, until eventually it flops on the dry gravel at his feet. It is a nine-pound salmon, the beginnings of dinner. Stell Newman catches another salmon, of about the same size. I catch one, a seven-pound adolescent, and let it go. Pat Pourchot, whose philosophical abstinence from fishing has until now been consistent, is suddenly aflush with temptation. Something like a hundred thousand salmon will come up the Kobuk in a summer. (They are counted by techniques of aerial survey.) The Kobuk is three hundred miles long and has at least fifty considerable tributaries—fifty branching streams to which salmon could be returning to spawn—and yet when they have come up the Kobuk to this point, to the mouth of the Salmon River, thirty thousand salmon turn left. As school after school arrives here, they pause, hover, reconnoitre—prepare for the run in the home stream. The riffles we see offshore are not rapids but salmon. Pourchot can stand it no longer. He may have phased himself out of fishing, but he is about to phase himself back in. Atavistic instincts take him over. His noble resolve collapses in the presence of this surge of fish.

He borrows Fedeler's rod and sends the lure on its way. He reels. Nothing. He casts again. He reels. Nothing. Out in the river, there may be less water than salmon, but that is no guarantee that one will strike. Salmon do not feed on the spawning run. They apparently bite only by instinctive reflex if something flashes close before them. Pourchot casts again. Nothing. He casts again. The lure this time stops in the river as if it were encased in cement. Could be a boulder. Could be a submerged log. The lure seems irretrievably snagged—until the river erupts. Pourchot is a big man with a flowing red beard. He is well over six feet. Blond hair tumbles across his shoulders. The muscles in his arms are strong from many hundreds of miles of paddling. This salmon, nonetheless, is dragging him up the beach. The fish leaps into the air, thrashes at the river surface, and makes charging runs of such thrust that Pourchot has no choice but to follow or break the line. He follows—fifty, seventy-five yards down the river with the salmon. The fish now changes plan and goes upstream. Pourchot follows. The struggle lasts thirty minutes, and the energy drawn away is almost half Pourchot's. He wins, though, because he is bigger. The fish is scarcely larger than his leg. When, finally, it moves out of the water and onto the gravel, it has no hook in its mouth. It has been snagged, inadvertently, in the dorsal fin. Alaska law forbids keeping any sport fish caught in that way. The salmon must take the lure in its mouth. Pourchot extracts the hook, gently lifts the big fish in his arms, and walks into the river. He will hold the salmon right side up in the water until he is certain that its shock has passed and that it has regained its faculties. Otherwise, it might turn bottom up and drown.

If that were my fish, I would be inclined to keep it, but such a thought would never cross Pourchot's mind. Moreover, one can hardly borrow the rod of a representative of the Alaska Department of Fish and Game, snag a salmon while he watches, and stuff it in a bag. Fedeler, for his part, says he guesses that ninety-five per cent of salmon caught that way are kept. Pourchot removes his hands. The salmon swims away.

Forest Eskimos, who live in five small villages on the Kobuk, do not tend to think in landscape terms that are large. They see a river not as an entity but as a pageant of parts, and every bend and eddy has a name. This place, for example—this junction of rivers—is Qalugruich paanga, which, tightly translated, means "salmon mouth." For thousands of years, to extents that have varied with cycles of plenty, the woodland Eskimos have fished here. The wall tent of an Eskimo fish

camp—apparently, for the time being, empty—stands a mile
or so downstream. We find .30–'06 cartridge cases sprinkled all
over the beach, and a G.I. can opener of the type that comes
with C rations. With the exception of some old stumps—of
trees that were felled, we imagined, by a hunting party cutting
firewood—we saw along the Salmon River no evidence whatever of the existence of the human race. Now we have crossed
into the outermost band of civilization—suggested by a tent,
by some cartridge cases, by a can opener. In the five Kobuk
River villages—Noorvik, Kiana, Ambler, Shungnak, and Kobuk
—live an aggregate of scarcely a thousand people. Kiana, the
nearest village to us, is forty miles downstream. In recent years,
caribou and salmon have been plentiful nearer home, and the
people of Kiana have not needed to come this far to fish, else
we might have found the broad gravel beach here covered with
drying racks—salmon, split and splayed, hanging from the
drying racks—and people seining for the fish going by.

We get back into the boats, shove off, and begin the run
down the Kobuk. Paddling on a big lake is much the same. You
fix your eye on a point two miles away and watch it until it puts
you to sleep. The river bottom, nearly as distinct as the
Salmon's, is no less absorbing. It is gravelled, and lightly covered with silt. In shallow places, salmon leave trails in the silt,
like lines made by fingers in dust. Eskimos know that one
school of salmon will follow the trails of another. In shallow
bends of the river, fishing camps are set up beside the trails.
"We must have fish to live," the people say; and they use every
part of the salmon. They eat the eggs with bearberries. They
roast, smoke, fry, boil, or dry the flesh. They bury the heads in
leaf-lined pits and leave them for weeks. The result is a delicacy
reminiscent of cheese. Fevers and colds are sometimes treated
by placing fermented salmon on the skin of the neck and nose.
A family might use as many as a thousand salmon a year. To
feed dogs, many salmon are needed. Dogs eat whole fish, and
they clean up the fins, intestines, and bones of the fish eaten

by people. Dog teams have largely been replaced by snowmobiles (or snow machines, as they are almost universally called
in Alaska), and, as a result, the salmon harvest at first declined.
Snow machines, however—for all their breathtaking ability to
go as fast as fifty miles an hour over roadless terrain—break
down now and again, and are thus perilous. A stranded traveller
cannot eat a snow machine. Dog teams in the region are
increasing in number, and the take of salmon is growing as well.

Now, for the first time in days of river travel, we hear the
sound of an engine. A boat rounds a bend from the west and
comes into view—a plywood skiff, two women and a man, no
doubt on their way from Kiana to Ambler. A thirty-five-horse-
power Evinrude shoves them upcurrent. They wave and go by.
There are a few kayaks in the villages, small ones for use in
stream and lake hunting, but the only kayaks we are at all likely
to see are the one-man Klepper and Snake Eyes.

Four miles from Qalugruich paanga, it is five in the day and
time to quit. We are, after all, officially an extension of bureaucracy. Walking far back from the water, Kauffmann picks
tent sites on beds of sedge. A big cottonwood log, half buried
in sand, will be a bench by the fire. Mosquitoes swarm. They
are not particularly bad. In this part of Alaska, nearer the coast,
they sometimes fly in dense, whirling vertical columns, dark as
the trunks of trees. But we have not seen such concentrations.
Kauffmann talks of killing forty at a slap in the Gates of the
Arctic, but the season is late now and their numbers are low.
I slap my arm and kill seven.

The temperature of the Kobuk is fifty-seven degrees—so
contrastingly warm after the river in the mountains that we
peel off our clothes and run into the water with soap. However,
by no possible illusion is this the Limpopo, and we shout and
yell at the cold water, take short, thrashing swims, and shiver
in the bright evening sun. The Kobuk, after all, has about the
same temperature—at this time of year—as the coastal waters
of Maine, for which the term most often heard is "freezing."

Wool feels good after the river; and the fire, high with driftwood, even better; and a dose of Arctic snakebite medicine
even better than that. In a memo to all of us written many
weeks ago, Pourchot listed, under "optional personal equipment," "Arctic snakebite medicine." There are no snakes in
Alaska. But what if a snake should unexpectedly appear? The
serum in my pack is from Lynchburg, Tennessee.

The salmon—filleted, rolled in flour, and sautéed on our
pancake grill—is superb among fishes and fair among salmon.
With few exceptions, the Pacific salmon that run in these
Arctic rivers are of the variety known as chum. Their flesh lacks
the high pink color of the silver, the sockeye, the king salmon.
Given a choice among those, a person with a lure would not
go for chum, and they are rarely fished for sport. After sockeyes
and humpbacks, though, they are third in the commercial
salmon fishery. Many millions of dollars' worth are packed each
year. Athapaskan Indians, harvesting from the Yukon, put king
salmon on their own tables and feed chum salmon to their
dogs. Hence, they call chum "dog salmon." Eskimos up here
in the Arctic Northwest, who rarely see another kind, are
piqued when they hear this Indian term.

We look two hundred yards across the Kobuk to spruce that
are reflected in the quiet surface. The expanded dimensions of
our surroundings are still novel. Last night, in forest, we were
close by the sound of rushing water. Sound now has become
inverse to the space around us, for we sit in the middle of an
immense and almost perfect stillness. We hear the fire and,
from time to time, insects, birds. The sound of an airplane
crosses the edge of hearing and goes out again. It is the first
aircraft we have heard.

Kauffmann says he is worried, from the point of view of park
planning, about the aircraft access that would probably be
developed for the Salmon River. "It's not a big world up there.
I'm not sure how much use it could take."

This reminds Fedeler of the cost of travel to wilderness, and makes him contemplate again who can pay to get there. "The Salmon is a nice enough river," he says. "But it is unavailable to ninety-nine point nine per cent of the people. I wouldn't go back to Fairbanks and tell everybody that they absolutely *have* to go and see the Salmon River."

"It's a fine experience."

"If you happen to have an extra six hundred bucks. Is the Park Service going to provide helicopter access or Super Cub access to some gravel bar near the headwaters?"

"Why does there have to be access?" Pourchot puts in.

"Why do there have to be wild and scenic rivers?" Fedeler wants to know. "And why this one—so far up here? Because of the cost of getting to it, the Salmon Wild River for most people would be just a thing on a map—an occasional trip for people from the Park Service, the Bureau of Outdoor Recreation, and the Alaska Department of Fish and Game. Meanwhile, with pressures what they are farther south, the sportsman in Alaska is in for some tough times."

"His numbers are increasing."

"And his opportunities are decreasing, while these federal proposals would set aside lands and rivers that only the rich can afford."

"The proposals, up here, are for the future," Kauffmann says, and he adds, after a moment, "As Yellowstone was. Throughout the history of this country, it's been possible to go to a place where no one has camped before, and now that kind of opportunity is running out. We must protect it, even if artificially. The day will come when people will want to visit such a wilderness—saving everything they have in order to see it, at whatever cost. We're talking fifty and more years hence, when there may be nowhere else to go to a place that is wild and unexplored."

I have a net over my head and cannot concentrate on this discussion, because something worse, and smaller, than mosquitoes—clouds of little flying prickers that cut you up—are in the air around us now and are coming through the mesh of the head net. They follow us into the tents, ignoring the netting there. They cut rashes in our faces all through the night.

(For two days, we stare at the hypnotizing vistas of the Kobuk, while its spacious novelty wears off. Uncannily, the river comes in almost precise two-mile segments, bend to bend. We move downstream a little more than twenty miles one day, only sixteen the next, in part because of stiff western head-winds. Having had one bad night with insects, we next choose to pitch our tents far out on a gravel point, on a dry part of the riverbed, two hundred yards from the nearest blade of vegetation, confident that the water will not rise, and prefer-ring anyway to be drowned outright than consumed piecemeal. The instant the bows touch shore, mosquitoes in grosses try to settle upon us. As we finish putting up the tents, a light rain begins to spit. The sky is slate gray in the east. We are camped on an island, and we fish the slough that goes behind it. Noth-ing there but six-inch grayling. Kauffmann and I try to walk around the island, but it is bigger than we imagined. Moreover, the beach runs out some distance down the slough. Plowing on through dense willow and alder, soaking wet, we give up the circumambulation and traverse the island to return to camp. We see wolf tracks seven inches long—amazing size, but there is a tape measure in my pocket and that is what it says. Less than a yard separates one set of prints from another—the tracks of a slow loper. Earlier in the day, fishing by the mouth of the Kallarichuk tributary, we saw wolf tracks intricately intertwined with the tracks of a running moose. There were changes of direction, overlapping circles. No other sign. The calligraphy seemed to report some unresolved encounter— unless two extremely odd animals had been through there at

different times. Now, after dinner, in light rain, we look upriver
and see a cow moose walk out of willows. She drinks from the
river. She stands, for a while, immobile, and stares across the
water. Slowly, she retreats into the thicket. Moose are so numerous now in this part of northwest Alaska that it is difficult
to imagine them absent, but they have been here scarcely fifty
years. The patterns of other creatures—the bear, the fish, the
caribou—run in long cycles over time, cycles of waxing, cycles
of waning; but they have been in the region for ten thousand
years, and when they have locally been gone for a time they
have always returned. In the case of the moose, though, there
is no evidence that they were ever here before the early part
of this century, and now they are established in the milieu and
in the native economy.

Eight boats, outboard-powered, going upriver, passed us in
the course of the day—all with at least three people in them,
some with children. Four have come back, and passed us again,
during the evening. It seems to be the rhythm of the Kobuk
that Eskimos go by about once an hour—at least on this part
of the river, many miles from the nearest village. I remember
Bob Waldrop saying how he counts on random Eskimos to
pick him up near the finish of certain trips he makes. Waldrop
is a Brooks Range guide, who leads long journeys, mainly on
foot, on both sides of the Arctic Divide. Much of the time, he
does not know exactly where he is. Maps lack detail, he explains; many mountains are unnamed. He generally has a fair
idea of his position, within eight miles or so, but he finds it
impossible to plan things more precisely than that, and people
who expect to know just where they are and to follow an exact
schedule, who are (in his words) "set in their ways," are likely
to be unhappy on such trips, and unenjoyable company. Waldrop, like Kauffmann, does not want his Brooks Range any
other way. He wants it imprecise. He wants to preserve its
surprises. When he goes up nameless mountains and finds on
their summits containers identifying someone or other as the

first visiting conqueror, he puts the containers in his pack and hauls them out. If you say to him, "You're altering history," Waldrop says, "The people were altering history who put the registers there." When Waldrop comes out of, say, the Sadlerochit Mountains, and makes his way across the wet tundra toward the Arctic Ocean, he has no idea when or where he will come to the water; nevertheless, he relies on "flagging the nearest Eskimo" for a ride to Barter Island, where mail planes land. An hour here, a day there, he waits with patience until one comes along.

The Eskimos on the Kobuk never seem surprised when they come upon us, as if nothing could be less extraordinary than the Grumman canoe, the small blue single kayak, and Snake Eyes—all afloat under five white faces. And now, as we watch from our campsite, another skiff approaches, coming downriver. It passes the sandspit where the moose was standing. A couple of hundred yards from us, a heavyset man in the stern cuts the motor. There are three people—two men and a woman. They drift and observe us. The woman is wearing a long calico dress, fringed at the bottom, rubber boots. The men are wearing short parkas with fur ruffs. There is an exchange of waves. At length, the man in the stern picks up an oar and sculls the boat toward the edge of the river. The boat is plywood, about eighteen feet long, apparently homemade, with a flat bottom, a square stern, and a thirty-five-horse Evinrude. The woman jumps out, into a couple of feet of water, where she firms the skiff against the current. She acts as an anchor while the heavyset man—her husband—talks with us. His name is Clarence Jackson, and he is from Noorvik. The other man is his uncle. In the boat is a full cartridge belt and a .45-calibre pistol. This is their annual trip upriver, he says, to visit his great-grandmother's grave. We ask about fish, and he says the runs have been mediocre this season. He says the caribou were plentiful near Kiana. He smiles amiably, somewhat diffidently, as he speaks. He wonders if we happen to know anything about a party of white people, far down the Kobuk, who had no boats, and who summoned a young Eskimo to shore and when he got out of his boat were extremely rough with him. We are surprised, and as dismayed as Clarence Jackson. He says, grinning, that if he had not seen our boats he would not have come so close. Up in the country where we have been no one much goes in summer, but Kobuk people sometimes hunt there in winter, he says, his friendly tone unaltered. His wife gets back into the boat. With toothy smiles, they say goodbye and move on down the river.

The people of the Kobuk are among the few Eskimos in Alaska whose villages are well within the tree line. They have a culture that reflects their cousinship to Eskimos of the coast and that borrows also from the Indians of the Alaskan interior. The combination is unique. At first glance—plywood boats, Evinrudes—they may seem to be even more a part of the world at large than they are of this Arctic valley. Much of their clothing is manufactured. They use rifles. They ride on snow machines. They seine whitefish and salmon with nylon nets that cost upward of four hundred dollars. Now and again, they leave the valley in search of jobs. They work on the pipeline. Without the river and the riverine land, though, they would be bereft of most of what sustains them. Their mail-order likeness to the rest of us does not go very deep. They may use Eagle Claw fishhooks from Wright & McGill, in Denver, but they still know how to make them from the teeth of wolves. They may give their children windup toys, but they also make little blowguns for them from the hollow leg bones of the sandhill crane. To snare ptarmigan, they no longer use spruce roots—they use picture wire—but they still snare ptarmigan. They eat what they call "white-man food," mainly from cans, but they also eat owl soup, sour dock, wild rhubarb, and the tuber *Hedysarum alpinum*—the Eskimo potato. Some of them believe that Eskimo food keeps them healthy and brown, and that too much white-man food will turn them white. Roughly half their carbohydrates come from wild food—and fully four-fifths of their protein. They eat—and, more to the point, depend on—small creatures of the forest. Rabbit. Beaver. Muskrat. Thousands of frozen whitefish will be piled beside a single house. At thirty below, whitefish break like glass. The people dip the frozen bits in seal oil and chew them. From fresh whitefish, as they squeeze, they directly suck roe. They trade mud-shark livers for seal oil from the coast. Mud sharks are freshwater, river fish, and for maritime Eskimos the liver of the mud shark is an exotic and delicious import. The forest Eskimo has a reciprocal yen for seal oil. When a Kobuk woman goes "fishing for seal oil," mud sharks are what she is after. Loon oil is sometimes substituted for seal oil, there being a great deal of oil in a loon. Sheefish, rare in the world and looking like fifteen-pound tarpon, make annual runs up the Kobuk. They are prized by the people.

On nothing, though, do the forest Eskimos depend so much as on caribou. They use the whole animal. They eat the meat raw and in roasts and stews. They eat greens from the stomach, muscles from the jaw, fat from behind the eyes. The hide goes into certain winter clothing that nothing manufactured can equal. Toward the end of the nineteenth century, the number of available caribou gradually declined in the Kobuk valley. Why the herd avoided the region perhaps had to do with climatic cycles and their effect on vegetation, but nobody knows. From the turn of the century until about 1940, people of the Kobuk had to go into the Brooks Range to find caribou, making prodigious journeys in winter, and feeding much of the kill to their dogs, on which they depended for the trip home with essential skins and sinew. In the nineteen-forties, the herd began to return—in numbers that increased each year. The caribou cycle—dearth to plenty and back again—seems to close itself in sixty to a hundred years. The Arctic herd numbered two hundred and forty thousand a few years ago, and has been fast decreasing. Some fifty thousand come over the mountains now.

With the rise and fall of such cycles, the people of the Kobuk from earliest times expanded and contracted over the riverine lands. Whenever caribou were plentiful, people were able to congregate in relatively large winter villages. Where caribou were scarce, people had to spread out—up and down the river in small family groups—for hunting small game and for fishing through the ice. Pursuit of furs for trading purposes tended to disseminate them as well. The arrival—seventy, eighty years ago—of white missionaries, schools, and trading posts tended to force the Eskimos together in places like Noorvik and Kiana, but Kobuk River people have not traditionally thought of their homes as permanent in location. Through much of their history, they built new houses—on sites shiftingly appropriate— each fall. With their Evinrudes and their Arctic Cat snowmobiles, their range has been extended—they can cover more miles from a fixed base—but cycles of climate, of salmon, of caribou cannot be levelled by gasoline. In order to continue existence as they have known it, the forest Eskimos must follow where the cycles may lead. So they are worried. It is difficult to see how the essential flexibility of their history is going to be advanced by the Alaska Native Claims Settlement Act and the so-called national-interest lands. By the terms of the law, the Eskimos must choose specific land—to become theirs according to the settlement—and the land must, by and large, be contiguous to the villages. When a boundary is established around native land, what if the caribou go somewhere else? Suppose the caribou concentrate for a time in the Kobuk Valley National Monument? Hunting is not permitted in national parks. Oh, but exceptions will be made in Alaska, where people can hunt on their traditional grounds. A tradition of 1920 may not be a tradition now, but will be again, in all likelihood, some decades in the future. The government understands that. The government may understand that today, but officials change, regulations change. Will the government understand in 1990? The Eskimos undeniably got a good deal in the Native Claims Settlement Act, but it was good only insofar as they agreed to change their way—to cherish money, and to adopt the concept (for centuries unknown to them) of private property. "No Trespassing" signs have begun to appear up here, around villages where those words would once have not been understood. Boundaries now have to be adjusted, adjudicated, where boundaries never existed. Kobuk societies once functioned like the clans of Scotland. Terrain was common to all. Kinship patterned things; ownership did not. Use determined use. If you had been using a place—say, a fishing spot—it was respected as yours while you used it. Now the enforced drawing of lines on the land has created tensions among the Kobuk villages that did not exist before. Under the ingratiating Eskimo surface is a sense of grave disturbance.

There is, as well, an added complication. In 1906, the Native Allotment Act provided that any Alaskan native could file a claim for a hundred and sixty acres of Alaska. This meant next to nothing to the people of the Kobuk valley, since they were not attracted to private ownership, and, in any case, could make little use of such a minuscule amount of land. Few people bothered to file. When the Native Claims Settlement Act came along, however, a final deadline was set for native allotments, and many people, thus pressed, decided to register claims after all. They took the allotments in violation of their own customary principles. Bad feeling inevitably followed and to some extent soured their society.

The sense of private property that has been jacketed upon them is uncomfortable, incompatible with subsistence harvesting and its changeful cycles. It is ironic that while the land-claim settlement is being effected relative plenty has been close to the villages. In 1900, the people could easily have shown that they needed a vast area in which to subsist. Of late, they have needed less. They will need more again. It is impossible to draw lines around a situation like this one, but the lines are being drawn.

The people of the National Park Service, for their part, seem to be amply sensitive to the effects their efforts might have. They intend to adjust their own traditions so that Alaskan national-park land will not abridge but will in fact preserve native customs. Under the direction of Douglas Anderson, of the Department of Anthropology at Brown University, an anthropological team commissioned by the Park Service has recently described and voluminously catalogued what must be every habit, tic, and mannerism, every tale and taboo—let alone custom—of the Kobuk River natives. The anthropologists make a convincing case for helping the people preserve their modus vivendi, but the most vivid words in the document occur when the quoted Eskimos are speaking for themselves:

> *Eskimos should make laws for those people outside. That would be just the same as what they try to do to us. We know nothing about how they live, and they know nothing about how we live. It should be up to us to decide things for ourselves. You see the land out there? We never have spoiled it.*
>
> *Too much is happening to the people. Too many outside pressures are forcing in on us. Changes are coming too fast, and we are being pushed in all different directions by forces that come from someplace outside. People thought that the land-claims settlement was the end of our problems, that it meant the future was secure; but it was only the beginning. Even before the lands were all selected the government wanted pipeline easements and road corridors right through our territory. These would take away strips miles wide, cutting right across our land. And instead of open access to the land, the Eskimos might be surrounded by huge pieces of country that are declared national resources for all the people. Land that has always belonged to the natives is being parcelled up and divided among the takers.*

The forest Eskimos' relationship with whites has made them dependent on goods that need to be paid for: nylon netting, boat materials, rifles, ammunition, motors, gasoline. Hence, part of the year some Eskimo men leave the river to find jobs. These pilgrimages to the wage economy are not a repudiation of the subsistence way of life. They make money so they can come back home, where they prefer to be, and live the way they prefer to live—foraging the wild country with gasoline and bullets. If subsistence living were to be, through regulation, denied to them, the probable result would be that the government would have to support them even more than at present —more aid to dependent children, more food stamps—for they would not be able to find sufficient work, at home or on seasonal trips outside, to support their families.

As long as I have the land and nobody tries to stop me from using it, then I'm a rich man. I can always go out there and make my living, no matter what happens. Everything I need—my food, clothes, house, heat—it's all out there.

And another thing, too. If we have nothing of our Eskimo food—only white-man food to live on—we can't live. We eat and eat and eat, but we never get filled up. Just like starvation.

Breakfast in the frying pan—freeze-dried eggs. If we were Kobuk people, one of us might go off into the watery tundra and find fresh eggs. Someone else might peel the bark from a willow. The bark would be soaked and formed into a tube with the eggs inside, and the tube would be placed in the fire. But this is not a group of forest Eskimos. These are legionaries from another world, talking "scenic values" and "interpretation." These are Romans inspecting Transalpine Gaul. Nobody's skin is going to turn brown on these eggs—or on cinnamon-apple-flavored Instant Quaker Oatmeal, or Tang, or Swiss Miss, or

on cold pink-icinged Pop-Tarts with raspberry filling. For those
who do not believe what they have just read, allow me to
confirm it: in Pourchot's breakfast bag are pink-icinged Pop-
Tarts with raspberry filling. Lacking a toaster, and not caring
much anyway, we eat them cold. They invite a question. To
a palate without bias—the palate of an open-minded Berber,
the palate of a travelling Martian—which would be the more
acceptable, a pink-icinged Pop-Tart with raspberry filling
(cold) or the fat gob from behind a caribou's eye?

It is raining. A wind is rising and pushing back a morning fog.
The air—fifty-four—is cooler than the Kobuk. We have twenty
miles to cover, downriver to Kiana. Each of us has put in
identical time in the various boats, so now we draw lots to see
who goes where, and Fedeler and I are the losers. We draw
Snake Eyes. Even before we shove off, whitecaps have formed
on the river, and waves two feet high. They are coming from the
west, and that is where we are going. As we pack up, Fedeler and
I are subjected to intense gratuitous ridicule because we are
condemned to Snake Eyes; and, indeed, a chill wet day on a
half-sunk log is about all we can expect. So we plow westward,
into the waves, and the wind is so strong it brings tears to the
eyes. They mix with the rain and the spray of the river. The
length of a mile varies. These are three-league miles. The
current flows west, the wind and waves come east, and they
more than cancel the force of the river. To stop paddling is to
move backward. The waves are so big they wash over the bow of
the Grumman. Light and bobbing in its ride down the Salmon,
the canoe here is too much up in the wind. John Kauffmann and
Stell Newman have to bend their paddles on every stroke. The
single Klepper, with Pourchot in it, is better off, but not much.
It is so light that he has to strain to drive it. Snake Eyes, however,
is thirty per cent submerged in its own leakings, another third by
the natural depth of its draft. Snake Eyes is in and of the river.
The wind cannot get to Snake Eyes, because the wind can't
swim. The waves that wash over us roll over the deck, asserting
an upstream thrust of zero. Snake Eyes, property of the United

States government, is today straight out of Groton, Connecticut—a nuclear-powered submarine. Fedeler and I, the nuclei, begin to suffer in a way unimaginable before. We become chilly, and a little stiff, waiting for the others—idling at the river bends, scanning the gray river through its flying spray to see where the others might be. After six or eight miles, we are so cold we stop. We build a bonfire of drifted cottonwood, and stand downwind of it at the edge of the flames.

The wind gradually subsides through the afternoon, and the low gray sky begins to pull itself apart. The weather here is like the weather in Scotland. It can change so abruptly—closing in, lifting, closing in again—that all in an hour, let alone a day, wind-driven rain may be followed by calm and hazy sunshine, which may then be lost in heavy mists that soon disappear into open skies. We pass under a high bluff and go around a final bend; then the water spreads open before us in a three-mile reach to Kiana. The village is quite lovely from this perspective, lifted on its own high bluff above a confluence of rivers—the Squirrel and the Kobuk—and with a European compactness of buildings that contributes emphasis and irony to the immense wilderness in which it is a dot. We stop three miles away and camp on a flat gravel bar. The sky over supper is shot with color —with washes of salmon light on accumulating clouds. Their edges are gray to black, growing heavy. To the north, we hear thunder and see lightning. Such storms are rare in much of Alaska, but they are common here. This one rolls on into the Brooks Range and leaves us bright and dry. The talk over the campfire is entirely about Alaska. We are at the end of this trip now, and from the moment it began no one has once mentioned anything that did not have to do with Alaska.

⁅ In the morning—cool in the forties and the river calm—we strike the tents, pack the gear, and move on down toward

Kiana. Gradually, the village spreads out in perspective. Its most prominent structure is the sheet-metal high school on the edge of town. Dirt-and-gravel streets climb the hill above the bluff. Houses are low, frame. Some are made of logs. Behind the town, a navigational beacon flashes. Drawing closer, we can see caribou antlers over doorways—testimony of need and respect. There are basketball backboards. We are closing a circuit, a hundred water miles from the upper Salmon, where a helicopter took us, from Kiana, at the start. Under the bluff, we touch the shore. Kiana is now high above us, and mostly out of sight. The barge is here that brings up supplies from Kotzebue. The river's edge for the moment is all but unpopulated. Fish racks up and down the beach are covered with split drying salmon—ruddy and pink. We disassemble the Kleppers, removing their prefabricated bones, folding their skins, making them disappear into canvas bags. I go up the hill for a carton, and return to the beach. Into envelopes of cardboard I tape the tines of the caribou antler that I have carried from the mountains. Protecting the antler takes longer than the dismantling and packing of the kayaks, but there is enough time before the flight to Kotzebue at midday. In the sky, there has as yet been no sound of the airplane—a Twin Otter, of Wien Air Alaska, the plane that brought us here to meet the chopper. Stell Newman has gone up the beach and found some people at work around their fish racks. He now has with him a slab of dried salmon, and we share it like candy.

Children were fishing when we were here before. They yanked whitefish out of the river and then pelted one another with the living fish as if they were snowballs. Women with tubs were gutting salmon. It was a warmer day then. The sun was so fierce you looked away; you looked north. Up at the airstrip behind the town—a gravel strip, where we go now with our gear—was the Grumman canoe. It had been flown in, and cached there, long before. The helicopter, chartered by the government and coming in from who knows where, was a new five-seat twin-engine Messerschmitt with a bubble front. On its shining fuselage, yellow-and-black heraldry identified it as the property of Petroleum Helicopters, Inc. The pilot removed a couple of fibre-glass cargo doors, took out a seat, and we shoved the canoe into an opening at the rear of the cabin. It went in halfway. The Grumman was too much for the Messerschmitt. The canoe was cantilevered, protruding to the rear. We tied it in place. It was right side up, and we filled it with gear. Leaving the rest of us to wait for a second trip, Pourchot and the pilot took off for the Salmon River. With so much canoe coming out of its body, the helicopter, even in flight, seemed to be nearing the final moment of an amazing pregnancy. It went over the mountains northeast.

There was a wooden sign beside the airstrip: "WELCOME TO THE CITY OF KIANA. 2nd Class City. Population 300 . . . Establish 1902 . . . Main Sources: Bear, Caribou, Moose, Geese, Salmon, Shee, Whitefish, Trout." The burning sun was uncomfortable. I walked behind the sign. In its shadow, the air was chill. I dragged the helicopter seat out of the sun and into the shade of a storage hut, sat down, leaned back, and went to sleep. When I woke up, I was shivering. The temperature a few feet away, in the sunlight, was above seventy degrees.

What awakened me were the voices of children. Three small girls had followed us up from the Kobuk, where we had watched them fish. They had crossed the runway and picked blueberries, and now were offering them from their hands. The berries were intensely sweet, having grown in the long northern light. The little girls also held out pieces of hard candy. Wouldn't we like some? They asked for nothing. They were not shy. They were totally unself-conscious. I showed them an imitating game, wherein you clear your throat—hrrrum—and then draw with a stick a figure on the ground. "Here. Try to do that." They drew the figure but did not clear their throats. "No. That's not quite right. Hrrrum. Here now. Try it again." They tried twice more. They didn't get it. I sat down again on the chopper seat. Stell Newman let them take pictures with his camera. When they noticed my monocular, on a lanyard around my neck, they got down beside me, picked it off my chest, and spied on the town. They leaned over, one at a time, and put their noses down against mine, draping around my head their soft black hair. They stared into my eyes. Their eyes were dark and northern, in beautiful almond faces, aripple with smiles. Amy. Katherine. Rose Ann. Ages nine and eleven. Eskimo girls. They looked up. They had heard the helicopter, and before long it appeared.

I sat in the co-pilot's seat, others in the seat I had been napping on. We lifted off, and headed out to join Pourchot, who was waiting on a gravel bar in the upper Salmon. The rotor noise was above conversation, but the pilot handed me a pair of earphones and a microphone. He showed me on a panel between us the mechanics of communicating. I couldn't think of much to say. I was awed, I suppose, in the presence of a bush pilot (mustache akimbo) and in the presence of the bush itself —the land and the approaching mountains. I didn't want to distract him, or myself. He kept urging me to talk, though. He seemed to want the company. His name was Gene Parrish, and he was a big man who had eaten well. He smoked a cigar, and on the intercom was garrulous and friendly.

Before us now was the first ridgeline. Flying close to ground, close to the mountainside, we climbed rapidly toward the crest, and then—crossing over it—seemed to plunge into a void of air. The ground ahead, which had been so near, was suddenly far below. We soon reached another mountainside, and again we climbed closely above its slope, skimmed the outcropping rocks at the top, and jumped into a gulf of sky.

Parrish said, "Y'all ever seen these mountains before?"

Some of the others had, I said, but I had not.

"Me, neither," he said. "Aren't they fabulous? Alaska is amazing, isn't it? Wherever you go, everything is different. These mountains sure are fabulous."

Indeed they were something like it—engaging, upsweeping

tundra fells. They were not sharp and knife-edged like the peaks of the central Brooks. They were less dramatic but more inviting. They looked negotiable. They were, as it happened, the last mountains of the range, the end of the line, the end of a cordillera. They were, after four thousand miles, the last statement of the Rocky Mountains before they disappeared into the Chukchi Sea.

Parrish went up the side of a still higher mountain and skimmed the ridge, to reveal, suddenly, a drainage system far below.

"Is that the Salmon River?" I said.

"Oh, my, no," he said. "It's a ways yet. Where y'all from?"

"I'm from New Jersey. And you?"

"Louisiana."

He said he had come to Alaska on a kind of working vacation. At home, where his job was to fly back and forth between the Louisiana mainland and oil rigs in the Gulf of Mexico, he seldom flew over anything much higher than a wave. Because the Messerschmitt had two engines, he said, he would not have to autorotate down if one were to fail. In fact, he could even climb on one engine. So it was safe to fly this way, low and close —and more interesting.

We flew up the sides of mountain after mountain, raked the ridges, fluttered high over valleys. In each new valley was a stream, large or small. With distance, they looked much alike. Parrish checked his airspeed, the time, the heading; finally, he made a sharp southward turn and began to follow a stream course in the direction of its current, looking for a gravel bar, a man, a canoe. Confidently, he gave up altitude and searched the bending river. He found a great deal of gravel. For thirty, forty miles, he kept searching, until the hills around the river began to diminish in anticipation of—as we could see ahead —the wet-tundra Kobuk plain. If the river was the Salmon, Pourchot was not there. If Pourchot was on the Salmon, Parrish was somewhere else.

The Salmon had to be farther east, he guessed, shaking his

head in surprise and wonder. We rollercoasted the sides of additional mountains and came upon another significant drainage. It appeared to Parrish to be the right one. This time, we flew north, low over the river, upstream, looking for the glint of the canoe. We had as much luck as before. The river narrowed as we went farther and farther, until it became a brook and then a rill, with steep-rising mountains to either side. "I don't believe it. I just *can't* believe it," Parrish said. There was nothing much below us now but the kind of streak a tear might make crossing a pilot's face. "This just isn't right," he said. "This is not working out. I was sure of the heading. I was sure this was the river. But nothing ever is guaranteed. Nothing— nothing—is guarandamnteed."

He turned one-eighty and headed downstream. Spread over his knees was a Nome Sectional Aeronautical Chart, and he puzzled over it for a while, then he handed it to me. Maybe I could help figure out where we were. The map was quite wonderful at drawing straight lines between distant airstrips, but its picture of the mountains looked like calves' brains over bone china, and the scale was such that the whole of the Salmon River was only six inches long. The chopper plowed on to the south. I held the map a little closer to my eyes, studying the blue veiny lines among the mountains. The ludicrousness of the situation washed over me. I looked back at Kauffmann and the others, who seemed somewhat confused. And small wonder. A map was being handed back and forth between a man from New Jersey and a pilot from Louisiana who were amiss in—of all places—the Brooks Range. In a sense—in the technical sense that we had next to no idea where we were— we were lost.

There are no geographical requirements for pilots in the United States. Anyone who is certified as a pilot can fly anywhere, and that, of course, includes anywhere in Alaska. New pilots arrive steadily from all over the Lower Forty-eight. Some are attracted by the romance of Alaska, some by the money around the pipeline. The Alyeska Pipeline Service Company, soon after it began its construction operations, set up its own standards for charter pilots who would fly its personnel—standards somewhat stiffer than those of the Federal Aviation Administration. Among other things, Alyeska insisted that applicants without flying experience in Alaska had to have fifty hours of documented training there, including a line check above the terrain they would be flying.

One effect of the pipeline charters has been to siphon off pilots from elsewhere in the Alaskan bush. These pilots are often replaced by pilots inexperienced in Alaska. Say a mail pilot quits and goes off to fly the pipeline. His replacement might be three days out of Teterboro. The mail must go through. Passengers in such planes (passengers ride with bush mail) sometimes intuit that they and the pilot are each seeing the landscape in a novel way. Once, for example, in the eastern-Alaska interior, I rode in a mail plane that took off from Fairbanks to fly a couple of hundred miles across mountains to Eagle, a village on the upper Yukon. It was a blustery, wet morning, and clouds were lower by far than summits. As rain whipped against the windshield, visibility forward was zero. Looking down to the side, the pilot watched the ground below —trying to identify various drainages and pick his way through the mountains. He frequently referred to a map. The plane was a single-engine Cessna 207 Skywagon, bumping hard on the wind. We went up a small tributary and over a pass, where we picked up another river and followed it downstream. After a time, the pilot turned around and went many miles back in the direction from which he had come. He explored another tributary. Then, abruptly, he turned again. The weather was not improving. Soon his confidence in his reading of the land seemed to run out altogether. He asked in what direction the stream below was flowing. He could not tell by the set of the rapids. He handed the map to a passenger who had apparently visited the region once or twice before. The passenger read the map for a while and then counselled the pilot to stay with the principal stream in sight. He indicated to the pilot which direction was downhill. At length, the Yukon came into view. I, who love rivers, have never felt such affection for a river. One would not have to be Marco Polo to figure out now which way to go. I had been chewing gum so vigorously that the hinges of my jaws would ache for two days. We flew up the Yukon to Eagle. When we landed, a young woman with a pickup was waiting to collect the mail. As the pilot stepped out, she came up to him and said, "Hello. You're new, aren't you? My name is Anna."

That was a scheduled flight on an American domestic airline. The company was Air North, which serves many bush communities, and its advertising slogan was "Experience Counts." Another Air North pilot told me once that he liked being a bush pilot in Alaska—he had arrived from New York several months before—but he was having a hard time living on his pay. He said there was better money to be made operating bulldozers on the pipeline than operating planes for Air North. As a result, experienced, able pilots had not only been drawn away to fly pipeline charters; experienced, able pilots were also flying bulldozers on the tundra.

Some people I know in the National Park Service who were studying a region near the upper Yukon chartered a helicopter in an attempt to find the headwaters of a certain tributary stream. When they had been in flight for some time and had not seen anything remotely resembling the terrain they were looking for, they grew uneasy. When they looked ahead and saw the bright-white high-rising Wrangells, mountain peaks two hundred miles from where they were going, they realized they were lost. The pilot, new in Alaska, was from Alabama. "This is different, unique, tough country," a pilot from Sitka once told me. "A guy has to know what he's doing. Flying is a way of life up here, and you have to get used to it. You can't drive. You can't walk. You can't swim."

In Anchorage, John Kauffmann had introduced me to his friend Charlie Allen, a general free-lance bush pilot with a wide reputation for having no betters and few peers. From the Southeastern Archipelago to Arctic Alaska, Allen had been flying for twenty-five years. He was dismayed by the incompetence of some people in his profession, and was not at all shy to say so. "Alaska is the land of the bush pilot," he said. "You have to think highly of this bush pilot, because he's dirty, he has a ratty airplane, and he's alive. It's a myth, the bush-pilot thing. It's 'Smilin' Jack.' The myth affects pilots. Some of them, in this magic Eddie Rickenbacker fraternity, are more afraid of being embarrassed than they are of death. Suppose they're low on gas. They're so afraid of being embarrassed they keep going until they have no recourse but to crash. They drive their aircraft till they cough and quit. Kamikaze pilots. That's what we've got up here—kamikaze pilots from New Jersey. Do you think one of them would ever decide the weather's too tough? His champion-aviator's manhood would be impugned. Meanwhile, he's a hero if he gets through. A while ago, some guy ran out of gas at night on the ice pack. He had been chartered for a polar-bear hunt. He chopped off his fuel tanks with an axe and used the fuel tanks as boats. He and the hunters paddled out. He was then regarded as a hero. He was regarded as Eddie Rickenbacker *and* Smilin' Jack. But he was guilty of outrageous technical behavior. He was the fool who got them into the situation in the first place.

"Aircraft-salvage operators have a backlog of planes waiting to be salvaged in Alaska. Helicopters go out for them. In the past year and a half, I have helped salvage six planes that have been wrecked by *one* pilot. Don't identify him. Just call him 'a government employee.' Why do passengers *go* with such pilots? Would they go to the moon with an astronaut who did not have round-trip fuel? If you were in San Francisco and the boat to Maui was leaking and the rats were leaving, even if you had a ticket you *would not go*. Safety in the air is where you find it. Proper navigation helps, but proper judgment takes care of all conditions. You say to yourself, 'I ain't going to go today. The situation is too much for me.' And you resist all pressure to the contrary."

Allen paused a moment. Then he said, "You don't have to run into a mountain. Only a pilot is needed to wreck an airplane."

Of reported accidents, there have lately been something like two hundred a year in Alaska. Upwards of twenty-five a year produce fatal injuries, killing various numbers of people. Another fifteen crashes or so produce injuries rated "serious." The figures seem to compliment the fliers in a state where a higher percentage of people fly—and fly more often—than they do anywhere else in the United States. Merrill Field, a light-plane airfield in Anchorage, handles fifty-four thousand more flights per year than Newark International. On the other hand, if you get into an airplane in Alaska your chances of not coming back are greater by far than they would be in any other part of the country. Only Texas and California, with their vastly larger populations, consistently exceed Alaska in aircraft accidents. Government employees in Alaska speak of colleagues who have been lost "in line of duty." In air accidents during the past two years, the Bureau of Land Management has lost four, Alaska Fish and Game has lost one, U.S. Fish and Wildlife has lost three, the U.S. Forest Service has lost five, and the National Park Service has lost seven (in a single crash). A gallery of thirteen of the great bush pilots in the history of Alaska was presented in an Alaska newspaper not long ago. Of the thirteen, ten—among them Carl Eielson, Russ Merrill, Haakon Christensen, Big Money Monsen—died flying. I dropped in at a bar one day, in a small Alaskan town, where a bush pilot had one end of a plastic swizzlestick clamped between his teeth and was attempting to stretch it by pulling the other end. He had apparently been there some time, and he was challenging all comers to see who could stretch a swizzlestick the farthest. Jay

Hammond, governor of Alaska, was himself a bush pilot for twenty-eight years, and a conspicuously good one. In an interview with him, I mentioned the sorts of things that cause disgust in pilots like Charlie Allen, and Hammond said, "There is nothing you can do by statute to assure competence." I wondered if that was altogether true—if, at the very least, regulations such as Alyeska's regarding pilots who come in from outside could not be extended to the state at large.

All this applies, of course, only to bush pilots and not to the big jet-flying commercial carriers, whose accidents are extremely rare and are not outstanding in national statistics. As we flew from Fairbanks to Kotzebue to begin the trip to the Salmon River, we were in a Boeing 737 of Wien Air Alaska. One Captain Clayton came on the horn and said he would be pleased to play the harmonica for us as soon as he had finished a Fig Newton. A while later, he announced that his mouth was now solvent—and, above clouds, he began to play. He played beautifully. The speaker system in that particular aircraft seemed to have been wired especially to meet his talent. He played three selections, and he found Kotzebue.

"This is not right. This just is *not* right," Gene Parrish said again, giving up on still another river and moving (west this time) to try again. Apparently, one of the streams he had passed over was, in fact, the Salmon. "I do my best," he said. "I do my best. I had the right heading—I'm certain of that. I do my best, but there ain't no guarangoddamntee." Of the next river he looked over perhaps twenty miles, without success. Then he began to mention fuel. He thought we should go back to Kiana and tap a drum. So he continued west, and crossed another mountain. Now he flew above a stream with a tributary coming into it that had a pair of sharp right-angled bends that formed the shape of a staple. Pictured on the Nome Sectional Aeronautical Chart was a staple-shaped pair of bends in a tributary of the Salmon River. The stream on the map and the stream on the earth appeared to be the same, but there was no guarangoddamntee. Forgetting Kiana for the time being, Parrish headed up the river. Down near the spruce, swinging around the bends, we hunted the gravel bars, looking for the shine of metal. There was much gravel but no aluminum. He turned once more for Kiana. There had been a hill on our left, and according to the map there should have been another tributary coming in on the far side of the hill. If the smaller stream was there, this was surely—so it seemed—the Salmon. Parrish could not resist having a look. He turned again, and flew north of the hill, which sloped down to the right bank of a tributary stream. We went on up the river. "This *must* be the Salmon, but it sure don't look right," Parrish said, and in the same instant Pourchot and the Grumman came into view. The chopper set down so near Pourchot it almost blew him over. We pulled out our gear, and wished Parrish well in his continuing tour of Alaska. In a whirling dust storm, the Messerschmitt took off, spattering us with sand and flying bits of dry debris. The dust would take a lot longer to settle than the laws of physics would suggest. Now we were alone between fringes of spruce by a clear stream where tundra went up the sides of mountains. This was, in all likelihood, the most isolated wilderness I would ever see, and that is how we got there.

《 The river was low, and Pat Pourchot had picked a site as far upstream as he judged we could be and still move in boats. We were on an island, with the transparent Salmon River on one side—hurrying, scarcely a foot deep—and a small slough on the other. Deeper pools, under bedrock ledges, were above us and below us. We built our fire on the lemon-sized gravel of what would in higher water be the riverbed, and we pitched the tents on slightly higher ground among open stands of willow, on sand that showed what Bob Fedeler called "the old tracks of a young griz." We would stay two nights, according to plan, before beginning the long descent to the Kobuk; and in the intervening day we would first assemble the kayaks and then be free to disperse and explore the terrain.

There was a sixth man with us, there at the beginning. His name was Jack Hession, and he was the Sierra Club's only salaried full-time representative in Alaska. Pourchot had invited him as an observer. The news that he was absent at the end of the trip could instantly cause hopes to rise in Alaska, where the Sierra Club has long been considered a netherworld force and Hession the resident Belial. Hession, though, was not going to perish on the Salmon. Pressures from Anchorage had travelled with him, and before long would get the better of him, and in cavalier manner—in this Arctic wilderness—he would bid us goodbye and set out early for home. Meanwhile, in the morning sun, we put together the collapsible kayaks— two single Kleppers and Snake Eyes. Hession's own single was the oldest of the three, and it had thirty-six parts, hardware not included. There were dowels of mountain ash and ribs of laminated Finnish birch, which fitted, one part to another, with hooks and clips until they formed a pair of nearly identical skeletal cones—the internal structures of halves of the boat. The skin was a limp bag made of blue canvas (the deck) and hemp-reinforced vulcanized rubber (the hull). The concept was to insert the skeletal halves into the skin and then figure out how to firm them together. We had trouble doing that. Hession, who ordinarily used rigid boats of fibre glass in his engagements with white water, could not remember how to complete the assembly. Stiff toward the ends and bent in the middle, his kayak had the look of a clip-on tie, and would do about as well in the river. We all crouched around and studied amidships—six men, a hundred miles up a stream, above sixty-seven degrees of latitude, with a limp kayak. No one was shy with suggestions, which were full of ingenuity but entirely failed to work. By trial and error, we finally figured it out. The last step in the assembly involved the center rib, and we set that inside the hull on a tilt and then tapped it with a rock and forced it toward the vertical. When the forcing rib reached ninety degrees to the longer axis of the craft, the rib snapped into place, and with that the entire boat became taut and yare. Clever man, Johann Klepper. He had organized his foldboat in the way that the North American Indians had developed the construction of their bark canoes. Over the years, the Klepper company had simplified its process. Our other single kayak, the more recent model, had fewer and larger skeletal parts, and it went together more easily; but it was less streamlined than the first. Snake Eyes, for its part—all eight hundred dollars' worth of Snake Eyes—was new and had an interior of broad wooden slabs, conveniently hinged. Snake Eyes had the least number of separate parts (only fifteen) and in the way it went together was efficient and simple. Its advanced design had been achieved with a certain loss of grace, however, and this was evident there on the gravel. The boat was lumpy, awkward, bulging—a kayak with elbows.

Toward noon and after an early lunch, we set off on foot for a look around. Pourchot went straight up the hills to the west, alone. Stell Newman and John Kauffmann intended lesser forays, nearer the campsite. I decided I'd go with Bob Fedeler, who, with Jack Hession, had the most ambitious plan. They were going north up the river some miles and then up the ridges to the east. I hoped my legs would hold up. I didn't want to embarrass myself, off somewhere in the hills, by snapping something, but I could not resist going along with Fedeler. After all, he was a habitat biologist, working for the state, and if the ground around here was not habitat then I would never be in country that was. The temperature had come up to seventy. The sky was blue, with moving clouds and intermittent sun. We stuffed our rain gear into day packs and started up the river.

Generally speaking, if I had a choice between hiking and

peeling potatoes, I would peel the potatoes. I have always had a predilection for canoes on rivers and have avoided walking wherever possible. My experience, thus, was limited but did exist. My work had led me up the Sierra Nevada and across the North Cascades, and in various eras I had walked parts of the Long Trail, the Appalachian Trail, trails of New Hampshire, the Adirondacks. Here in the Brooks Range, of course, no one had been there clearing the path. A mile, steep or level, could demand a lot of time. You go along with only a general plan, free lance, guessing where the walking will be least difficult, making choices all the way. These are the conditions, and in ten minutes' time they present their story. The country is wild to the limits of the term. It would demean such a world to call it pre-Columbian. It is twenty times older than that, having assumed its present form ten thousand years ago, with the melting of the Wisconsin ice.

For several miles upstream, willow and alder pressed in on the river, backed by spruce and cottonwood, so the easiest path was the river itself. Gravel bars were now on one side, now the other, so we crossed and crossed again, taking off our boots and wading through the fast, cold water. I had rubber-bottomed leather boots (L.L. Bean's, which are much in use all over Alaska). Fedeler was wearing hiking boots, Hession low canvas sneakers. Hession had a floppy sun hat, too. He seemed to see no need to dress like Sir Edmund Hillary, or to leave the marks of waffles by the tracks of wolves. He was a brief, trim, lithe figure, who moved lightly and had seen a lot of such ground. He stopped and opened his jackknife, and stood it by a track in sand at the edge of the river. Other tracks were near. Two wolves running side by side. He took a picture of the track. We passed a deep pool where spring water came into the river, and where algae grew in response to its warmth. Grayling could winter there. Some were in the pool now—bodies stationary, fins in motion, in clear deep water as green as jade. Four mergansers swam up the river. We saw moose pellets in sand beyond the pool. I would not much want to be a moose just there, in a narrow V-shaped valley with scant protection of trees. We came, in fact, to the tree line not long thereafter. The trees simply stopped. We took a few more northward steps and were out of the boreal forest. Farther north, as far as land continued, there would be no more. I don't mean to suggest that we had stepped out of Sequoia National Park and onto an unvegetated plain. The woods behind us were spare in every sense, fingering up the river valley, reaching as far as they could go. Now the tundra, which had before been close behind the trees, came down to the banks of the river. We'd had enough of shoelaces and of bare feet crunching underwater stones, so we climbed up the west bank to walk on the tundra—which from the river had looked as smooth as a golf course. Possibly there is nothing as invitingly deceptive as a tundra-covered hillside. Distances over tundra, even when it is rising steeply, are like distances over water, seeming to be less than they are, defraying the suggestion of effort. The tundra surface, though, consists of many kinds of plants, most of which seem to be stemmed with wire configured to ensnare the foot. For years, my conception of tundra—based, I suppose, on photographs of the Canadian north and the plains of the Alaskan Arctic slope —was of a vast northern flatness, water-flecked, running level to every horizon. Tundra is not topography, however; it is a mat of vegetation, and it runs up the sides of prodigious declivities as well as across the broad plains. There are three varying types —wet tundra, on low flatland with much standing water; moist tundra, on slightly higher ground; and alpine tundra, like carpeted heather, rising on mountains and hills. We moved on, northward, over moist tundra, and the plants were often a foot or so in height. Moving through them was more like wading than walking, except where we followed game trails. Fortunately, these were numerous enough, and comfortably negotiable. They bore signs of everything that lived there. They were highways, share and share alike, for caribou, moose, bears,

wolves—whose tracks, antlers, and feces were strewn along the
right-of-way like beer cans at the edge of a road. While these
game trails were the best thoroughfares in many hundreds of
square miles, they were also the only ones, and they had a
notable defect. They tended to vanish. The trails would go
along, well cut and stamped out through moss campion, reindeer moss, sedge tussocks, crowberries, prostrate willows, dwarf
birch, bog blueberries, white mountain avens, low-bush cranberries, lichens, Labrador tea; then, abruptly, and for no apparent reason, the trails would disappear. Their well-worn ruts
suggested hundreds of animals, heavy traffic. So where did they
go when the trail vanished? Fedeler did not know. I could not
think of an explanation. Maybe Noah had got there a little
before us.

On the far side of the river was an isolated tree, which had
made a brave bid to move north, to extend the reach of its
progenitive forest. The Brooks Range, the remotest uplift in
North America, was made a little less remote, fifty years ago,
by the writing of Robert Marshall, a forester, who described
several expeditions to these mountains in a book called "Alaska
Wilderness." Marshall had a theory about the tree line, the
boundary of the circumboreal world. He thought that white
spruce and other species could live farther north, and that they
were inching northward, dropping seeds ahead of them, a
dead-slow advance under marginal conditions. Whatever it
may have signified, the tree across the river was dead, and out
of it now came a sparrow hawk, flying at us, shouting *"kee kee
kee,"* and hovering on rapidly beating wings to study the creatures on the trail. There was not much it could do about us,
and it went back to the tree.

The leaves of Labrador tea, crushed in the hand, smelled like
a turpentine. The cranberries were early and sourer than they
would eventually be. With the arrival of cold, they freeze on
the vine, and when they thaw, six months later, they are somehow sweeter and contain more juice. Bears like overwintered

berries. Blueberries, too, are sweeter after being frozen on the
bush. Fried cranberries will help relieve a sore throat. Attacks
in the gall bladder have been defused with boiled cranberries
mixed with seal oil. The sedge tussocks were low and not as
perilous as tussocks can be. They are grass that grows in
bunches, more compact at the bottom than at the top—a
mushroom shape that can spill a foot and turn an ankle. They
were tiresome, and soon we were ready to move upward, away
from the moist tundra and away from the river. Ahead we saw
the configurations of the sharp small valleys of three streams
meeting, forming there the principal stem of the Salmon. To
the east, above the confluence, a tundra-bald hill rose a thousand feet and more. We decided to cross the river and go up
the hill. Look around. Choose where to go from there.

The river was so shallow now that there was no need for
removing boots. We walked across and began to climb. The
going was steep. I asked Jack Hession how long he had been
in Alaska, and he said seven years. He had been in Alaska
longer than two-thirds of the people in the state. He was from
California, and had lived more recently in western Washington, where he had begun to acquire his expertise in boats in
white water. Like Fedeler—like me, for that matter—he was
in good condition. Hession, though, seemed to float up the
incline, while I found it hard, sweaty work. From across the
river it had looked as easy as a short flight of stairs. I went up
it a trudge at a time—on reindeer moss, heather, lupine. The
sun had suddenly departed, and a cool rain began to fall. At
the top of the hill, we sat on a rock outcropping and looked
back at the river, twelve hundred feet below. Everywhere
around us were mountains—steep, treeless, buff where still in
the sun. One was bright silver. The rain felt good. We nibbled
M&M's. They were even better than the rain. The streams far
below, small and fast, came pummelling together and made the
river. The land they fell through looked nude. It was all tundra,
rising northward toward a pass at the range divide. Looking at

so much mountain ground—this immense minute fragment of wilderness Alaska—one could wonder about the choice of words of people who say that it is fragile. "Fragile" just does not appear to be a proper term for a rugged, essentially uninvaded landscape covering tens of thousands of square miles— a place so vast and unpeopled that if anyone could figure out how to steal Italy, Alaska would be a place to hide it. Meanwhile, earnest ecologues write and speak about the "fragile" tundra, this "delicate" ocean of barren land. The words sound effete, but the terrain is nonetheless vulnerable. There is ice under the tundra, mixed with soil as permafrost, in some places two thousand feet deep. The tundra vegetation, living and dead, provides insulation that keeps the summer sun from melting the permafrost. If something pulls away the insulation and melting occurs, the soil will settle and the water may run off. The earth, in such circumstances, does not restore itself. In the nineteen-sixties, a bulldozer working for Geophysical Service, Inc., an oil-exploration company, wrote the initials G.S.I. in Arctic Alaskan tundra. The letters were two hundred feet from top to bottom, and near them the bulldozer cut an arrow—an indicator for pilots. Thermokarst (thermal erosion) followed, and slumpage. The letters and the arrow are now odd-shaped ponds, about eight feet deep. For many generations that segment of tundra will say "G.S.I." Tundra is even sensitive to snow machines. They compress snow, and cut off much of the air that would otherwise get to the vegetation. Evidence appears in summer. The snow machines have left brown trails on ground they never touched.

Both sunlight and rain were falling on us now. We had a topographic map, of the largest scale available but nonetheless of scant detail—about five miles to half a thumb. Of the three streams that met below us, the nearest was called Sheep Creek. A rainbow wicketed its steep valley. The top of the arch was below us. The name Sheep Creek was vestigial. "Historically, there were Dall sheep in these mountains," Fedeler said.

"What happened to them?"

"Who knows?" He shrugged. "Things go in cycles. They'll be back."

Alders had crept into creases in the mountainside across the Salmon valley. I remarked on the borderline conditions in evidence everywhere in this spare and beautiful country, and said, "Look at those alders over there, clinging to life."

Fedeler said, "It's hungry country, that's for sure. Drainage and exposure make *the* difference."

We ate peanuts and raisins and more M&M's—and, feeling rested, became ambitious. On a long southward loop back to camp, we would extend our walk by going around a mountain that was separated from us by what looked to be the fairly steep declivity of a tributary drainage. The terrain sloped away to the southwest toward the mouth of the tributary. We would go down for a time, and then cross the tributary and cut back around the mountain.

We passed first through stands of fireweed, and then over ground that was wine-red with the leaves of bearberries. There were curlewberries, too, which put a deep-purple stain on the hand. We kicked at some wolf scat, old as winter. It was woolly and white and filled with the hair of a snowshoe hare. Nearby was a rich inventory of caribou pellets and, in increasing quantity as we moved downhill, blueberries—an outspreading acreage of blueberries. Fedeler stopped walking. He touched my arm. He had in an instant become even more alert than he usually was, and obviously apprehensive. His gaze followed straight on down our intended course. What he saw there I saw now. It appeared to me to be a hill of fur. "Big boar grizzly," Fedeler said in a near-whisper. The bear was about a hundred steps away, in the blueberries, grazing. The head was down, the hump high. The immensity of muscle seemed to vibrate slowly —to expand and contract, with the grazing. Not berries alone but whole bushes were going into the bear. He was big for a barren-ground grizzly. The brown bears of Arctic Alaska (or grizzlies; they are no longer thought to be different) do not grow to the size they will reach on more ample diets elsewhere. The barren-ground grizzly will rarely grow larger than six hundred pounds.

"What if he got too close?" I said.

Fedeler said, "We'd be in real trouble."

"You can't outrun them," Hession said.

A grizzly, no slower than a racing horse, is about half again as fast as the fastest human being. Watching the great mound of weight in the blueberries, with a fifty-five-inch waist and a neck more than thirty inches around, I had difficulty imagining that he could move with such speed, but I believed it, and was without impulse to test the proposition. Fortunately, a light southerly wind was coming up the Salmon valley. On its way to us, it passed the bear. The wind was relieving, coming into our faces, for had it been moving the other way the bear would not have been placidly grazing. There is an old adage that when a pine needle drops in the forest the eagle will see it fall; the deer will hear it when it hits the ground; the bear will smell it. If the boar grizzly were to catch our scent, he might stand on his hind legs, the better to try to see. Although he could hear well and had an extraordinary sense of smell, his eyesight was not much better than what was required to see a blueberry inches away. For this reason, a grizzly stands and squints, attempting to bring the middle distance into focus, and the gesture is often misunderstood as a sign of anger and forthcoming attack. If the bear were getting ready to attack, he would be on four feet, head low, ears cocked, the hair above his hump muscle standing on end. As if that message were not clear enough, he would also chop his jaws. His teeth would make a sound that would carry like the ringing of an axe.

One could predict, but not with certainty, what a grizzly would do. Odds were very great that one touch of man scent would cause him to stop his activity, pause in a moment of absorbed and alert curiosity, and then move, at a not undignified pace, in a direction other than the one from which the scent was coming. That is what would happen almost every time, but there was, to be sure, no guarantee. The forest Eskimos fear and revere the grizzly. They know that certain individual bears not only will fail to avoid a person who comes into their country but will approach and even stalk the trespasser. It is potentially inaccurate to extrapolate the behavior of any one bear from the behavior of most, since they are both intelligent and independent and will do what they choose to do according to mood, experience, whim. A grizzly that has ever been wounded by a bullet will not forget it, and will probably know that it was a human being who sent the bullet. At sight of a human, such a bear will be likely to charge. Grizzlies hide food sometimes—a caribou calf, say, under a pile of scraped-up moss—and a person the bear might otherwise ignore might suddenly not be ignored if the person were inadvertently to step into the line between the food cache and the bear. A sow grizzly with cubs, of course, will charge anything that suggests danger to the cubs, even if the cubs are nearly as big as she is. They stay with their mother two and a half years.

None of us had a gun. (None of the six of us had brought a gun on the trip.) Among nonhunters who go into the terrain of the grizzly, there are several schools of thought about guns. The preferred one is: Never go without a sufficient weapon—a high-powered rifle or a shotgun and plenty of slug-loaded shells. The option is not without its own inherent peril. A professional hunter, some years ago, spotted a grizzly from the air and—with a client, who happened to be an Anchorage barber—landed on a lake about a mile from the bear. The stalking that followed was evidently conducted not only by the hunters but by the animal as well. The professional hunter was found dead from a broken neck, and had apparently died instantly, unaware of danger, for the cause of death was a single bite, delivered from behind. The barber, noted as clumsy with a rifle, had emptied his magazine, missing the bear with every shot but one, which struck the grizzly in the foot. The damage the bear did to the barber was enough to kill him several times. After the corpses were found, the bear was tracked and killed. To shoot and merely wound is worse than not to shoot at all. A bear that might have turned and gone away will possibly attack if wounded.

Fatal encounters with bears are as rare as they are memorable. Some people reject the rifle as cumbersome extra baggage, not worth toting, given the minimal risk. And, finally, there are a few people who feel that it is wrong to carry a gun, in part because the risk is low and well worth taking, but most emphatically because they see the gun as an affront to the wild country of which the bear is sign and symbol. This, while strongly felt, is a somewhat novel attitude. When Robert Marshall explored the Brooks Range half a century ago, he and his companions fired at almost every bear they saw, without pausing for philosophical reflection. The reaction was automatic. They were expressing mankind's immemorial fear of this beast —man and rattlesnake, man and bear. Among modern environmentalists, to whom a figure like Marshall is otherwise a hero, fear of the bear has been exceeded by reverence. A notable example, in his own past and present, is Andy Russell, author of a book called "Grizzly Country." Russell was once a professional hunter, but he gave that up to become a photographer, specializing in grizzlies. He says that he has given up not only shooting bears but even carrying a gun. On rare instances when grizzlies charge toward him, he shouts at them and stands his ground. The worst thing to do, he says, is to run, because anything that runs on open tundra suggests game to a bear. Game does not tend to stand its ground in the presence of grizzlies. Therefore, when the bear comes at you, just stand there. Charging something that does not move, the bear will theoretically stop and reconsider. (Says Russell.) More important, Russell believes that the bear will *know* if you have a gun, even if the gun is concealed:

Reviewing our experiences, we had become more and more convinced that carrying arms was not only unnecessary in most grizzly country but was certainly no good for the desired atmosphere and proper protocol in obtaining good film records. If we were to obtain such film and fraternize successfully with the big bears, it would be better to go unarmed in most places. The mere fact of having a gun within reach, cached somewhere in a pack or a hidden holster, causes a man to act with unconscious arrogance and thus maybe to smell different or to transmit some kind of signal objectionable to bears. The armed man does not assume his proper role in association with the wild ones, a fact of which they seem instantly aware at some distance. He, being wilder than they, whether he likes to admit it or not, is instantly under even more suspicion than he would encounter if unarmed.

One must follow the role of an uninvited visitor—an intruder—rather than that of an aggressive hunter, and one should go unarmed to insure this attitude.

Like pictures from pages riffled with a thumb, all of these things went through my mind there on the mountainside above the grazing bear. I will confess that in one instant I asked myself, "What the hell am I doing *here?*" There was nothing more to the question, though, than a hint of panic. I knew why I had come, and therefore what I was doing there. That I was frightened was incidental. I just hoped the fright would not rise beyond a relatively decorous level. I sensed that Fedeler and Hession were somewhat frightened, too. I would have been troubled if they had not been. Meanwhile, the sight of the bear stirred me like nothing else the country could contain. What mattered was not so much the bear himself as what the bear implied. He was the predominant thing in that country, and for him to be in it at all meant that there had to be more country like it in every direction and more of the same kind of country all around that. He implied a world. He was an affirmation to the rest of the earth that his kind of place was extant. There had been a time when his race was everywhere in North America, but it had been hunted down and pushed away in favor of something else. For example, the grizzly bear is the state animal of California, whose country was once his kind of place; and in California now the grizzly is extinct.

> *The animals I have encountered in my wilderness wanderings have been reluctant to reveal all the things about them I would like to know. The animal that impresses me most, the one I find myself liking more and more, is the grizzly. No sight encountered in the wilds is quite so stirring as those massive, clawed tracks pressed into mud or snow. No sight is quite so impressive as that of the great bear stalking across some mountain slope with the fur of his silvery robe rippling over his mighty muscles. His is a dignity and power matched by no other in the North American wilderness. To share a mountain with him for a while is a privilege and an adventure like no other.*
>
> *I have followed his tracks into an alder hell to see what he had been doing and come to the abrupt end of them, when the maker stood up thirty feet away with a sudden snort to face me.*
>
> *To see a mother grizzly ambling and loafing with her cubs across the broad, hospitable bosom of a flower-spangled mountain meadow is to see life in true wilderness at its best.*

If a wolf kills a caribou, and a grizzly comes along while the wolf is feeding on the kill, the wolf puts its tail between its legs and hurries away. A black bear will run from a grizzly, too. Grizzlies sometimes kill and eat black bears. The grizzly takes what he happens upon. He is an opportunistic eater. The predominance of the grizzly in his terrain is challenged by nothing but men and ravens. To frustrate ravens from stealing his food, he will lie down and sleep on top of a carcass, occasionally swatting the birds as if they were big black flies. He prefers a vegetable diet. He can pulp a moosehead with a single blow, but he is not lusting always to kill, and when he moves through his country he can be something munificent, going into copses of willow among unfleeing moose and their calves, touching nothing, letting it all breathe as before. He may, though, get the head of a cow moose between his legs and rake her flanks with the five-inch knives that protrude from the ends of his paws. Opportunistic. He removes and eats her entrails. He likes porcupines, too, and when one turns and presents to him a pygal bouquet of quills, he will leap into the air, land on the other side, chuck the fretful porpentine beneath the chin, flip it over, and, with a swift ventral incision, neatly remove its body from its skin, leaving something like a sea urchin behind him on the ground. He is nothing if not athletic. Before he dens, or just after he emerges, if his mountains are covered with snow he will climb to the brink of some impossible schuss, sit down on his butt, and shove off. Thirty-two, sixty-four, ninety-six feet per second, he plummets down the mountainside, spray snow flying to either side, as he approaches collision with boulders and trees. Just short of catastrophe, still going at bonecrushing speed, he flips to his feet and walks sedately onward as if his ride had not occurred.

His population density is thin on the Arctic barren ground. He needs for his forage at least fifty and perhaps a hundred square miles that are all his own—sixty-four thousand acres, his home range. Within it, he will move, typically, eight miles a summer day, doing his travelling through the twilight hours of the dead of night. To scratch his belly he walks over a tree—

where forest exists. The tree bends beneath him as he passes. He forages in the morning, generally; and he rests a great deal, particularly after he eats. He rests fourteen hours a day. If he becomes hot in the sun, he lies down in a pool in the river. He sleeps on the tundra—restlessly tossing and turning, forever changing position. What he could be worrying about I cannot imagine.

His fur blends so well into the tundra colors that sometimes it is hard to see him. Fortunately, we could see well enough the one in front of us, or we would have walked right to him. He caused a considerable revision of our travel plans. Not wholly prepared to follow the advice of Andy Russell, I asked Fedeler what one should do if a bear were to charge. He said, "Take off your pack and throw it into the bear's path, then crawl away, and hope the pack will distract the bear. But there is no good thing to do, really. It's just not a situation to be in."

We made a hundred-and-forty-degree turn from the course we had been following and went up the shoulder of the hill through ever-thickening brush, putting distance behind us in good position with the wind. For a time, we waded through hip-deep willow, always making our way uphill, and the going may have been difficult, but I didn't notice. There was adrenalin to spare in my bloodstream. I felt that I was floating, climbing with ease, like Hession. I also had expectations now that another bear, in the thick brush, might come rising up from any quarter. We broke out soon into a swale of blueberries. Hession and Fedeler, their nonchalance refreshed, sat down to eat, paused to graze. The berries were sweet and large.

"I can see why he's here," Hession said.

"These berries are so big."

"Southern exposure."

"He may not be the only one."

"They can be anywhere."

"It's amazing to me," Fedeler said. "So large an animal, living up here in this country. It's amazing what keeps that big body alive." Fedeler went on eating the blueberries with no apparent fear of growing fat. The barren-ground bear digs a lot of roots, he said—the roots of milk vetch, for example, and Eskimo potatoes. The bear, coming out of his den into the snows of May, goes down into the river bottoms, where over-wintered berries are first revealed. Wolf kills are down there, too. By the middle of June, his diet is almost wholly vegetable. He eats willow buds, sedges, cotton-grass tussocks. In the cycle of his year, roots and plants are eighty per cent of what he eats, and even when the salmon are running he does not sate himself on them alone but forages much of the time for berries. In the fall, he unearths not only roots but ground squirrels and lem-mings. It is indeed remarkable how large he grows on the provender of his yearly cycle, for on this Arctic barren ground he has to work much harder than the brown bears of southern Alaska, which line up along foaming rivers—hip to hip, like fishermen in New Jersey—taking forty-pound king salmon in their jaws as if they were nibbling feed from a barnyard trough. When the caribou are in fall migration, moving down the Salmon valley toward the Kobuk, the bear finishes up his year with one of them. Then, around the first of November, he may find a cave or, more likely, digs out a cavern in a mountainside. If he finds a natural cave, it may be full of porcupines. He kicks them out, and—extending his curious relationship with this animal—will cushion his winter bed with many thousands of their turds. If, on the other hand, he digs his den, he sends earth flying out behind him and makes a shaft that goes upward into the side of the mountain. At the top of the shaft, he excavates a shelf-like cavern. When the outside entrance is plugged with debris, the shaft becomes a column of still air, insulating the upper chamber, trapping the bear's body heat. On a bed of dry vegetation, he lays himself out like a dead pharaoh in a pyramid. But he does not truly hibernate. He just lies there. His mate of the summer, in her den somewhere, will give birth during winter to a cub or two—virtually hairless, blind, weighing about a pound. But the male has nothing to do. His heart rate goes down as low as eight beats a minute. He sleeps and wakes, and sleeps again. He may decide to get up and go out. But that is rare. He may even stay out, which is rarer—to give up denning for that winter and roam his frozen range. If he does this, sooner or later he will find a patch of open water in an otherwise frozen river, and in refreshing himself he will no doubt wet his fur. Then he rolls in the snow, and the fur acquires a thick plate of ice, which is less disturbing to the animal than to the forest Eskimo, who has for ages feared—feared most of all—the "winter bear." Arrows broke against the armoring ice, and it can be heavy enough to stop a bullet.

We moved on now, in continuing retreat, and approached the steep incline of the tributary valley we'd been skirting when the bear rewrote our plans. We meant to put the valley between us and him and reschedule ourselves on the other side. It was in fact less a valley than an extremely large ravine, which plunged maybe eight hundred feet, and then rose up an even steeper incline some fifteen hundred feet on the other side, toward the top of which the bushy vegetation ceased growing. The walking looked promising on the ridge beyond.

I had hoped we might see a den site, and this might have been the place. It had all the requisites but one. It was a steep hillside with southern exposure, and was upgrown with a hell of alders and willows. Moreover, we were on the south side of the Brooks Range divide, which is where most of the dens are. But we were not high enough. We were at something under two thousand feet, and bears in this part of Alaska like to den much higher than that. They want the very best drainage. One way to become a "winter bear" is to wake up in a flooded den.

The willow-alder growth was so dense and high that as we went down the hillside we could see no farther than a few yards ahead. It was wet in there from the recent rain. We broke our way forward with the help of gravity, crashing noisily, all but trapped in the thicket. It was a patch of jungle, many acres of jungle, with stems a foot apart and as thick as our arms, and canopies more than twelve feet high. This was bear habitat, the sort of place bears like better than people do. Our original choice had been wise—to skirt this ravine-valley—but now we were in it and without choice.

"This is the sort of place to come upon one of them unexpectedly," Hession said.

"And there is no going back," Fedeler said. "You can't walk uphill in this stuff."

"Good point," Hession said.

I might have been a little happier if I had been in an uninstrumented airplane in heavy mountain cloud. We thunked and crashed for fifteen minutes and finally came out at the tributary stream. Our approach flushed a ptarmigan, willow ptarmigan; and grayling—at sight of us—shot around in small, cold pools. The stream was narrow, and alders pressed over it from either side. We drank, and rested, and looked up the slope in front of us, which must have had an incline of fifty degrees. The ridge at the top looked extremely far away. Resting, I became aware of a considerable ache in my legs and a blister on one of my heels. On the way uphill we became separated, Hession angling off to the right, Fedeler and I to the left. We groped for handholds among bushes that protruded from the flaky schist, and pulled ourselves up from ledge to ledge. The adrenalin was gone, and my legs were turning to stone. I was ready to dig a den and get in it. My eyes kept addressing the ridgeline, far above. If eyes were hands they could have pulled me there. Then, suddenly, from far below, I saw Jack Hession lightly ambling along the ridge—in his tennis shoes, in his floppy cotton hat. He was looking around, killing time, waiting up for us.

Things seemed better from the ridge. The going would be level for a time. We sat down and looked back, to the north, across the deep tributary valley, and with my monocular tried to glass the grazing bear. No sight or sign of him. Above us now was a broadly conical summit, and spread around its western flank was a mile, at least, of open alpine tundra. On a contour, we headed south across it—high above, and two miles east of, the river. We saw what appeared to be a cairn on the next summit south, and decided to go to it and stand on it and see if we could guess—in relation to our campsite—where we were. Now the walking felt good again. We passed a large black pile of grizzly scat. "When it's steaming, that's when you start looking around for a tree," Hession said. This particular scat had sent up its last vapors many days before. Imagining myself there at such a time, though, I looked around idly for a tree. The nearest one behind us that was of more than dwarf or thicket stature was somewhere in Lapland. Ahead of us, however, across the broad dome of tundra, was a dark stand of white spruce, an extremity of the North American forest, extending toward us. The trees were eight hundred yards away. Black bears, frightened, sometimes climb trees. Grizzlies almost never climb trees.

At seven in the evening, after wading up a slope of medium to heavy brush, we came out onto more smooth tundra and reached the hilltop of the apparent cairn. It was a rock outcropping, and we sat on it in bright sunshine and looked at the circumvallate mountains. A great many of them had such outcroppings projecting from their ridges, and they much resembled the cairns shepherds build on bald summits in Scotland. For that matter, they suggested the cairns—closer to the Kobuk—that forest Eskimos once used in methodical slaughter of caribou. The cairns were built on the high tundra in a great V, open end to the north, and they served as a funnel for the southbound herd. To the approaching caribou, the cairns were meant to suggest Eskimos, and to reinforce the impression Eskimos spaced themselves between cairns. At the point of the V, as many caribou as were needed were killed and the rest were let through.

Before us now, lying on the tundra that stretched away toward the river we saw numerous caribou antlers. The Arctic herd cyclically chooses various passes and valleys in making its way south across the range, and of late has been favoring, among other places, the Salmon and Hunt River drainages. Bleached white, the antlers protruded from the tundra like the dead branches of buried trees. When the forest Eskimo of old went to stalk the grizzly bear, he carried in his hand a spear, the tip of which was made from bear bone or, more often, from the antler of the caribou. A bearskin was the door of an Eskimo's home if the occupant had ever killed a bear, for it symbolized the extraordinary valor of the hunter within. When the man drew close and the bear stood on its hind legs, the man ran under this eave of flesh and set the shaft of the spear firmly on the ground, then ducked out from under the swinging, explosive paws. The bear lunged forward onto the spear and died.

Eskimo knife handles were also made from caribou antlers, and icepicks to penetrate the surface of the river, and sinkers for the bottoms of willow-bark seines, and wood-splitting wedges, and arrowheads. All caribou, male and female, grow antlers. The horns of sheep, cattle, buffalo consist of extremely dense, compactly matted hair. The antler of the caribou is calcareous. It is hard bone, with the strength of wrought iron. Moving downhill and south across the tundra, we passed through groves of antlers. It was as if the long filing lines of the spring migration had for some reason paused here for shedding to occur. The antlers, like the bear, implied the country. Most were white, gaunt, chalky. I picked up a younger one, though, that was recently shed and was dark, like polished brown marble. It was about four feet along the beam and perfect in form. Hession found one like it. We set them on our shoulders and moved on down the hill, intent to take them home.

We headed for the next of the riverine mountains, where we planned to descend and—if our calculations were accurate—

meet the river at the campsite. The river, far below us, now and again came into view as we walked abreast over open tundra. Fedeler, even more alert than usual, now stopped and, as before, touched my arm. He pointed toward the river. If a spruce needle had been floating on the water there, Fedeler would have seen it. We saw in an instant that we had miscalculated and were heading some miles beyond the campsite and would have come eventually to the river not knowing—upstream or downstream—which way to go. Fedeler was pointing toward a gravel bar, a thin column of smoke, minute human figures near the smoke, and the podlike whiteness of the metal canoe.

Another two miles, descending, and we were barefoot in the river, with pink hot feet turning anesthetically cold. We crossed slowly. The three others were by the campfire. On the grill were grayling and a filleted Arctic char. The air was cool now, nearing fifty, and we ate the fish, and beef stew, and strawberries, and drank hot chocolate. After a time, Hession said, "That was a good walk. That was some of the easiest hiking you will ever find in Alaska."

We drew our route on the map and figured the distance at fourteen miles. John Kauffmann, tapping his pipe on a stone, said, "That's a lot for Alaska."

We sat around the campfire for at least another hour. We talked of rain and kestrels, oil and antlers, the height and the headwaters of the river. Neither Hession nor Fedeler once mentioned the bear.

When I got into my sleeping bag, though, and closed my eyes, there he was, in color, on the side of the hill. The vision was indelible, but fear was not what put it there. More, it was a sense of sheer luck at having chosen in the first place to follow Fedeler and Hession up the river and into the hills—a memento not so much of one moment as of the entire circuit of the long afternoon. It was a vision of a whole land, with an animal in it. This was his country, clearly enough. To be there was to be incorporated, in however small a measure, into its

substance—his country, and if you wanted to visit it you had
better knock.

> *His association with other animals is a mixture of enter-*
> *prising action, almost magnanimous acceptance, and just*
> *plain willingness to ignore. There is great strength and*
> *pride combined with a strong mixture of inquisitive curios-*
> *ity in the make-up of grizzly character. This curiosity is*
> *what makes trouble when men penetrate into country*
> *where they are not known to the bear. The grizzly can be*
> *brave and sometimes downright brash. He can be secretive*
> *and very retiring. He can be extremely cunning and also*
> *powerfully aggressive. Whatever he does, his actions match*
> *his surroundings and the circumstance of the moment. No*
> *wonder that meeting him on his mountain is a momentous*
> *event, imprinted on one's mind for life.*

❰ In the night, the air and the river balanced out, and both
were forty-six at seven in the morning. Walking in the water
promised to be cold, and, given the depth of the river at the
riffles, that is apparently what we were going to do. We took
a long time packing, as anyone would who apparently had
twenty per cent more cargo than there was capacity in the
boats. Duffel was all over the gravel bar. I had brought my gear
in a Duluth sack—a frameless canvas pack in every way out-
sized. It had a tumpline and shoulder straps, all leather, and,
stuffed to the bulge point, it suggested Santa Claus on his way
south. My boat for the day was one of the single kayaks. I
spread out the gear on the gravel beside it, turned the empty
Duluth sack inside out and rolled and trussed it so that it was
about the size of a two-pound loaf of bread. This went into the

bow of the kayak. I poked it up there with a stick. Anyone with a five-foot arm could easily pack a Klepper. The openings in the rib frames were less than the breadth of two spread hands. Stowing gear fore and aft was like stuffing a couple of penholders, but an amazing amount went in. All excess was taken by the canoe, and it was piled high—our aluminum mule. I tied the caribou antler across the stern deck of the kayak, and we moved out into the river. The current was going about four miles an hour, but we travelled a great deal more slowly than that, because we walked almost as far as we floated. If we had a foot of water, we felt luxuriously cushioned. Often enough, we had an inch or two. Pool to riffle, pool to riffle, we rode a little and then got out and walked, painters in our hands. The boats beside us were like hounds on leashes, which now and then stopped and had to be dragged. Getting into a kayak just once is awkward enough, let alone dozens of times a day. You put your hands behind you on the coaming, then lower yourself into place, all in the same act removing your legs from the river and shaking off water. Hession, at the start, showed me how to do this, and then he sat down lightly in his own kayak and floated away. I flopped backward into mine and nearly rolled it over; but the day would hold, if nothing else, practice in getting in and out of a kayak. When the boats scraped bottom at the tops of riffles, we got out, sought the channel of maximum depth, moved the boats through, and then got back into them where the water was fast and deepening in the lower parts of the rips. The problem of getting in was therefore complicated by generally doing so in the middle of rapids. In the first such situation, I lost all coördination, lurched backward onto the boat, nearly sat in the river, and snapped a toe, ripping the ligaments off the second joint. By noon, however, I was more or less competent, and further damage seemed unlikely.

I was not disappointed that the Salmon was low. In a lifetime of descending rivers, this was the clearest and the wildest

river. Walking it in places made it come slow, and that was a
dividend in itself. A glance at the gravel bars, ledges, and cut
banks told where the river at times would be—high, tumbling,
full of silt, and washing down. I would prefer to walk in water
so clear it seemed to be polished rather than to ride like a rocket
down a stream in flood. For all of that, another two inches
would have helped the day.

The water was cold by anyone's standards, for had it been
much colder it would not have been water. Pourchot and
Hession were wearing sneakers, and I did not envy them.
Fedeler and Newman wore hip boots. Kauffmann and I had
wet-suit boots—foam-rubber socks, more or less, that keep wet
feet completely warm. The water that is arrested in the foam
takes on the temperature of blood. I had on thick wool socks
as well, and my feet were never cold. The sun was circling a
cloudless sky, and needles of light came flashing off the river.
The air went into the seventies. We walked along in T-shirts
—feet warm, legs cool in soaking trousers, shoulders hot in the
Arctic sun.

A couple of tributaries came into the river, the first from the
east, the second from the west, and they deepened the pools
and improved the rips. Somewhere up the easterly stream, said
Pourchot, nineteen placer gold claims had been filed in 1968.
The claims had not been kept up with yearly "assessment
work," however. No mining had begun, and now would not
begin as long as the claims were in national-interest land. This
was not important gold country. Perhaps the most unusual
event in the experience of the forest Eskimos was the arrival
in 1898 of more than a thousand prospectors who had heard
glistering rumors about the Kobuk valley. They looked around,
did not find much, and lasted, for the most part, a single
winter. About ten years later, gold of modest but sufficient
assay was discovered on a creek near Kiana. Claims there were
worked by placer mining—sluicing gravels, flushing out the
gold. Where gold is mined in Alaska now, bulldozers, for the

most part, move the gravels. The clear water that comes in from the upstream side goes on its way—brown and turbid— with a heavy load of fresh debris. Early in Fedeler's time with the Habitat Section of the Alaska Department of Fish and Game, he was shifted from pipeline surveillance to gold-mining surveillance—going from one site to another to check effluent standards in placer operations. He might better have waltzed with grizzlies than approach some of the miners, who told him to pack up his permit applications and get the hell off their claims. So what if some fish got a gutful of silt? Fedeler was only a few short years from his family's farm in Iowa, his master's thesis on the life cycle of pheasants, but he was quickly learning the folkways of Alaska. "Get out!" the miners suggested. "We've always done things when we want to, where we want to, how we want to, and that is what we're going to do now."

The forest around us, to the extent that it could be called forest, consisted of bands of spruce and cottonwood. Occasionally, it made sallies up the hillsides onto protected slopes or into dry ravines, but mainly it pointed north like an arrow, and gradually it widened as we moved downstream. Close to the river edge, much of the way, were clumps of willow and alder, backed by the taller trees, which in turn had bands of alder backing them, before the woods gave way altogether to open, rising ground—to the lichens, the sedges, and mosses of the high tundra. The leaves of alder, chewed to break out the sap, relieve itching when rubbed on mosquito bites. The forest Eskimos make red dyes from alder bark—American green alder, the only species that grows so far north. Willow, as a genus, is hardier. The Sitka spruce is the state tree, in recognition of its commercial distinction, for Sitka spruce is the most negotiable thing that grows from roots in Alaska. It grows only in the south, however, and while the Sitka spruce goes off to the sawmill, the willow vegetates the state. There are only a hundred and thirty-three species of trees and shrubs in all

Alaska, and thirty-three of those are willows. Before the impor-
tation of nylon, fishnets were made from willow—from long
pliant strips of the bark, braided with the split roots of spruce.
Rope, dog collars, and hunters' bows were made from willow,
and snares for small game and birds. Willow still goes into
snowshoe frames, and fish traps, and wicker baskets. Young
leaves, buds, and shoots of willow are edible and nourishing.
The inner bark, chewed like cane, is full of sugar. Willow sap,
scraped together with a knife, is sweet and delicious. At least
twelve kinds of willow were growing along the Salmon—among
them little-tree willow, halberd willow, netleaf, skeleton-leaf,
and diamond-leaf willow, Arctic willow, barren-ground willow,
Alaska bog willow. Oranges are easier to tell apart. We called
all willows willows. The wood was agreeable in fires, and became almost as hot as the coals of alder.

On a broad acreage of gravel, we stopped now for lunch, and
built a fire of willow and alder. The sun was hot to the point
of headache, but there was a factor of chill in the day. Gradually the kayaks were acquiring water, dripping from us as we
got out and in. One's buttocks, after several hours in cold kayak
bilge, began to feel like defrosting meat. However warm one's
head and shoulders might have been, a shiver went into the
bones. The fire was piled high with wood that had bleached on
the gravel in the sun, and a light breeze tilted the flame.
Standing in the downwind heat was like standing in the Grand
Canyon on a summer day. In a few minutes, our clothes had
dried.

Three more tributaries came into the river, and its navigable
stretches lengthened through the afternoon. Still, though, we
did a lot of walking. Mergansers—a mother and six—fled
ahead of us, running on the water like loons. Now and again,
big ledges of bedrock jutted into and under the river, damming
water, framing pools. Below one ledge, where water ran white
from a pool, we stopped to fish. Stell Newman caught an Arctic
char. Bob Fedeler caught another. They were imposing speci-

mens, bigger than the Salmon's salmon. They were spotted orange and broad-flanked, with lobster-claw jaws. Sea-run Arctic char. They could be described as enormous brook trout, for the brook trout is in fact a char. They had crimson fins with white edges and crimson borders on their bellies. Their name may be Gaelic, wherein "blood" is *"cear."* The Alaska record length for an Arctic char is thirty-six inches, and ours were somewhat under that. I tossed a small Mepps lure across the stream, size zero, and bringing it back felt a big one hit. The strike was too strong for a grayling—more power, less commotion. I had, now, about ten pounds of fish on a six-pound line. So I followed the fish around, walking upstream and down, into and out of the river. I had been walking the kayak all day long, and this experience was not much different. After fifteen minutes or so, the fish tired, and came thrashing from the water. I took out my tape and laid it on him, from the hooking jaw to the tip of the tail. Thirty-one and a half inches. Orange speckles, crimson glow, this resplendent creature was by a long measure the largest fish I had ever caught in fresh water. In its belly would fit ten of the kind that I ordinarily keep and eat. For dinner tonight we would have grilled Arctic char, but enough had been caught already by the others. So, with one hand under the pelvic fins and the other near the jaw, I bent toward the river and held the fish underwater until it had its equipoise. It rested there on my hands for a time, and stayed even when I lowered them away. Then, like naval ordnance, it shot across the stream. The best and worst part of catching that fish was deciding to let it go.

Floating for a time, we moved on downstream. When Eskimos returning from long summer hunting trips rode down the Salmon River, they travelled on rafts. In June, when they had established their seine-fishing camps along the Kobuk, the men left the women and went off into the mountains in small groups to spend the summer killing creatures whose skins were needed for winter—marmots, lone caribou, caribou fawns (for

undergarments). The hunters had long hours of leisure, and
they sat around campfires, as we do, telling tales. They repeated
the narratives night after night, yet no one ever told someone
else's story; a sense of copyright was inherent, and plagiarism
was seemingly unknown. Sons inherited stories from their fathers. Needless to say, many tales had to do with the hunt—
hunting the wolf, hunting the caribou, fall and winter hunting
the bear. Tramping up the mountains on snowshoes, they
searched for signs of denning—watching, in otherwise uniform
snow, for a glaze of ice, the product of the vapors of breath.
Finding such evidence, they carefully removed the ice, quietly,
gingerly, revealing a vent hole. An exploring spear was inserted
in the hole and moved about until it touched something soft.
Resting there, the spear would slowly move up and down. The
hunter then rammed it home, and leaned on it with all his
weight as the bear heaved in torment, lifting the hunter off the
ground. The modern method is to poke for the bear with a long
rod and when contact is established place a rifle by the rod and
fire. When the bear is still, the hunters go into the den. Sometimes, living bears are in there, too—new cubs, or full-grown
cubs, or a living mother and a dead cub. There is no need for
fear, the hunters say, because a bear will not fight in its den.
The bear is the animal whose intelligence they respect above
all others', and around which they have spun over centuries
skeins of ritual and taboo. In times past, the skull of a killed
bear was ceremonially touched to the bear's heart and was then
placed atop a living spruce and left in the forest with its eye
sockets facing north.

With signs of autumn, hunters came down from the mountains to the upper waters of the river. They cut dead spruce,
built their rafts, and piled them high with fur. In the upper
river, in shallow water, rafts consisted of just a few logs, tied
together with thongs of bear hide. The narrow ends of the logs
all faced downstream; the wide ends formed the stern. Thus,
the raft was a wedge, pointing down the river. Afloat, it was
guided with a spruce pole at the bow. When it ran aground,

it was dragged, like a Klepper, through the shallow rips. As the river deepened, the rafts of two or more parties were joined together. The bigger the river, the bigger the total raft—a stable vessel anytime, even in thundering flood.

Some of the wood in the rafts was for winter fires, but most was used for housing, a need that has waned on the Kobuk. Houses now come from the government, in three choices—A, B, and C—at so much a month for twenty years. They are frame structures, gabled, nondescript. They could be garages with windows. In winter the walls sweat, and show a frost line four feet high. Their exterior sheds are not large enough for the storage of meat and equipment. There is a new house today in Kiana made of river-floated logs.

We stopped for the night below a bedrock pool, pitching the tents on a sandy bank under woolly mountains whose ridgelines were a couple of thousand feet above the river. The forest now filled in most of the valley floor and went up the slopes maybe three hundred feet. Bear tracks in the sand by the river were eleven inches long, six inches wide. We fished—take-and-put —catching and releasing half a dozen grayling and several char. Eskimos, on their journeys, now cook char in aluminum foil, which is what we did. The pink flesh steamed in its own moisture, and each of us ate at least two pounds. Looking up from dinner, we saw a black bear, long and leggy, crossing a steep hillside at a slow lope. It stopped to graze for a time, and then, apropos of nothing, suddenly ran and took a crashing leap into a stand of willow and alder, breaking its way through, coming out the other side onto a high plain of pale-green caribou moss.

❆ In the morning there was wind. A front as dank as an oyster was moving in over the eastern mountains. Rain was coming —an uninviting day to frog kayaks in the river. We ate oatmeal, and then, after coffee, Jack Hession said he thought he'd be going. He had deadlines to meet and simply had to get back to the office. The office—in Anchorage—was six hundred miles away. If there was a wild place in the United States, we were in it, and Hession was about to take off on his own, pressed for time. Terribly sorry, he said. He would have enjoyed staying with us, but he had pressures from home. He had decided to make the trip with us more or less at the last moment, and now he was deciding to leave at the last moment plus one. He would take the mail plane from Kiana, which was something like ninety miles downstream. With a packet or two of freeze-dry and six pieces of pilot bread, he got into his single Klepper and bobbed down the river. The two blades of his paddle wagged like a semaphore, and he was gone. He had no tent. Rain fell through much of the day, and all through the night.

Hession told us, many days later, stories of his solo run. Not long after he left us, he became preoccupied with his thoughts and overshot a channel in a riffle. Near the far ends of pools, where loose-stone deposits had built up as dams, the river would characteristically become fast and shallow and would tumble to one side over a brink of gravel—racing white toward a lower pool. The knack of navigation was to read the riffle, sense the heaviest flow there, and get into it before the broad general current could take the boat a little farther and run it aground; for while much water went down the riffle even more simply disappeared into the earth, passing into the porous basements of high, dry bars of gravel. Often enough, there was just a narrow slot, angling left or right, through which the kayak could proceed, and now Hession had missed such a place, so he would have to backferry—moving, stern first, across the stream, to realign his course and shoot the rip. He was close to a bank. Realizing his mistake, he reached backward with his paddle. He happened to look up as well. On the bank above him were a sow grizzly and a huge two-year-old cub. Across a distance of no more than fifteen feet Hession and the mother grizzly looked each other in the eye. Staring steadily at her, he slowly moved the paddle, retreating at an angle to the current. He felt helpless, because he could think of nothing to do if the bear attacked. He thought of turning the boat over in order to disappear beneath it, but there was nowhere to hide in less than a foot of water. Therefore, all decisions belonged to the bear. Hession kept on gazing fixedly into her eyes, making no gesture of fear or flight. The bears themselves retreated. But after a few steps they turned, and both stood up on their hind legs, squinting. Hession thought they were going to come for him, after this second look. But they dropped down, turned, and went. He told this story without modulation, without a hint of narrative excitation; and in the same flat manner he went on to say that he had later seen a pair of sandhill cranes and, some time after that, a golden eagle. It was all wildlife to him. When you are the Sierra Club's man in Alaska, the least of your problems is bears.

That evening, when he decided it was time to sleep, the rain was steady and miserable, and he looked around for shelter. He looked for big driftwood. He finally came to an uprooted spruce, washed downriver probably in June. Resting on its root structure, it was partly off the ground. He tipped the kayak so that it leaned against the tree, and put his sleeping bag in the space formed between them. (As an alternative, he might have cut a number of young spruce and arranged them in a circle with their tips together at the top—a form of tepee that the forest Eskimos call "poor people's camp.") Hession slid himself into place. The rain fell on the boat and tree. "I passed out," he said, "and the next thing I knew it was morning." When he arrived at the confluence of the Salmon and the Kobuk, two Eskimos were fishing there. They shared their boiled salmon with him, in a sauce of seal oil. Their Evinrude took him to Kiana.

John Kauffmann and I paddled Snake Eyes the day Hession left, and we spent a lot of time in the river beside it, making

Klepper trails in the gravel. We had to bail frequently, because water was accumulating inside the hull not only from the rain and from our dripping boots but also through leaks in the vulcanized rubber. The shallow river was grinding Snake Eyes down. The hull, advertised to be as "strong as a heavy-duty conveyor belt," was losing its capability to convey us. We were coming into many deep pools and fine stretches of water now, but the momentum and response of Snake Eyes afloat were not much better than of Snake Eyes aground, so the others—in their maneuverable, shallow-draft canoe and light kayak— often had to wait. On the slope above the left bank we saw a lone grizzly walking north in the rain. Since the river was narrow and bending, the boats were sometimes out of sight from one another. Fedeler, in the single Klepper, saw a grizzly that was gone when the rest of us came along. There was no telling how many bears we may have failed to notice—or, for that matter, how many bears we may have seen twice. The Nikok, a tributary, came into the Salmon from the west, and we stopped for lunch beside it, and cast lures from smooth ledges into deep holes that were clear and green.

After the Nikok, there was more river to float us. The rain turned to mist and put a soft gray light on the hills. No matter what the weather might be, Kauffmann said, the Brooks Range for him was the best of Alaska—in the quality of its light, in the clarity of its flowing water, in the configuration of its terrain. He did not much care for the glacier country—the south. "It's too raw," he went on. "Up here in the north, you have all the effects of the glacier land forms without the glaciers themselves. You have clear streams." Studying the Salmon as a national wild river had been Kauffmann's idea. If Kauffmann could have his way, at least a quarter of Alaska would be held as wilderness forever. After his five years of study and planning for Gates of the Arctic National Park—an area twice as large as the state of Hawaii, four times the size of Yellowstone—odds seemed favorable that it would be congres-

sionally confirmed. Kauffmann's total plans for the park's development—his intended use of airstrips, roadways, lodges,
lean-tos, refreshment stands, trash barrels, benches—added up
to zero. The most inventive thing to do, as he saw it, was
nothing. Let the land stand wild, without so much as a man-
made trail.

Kauffmann, among Alaskans, represented only a small arc or
two in a wheel of attitudes toward the land. For one thing, he
was a "fed" and thus an "outsider," who—in the view of some
—was trying to "grab" and "lock up" prime terrain. Yet he was
also an Alaskan. In a state largely populated by aggressive
transients, he was at least as Alaskan as most. He had built a
home and had become an earnest Alaskan citizen. As such, and
not merely as a fed, he did indeed favor locking up land, if that
meant saving it for the future of the future.

In the time Kauffmann had lived in Alaska, the number of
voters with views sympathetic to his own had risen from very
low to modest. Yet the presence of this minority (backed by
support from outside) had produced a tension that underlay
much of what was happening in the state. It was tension over
the way in which Alaska might proceed, tension somewhat
reminiscent of the matters (water rights, grazing rights) that
divided earlier pioneers. In its modern form, it was the tension
of preservation versus development, of stasis versus economic
productivity, of wilderness versus the drill and the bulldozer,
and in part it had caused the portentous reassignment of land
that now, in the nineteen-seventies, was altering, or threaten-
ing to alter, the lives of everyone in the state.

The federal government, long ago, used to watch over Alaska
with one eye, and with so little interest that the lid was generally closed. In all that territorial land, so wild and remote,
emigrants from the United States easily established their frontier code: breathe free, do as you please, control your own
destiny. If you had much more in mind than skinning hares,
though, it was difficult to control much of a destiny—to plan,

for example, any kind of development on a major scale—since the federal government owned more than ninety-nine per cent of the land. The push for statehood was seen as a way to gain more control; but, to their frustration and disappointment, Alaskans found that the big decisions continued to be made (or postponed, as the case might be) in Washington. After some years, and under pressure to find new energy resources, the federal government awakened to the potentialities of Alaska. With the development of the oil field at Prudhoe Bay, state and federal interests at last seemed to complement each other. The discovery of oil felt like the discovery of gold, and the future seemed lighted from behind. With the pipeline, however, Alaska suddenly had more development than it could absorb. It suddenly had manifold inflation and a glut of trailer parks. It had traffic jams. You could pick up a telephone and "dial a date." In the reasonably accessible bush, fishing and hunting—the sorts of things many people had long sought in Alaska—became crowded and poor. A boom was on, money was around, and buildings were going up; but a dream may have come too true. Most of the money was passing over the heads of Alaskans long established in the state. Confused and disillusioned, many were forced to ponder if big-scale development meant bonanza after all.

The people's new hesitation about the wisdom of development was expressed in 1974 in the election, by a narrow margin, of Jay Hammond as governor. Hammond had homesteaded land in Alaska. His wife was an Alaskan native. His approach to Alaska's future was to attempt to go slow, to build with caution, to try to find a middle course—not only *between* conservation and economic development but *within* them as well. He appointed Robert Weeden, a wildlife biologist from the University of Alaska, as State Policy Development and Planning Director, and set him the task of drawing together a state proposal for the future of the designated national-interest lands. Unsurprisingly, the state soon informed Congress that it would like to participate in the management of these lands, and hence was willing to put some of its own land into the total. The state would like various options to be left open for the future and not to be written away in legislation. "We're interested in sharing in the decisions on federal lands forever," Weeden told me one day in the capitol, in Juneau. "The federal proposals reflect the territorial imperative of agencies rather than the long-term interests of the state as the nation relates to it. The state has gone from a development urge to development plus conservation, while the federal trajectory— in general—has been from neglect and preservation to exploita- tion of resources. We've almost changed roles. Meanwhile, federal agencies are scrapping among themselves. The Na- tional Park Service wants the land as it is, and the Forest Service and the Bureau of Land Management would like to see it exploited. The Fish and Wildlife Service is closer to the middle. Their lands are available for 'compatible uses.' For example, their Kenai National Moose Range has oil wells in it. The Moose Range was the first oil field in Alaska. The National Park Service and Fish and Wildlife are the conservationists' favorites. Developers favor the Bureau of Land Management. We need an additional approach. Suppose you have good park- land that also has minerals. You say a firm decision should not be made there—not right now. There are places where a rea- sonable man would not want to make decisions yet. Our posi- tion has been described by some as a middle-of-the-road stance. Perhaps so, but in this road all the traffic seems to be hugging the two ditches. These days, man should be somewhat humble about his *capacity* to make permanent decisions." On a wall in Weeden's offices, a sign said, "Earth, this is God. I want all you people to clear out before the end of the month. I have a client who is interested in the property."

I had lunch one day in Anchorage with an entrenched Alas- kan boomer—Robert Atwood, editor and publisher of the An- chorage *Times*. If the state government and its Robert Weed-

ens were about ninety degrees around from the attitude represented by John Kauffmann, Atwood was a hundred and eighty.
"We should preserve wilderness only in areas that are without
other resources," he said. "The U.S. needs our oil. We're not
going to prevent it going. God damn it, they should take it.
They need it. The ultimate destiny of Alaska is to help the
nation be self-sufficient. We should bend and help, not tie the
land up in a knot to save a tree or a bear or a fond dream. A
state develops by developing its resources. Prudhoe Bay was a
big start for this little state. Then what happened? The pipeline was stopped for years by conservationists. It was the first
time in history that a state was told it could not take its
resources to market. Some people think anybody who wants to
do anything with a shovel is bad. They should see Prudhoe Bay.
It's so damned clean and neat and sterile—with refrigerated
pilings, so the tundra won't melt. The pipeline will be the
biggest tourist attraction in Alaska. Caribou will move close to
it for heat. Meanwhile, these wilderness buffs, like your friend
Kauffmann, have an insatiable appetite for wilderness. They
have drawn lines on the map according to what is best and
beautiful from their point of view. What they are trying for is
a land grab, but they see it as the last chance to preserve
something. From their point of view, it *is* the last chance. But
locking the land up is unfair to future generations. Nobody
knows wholly what is under it, in coal or oil or minerals."

Alaskan natives, for their part, were somewhere on the way
back to Kauffmann. They saw the federal park and refuge
proposals as possibly—but not necessarily—the least disturbing
of the changes that could come to, for example, the Salmon
River and the Kobuk valley. Willie Hensley, an Eskimo leader,
once described it this way for me: "If we can hunt, fish, trap,
we're not concerned. We don't have that assurance yet. If we
can't drive our boats up the river, we're going to have problems.
If we can't take our dog teams or snow machines after caribou,
we're going to have problems. Now is a time of transition for

the native people. We have long used the land as if we owned
it. We thought we *did* own it. We had lived here ten thousand
years and assumed it was ours. But in the past we never had
the political or economic clout to make a single bit of difference in Alaska. The Native Claims Settlement Act has given
us a voice that we did not have before. It has also given us the
problem of the national-interest lands. If these lands can be
used for subsistence hunting, fishing, trapping, we don't have
many qualms." No less wary of the coming of the parkland
were any number of whites living in the bush, who had also
been trapping and hunting and fishing for (in many cases)
generations, and who now found themselves confronted with
much the same worries the natives had—but without the incidental benefits of a billion dollars and forty million acres of
land.

Paddling on through the light rain, Kauffmann now began
to fulminate. He said he had once drawn up an Alaskan coat
of arms, its shield quarterly gules and gold with a motto written
in each quarter, expressing what he took to be the core attitudes of the people of Alaska toward—as the Aleut word
"Alaska" means—"the great land." The motto written on one
quarter of the shield was "Dig It Up." On another, "Chop It
Down." On another, "Fish It Out." On the fourth, "Shoot
It." He said the forty million acres involved in the Native
Claims Settlement Act amounted to something over six hundred acres for each native. He said the Statehood Act had
provided what now amounted to two hundred and fifty acres
for each Alaskan. And that left roughly one acre of Alaska for
each citizen of the United States as a whole—an amount he
considered minimal. "People who have come to Alaska, worked
hard, and grubbed out a living feel resentment toward people
whom they call 'Lower Forty-eight meddlers,' " he went on.
"People here take a proprietary attitude. They say, 'Don't tie
our hands.' They forget that we *all* own Alaska. They call it
their land, but it's everybody's land. Alaska is the last great

opportunity this nation has to set aside adequate chunks of natural landscape for a variety of conservation purposes. The land is still open. It is uncommitted. Think what the East would look like if Thoreau had been heeded. Think of the rivers and lakes of New Hampshire and Maine—Lake Winnipesaukee, Moosehead Lake. The opportunity exists in Alaska on a scale incomprehensible to anyone who hasn't seen it. Local interests should be satisfied, certainly, and state interests as well—but so should *national* interests. This river, this land around us, is of national interest, and it belongs to everybody in the United States."

In part to make him paddle harder, I said, "Yes, but why do all you sneakerfaces, you ecocentrics, think you need so much of it? Why do you need eighty million acres?"

"Everything in Alaska is on a bigger scale," he said. "There is a need for a place in which to lose yourself, for more space than you can encompass. It's not sufficient just to set aside sights to see. We need whole ecosystems, whole ranges, whole watersheds."

"Entire mountain ranges?"

"We're going to have to live in close harmony with the earth. There's a lot we don't know. We need places where we can learn how. The carrying capacity for plants and animals is limited here. They need plenty of space and time. Think of the years it takes a grayling to grow. If we do our thing, if we exploit shortsightedly, we impoverish even the biggest landscapes. There is no such thing as superabundance. I think many people have come to realize this. A sense of spaciousness has shaped the character of this country. We don't want to let that sense entirely pass. The frontier society feels it is here to exploit the land, though—to grow, to build, to tame, to extract, to realize the wealth that is here. They don't like regulation. They don't like to be told they can't do something. They want to do what they want to where and when they please. Between their interests and the interests of the nation as a whole the Native Claims Settlement Act tried to strike a balance."

"Some balance," I said. "The map is covered with proposed parks."

"The parks are ten per cent of the state, God damn it. Tithed to the future. The proposals are not repetitious. They are different. They complement each other. This river and the Gates of the Arctic are at the wilderness end of the spectrum. This is the last big piece of magnificent mountain wilderness we have left. First it was the Appalachians, then the Rockies, then the Sierra Nevada, then Alaska, and this is the last part of Alaska. This is America's ultimate wilderness; it goes no farther. This is our last opportunity to provide, admittedly in a contrived way, the chance to go adventuring in country so wild that valleys and mountains are without names."

"But why lock it up forever?"

"It will *not* be locked up. The resources aren't going to go anywhere. In some dire situation, they are there. People say, 'Study it first.' This is a delaying tactic by people who want to exploit it later. There's always someone who wants another look. Meanwhile, the time has historically come for preserving major pieces of land in Alaska, to have the freshness of Alaska —large landscapes, habitats—perpetuated, not tarnished and degraded as man grubs his way along with awesome power. The locations of oil reserves are largely determined. The national-interest lands include very little oil. What the contention comes down to is mining. Nineteenth-century laws let the miner onto most government land, but the miner is no longer the quaint old man with the burro and the pick."

Having goaded him, I thought I should reward him. I said, "In Alaska, we appear to be recapitulating ourselves. This may be our last chance to suggest that we've learned anything at all." I felt the momentum of Snake Eyes perceptibly increase.

We came to the end of a pondlike pool, and Snake Eyes ran aground. Salmon were thrashing up the riffle there—backs exposed, sculling against water and stones. Toward the bottom of the rip, water collected, becoming heavy and white and two feet deep. The river then curved right—a bending chute with a cut bank on one side and an apron of gravel on the other. Over the cut bank a sweeper had recently fallen, a spruce whose trunk reached into the river. Its green boughs spread over the white water. The swiftest of the current went under the branches, so the problem presented to Kauffmann and me was to get into the kayak in fast water and then collect ourselves at once for a move around the tree. Sweepers tend to trap boats and hold them almost broadside to the current while the weight of the river rolls them over. Kauffmann and I attacked the situation with the same easy confidence we had displayed over the years on a number of analogous occasions, beginning with a near double drowning in 1955. Standing in the rain in the fast water, we settled into Snake Eyes and flew at the sweeper. In concept, we would skirt it to the right. In practice, we hit it dead center. Kauffmann was still reminding me that this was our last opportunity to save the final American wilderness when Snake Eyes bought the river. The thought occurred to me as I pitched head first into the rushing water that I had not often involuntarily overturned on a river trip, and that on almost all the occasions when I had the last thing I had seen on my way to the bottom was Kauffmann. Tact restrained me from mentioning this to him until he had come up out of the river. Meanwhile, I jumped to my feet. The water was waist deep, cold as a wine bucket. I retrieved Kauffmann's hat. Under the gin-clear water, his head, with its radical economy of hair, looked like an onion. Snake Eyes was upside down. I wrenched it right side up, then took its painter and hurried out of the river. From the moment we spilled until I was standing on dry gravel, scarcely fifteen seconds went by. Kauffmann was soaked, but I was not. My rain gear had been drawn tight at the neck and had elastic cuffs. I was half wet—in harlequin patches, and not much on the chest or the back. A piece at a time, we floated our duffel out of Snake Eyes—sleeping bags, clothes bags. Then we dumped out the water, repacked the duffel, and got back onto the river.

We were chilled, and that was a long cold afternoon. Snake Eyes continued to move downstream like a sea anchor, and in the miserable rain we chose not to stop and build a fire. A few hours later, we embraced the fire that ended the day.

(Pourchot, after dinner in the bright evening light, began repairing the Kleppers. The hulls were so abraded, the damage so extensive, that he interrupted the job for his night's sleep and finished it after breakfast. Kleppers afloat, it is only fair to insert, are tough and sturdy boats; and, as someone pointed out, an almost identical twin of Snake Eyes in 1956 had crossed the Atlantic Ocean. "Good God!" Kauffmann said on receiving this news. But the Salmon River in low water—with its limestones, its dolomite, its sharp miscellaneous schists—was too much for the rubber-coated kayaks. Both had been leaking seriously, and as I watched Pourchot taping their hulls I could not help thinking that we would be a stone's throw from nowhere without them. He worked slowly, with fibre-glass tape, trying through applied friction to enhance the strength of the sticking.

"We're up some creek," I said, "without those boats."

Pourchot said, "I always pack an extra day's food in case everything does not go right."

Since he had advised bringing emergency rations, I had along a bacon bar, a can of mixed nuts, a bag of dried fruit, and half a dozen packets of M&M's. Their octane seemed low for a walk to Kiana. I had waterproof matches strewn around in various places in my pack. I asked Pourchot if he ever took along a radio, and he said no. He said there was a choice of two types and both were disadvantageous. One was an FM transmitter that was much like a walkie-talkie, but it worked only on line of sight, and, even from a ridge, would at best carry twenty miles. Twenty miles is not an impressive radius in Alaska. Anyway, almost no one ever monitored the frequency. On the other hand, if you had a single-side-band, you could, with a properly laid-out antenna, call anywhere in Alaska. But the single-side-band was big as a breadbox, bulky, heavy (thirty pounds), and extremely expensive. So Pourchot could not be bothered with that, either. We had no axes with us, which at least reduced chances of injury. Pourchot said he had brought along a ten-dollar first-aid kit, but it had no sutures and no prescription drugs, and "a doctor would laugh at it."

He cut a short piece of tape and laid it over a particularly open break in the hull of Snake Eyes, then put a longer strip over that. "These trips are not fail-safe," he went on. "You can get hurt and not get attention for several days. There's nothing you can do, short of staying home all the time."

"You come to the place on its terms," Kauffmann put in. "You assume the risk."

"When people come to Alaska, there's a sifting and winnowing process that follows," Pourchot said. "Some just make day trips out of Anchorage into the bush. Others go out for more than one day—fishing or whatever—but they stay in one place, at an established camp or lodge. After that come the hikers and canoers, and from them you get many stories of, say, the boat that breaks up and the guy who sits on the gravel bar for two weeks and walks out in five miserable days. He makes it, though. It's a rare day when somebody starves or bleeds to death. You're just not going to make a trip perfectly safe and still get the kind of trip you want. There are no what-if types out here. People who come this far have come to grips with that problem."

Pourchot was apparently unaware that he was addressing a what-if type—an advanced, thousand-deaths coward with oak-leaf clusters. If I wanted to, I could always see disaster running with the river, dancing like a shadow, moving down the forest from tree to tree. And yet coming to grips with the problem may have been easier for me than for the others, since all of them lived in Alaska. Risk is everywhere, but it is in some places more than others, and this was the safest place I'd been all year. I live in New Jersey, where risks to life are statistically higher than they are along an Arctic river.

Fedeler pointed out that on the back of Alaska fishing licenses are drawings of a signal system for people in trouble who are fortunate enough to be seen by an airplane. I looked at my license. It showed a figure holding hands overhead like a referee indicating a touchdown. That meant, "Please pick me up." A pair of chevrons, sketched on the ground, was a request for firearms and ammunition. An "I" indicated serious injury. An "F" called for food and water, and an "X" meant "Unable to proceed."

"To get a plane to see you, a big smoky fire will help," Fedeler said.

What had struck me most in the isolation of this wilderness was an abiding sense of paradox. In its raw, convincing emphasis on the irrelevance of the visitor, it was forcefully, importantly repellent. It was no less strongly attractive—with a beauty of nowhere else, composed in turning circles. If the wild land was indifferent, it gave a sense of difference. If at moments it was frightening, requiring an effort to put down the conflagrationary imagination, it also augmented the touch of life. This was not a dare with nature. This was nature.

The bottoms of the Kleppers were now trellised with tape. Pourchot was smoothing down a final end. Until recently, he had been an avocational parachutist, patterning the sky in star formation with others as he fell. He had fifty-one jumps, all of them in Colorado. But he had started waking up in the night with cold sweats, so—with two small sons now—he had sold his jumping gear. With the money, he bought a white-water kayak and climbing rope. "You're kind of on your own, really. You run the risk," he was saying. "I haven't seen any bear incidents, for example. I've never had any bear problems. I've

never carried a gun. Talk to ten people and you get ten different bear-approach theories. Some carry flares. Ed Bailey, in
Fish and Wildlife, shoots pencil flares into the ground before
approaching bears. They go away. Bear attacks generally occur
in road-system areas anyway. Two, maybe four people die a
year. Some years more than others. Rarely will a bear attack a
person in a complete wilderness like this."

Kauffmann said, "Give a grizzly half a chance and he'll avoid
you."

Fedeler had picked cups of blueberries to mix into our breakfast pancakes. Finishing them, we prepared to go. The sun was
coming through. The rain was gone. The morning grew bright
and warm. Pourchot and I got into the canoe, which, for all
its heavy load, felt light. Twenty minutes downriver, we had
to stop for more repairs to the Kleppers, but afterward the
patchwork held. With higher banks, longer pools, the river was
running deeper. The sun began to blaze.

Rounding bends, we saw sculpins, a pair of great horned
owls, mergansers, Taverner's geese. We saw ravens and a gray
jay. Coming down a long, deep, green pool, we looked toward
the riffle at the lower end and saw an approaching grizzly. He
was young, possibly four years old, and not much over four
hundred pounds. He crossed the river. He studied the salmon
in the riffle. He did not see, hear, or smell us. Our three boats
were close together, and down the light current on the flat
water we drifted toward the fishing bear.

He picked up a salmon, roughly ten pounds of fish, and,
holding it with one paw, he began to whirl it around his head.
Apparently, he was not hungry, and this was a form of play. He
played sling-the-salmon. With his claws embedded near the
tail, he whirled the salmon and then tossed it high, end over
end. As it fell, he scooped it up and slung it around his head
again, lariat salmon, and again he tossed it into the air. He
caught it and heaved it high once more. The fish flopped to
the ground. The bear turned away, bored. He began to move

upstream by the edge of the river. Behind his big head his hump projected. His brown fur rippled like a field under wind. He kept coming. The breeze was behind him. He had not yet seen us. He was romping along at an easy walk. As he came closer to us, we drifted slowly toward him. The single Klepper, with John Kauffmann in it, moved up against a snagged stick and broke it off. The snap was light, but enough to stop the bear. Instantly, he was motionless and alert, remaining on his four feet and straining his eyes to see. We drifted on toward him. At last, we arrived in his focus. If we were looking at something we had rarely seen before, God help him so was he. If he was a tenth as awed as I was, he could not have moved a muscle, which he did, now, in a hurry that was not pronounced but nonetheless seemed inappropriate to his status in the situation. He crossed low ground and went up a bank toward a copse of willow. He stopped there and faced us again. Then, breaking stems to pieces, he went into the willows.

We drifted to the rip, and down it past the mutilated salmon. Then we came to another long flat surface, spraying up the light of the sun. My bandanna, around my head, was nearly dry. I took it off, and trailed it in the river.

WHAT
THEY WERE
HUNTING FOR

———

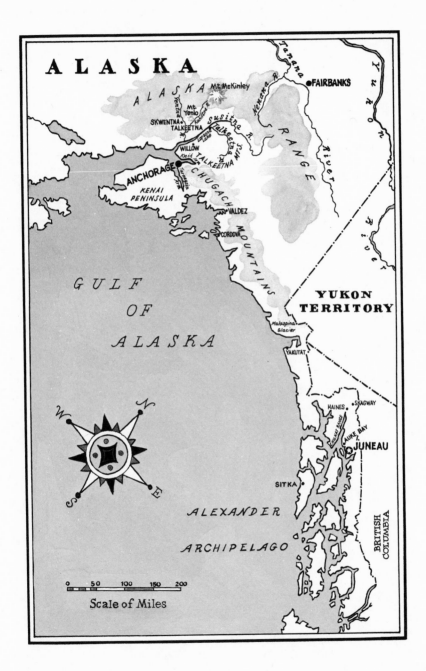

ALASKA

ALASKA RANGE

Mt. McKinley

●FAIRBANKS

Tanana R.

Nenana R.

Yentna R.

Mt. Yenlo

SKWENTNA●

TALKEETNA

Kashitna R.

Susitna R.

Talkeetna River

Lake Louise

WILLOW

Knik

TALKEETNA

ANCHORAGE

Turnagain Arm

KENAI
PENINSULA

CHUGACH MOUNTAINS

●VALDEZ

CORDOVA

Yukon River

YUKON
TERRITORY

Malaspina
Glacier

YAKUTAT

GULF

OF

ALASKA

HAINES●

●SKAGWAY

Chilcoot Range

AUKE BAY

JUNEAU

N

W

E

S

●SITKA

ALEXANDER

ARCHIPELAGO

BRITISH
COLUMBIA

0   50   100   150   200

Scale of Miles

❮ One morning in the Alaskan autumn, a small sharp-nosed helicopter, on its way to a rendezvous, flew south from Fairbanks with three passengers. They crossed the fast, silted water of the Tanana River and whirred along over low black-spruce land with streams too numerous for names. The ground beneath them began to rise, and they with it, until they were crossing broad benchlands and high hills increasingly jagged in configuration as they stepped up to the Alaska Range.

At about the same time, another and somewhat larger group took off from Anchorage in a de Havilland Twin Otter, and this sturdy vehicle, firm as iron in the air, flew north up the valley of the Big Su—Susitna River, a big river in a land of big rivers—and on up over alpine tundra that now, in the late season, was as red as wine. After moving over higher and higher hills, the plane moved in among mountains: great, upreaching things, gray on the rockface and then—above the five-thousand-foot contour and far on up, too high to see without pressing to the window—covered with fresh snow.

"Is the mountain out?" someone on the right side of the plane wanted to know. In so many mountains, there was one mountain. "Is the mountain out?"

"It surer than hell is."

"It never looks the same."

The mountain was a megahedron—its high white facets doming in the air. Long snow banners, extending eastward, were pluming from the ridges above twenty thousand feet.

"What would you call that mountain, Willie?"

"Denali. I'll go along with the Indians that far."

Everyone aboard was white but Willie (William Iġiaġruq Hensley), of Arctic Alaska, and he said again, "Denali. What the hell did McKinley ever do?"

The Twin Otter by now was so deep in the Alaska Range that nothing could be seen but walls of mountain in a pass. Then, finally, the pass widened the way to the north. Banking over terraces and high riverine bluffs—Nenana River—the plane landed on gravel near a small group of buildings, a mining town. The helicopter from Fairbanks was already there. Handshakes all around. Brisk, nippy morning, right? Won't be long now. And then, in threes and fours, the group made successive flights in the small helicopter—down the right bank of the Nenana over the broad high benchland, back and forth in loosely patterned flight. Four grizzly bears—large and small, perhaps a ton or so of bear—were grazing a meadow below, eating blueberry bushes rich with fruit. The helicopter ignored the bears. It crossed the river and flew back to the north in vectors, as if looking for something. A small lake. Then a larger lake. This was indeed a hunt, and what the people in the air were hunting for was a new capital of Alaska.

❴ When states move their capitals, as most of them have done at one time or another, the usual aim is to have a seat of government somewhere near the centers of geography and population—criteria that distinctly fail to describe Juneau. Juneau, capital of Alaska since 1900, is in the eccentric region that Alaskans call Southeastern—a long, archipelagic claw that dangles toward Seattle and is knuckled to the main body of Alaska by a glacier the size of Rhode Island. Southeastern Alaska reaches so far east that all the land north of it is Canadian. British Columbia. Yukon Territory. Juneau is two time zones from Anchorage, from Fairbanks, from the center of the state. It is twenty-five hundred miles from the other end of Alaska. Many Alaskans do not regard Southeastern as part of Alaska but, rather, as an appendage of inconvenience, because Juneau is there. Juneau is an outport—cannot be reached, or even approached, by road. Juneau was the site of a gold strike that attracted people enough to make a town, and the town's importance increased when strikes of bonanza quantity were made in mountains to the north, along the Klondike River and other tributaries of the upper Yukon. Juneau, already a mining town, was also a way station on trips to the Klondike, and it became—for the duration of the gold boom—a center of Alaskan commerce.

Anchorage is the commercial center now, and roughly half of political Alaska. As a result of a petition signed by sixteen thousand, an initiative appeared on the 1974 primary ballot through which the voters could indicate a wish to move their capital. Similar initiatives in 1960 and 1962 had been defeated, perhaps in part because Alaskans elsewhere in the state did not want to see even more power concentrated in Anchorage. Anchorage, for its part, wished to yield nothing to Fairbanks. Their rivalry is intense to the point of unseemliness. So the 1974 initiative was written to exclude both cities—the new capital could not be within thirty miles of either one—and in strong majority (fifty-seven per cent) the voters went for it.

The state is more or less broke—if that term can be used to describe a budget that regularly expends a great deal more than it ingests. For this reason, it might seem an act of bravado to contemplate building anything at all, let alone a new capital city. Bravado, on the other hand, is a synonym for Alaska. A high proportion of the white people who have tried to make their way in Alaska have lived from boom to boom. The first boom was in fur, and then came gold, followed by war, and now oil. How could it matter that the treasury was atilt when the Alyeska Pipeline Service Company was moving toward completion of a tube that would draw so much oil out of the north of Alaska that the state government alone would collect in royalties as much as three and a half million dollars a day? Some Alaskans were already spending the money. Others were dreaming of ways to spend it. One of the dreams was of a new capital, in a wild setting, preferably within sight of the summits of North America's highest massif.

Following the terms of the initiative, the governor of Alaska appointed a Capital Site Selection Committee, most of whose nine members had been—like the governor himself—opponents of the initiative. One might think that only Gilbert and Sullivan could work out the story from there. The committee, though—representing a geographical spread of the state, including Southeastern—had taken up its work with a seriousness Alaskan in grandeur, and would spend well over a million dollars to narrow its choices down.

⟮ The move to move the capital has "bestirred the community," as one Alaska senator has put it, and from the community has come a chorus of comment. The dialogue assembled here contains voices from Seward, Sitka, Fort Yukon, Kotzebue, Fairbanks, Juneau, Anchorage.

"Despite the terms of the initiative, Anchorage is the logical place for the capital. The move would cost the least, and Anchorage would serve best. Anchorage should *be* the capital."

"There are more state-government employees in Anchorage now than there are in Juneau."

"Everyone is afraid of, and is envious of, Anchorage."

"Anchorage has got enough."

"People don't want the Anchorage scourge to spread."

"The initiative was a vendetta."

"The capital move started with people in Anchorage who thought they were getting screwed by the legislature in Juneau."

"Make no mistake. Anchorage wants the capital in Anchorage and will somehow get it."

"Anchorage works hard to get things from other towns. It has from the start. When Anchorage was just a few people in tents, they tried to take the headquarters of the railroad from Seward and the U.S. District Court from Valdez. In both instances, they succeeded. Recently, they have tried hard to take the university from Fairbanks. They have part of it already. They wooed the U.S. land office away from Juneau. 'Proud' is a word still used here in Alaska—but not about Anchorage."

A single voice can be particularly audible in Alaska, because there are so few people. Much is made of Alaska's great size. It is worth remembering, as well, how small Alaska is—a handful of people clinging to a subcontinent. There are nearly twice as many people in the District of Columbia as there are in the State of Alaska. In ten square miles of the eastern state I live in are more people than there are in the five hundred and eighty-six thousand square miles of Alaska.

"The capital must be a new city."

"Pipeline or no pipeline, the state would go broke buying land in Anchorage. On top of that, because everybody in Alaska hates Anchorage it is politically expedient to put the capital in a new place, an undeveloped place."

"The land out there is of no great value. It's just wilderness, standing there."

❨ The committee's flight through the mountains that morning appeared to be, as much as anything else, a gesture of courtesy to Fairbanks, *de facto* capital of the terrain that is called the Interior. Fairbanks is the pivot from which travellers fan out to the north—the usual departure point for Arctic Alaska, and the departure point, as well, for mail planes and bush craft that serve the Interior villages. A look at a map would suggest a site near Fairbanks as an obvious capital for the state as a whole, because of Fairbanks' position near the center of the Alaskan mainland. There are drawbacks, however, in climate. The Interior is so named because it lies between the Brooks Range, which traverses the far north, and the Alaska Range, which is the climax of the mountain chain that comes up the Pacific coast and then bends across south-central Alaska to indicate the Aleutians. The Interior is the hottest region of Alaska. It is also the coldest. Temperatures there can go into the nineties in summer and into the minus-seventies in winter, and at times of deep cold large areas of the Interior will be palled with ice fog. Fairbanks has more motor vehicles per capita than does Los Angeles, and as the cars toot and tap bumpers on the long crawls through the ice fog the warm gases of their exhaust plumes seem to stick in the air close around them—an especially pernicious, carcinogenic subarctic variety of smog. This experience would suggest—too late to help Fairbanks—that it might be imprudent to plan deliberately to attract numerous vehicles to a single site in the Interior.

The capital committee got into the Twin Otter and flew back through the mountains toward the south. "A great place for grizzlies," said Willie Hensley, looking over his shoulder.

In its many months of sorting possibilities, the committee had discovered that there were few places in Alaska that could meet the criteria of the search. By law, resulting from the terms of the initiative, they had to find a hundred square miles of land somewhere near a road and a railroad and in terrain appropriate for a new airport that would consistently experience negotiable weather. The land had to belong to the state, or, in any case, to be available to the state for nothing. In addition, the committee and its consultants established standards of their own. Since weather and cold worsen with altitude, they would look for a site below two thousand feet. It should have, among other things, good soil, ample water, topography both practical and aesthetically appealing, relatively modest annual snowfall. It should not inconvenience resident wildlife—should not invade bear-denning grounds, salmon-spawning areas—and it should not be in zones of earthquakes or volcanism.

A simple task. In Indiana. Corydon was the capital of Indiana until a new-capital-site-selection committee drew a state-size X on the map and noted where the legs crossed. The spot was in deep forest. Indians owned the land. A treaty took care of them. Indianapolis, Indiana.

This was Alaska, though, where people are even more marginal than plants, and the choice was truly complex. About a third of Alaska is above two thousand feet. Something like two-thirds is demarcated for the natives and the federal government. It would be unwise to build in an area of permafrost. Two-thirds of Alaska is underlaid by permafrost. Alaska has two railroads. One is twenty-six miles long. The other runs four hundred and seventy miles, from Seward—a port on the Gulf of Alaska—through Anchorage and on to Fairbanks. The Alaska Highway comes into the Interior from Yukon Territory. The rest of the state's highway system principally consists of two roads. One goes from Fairbanks to Anchorage, and the other, by a newer and more westerly route, goes from Anchorage to Fairbanks. Roughly speaking, the land that has been built upon, pipelined, or otherwise trammelled in Alaska—all the land that is now taken up by towns, villages, cities, airports, trapper cabins, motels, roads—consists agglomerately of less than a hundred thousand acres. That leaves, untouched, nearly three hundred and seventy-five million acres. By almost any standards drawn from the North Temperate Zone, human settlement is still the next thing to nonexistent in Alaska.

Juneau, a relatively small town of eighteen thousand, is Alaska's third-largest "city." The celebrated Trans-Alaska Pipeline is, in scale, comparable to a thread laid across Staten Island. With it, the "destruction of Alaska" may have begun, as some people will say, but utter wilderness—uncompromising, unhuman wilderness—is almost wholly what Alaska is now. So if a group of people had to choose a townsite near a road and a railroad, off permafrost and on fairly low but well-drained ground, and not inordinately far from the main pockets of existing population, nearly all of Alaska would recede from the conversation and by the facts the people would be ushered into the Susitna Valley.

The Twin Otter, coming out of the mountains, moved south above the Susitna, whose water, flowing swiftly, bore so much glacially pulverized rock that it was gray and glisteningly opaque, and appeared to be ready to set. The upper Susitna has cut a canyon—Devils Canyon—where rapids pile up almost to the scale of the Colorado; and then the currents spread out and braid their way among uncountable islands. The Susitna Valley —to a point more than a hundred miles above Anchorage— includes the most northerly penetration in Alaska of land that is generally free from permafrost. The Alaska Railroad goes up the valley, as does the Anchorage-Fairbanks Highway, which was opened in 1974—significant marks, to be sure, of advancing humanity, but from the low-flying plane they looked in the forest like a slim ribbon and a set of sutures. An occasional roadhouse, cabin, or clearing appeared along the highway, and there were other cabins beside streams splaying out from the railway. A train—Lionel in appearance among the black lowland spruce—was stopped near a stream in the undepoted wild. Someone was collecting supplies. Or getting off to go home. The railway serves many dozens of people who have abandoned the civilization the railway represents. The train, typically, drops them at a stream and they go in canoes or skiffs to cabins some miles away. They chose the cabin sites and staked them out as "Open to Entry" land, which was available for low sums until 1973, when the program was at least temporarily stopped, pending the resolution of all the major and interlocking events in the subdivision of Alaskan land: final selection by the state of the one hundred and three million acres allotted to it in the Statehood Act, in 1958; final designation of intended use— parks, refuges, national wild rivers—for vast segments of federal lands; and selection by the natives of the tracts to be deeded to them. When the Open to Entry program was set up, recreation was what its creators had in mind. But a number of people who staked lots went to live on them year round—to combat the winter, to live in wilderness, to kill and eat game, to trap fur, to simplify their lives and be relatively self-sufficient, albeit in some dependence on the Alaska Railroad. Making money was emphatically not their objective. They sought little more than permanent relief from the larger society. To place a city down among them would be to flick them from the earth. Willie Hensley and the committee, overhead, looked down over the spruce-and-hardwood forest. A couple of cabins were barely visible among the trees. Aspen leaves, yellow, were quaking in the fall air. "Too mundane," Willie Hensley said as the Twin Otter moved on toward Talkeetna.

A minor but handsome run of mountains—the Talkeetna Mountains—now framed the valley with a six-thousand-foot ridgeline to the east. To the west, the land was at first low and then rose toward mountains beyond which were only a few specks of settlement in the five hundred miles to the Bering Sea. To the north, roughly forty miles distant now, was the topographical mural that closed off the Interior. Mount McKinley, veiled in snow haze, was fast removing itself to obscurity. The big mountain, sometimes described as the Weathermaker, creates its own integument, because it is so high and cold that when it interrupts flows of warm and often moist summer air it causes violent reactions: roiling clouds that form in a moment, sudden storms, gale-driven blizzards. High up the

mountain, the windchill—even during the elsewhere-warm
Alaskan summer—can go down to (and beyond) a hundred
below zero. From within its vapors, the mountain can emerge
as swiftly as it disappeared, and when it is out only the distant
curve of the earth can reduce its dominance, for it is the most
arresting sight from forty million acres around. The Alaska
Range elevates with a rapidity rare in the world. Its top is about
two-thirds as high as the top of the Himalayas, but the
Himalayan uplift is broad and extensive. If you were looking
toward Mount Everest from forty miles away, you would lift
your gaze only slightly to note the highest in a sea of peaks.
Forty miles from McKinley you can stand at a bench mark of
three hundred and climb with your eyes the other twenty
thousand feet. The difference—between your altitude near sea
level and the height of that flying white mountain—is much
too great to be merely overwhelming. The mountain is a sky
of rock, seemingly all above you, looming. Until it takes itself
away, you watch it as you might watch a hearth fire or a show
in color of aurorean light. The provocative immensity of
Mount McKinley seems to symbolize Alaska to many Alaskans.
No wonder they would have a capital with the mountain much
in view. Some of those Alaskans, as it happens, are Athapaskans, and their regard for the big mountain is understandably
deeper (in time, in metaphor, in spiritual mystery) even than
the regard of white Alaskans. The Athapaskans are not much
impressed that a young Princeton graduate on a prospecting
adventure in the Susitna Valley in 1896 happened to learn, on
his way out of the wilderness, that William McKinley had
become the Republican nominee for President of the United
States. In this haphazard way, the mountain got the name it
would carry for at least the better part of a century, notwithstanding that it already had a name, for uncounted centuries
had had a name, which in translation has been written, vari-
ously, as The Great One, The Mighty One, The High One.
The Indians in their reverence had called it Denali. Toponymi-

cally, that is the mountain's proper name; and if a city were deliberately to seek the mountain and appear before it, the city might be Denali, too.

⟨ Talkeetna, the only community of any size in the upper part of the valley, voted sixty-nine to forty-two in favor of moving the capital. Talkeetna is a prime collecting point for climbers on their way to McKinley. I once saw a Japanese climber in Richard and Dorothy Jones's store there, buying a cabbage. It was a purple cabbage and somewhat larger than his own head, which was purple as well, in places, from contusions and sunburn, and probably windburn, suffered in his bout with the mountain. On his cheek was a welted wound, like a split in a tomato. Leaving the store, he walked out of town, ate his cabbage, and slept it off in a tent. I had asked Mrs. Jones what she thought of the idea of moving the capital away from Juneau, and she said she was all for it, but she did hope the new town would not be placed near Talkeetna. "Please may they leave this beautiful section of Alaska alone," she said. "Nature is part of us. We moved here for the out living—for the river. The capital has to have big buildings, a superhighway—and that takes care of the blueberry patches."

A genial person, easygoing and garrulous, she was somewhat beyond athletic weight. Her husband, wry and spare, smiled and nodded while she talked. "A new city, built from scratch in the bush, would be sterile," she said. "The state will probably sell off land to meet some of the cost. I can't see anything of value coming out of a place where people go in with speculation in mind. Meanwhile, we're so naïve we'd be stepped on like bugs. Like June bugs. We're all neighbors here, and together. Your neighbor might need you to help put out a fire in his cabin. But Anchorage and Fairbanks are crooked. If you don't wear pointed-toe boots and a Texas hat, you're not with it. And that is what would come with a capital here. The capital should go to Fairbanks or Anchorage. They're already ruined. But it goes in the bush because the cities are arch-rivals. If it comes here, it will be the end of this community as it stands."

Talkeetna was a random miscellany of log cabins, cabbage patches, some frame houses, house trailers, Quonsets, lettuce-onion-carrot gardens, two or three roadhouses, and an inn from the first part of the century, with a dusty moose rack in velvet on the wall and old colored-glass shades on the hanging lights above the bar. There were two hundred and fifty gold and silver claims around Talkeetna once. Talkeetna has a Historical Society. Dorothy Jones is on the board of directors. Unlike most of her neighbors, she grew up in Alaska. Her father home-steaded, in the Matanuska Valley, nearer Anchorage.

"I was brought up here, too," said her husband. "By Uncle Sam." He, also, was for moving the capital, but he seemed just a little less concerned than his wife did for the environs of Talkeetna. He was a disaffected fisherman. Things had been better when Talkeetna was more isolated, when it was served only by the railroad and bush aircraft; but now, with the new highway, and Anchorage only a little more than two hours away, the fish had been beaten down and you couldn't find a rainbow more than twelve inches long.

Looking down from the Twin Otter at Talkeetna—close by the confluence of three rivers, where the Chulitna and the Talkeetna pile into the Susitna—I could see the Joneses' place and, facing it, an old and ramblingly extended cottonwood-log cabin called the Roadhouse, and near that the small Quonset home of a bush pilot named Cliff Hudson. Climbers stay in the Roadhouse—gather there, go over and over their gear, and wait for the mountain to come out, or, at least, for weather promis-ing enough so that Hudson (among others) can fly them to the Kahiltna Glacier, on the mountain's south side, landing on skis at seven thousand feet. A gravel airstrip runs from behind

Hudson's Quonset on out to the edge of the Susitna. I had once
flown with him, not to the glacier but into the country around
Talkeetna, looking for the dragon's teeth of capitals. Hudson
will take anything that comes along—trappers and miners to
their cabins, hunters, Oriental alpinists. Bearded, bespectacled,
with tousled thinning curly hair, Hudson flew in ten-inch boots
and a brown wool shirt that had seen a lot of time on his back.
In fact, he appeared to have been *in* the bush instead of flying
it—to have lost his plane there and to have just walked out. In
1948, he had come to Alaska (from the Pacific "northwest")
for all the great hunting and fishing, and he had become a bush
pilot because it was "the only way you could get around." He
was disappointed, bitterly, with Alaskan progress. Would he
vote—now—for statehood? "Hell, no. They're ripping us off
every way they can think of. It's bad enough just to have to
feed all those politicians. We've got nine-tenths too many of
them. They're a bunch of kids. It's just a big playpen—Juneau
—at our expense. They argued once for eleven days over who
would be the House Speaker." Flying me around the valley,
bumping along on the wind over the spruce and the high
tundra, he said he did not really care now if a capital were to
come springing up from the land below. The plan was "ridiculous" and "expensive," but if a new city was to be built, it
would be "O.K. anywhere." He said, "The game is all gone,
anyway. Those asses in Juneau won't let us hunt wolves from
airplanes anymore. Three packs of wolves roam this area in
winter and kill at least three moose a week—sometimes that
many in one day. The fishing is going downhill, too, like everything else up here. When I came up here, you could catch fish
till your arm was tired. That's Montana Creek down there.
Used to be good. The air is cooler beyond Montana Creek. If
you're driving south in the winter and it's, say, ten below in
Talkeetna, it's suddenly forty below when you cross Montana
Creek, and you feel the car tighten up—the steering gets stiff.
Talkeetna is a little higher and warmer than the lower part of

the valley." Montana Creek, having unglacial waters, was pebbly clear. A day or two before, I had caught a four-pound humpback salmon there.

The Roadhouse was a good place to stay. Climbers on the mountain had returned to the glacier, and were waiting day upon day for clear enough sky to get off; meanwhile, the Roadhouse, except at mealtime, was quiet. It was run, somewhat stringently, by Carroll Close and his wife, Verna, with an unnegotiable ten-thirty curfew, and signs here and there to remind you that you were not in your own home. "DON'T TOUCH." "NOTICE: In meeting the public the proprietors of this Roadhouse do not employ profane or obscene language. We ask you to display similar restraint while quartered here." At seven in the morning in an upstairs room, cracks in the floorboards become fumaroles of coffee, and the scent draws you down from the summit. In the kitchen, under racks of utensils, is a big wood stove, and Verna Close is sprinkling salt on its hot iron surface. She is dour, silent, stolid as a ceramic cat. She places thick slices of bread over the salt to toast. Each day, she bakes forty-six loaves of bread. Carroll Close, who is in his seventies and has been out splitting spruce, brings a load of it in and commits some to the fire. He is thin, thewy, with snowy hair and eyes that flash. With his wife, he makes and serves the standard breakfast: a mound of potatoes fried in white lard, scrambled eggs, four thick hunks of buttered toast, juice, coffee, ham, jam. Only a long-distance run at fifty below zero could work down such a meal, but the temperature outside is in the easygoing seventies and for the future there is no hope. There is dinner. No one is allowed to be late for dinner, so throughout the hour beforehand, in twos and threes, people drift in. They come from Talkeetna and from down the valley. Weekends, they come from Anchorage. They wait quietly in the sitting room before the unlighted face of the television, gray like the river ("DON'T TOUCH"), and at six they file to the table, and Carroll Close tells them where to sit. Eighteen is the capacity. Eighteen are there—around an oilcloth-covered table. They will make friends quickly. They are, for the most part, long in Alaska. But they are relatively silent in the early minutes of the meal, passing platters and bowls of potatoes, rice, meat-loaded gravy, beans, salad, corned beef, fried chicken, carrots, peas, bread, jam, and butter, leaving room for cake. And all the while Close circles the table, alert, attentive.

He came to Alaska from Oregon when he was in his thirties. I asked him, one afternoon, why. "Poverty," he said. When the war came, he found work around Anchorage, and eventually he had enough money to move north and, with his wife, buy the original part of the Roadhouse. He had built the extensions. "People voted five to one for statehood," he said. "You weren't a good citizen if you were against it. It was a lost cause."

"You were against statehood?"

"Oh, sure. Oh, sure. Before then, three-quarters of the people here weren't here. Eight or nine hundred people ran the Territory. Ten thousand now run the state. Where it used to take one person to investigate you, it now takes two to four. The state spends too much. If a tree blows down, two guys from the state come with a chain saw. The state has sold the state out. To the unions. To the oil companies. The oil companies have more power than the legislature. The capital move is a lot of talk. That's all it is, a lot of talk. What we need is not a new capital but better legislators than we have. I'd say leave the capital where it's at. The state can't afford it. There *is* no economy. They're dreaming about all this oil money. You do more good with a letter into Juneau than going there, anyway. Up here, we have the severest winters this side of the range. This is no place for a capital. If it does move, the proper place for it is in Anchorage."

He opened the stove and flung in some spruce. Spruce tends to be tough, stronger than most people who try to split it. "Since statehood," he said, "this country's went sour."

The unofficial mayor of Talkeetna was Evil Alice Powell. She

did not seem to mind her nickname. She had worked, years
ago, for the Alaska Territorial Department of Health in Anchorage—inspecting bars, bakeries, groceries, private sewage
systems—and the doctor she worked for gave her the title
because she scoured Augean Anchorage as few people have
ever done. Her husband had come to Alaska as a highway- and
railway-bridge engineer, and they moved out to Talkeetna in
1960. She ran a sort of roadhouse up the road from the Roadhouse, but she had attempted to upgrade it with the word
"motel." I found her there, ironing linen, and she said, "It's
reached the point now where if someone wants to see an
old-timer they come to me." She looked the part and she didn't
—in slacks and a sweater, white hair streaked blond. She was
small, gentle, amiable, accommodating, grandmotherly. Evil
Alice. She said yes, the capital should move, and move up here
to the valley. On various private and public missions, she had
had it with Juneau—too hard to get there, too much chance
of being weathered in there. Anybody in Talkeetna with a little
property was for the capital move. The people who were not
for it were "food-stampers" and "welfarers" and some of the
hippies up the track, in cabins in the woods north of town.
"They have Mary Jane and hard stuff up there," she said.
"Some of them are on welfare, too. If the capital came, there
might be a job and they'd have to go to work. Some are on the
God Squad. They got religion a while back—Mickey Mouse
religion—and they spun off from the others. A number came
down to Talkeetna to live. A few work for me. They're O.K.
I don't have to worry. They won't rip off the cigarettes and the
booze."

She knew where the capital should be, she said. She had the
spot picked out. It was just a few miles east of town. Talkeetna's air facilities could be expanded. Road and rail service
already existed. Hydroelectric power could come from Devils
Canyon, up the Big Su. Money had already been appropriated
for a study of a dam there. The capital site she had in mind

was up near the headwaters of Montana Creek, in a lovely world of birches, on elevated ground, with an unimpeded view of the mountain.

❲ Alice Powell might have been holding a forked stick that had just swung down. The terrain she described had become prominent on a list of what the Capital Site Selection Committee called "footprints"—feasible, desirable places to build. The capital would be a footprint in the wilderness. On an earlier outing, the committee had flown in a helicopter to the top of Bald Mountain, seven miles east of Talkeetna, and there, from a vantage altitude of thirty-six hundred feet, had looked down on everything that had been ordered but a gold dome. It was heavily wooded country with few muskeg pockets and good soil. Divisioning the woodland, clear streams ran down out of the mountains—Sheep Creek, Montana Creek, Sheep River, Talkeetna River—and at the time they were viscous with salmon. One stream was interrupted by a three-mile lake— Larson Lake—which was only six hundred feet above sea level, was surrounded by spruce-and-birch forest, and had behind it a rising slope that yielded a view over the lake to the big river valley overtowered by the imminent Denali. The mean January temperature at Larson Lake is nine degrees; July, fifty-seven. Here and there in sight was a strip of homestead plowing, but virtually all the land in the immediate area was still untouched. This was fine moose range, too. Moose are up in the mountains in the summer, and they go down toward the Susitna in winter. Whatever a capital might do for people, it would surely repel wolves and thus, to an extent, be good for moose. As had been learned when oil wells were drilled south of Anchorage, in the Kenai National Moose Range, moose get along with progress.

Now, off to the left of the Twin Otter, the Talkeetna Mountains, behind Larson Lake, were topped with a dusting of snow, and along the whole range the snowline was drawn absolutely level somewhere near five thousand feet, as if someone painting a wall had carefully cut in with a brush to whiten just the high part. Gradually, through the autumn, the level line comes down—down the sides of the Alaska Range, down the Talkeetnas, down the Chugach Mountains in view of Anchorage. It is watched like a river gauge: six thousand feet, five thousand, four thousand, three. Day by day, it is somewhat lower, until the mountains are totally white. The snow then comes over the people. Six months. Then Alaska turns green again: green in the Susitna Valley, green in the Interior, the Arctic green and reddish and buff. The snow stays only in the high cols of most of the mountain chains but all over the peaks of the Alaska Range.

The Twin Otter, some minutes later, gave up altitude toward the southwest and approached the gravel airstrip at Skwentna. Some forty miles from the highway over streams and muskeg bogs and island patches of black spruce, Skwentna was an air and river stopping place, remote, unconnected. Willie Hensley said, "When these people find out who we are, they will probably run us off. They don't want their homesteads ruined." But the population of Skwentna, Alaska 99667 (fifteen people), was otherwise occupied, and the airstrip, when the Twin Otter engines shut down, was a silent clearing in the forest. A large percentage of a moose, reduced to bloody chunks, with flies on the chunks like cloves in ham, lay waiting on the ground for its hunter to return and fly it away. By prearrangement—the better to present certain landscapes for scrutiny—a big Bell Huey, a kind of helicopter that carried troops in Vietnam, was waiting for the committee. Its transmission was in the middle of the fuselage and resembled a home oil-burner of the vertical type, covered with heavy padding. The ceiling and interior walls were covered with the same padding, as if heavy furniture were about to go up in an elevator. Passenger seats were in two benchlike rows, facing one another. The committee compacted itself into the chopper, knees touching: Cook, Bettisworth, Ward, Hensley, Sturgulewski, Kellogg, Corbus. A flying quorum. Only two members had failed to join the day—Guy Martin, Alaska's Commissioner of Natural Resources, and Dwayne Carlson, an Anchorage carpenter who had reached a high position in the Alaska State Federation of Labor. The big Huey took off in its own din, and headed miscellaneously east and north, tilting now and again to circle a footprint—a site by a lake on the valley floor, a site on a high slope, a site by a gold-claim creek. Much of the way, great fingers of muskeg reached through the spruce like fairways—soft, morassic, mosquito muskeg, virtually construction-proof. Someone cried out above the engine noise, "Corbus, you're looking better all the time! There's not enough land suitable for building!" William Corbus did not disagree. His home was Juneau. For the better part of two years, he had concentratedly fought the capital move. He had helped found, and was chief financial officer of, Alaskans United, a statewide organization dedicated to snuffing out the idea. And now that the state had voted to move the capital, Corbus, paradoxically, had become a member of the committee to pick the new site. The initiative required that two members be from Southeastern Alaska, and one of these could hardly *not* be from Juneau. So Corbus had agreed to serve. He saw himself as a kind of monitor, attempting to make sure that the committee as a whole was "straightforward as to how much it's really going to cost the state to make the move." A modest, self-effacing man—with a young face, wide-eyed, blue-eyed, and with bits of an almost-crew haircut sticking up here and there—he was given to gray suits and striped ties, and carried himself in a manner that suggested an Ivy League athlete still in shape twenty years after college. He had gone to the Tuck School of Finance, at Dartmouth, and had worked for Stone & Webster Securities Corporation, in Manhattan, before deciding, in 1970, that he wanted to move to, as he put it, "a place where you could feel you were playing a bigger role." The roles he was playing in separate aspects of the capital situation caused no apparent conflict within him; and, like everyone on the committee, he actually enjoyed the work and—all other considerations aside—felt caught up in "an interesting intellectual exercise."

Natchez and other towns were, in turn, the capital of Mississippi until a three-member site-selection committee chose the place where Jackson was cleared in the woods. Columbus, Ohio, was a forest, too. Detroit, for many years, was the capital of Michigan. Villages in the Michigan interior feared and resented what was known as the "Detroit influence." People were jealous, and thought Detroit had enough. Someone in the legislature proposed moving the capital to the township of Lansing. This was regarded as a joke. *Lansing?* "Amid choking miasma . . . where the howl of wolves and the hissing of massaugas, and groans of bull frogs resound to the hammer of the woodpecker and the solitary note of the nightingale?" Lansing? "A howling wilderness?"

The other member from Southeastern Alaska was C. B. Bettisworth, who came from Ketchikan, which is about as close to Seattle as you can get and still be in Alaska. Bettisworth represented Southeastern, but he had a particular interest in Fairbanks, because Fairbanks was his home town. When votes were taken in committee meetings, his tended to follow the Fairbanks view. A young man with a beard and boots and wide-wale trousers and tumbling light-brown hair, he had a backpackery, environmental look, a suggestion in his face of early Lincoln. (Young Lincoln's first successful activity as an Illinois legislator was the moving of the capital from Vandalia to Springfield.) By training, Bettisworth was an architect and planner, and he seemed much absorbed in the selection process, the sheer excitement of pressing the land and releasing a city.

Earl Cook, of Fairbanks, did not seem to relish being up in the air—a sane reaction in this machine, which shivered and lurched like a long-since-depreciated railroad car, occasionally spilling everybody sidewise for selected glimpses of prime terrain. The cockpit was partitioned off, and for the passengers there was no view forward. Cook's smile had thinned with altitude. He was a slim man, with receding hair combed straight back, a real-estate man, who somehow seemed formal in a Levi jacket and Levi pants and hiking boots. He had been in Alaska thirty-seven years. He was an advocate of the capital move, and he still held hopes for a site on the Fairbanks side of the Alaska Range. Among his six children was a young accountant who, opposing the move, had helped organize the Fairbanks chapter of Alaskans United. Like father and son, Fairbanks as a whole had split on the issue, and Fairbanks' vote on the initiative was almost a balance, with a slight tip toward the proponent side.

Austin Ward—more or less a unit vote with Cook—was the other Fairbanksan on the committee. He came from Pontiac, Michigan, and had lived in Alaska twenty-two years. Light and compact, a haberdasher (and now wearing bright-red-and-gray checked slacks), he looked jaunty—if anyone could, shaking in the air—and a great deal jauntier after the helicopter touched down for recess near the summit of a long loaf of tundra called Little Peters Hills. The committee and its consultants—Barry Quinn, a planner; William Pyle, a geologist—bent their heads under the rotors and ran away from the machine a hundred yards or so, to a swale of relative quiet, although the constant roar of the vehicle was practically inescapable, even with the help of a mountain wind. The altitude was two thousand feet, and the view to the east, toward Talkeetna, was over moist green tundra and high red alpine tundra, with gray bedrock sticking through. To the north, the big white peaks were now partly visible, but only careful study of the sky would suggest what was cloud and what was mountain. Over broad miles of nearby tundra, isolated spruce stood like incense cones. On the low eastern slope of the hill were a couple of homesteads, neat in appearance, neatly sculptured out of the forest, and a clear rainbow stream—Peters Creek—with the core of a capital city in contemplation beside it. The committee was not contemplating much of anything, though. Voluble after their release from the helicopter, the people smoked and chattered and took one another's picture eating bearberries and blueberries. Some of the tundra blueberry plants were so small that an entire bush might consist of one short stem, like a golf tee, with a single blueberry, much larger than the bush itself, resting upon it. "You stay out of my berry field," said Arliss Sturgulewski, and Bill Pyle—short, dark, bearlike—shifted his forage.

Pyle had been assigned to the capital project by Dames & Moore, international experts in geophysics. Looking up from time to time and across the valley, he offhandedly indicated moraines that had been bulldozed by advancing ice, silt deposits in what had been lakes, the pitted outwash plains of melted glaciers. He was like a radiologist reading a picture. There were in this area some beautiful sites, he said, for vegetation and topography, but there were problems, too: an uncomfortable level of seismic risk, for one thing, and a few too many bogs, and possibilities of permafrost. We were beyond the area that was usually free of it. Pyle had been in Alaska fifteen years. With his bald pate and handlebar mustache, he appeared to have been there since the discovery of gold. He spoke not just with knowledge but with ample affection for the Alaskan land. He had worked for a time in Chicago, and when he left for Alaska someone asked him why he was going. He said, "If you have to ask that question, you wouldn't understand the answer."

Louise Kellogg, of Palmer (thirty-five miles northeast of Anchorage), had been a vigorous proponent of the capital move —unlike most of the committee. And now she smiled and said to me, "Has Willie brainwashed you yet?"

I said, "How would I know?"

Beyond the big Huey, on down the ridge, Willie Hensley stood alone, looking southeastward over the valley. In time, I left the berry-picking and went to join him. In his Western boots, his dungarees, his bright-red down jacket with blue-banded shoulders, he seemed somewhat incongruous there—an Eskimo, many miles from home, dressed apparently for a rodeo or a basketball game in which he might star. He was slender, physically adroit, and his high Mongolian cheekbones, his soft black hair ruffling in the wind, his Asian-myna-bird look all seemed to suggest that he had recently walked across the land bridge to have a look around. Willie in the committee was first among equals. The others had long since made him their chairman.

⟨ Willie Hensley was born in Kotzebue, in Arctic Alaska, and grew up some ten miles out of town in a kind of family commune, with uncles, aunts, and cousins all around him as well as his immediate family. In winter, they lived in an *ivrulik,* which was an *iglu* made of sod. *"Iglu"* means "house"—any kind of house—and the kind that is made of blocks of snow in the shape of a dome was unknown to Willie, the nearest one being in Arctic Canada, more than a thousand miles away. Kotzebue was distant, too ("It seemed like a thousand miles"), and during Willie's early youth the whole family went there only twice a year, at Thanksgiving and at Christmas, for dinners, pageants, and the communal opening of what he remembers as "a mountain of gifts." All this took place in Friends Church—a mission derived from Whittier, California—and Willie grew up a titular Quaker, but the most lasting impression he took away with him was of the great amounts of food there: seal oil, piles of frozen fish to dip into the seal oil, and

pyramids of berries—altogether "so much you took it home."
The sod house was across an arm of Kotzebue Sound of the
Chukchi Sea of the Arctic Ocean, two hundred miles from
Siberia, six hundred miles from Anchorage. In chicken-wire
traps the family caught whitefish in the late fall, and stored
them in gunnysacks outside for the winter. Later on, they
netted sheefish under the ice and stacked them up frozen, like
cordwood. In summer they moved upriver—up the Noatak—
and lived in tents, and hunted ducks and muskrats. In early fall,
toward the end of August, they gathered berries and took them
by the barrel back home.

They had no radio, no magazines, and, in Willie's words,
"formal education was not that critical." There was a Bureau
of Indian Affairs school in Kotzebue, and when Willie learned
about it he decided, on his own, that he wanted to go there.
He remembers his mother saying, "Go ahead. Go ahead, then.
Go to school." He stayed with relatives in Kotzebue, and
worked his way through what he has called "a highly sporadic
primary education"—as little as a month a year. As he grew up,
he became the family scribe.

Kotzebue is in an election district that is larger than most
of the states of the United States, yet its population warrants
only one representative in Alaska's forty-member House. In
1966, Willie—age twenty-five—was elected to the job. Two
years later, he was head of the Democratic Party in Alaska. In
1970, he was elected to the Alaska Senate. In all, he spent eight
years—eight legislative sessions—in Juneau. He emerged with
certain goods. He brought high schools to his district, and a
radio station (KOTZ) to Kotzebue, and an old people's home.
He made himself unpopular with the liquor lobby by sponsor-
ing legislation that created municipally owned liquor licenses,
with the idea that communities could derive money from liquor sales and use it to pay the costs that liquor incurs. He
brought electric generators to small villages in the north. But
with all this, he seldom brought himself. Juneau was a thousand

miles from Kotzebue, and he could rarely afford the trip. Nonetheless, when the initiative to move the capital came along he decided that in the interests of the Alaskan treasury the capital should remain in Juneau.

In 1974, he ran for Alaska's single seat in the United States House of Representatives. The capital-move initiative had been on the primary ballot, and Hensley had spoken against it wherever he went. He thought that Alaska, whose budget had more than quadrupled in a few years' time, was heading for failure and could ill afford to crown it with a billion-dollar capital city. Privately, he regarded his achievements in the legislature as "crumbs" begged for and sent back to his people. If so much money were to go for a capital, he feared for the faraway villages. There would be funds not even for crumbs. "When there is a budget crunch, the bush loses," he said. He compared the capital-movers to a young couple whose eyes shine at the prospect of a new house but who find themselves unable to cope with the terms of the mortgage. A federal building then projected for Anchorage was going to cost at least a hundred million dollars. So how much would an entire city cost? If Alaska were to build a capital, state-federal sharing money would be applied to the airport, utilities, highways, housing—money that would otherwise go to existing communities. The capital-move prevailed, but Hensley lost. Before long, he found himself on the Capital Site Selection Committee, the lone native, the lone northwestern member.

I had met him for the first time some months after the election, quite by chance, in Kotzebue, where he was trailing a cone of dust from his Chevrolet pickup, in a town whose streets—four hundred miles from the nearest highway—were connected only to themselves. He stopped at the airfield to complete an errand, and I talked with him briefly and wondered if his attitudes about the capital had changed since the election. He said that, like everyone else on the committee, he had become caught up by the inherent excitement in the idea of creating a new town, but he was still a pessimist about the financial future of Alaska, and nothing had happened to alter that view. Kotzebue was almost painfully decibelled, Yamahas and Hondas ratchetting the air. I was struck, the more, by the lilting modulation of Hensley's voice, calm as (that day) the Chukchi Sea. Detached humor played across his eyes. He said he would like to see a new referendum on a future ballot presenting to Alaskan voters a more extensive set of choices. Choice No. 1: Juneau. Choice No. 2: Anchorage. Choice No. 3: A wholly new capital city, its cost realistically estimated and included on the ballot. Cost—the essential factor—was being too widely ignored, he said. "In Alaska, too many people seem to think they are floating to Heaven on a sea of oil."

◖ If Boston was once the most provincial place in America (the story goes that after a six-megaton bomb exploded in Times Square a headline in a Boston paper would say, "HUB MAN KILLED IN NEW YORK BLAST"), Alaska, in this respect, may have replaced Boston. In Alaska, the conversation is Alaska. Alaskans, by and large, seem to know little and to say less about what is going on outside. They talk about their land, their bears, their fish, their rivers. They talk about subsistence hunting, forbidden hunting, and living in trespass. They have their own lexicon. A senior citizen is a pioneer, snow is termination dust, and the N.B.A. is the National Bank of Alaska. The names of Alaska are so beautiful they run like fountains all day in the mind. Mulchatna. Chilikadrotna. Unalaska. Unalakleet. Kivalina. Kiska. Kodiak. Allakaket. The Aniakchak Caldera. Nondalton. Anaktuvuk. Anchorage. Alaska is a foreign country significantly populated with Americans. Its languages extend to English. Its nature is its own. Nothing seems so unexpected as the boxes marked "U.S. Mail." Alaskans talk and talk about their pipeline—about the big welders from Tulsa ("Animals, sheer animals"), whose power showdowns with the Teamsters so terrified the Teamsters that the Teamsters turned to petroleum jelly. Years in advance, they talked about the royalties the pipeline would bring them, and, to some extent, about the devastation it could bring to Prince William Sound, which, starred with islands, is one of the marine splendors of the subarctic.

"There is the real problem—not the possible spills on land but the spills that could happen in Prince William Sound."

In recent time, the entrenched, traditional boomers of Alaska, the develop-it majority, have been challenged by a growing body of people who wonder if the boom philosophy is good for the state. Fairbanks, under the impact of the pipeline, has become (in Willie Hensley's word) "scroungy"—prostitutes, Texans, ticky-tacky. Maybe Alaska should take a more circumspect look before entering such arrangements again. This was the novel body of thought that helped to produce the 1974 election victory of Governor Jay Hammond —fisherman, homesteader, wilderness man. Hammond was hardly a fierce and fighting conservationist. Alaska had not molted. But Hammond's prudent, balanced approach to things was an attempt to reconcile what his first Commerce Commissioner, Langhorne Motley, once called "the Sierra Club syndrome and the Dallas scenario." In the ongoing debate about the new capital, among all the varied reasons for and against the move, those two strands were prominently braided.

"The new capital will be a growth center for Alaska. It will take the pressure off Anchorage."

"In a state this size, if you put everything in one area you detract from the reasons we're all here. The new capital won't be all that far from Anchorage. You put all the people in one place, you create an unattractive state, and you pull out the employment from people who would like to live in the Juneau area."

"Juneau will die."

"The people of Alaska have mandated this, and the people of Alaska have darned good judgment."

"I don't think anyone is smart enough to plan a place like that. In Valdez, after the '64 earthquake, up we went and moved the city. Four or five miles, to a safer place. What a mess! The new Valdez is full of cul-de-sacs. What do you do with twenty-five feet of snow at the end of a cul-de-sac? A mess. And I was the mayor."

"Places like that are sterile. Salt Lake is the only planned city worth a damn. Have you ever seen a town planned by an American planner?"

"Savannah was sketched out in England."

"The purpose is better government. Move the seat of government to the Susitna Valley and seventy per cent of the population is within driving distance."

"Legislators could drive home for the weekend to Fairbanks, Homer, and anywhere between. To Anchorage they could drive home evenings."

"You want to drive home evenings at fifty below?"

"Try flying to Juneau. Socked in. You end up in Seattle."

"Lobby groups have an advantage in Juneau. They can afford to stay there, and they are unhampered by people coming down and butting in. They have the legislators to themselves."

"The highway people down there have to fly five hundred miles to see the roads they're working on."

"People voted for the move because they thought the money would be coming in. It won't be there. We have virtually already spent the money from the pipeline. To me, it's that bleak. The state has been taking in about three hundred million a year—from petroleum revenues, highway-fuel revenues, income tax—and it is spending five hundred million. By 1980, Alaska's annual expenditures will be around one billion. The legislature spends money faster than they can get it, and nobody sees where it goes. To try to cover themselves, they hit the oil companies. They enacted a reserves tax on oil that is still in the ground, deductible from future royalties. I guess it's legal, but it sure doesn't sound moral."

"The state parking garage in Fairbanks cost four and a quarter million—or fourteen thousand dollars a parking slot. So who can pay for a city?"

"Having Juneau the capital provides one more reason for tourists to travel around the state."

"Putting it up here near Anchorage is like putting the barn close to the fields. Better, more responsible people would agree to be legislators. Doctors and lawyers are out of business when they're in Juneau."

"The new city would grow here, grow naturally, the way Alaska will grow."

"Not so fast! The flow of oil will not do everything. We'd better sit back and look at our hole card."

❨ There are those who would say that tens of thousands of barrels of oil erupting from a break in the Trans-Alaska Pipeline would be the lesser accident if, at more or less the same time, a fresh Anchorage were to spill into the bush. While the dream of the capital city plays on in the mind, Anchorage stands real. It is the central hive of human Alaska, and in manner and structure it represents, for all to see, the Alaskan dynamic and the Alaskan aesthetic. It is a tangible expression of certain Alaskans' regard for Alaska—their one true city, the exemplar of the predilections of the people in creating improvements over the land.

As may befit a region where both short and long travel is generally by air, nearly every street in Anchorage seems to be the road to the airport. Dense groves of plastic stand on either

side—flashing, whirling, flaky. HOOSIER BUDDY'S MOBILE
HOMES. WINNEBAGO SALES & SERVICE. DISCOUNT
LIQUORS OPEN SUNDAY. GOLD RUSH AUTO SALES.
PROMPT ACTION LOCKSMITHS. ALASKA REFRIGERATION
& AIR CONDITION. DENALI FUEL. . .

"Are the liquor stores really open Sundays?"

"Everything in Anchorage is open that pays."

Almost all Americans would recognize Anchorage, because
Anchorage is that part of any city where the city has burst its
seams and extruded Colonel Sanders.

"You can taste the greed in the air."

BELUGA ASPHALT.

Anchorage is sometimes excused in the name of pioneering.
Build now, civilize later. But Anchorage is not a frontier town.
It is virtually unrelated to its environment. It has come in on
the wind, an American spore. A large cookie cutter brought
down on El Paso could lift something like Anchorage into the
air. Anchorage is the northern rim of Trenton, the center of
Oxnard, the ocean-blind precincts of Daytona Beach. It is
condensed, instant Albuquerque.

PANCHO'S VILLA, MEXICAN FOOD. BULL SHED, STEAK
HOUSE AND SONIC LOUNGE. SHAKEY'S DRIVE-IN
PIZZA. EAT ME SUBMARINES.

Anchorage has developed a high-rise city core, with glass-box
offices for the oil companies, and tall Miamian hotels. Zone-
lessly lurching outward, it has made of its suburbs a carnival of
cinder block, all with a speculative mania so rife that sellers of
small homesites—of modest lots scarcely large enough for
houses—retain subsurface rights. In vacant lots, queen-post
trusses lie waiting for new buildings to jump up beneath them.
Roads are rubbled, ponded with chuckholes. Big trucks, grad-
ers, loaders, make the prevailing noise, the dancing fumes, the
frenetic beat of the town. Huge rubber tires are strewn about

like quoits, ever ready for the big machines that move hills of earth and gravel into inconvenient lakes, which become new ground.

FOR LEASE. WILL BUILD TO SUIT.

Anchorage coins millionaires in speculative real estate. Some are young. The median age in Anchorage is under twenty-four. Every three or four years, something like half the population turns over. And with thirty days of residence, you can vote as an Alaskan.

POLAR REALTY. IDLE WHEELS TRAILER PARK. MOTEL MUSH INN.

Anchorage has a thin history. Something of a precursor of the modern pipeline camps, it began in 1914 as a collection of tents pitched to shelter workers building the Alaska Railroad. For decades, it was a wooden-sidewalked, gravel-streeted town. Then, remarkably early, as cities go, it developed an urban slum, and both homes and commerce began to abandon its core. The exodus was so rapid that the central business district never wholly consolidated, and downtown Anchorage is even more miscellaneous than outlying parts of the city. There is, for example, a huge J. C. Penney department store filling several blocks in the heart of town, with an interior mall of boutiques and restaurants and a certain degree of chic. A couple of weedy vacant lots separate this complex from five log cabins. Downtown Anchorage from a distance displays an upreaching skyline that implies great pressure for land. Down below, among the high buildings, are houses, huts, vegetable gardens, and bungalows with tidy front lawns. Anchorage burst out of itself and left these incongruities in the center, and for me they are the most appealing sights in Anchorage. Up against a downtown office building I have seen cordwood stacked for winter.

In its headlong, violent expansion, Anchorage had considerable, but not unlimited, space to fill. To an extent unusual among cities, Anchorage has certain absolute boundaries, and in that sense its growth has been a confined explosion. To the north, a pair of military bases establish, in effect, a Roman wall. To the west and south, fjordlike arms of the Pacific—Knik Arm, Turnagain Arm—frame the city. Behind Anchorage, east, stand the Chugach Mountains, stunning against the morning and in the evening light—Mount Magnificent, Mount Gordon Lyon, Temptation Peak, Tanaina Peak, Wolverine Peak, the Suicide Peaks. Development has gone to some extent upward there. Houses are pushpinned to the mountainsides—a Los Angelized setting, particularly at night, above the starry lights of town. But the mountains are essentially a full stop to Anchorage, and Anchorage has nowhere else to go.

Within this frame of mountains, ocean, and military boundaries are about fifty thousand acres (roughly the amount of land sought by the Capital Site Selection Committee), and the whole of it is known as the Anchorage Bowl. The ground itself consists of silt, alluvium, eolian sands, glacial debris—material easy to rearrange. The surface was once lumpy with small knolls. As people and their businesses began filling the bowl, they went first to the knolls, because the knolls were wooded and well drained. They cut down the trees, truncated the hills, and bestudded them with buildings. They strung utility lines like baling wire from knoll to knoll. The new subdivisions within the bowl were thus hither and yon, random, punctuated with bogs. Anchorage grew like mold.

WOLVERINE ALUMINUM SIDING. ALASKA FOUR-WHEEL DRIVE. JACK BENNY'S RADIO-DISPATCHED CESS-POOL PUMPING.

Low ground is gradually being filled. The bowl has about a hundred and eighty thousand people now, or almost half of human Alaska. There are some in town—notably, Robert Atwood, of the *Times*—who would like to see Anchorage grow to seven hundred thousand. Atwood is a big, friendly, old-football-tackle sort of man, with whitening hair and gold-rimmed glasses. Forty years on the inside, this impatient advocate of the commercial potentialities of Alaska is said to be one of the two wealthiest people in the state, the other being his brother-in-law. "Idealists here in town see a need for a park in every housing development," Atwood told me one day. "They want to bury utility lines, reserve green belts, build bicycle paths. With these things, the bowl could only contain three hundred and fifty thousand. They're making it very difficult for man, these people. They favor animals, trees, water, flowers. Who ever makes a plan for man? Who ever *will* make a plan for man? That is what *I* wonder. I am known among conservationists as a bad guy."

In Anchorage, if you threw a pebble into a crowd, chances are you would not hit a conservationist, an ecophile, a wilderness preserver. In small ghettos, they are there—living in a situation lined with irony. They are in Alaska—many of them working for the federal government—because Alaska is everything wild it has ever been said to be. Alaska runs off the edge of the imagination, with its tracklessness, its beyond-the-ridgeline surprises, its hundreds of millions of acres of wilderness— this so-called "last frontier," which is certainly all of that, yet for the most part is not a frontier at all but immemorial landscape in an all but unapproached state. Within such vastness, Anchorage is a mere pustule, a dot, a minim—a walled city, wild as Yonkers, with the wildlife riding in a hundred and ninety-three thousand trucks and cars. Yet the city—where people are, where offices are—is perforce the home address of wilderness planners, of wildlife biologists, of Brooks Range guides.

The first few days I spent in Alaska were spent in Anchorage, and I remember the increasing sense of entrapment we felt (my wife was with me), knowing that nothing less than a sixth of the entire United States, and almost all of it wilderness, was out there beyond seeing, while immediate needs and chores to do were keeping us penned in this portable Passaic. Finally, we couldn't take it any longer, and we cancelled appointments and rented a car and revved it up for an attempted breakout from town. A float plane—at a hundred and ten dollars an hour—

would have been the best means, but, like most of the inmates
of Anchorage, we could not afford it. For a great many residents, Anchorage is about all they ever see of Alaska, day after
day after year. There are only two escape routes—a road north,
a road south—and these are encumbered with traffic and, for
some miles anyway, lined with detritus from Anchorage. We
went south, that first time, and eventually east, along a fjord
that would improve Norway. Then the road turned south
again, into the mountains of Kenai—great tundra balds that
reminded me of Scotland and my wife of parts of Switzerland,
where she had lived. She added that she thought these mountains looked better than the ones in Europe. Sockeyes, as red
as cardinals, were spawning in clear, shallow streams, and we
ate our cheese and chocolate in a high meadow over a torrential
river of green and white water. We looked up to the ridges for
Dall sheep, and felt, for the moment, about as free. Anchorage
shrank into perspective. It might be a sorry town, but it has the
greatest out-of-town any town has ever had.

BIG RED'S FLYING SERVICE. BELUGA STEAM & ELEC-
TRIC THAWING. DON'T GO TO JAIL LET FRED GO YOUR
BAIL.

There is a street in Anchorage—a green-lights, red-lights,
busy street—that is used by automobiles and airplanes. I remember an airplane in someone's driveway—next door to the
house where I was staying. The neighbor started up its engine
one night toward eleven o'clock, and for twenty minutes he ran
it flat out while his two sons, leaning hard into the stabilizers,
strained to hold back the plane. In Alaska, you do what you feel
like doing, or so goes an Alaskan creed.

There is, in Anchorage, a somewhat Sutton Place. It is an
enclave, actually, with several roads, off the western end of
Northern Lights Boulevard, which is a principal Anchorage
thoroughfare, a neon borealis. Walter Hickel lives in the enclave, on Loussac Drive, which winds between curbs and lawns,
neatly trimmed, laid out, and landscaped, under white birches
and balsam poplars. Hickel's is a heavy, substantial home, its

style American Dentist. The neighbors' houses are equally expensive and much the same. The whole neighborhood seems to be struggling to remember Scarsdale. But not to find Alaska.

I had breakfast one morning in Anchorage with a man who had come to Alaska from The Trust for Public Land, an organization whose goal is to buy potential parkland in urban areas and hold it until the government, whose legislative machinery is often too slow for the land market, can get up the funds for the purpose. In overbuilt urban settings—from Watts to Newark and back to Oakland—The Trust for Public Land will acquire whatever it can, even buildings under demolition, in order to create small parks and gardens that might relieve the compressed masses. And now The Trust for Public Land had felt the need to come to Anchorage—to the principal city of Alaska—to help hold a pond or a patch of green for the people in the future to have and see.

Books were selling in Anchorage, once when I was there, for forty-seven cents a pound.

There are those who would say that the only proper place for a new capital of Alaska—if there has to be a new one—is Anchorage, because anyone who has built a city like Anchorage should not be permitted to build one anywhere else.

At Anchorage International Airport, there is a large aerial photograph of Anchorage formed by pasting together a set of pictures that were made without what cartographers call ground control. This great aerial map is one of the first things to confront visitors from everywhere in the world, and in bold letters it is titled "ANCHORAGE, ALASKA. UN-CONTROLLED MOSAIC."

⟨ To place its government nearer the center of things, Missouri moved its capital from St. Charles to Jefferson City; West Virginia from Wheeling to Charleston; South Carolina from

Charleston to Columbia; North Carolina from New Bern to Raleigh. The first capital of California was San Jose. Then General Mariano Vallejo offered to underwrite a new capital in, as it happened, Vallejo. The capital soon moved to Benicia, to Sacramento. New York has moved its capital more times than can conveniently be counted. New York City, White Plains, Harlem, Fishkill, Kingston, Marbletown, Hurley, Poughkeepsie . . . When you have been espoused that often, you are possibly in no hurry to make matters legal the next time around. Such was the case with Albany. The legislation designating Albany the capital of New York was finally written and passed in 1971. Santa Fe became the capital of the Kingdom of New Mexico ten years before Plymouth Rock.

Now, from the Arctic to Southeastern, the committee had been holding "workshop hearings," inviting and even recruiting people to come and help "relocate" the capital of Alaska. The total attendance each evening would first be separated into small conversational units, and after an hour or so of that a mass parliamentary fracas would follow, during which the various groups reported what had turned up in their discussions.

"Our group is not really familiar with the Susitna area. To us, it's a swamp."

"A swamp is an appropriate place for government."

"Swamp or no swamp, get those legislators up here where we can watch them."

"Even if we don't go to see them many times during a session, just the thought that we can will keep them on their toes."

Maps were put up on the walls, and people were invited to offer their suggestions on the maps. Someone drew an X in the ocean near Anchorage and wrote, "Just the place for watered-down politicians."

Someone else said, "Put the capital on a barge. It can travel around the state."

Quickly the maps were covered with advice.

"Put the money into education."

"Why destroy one town and at the same time destroy more wild land to build another?"

"Don't mess up more of Alaska."

"I strongly suggest that the capital not be placed in a wilderness site. We are not Brazil. I don't think we need a new city in Alaska."

Brasília, unsurprisingly, had been much on the minds of Alaskans, and they tended to assess Brasília in the light of their opinions of the Alaskan initiative. Certain promoters of the new city recommended that the Capital Site Selection Committee go to Brasília to see a vital new capital at work. Others believed what they had read, and saw Brasília as an airplane (it is laid out in the shape of an airplane) that had made a long flight inland and crashed.

In one of the seminar discussions in a workshop hearing I attended, everyone kept nodding in agreement as grandiose assumptions circled the table.

"I don't know if anybody should even bother to figure the cost of something as important as this."

"We're going to be Arabs when the royalties come from the pipeline."

"Alaska will be another Saudi Arabia."

Then someone compared Anchorage to the slums around Brasília.

Someone else said, "Yes sirree. What we do not need is a Brasília in our wilderness."

And someone else said, "At least, we should profit by others' mistakes."

Whereupon a distinguished-looking gray-haired man, whose spine was straighter than a T-square, straightened it a little more and gave a short-bark cough for attention. He appeared to have received in his lifetime an unquestioning lot of attention. He said firmly that he felt the moment had come for him to make himself known. His name was B. B. Talley, he said, and he lived in Kenai and was a retired brigadier general in the United States Army Corps of Engineers. During the Second World War, he had built bases in Alaska. Later on, as a civilian contractor, he had been "in on the planning of Brasília from beginning to end." When building began, his company was the only foreign firm with a construction contract there. "We poured the concrete for Brasília."

He paused, and looked around the table. A woman across from him said, "Beg your pardon, sir. Are you bragging or complaining?"

General Talley went on to say that Brasília had been placed far out in the wilderness because various parts of Brazil despise one another and would agree only on a wilderness site. Surely, he said, that's not the case in Alaska.

"Begging your pardon, sir. It surely is."

Canberra, to a lesser extent, came into the workshop conversations. Canberra, set in the Australian bush between Sydney and Melbourne, had been designed in Chicago by Walter Burley Griffin and had won, through the years, the acceptance of Australians. A somewhat sterile place, undeniably attractive, it has tended to depress some visitors because it offers nothing but government, no relief from government.

In groups formal and informal, small and large, however, the city that was talked about more than any other was Juneau.

"Juneau will be decimated in its spirit as well as in its pocketbook."

"Juneau's fishing industry is almost gone. The gold mine closed thirty years ago. The logging industry is down—cut down by the Sierra Club. What a shame! The timber is rotting on the vine."

"The capital is Juneau's only economic base."

"They will move the capital over my dead body."

"That condition is acceptable."

"This move in effect puts up a fence across the hundred-and-forty-first meridian and says, 'We don't care what happens to you in Southeastern Alaska.' "

"Juneau snatched the capital from Sitka in 1900. They lobbied secretly in Washington."

"Anchorage thinks Juneau exercises an undue and malign influence over the entire state—in matters of money, land speculation, capital improvements."

"Juneau, with the legislature, has had more than its share of appropriated funds. People want to get the money up here in Anchorage."

"People maneuver, and they put on masks to cloak their maneuvers. Those behind the scenes don't really want to have the legislature close to the people, but that's been the way to peddle the move. What they want is the money."

"To make a power play work, you have to give lip service to the people."

"Juneau will survive. Many government employees will stay there in service jobs for Southeastern."

"Tourists will still come. Every spring, they can't wait, in Juneau, for the legislators to leave, so they can fill the houses with tourists."

"Juneau will just have to broaden its base."

"Long before Juneau was ever the capital, Juneau was making a living."

"They might even start digging some more gold out down there and spending it up here in Alaska."

(Gold prospectors in the nineteenth century had little to go on except an association of gold with quartz and pyrite, and, since that required neither a great deal of intelligence nor academic training, many gold prospectors were the sort of people who had little to go on whatsoever. Two such were

Richard Harris and Joe Juneau, whose most noted employer described Harris as "an inveterate drunkard" and said of Juneau, "Between hooch and squaws he never had a cent to get away on."

The employer was George Pilz, a mining engineer who set up a mill near Sitka to extract gold from bearing rock. Sitka, in the Alexander Archipelago, had been the Russian capital and was now the American capital of Alaska. The year was 1879, and three events of that season led, ultimately, to the moving of the capital away from Sitka. First, Kowee, principal chief of the Auks, travelled a hundred and fifty miles to Sitka to show the mining engineer certain rock he had collected along Gastineau Channel, near his home. Pilz had promised a hundred Hudson's Bay blankets and steady employment to any tribe that led him to a place where mining could successfully follow. Kowee wanted the work and the blankets. Then, by odd coincidence, the naturalist John Muir passed by on an eight-hundred-mile canoe trip. He reported that he had been through Gastineau Channel and had seen interesting mineralization there. And, third, Joe Juneau and Dick Harris—each about forty-five years old—came wobbling down a gangplank off a ship from Wrangell. They owed the purser and the captain for passage, and they were looking around for work.

There was no special hurry about checking out the leads of Muir and Kowee. Pilz had prospectors all over the archipelago —from the Taku Inlet to the Peril Strait, Admiralty Island, Chichagof Island—playing hunches or following the reports and hunches of others. He grubstaked prospectors and salaried them at four dollars a day. In return, he reserved the right to choose two claims from every three they might make. He himself was little more than a middleman. He had to go to the merchants of Sitka, or even to San Francisco, for money to keep all his prospectors active. In attempting to cover an archipelago four hundred miles in length, Pilz in his employment practices could not impose high standards. He took what came

along. Joe Juneau and Dick Harris had been around mining
camps much of their lives, and they had come along.

Harris had been educated—Girard College, Philadelphia.
Juneau had avoided school. He had fished and hunted, and
projected himself into later life able only to write a little
French. Harris had a large nose and lenticular eye sockets and
a certain look—in the wings of the mustache, perhaps—of the
schemingly disenchanted. Juneau—slim, sad-eyed Juneau, lip
hair tumbling, crown hair short and flat—appeared to be a
Yonne Valley farmer, an eel fisherman, the mayor of an embarrassed village, a waiter in a one-fork brasserie. Actually, he was
born near Quebec and raised in Wisconsin, where his uncle,
Solomon Juneau, built the first cabin in what is now Milwaukee
but did not have the honor of seeing his name transferred to
the town. In July, 1880, Harris and Juneau set out from Sitka
Harbor with three months' provisions. Following a northeast-
erly route, they panned streams here and there but came up
with only "light prospects"—some float quartz and colors of
gold, but not enough for a profitable claim. They had several
Auks with them, who were guiding for one dollar, a few hard-
tacks, and a cup of seal oil per day. The Auks took Harris and
Juneau to Auk Village, and the two prospectors then spent
three weeks in a condition—even by the standards of the
Indians who would tell the story—of total bibacity. The Indians of the archipelago distilled a drink they called *hoochinoo*.
They were adding its first syllable to the American language,
with the help of Harris and Juneau. The prospectors paid with
equipment and grub, and to buy more drink, and squaw-pleas-
ures as well, they gave up more food, more equipment, until,
scarcely a month out of Sitka, their three months' supplies were
all but gone. Moreover, they lost their boat. It floated away
with the tide in mid-binge. So, having no alternative, they
decided to return to Sitka. They paid the tribe a rifle to take
them home. But first the Indians took them down Gastineau
Channel to a small anchorage near the mouth of a stream.

Its water ran white over ledges of rock and down through the cleavage of two sheer mountains—mountainsides stiff with big Sitka spruce, rising on up to avalanchine balds with declivities so steep that brooks fell down them in veils. When you look up from the streets of Juneau, that is what you see, for Juneau is compacted where the mountains touch, and the mountains loom behind the town in shades of green with snow-covered summits and alpine ice. The channel, Gastineau, is deep-water and blue, three-quarters of a mile wide, nineteen miles long, mountainsided all the way. Big white ships come up the channel to the town. In the opposite direction, sometimes, travel the Taku winds—off Taku Glacier, some thousands of feet above—winds so fierce and flattening that in 1880 it was on some days impossible to build a fire, and tents were not up long before they blew away. A pedestrian today in Juneau, head down and charging, can be stopped for no gain by the wind. There are railings along the streets by which senators and representatives can haul themselves to work. In recent years, a succession of wind gauges were placed on a ridge above the town. They could measure velocities up to two hundred miles per hour. They did not survive. The Taku winds tore them apart after driving their indicators to the end of the scale. The weather is not always, or even generally, so bad; but under its influence the town took shape, and so Juneau is a tight community of adjacent buildings and narrow European streets, adhering to its mountainsides and fronting the salt water.

There is a characteristic, too, of frequent rain. It rains in Juneau about two hundred and twenty days a year. Clouds hang like bunting on the mountains. Many sidewalks of the town are covered with permanent roofs that are cantilevered from building sides and held in place by coupled rods. Houses go unpainted, because it is so hard to find an appropriate time to paint them. Old-timers, eating halibut cheeks in the City Cafe, talk about putting a dome over Juneau. Rain does not fall around the clock, however, and the weather will shift with tonic swiftness, the gray above the channel brightening to cotton and tearing apart to show blue sky, with tilted shafts of sunlight coming through, a rainbow forming.

There is no permafrost in Juneau. It is six hundred miles from the Arctic Circle. The temperature in winter seldom goes below zero, and in summer it holds under eighty. Out past the airport are forested bays that suggest Washington, Oregon, northern California, with the difference that the Mendenhall Glacier approaches them—all blue ice and powdered rock, like a huge white earth-fill dam. In streams near the glacier run cutthroat trout and Dolly Vardens two feet long. When the king salmon come into nearby waters they weigh as much as eighty pounds.

Juneau, bright at night from across the channel, is dense and galactic under the dark shapes of the mountains. From the same perspective in the day—with its ships at wharfside, its small-craft anchorage, its buildings all crowded before an uprising wilderness—it is a pocket city in a setting as wondrous as the setting of a city could ever be. Juneau is Alaskan, and American, and it has its oil-storage tanks in the heart of town. It holds its own in junk and crud. Gold Creek, the rushing stream that was named by Harris and Juneau, now runs through town in a concrete trough, a large storm sewer. The State Capitol is a six-story yellow brick-and-limestone building with big windows of the sort that are opened with a pole. In appearance, it is an abandoned junior high school. The governor's mansion is Southern and decadent, tired in its innards. On the edge of town is the abandoned mine—abandoned during the Second World War—of the Alaska-Juneau Gold Mining Company, a flooded ruin now, fronting the mountain like the façade of a theatre that has long since played its last show. From Calhoun Avenue to Willoughby Avenue, old wooden steps go far down the cliffside and around the new State Office Building, which soars into the air and goes down the hill, too. People approaching the building on the uphill side walk in on the eighth floor—into a high atrium of light and space, of glass-walled, unpartitioned offices that look down into the interior as well as out upon the mountains and the channel. A sign on the ground floor says, "POSITIVELY NO DOGS." So much for old Alaska.

After the United States bought the territory from Russia, Juneau was the first city to be founded there. Juneau was also the first city in Alaska to be founded in result of a discovery of gold.

Through the cleft in the mountains, the two prospectors went up the stream a mile and more, panning. They found promising color in their pans, and in the creek bed "very good float gold quartz." And, having done that and no more, they left. Back to Sitka went Richard Harris and Joe Juneau. They had staked no claims. They had gone only a short way upstream. They had only guessed at the gold beyond. Hungry, hung over, out of hooch and barter, they—prospectors!—had found the underbrush forbidding, the going too tough, so they had taken with them a hundred pounds of the river quartz and departed.

Chief Kowee, amazed, saw his chances for a hundred blankets going straight down the channel with these fools. So he chased after them to Sitka and complained to the mining engineer that Harris and Juneau had not been inclined to follow him far enough upstream, and he laid on the table some rich gold quartz as an example of what was there. Pilz arranged the grubstake for another expedition, and he paid for a canoe. For prospectors, now, in the fall, with the season running short, he had to use whatever he could find, and the pickings were limited to Harris and Juneau. After naming the canoe the Alaska Chief of Gold Creek, they started out in mid-September from Sitka.

Chief Kowee made extremely sure this time that they found the proper gold. En route, they prospected a stream or two that they had prospected before, apparently not remembering where they had been. But the guiding Indians firmly led them on to the small anchorage in Gastineau Channel near the stream they had named Gold Creek. This time they went for the headwaters, and the brush was indeed so dense that to get around it they went up a gulch—calling it Snowslide Gulch—and on up the mountainside to a commanding view of an El Dorado. It was a stream-sculptured dish of ground into which long eras of erosion—glacial, fluvial, ice-spall erosion—had (from the mineralized mountains) poured a deep filling of gravels of gold. "I broke some with a hammer and Juneau and myself could hardly believe our eyes. We knew it was gold, but so much and not in particles, streaks running through the rock and little lumps as large as peas or beans." (These quotations are from "The Founding of Juneau," a careful history by R. N. De Armond which was published in 1967 by the Gastineau Channel Centennial Association.) In days that followed, claims were staked in the names of Juneau and Harris and their assorted grubstakers, backers, and creditors. Harris called a meeting—consisting of himself, Juneau, and three Indians—to formalize a code of local laws, the usual procedure under the Mining Act of 1872. Harris took the power job—district recorder—and two hundred square miles around the discovery was designated the Harris Mining District. Then, beside Gastineau Channel, a townsite of a hundred and sixty acres was staked and claimed. The name given the town was Harrisburgh. Pressed, at a later date, for his reasons for choosing that name, Harris said he wished to honor the state of Pennsylvania. Five bona-fide miners—not two miners and three Indians—were by custom required for the approval of a code of laws; and as the gold rush developed in Harrisburgh other miners quickly challenged Harris's power and, in the process, relieved the town of his name. The honor was transferred to Juneau. In a dispute about overlapping claims, the new Alaska court system a few years later deprived Harris of nearly all his property in and around the town. He eventually died in a sanatorium in

Oregon, his way there paid by friends. Juneau died in Dawson, in Yukon Territory, after a lifetime in the wild, always, but perhaps not primarily, in search of gold. It was his wish to be buried in Juneau, and four hundred dollars was raised there to bring the body south. In 1900, the year after he died, the town became the capital of Alaska.

⦗ The man who caused the initiative to select a new capital for Alaska to be placed on the 1974 ballot—the man who took up the idea and organized a group of volunteer workers and collected signatures and raised money and administered the entire successful procedure—was named, as it happens, Harris. He was not a descendant of the eponymous Harris of Harris-burgh. He had found his own lode in Anchorage in the nine-teen-forties when he quit as a deliveryman for a dry-cleaning company and, with another driver, borrowed something over three thousand dollars and started the Alaska Cleaners, 610 Fireweed, Anchorage—a hanging-clothes forest, wherein someone presses a button and twenty miles of garments begin to move. Frank Harris is a lean man, bald, gentle in voice, with long jaws, an English face. He was elected to the Alaska State Senate in 1966, defeated in 1968. The urge to move the capital came over him during those two years. Sessions began in January and ran on at least three months (of late they have been extending through June), and Harris in Juneau developed what he called "a complete feeling of isolation—stuck there." He found Juneau "a dilapidated city, buildings unpainted, streets dirty, sidewalks crumbling," and could not imagine "people having pride in a state capital in such condition." He lived in a big concrete coop that was painted pink—the Mendenhall Apartments. The wind blew so hard it seemed to come through the paint. He covered his windows with sheets and masking tape, and, even so, he could not stay warm. "The Capitol Building was cold, too, if you could get to it, leaning into the Taku wind. The rain didn't bother me. I come from Oregon. I could not imagine how any place could be so isolated. People couldn't get at you. You were in a cage. You talked to the hard lobbyists every day. Every day the same people. What was going on there needed more airing." So he sponsored a bill to move the capital. The day he introduced it, the news went out over the radio, and when he went to have lunch in the Baranof Hotel a waitress refused to serve him. In the State Affairs Committee, a legislator from Juneau killed the bill. Each of the three times that a capital-move initiative has appeared on the Alaska ballot, it has been as a result of a people's petition. "The legislature could do it," Harris has explained, "but they don't have the guts."

In Minnesota, when a bill was introduced to move the capital from St. Paul to St. Peter, Joe Rolette, legislator and fur trader, disappeared with the bill itself until the legislature adjourned. In Nevada, when the count was shaping up as close, one delegate shot another, and Carson City became the capital by a single vote.

Harris, in his effort, was taking up an idea that had come from nowhere so concentratedly as from Robert Atwood, of the Anchorage *Times*. All through the statehood years, Atwood had been writing columns advocating that the capital be moved. Atwood had, in Harris's words, "always been ve-*he*-ment on the subject." When initiatives made the ballot in 1960 and again in 1962, Juneau taxed property owners to raise money to fight and defeat them. Twelve years went by, during which oil was discovered at Prudhoe Bay, in Arctic Alaska. Money was on the way. In the same period, the population of the Anchorage Bowl a great deal more than doubled. "Fairbanks and Juneau and the bush always combined and defeated the previous initiatives," Harris told me one day at the cleaners. "But now we had the votes."

The legislature, in the end, is to pick a name for the new capital. Meanwhile, astonishingly, almost no one shows interest in what the city might be like. I guess I have talked with several hundred Alaskans about the moving of the capital, and among them virtually no one has offered any concept, any vision, of how the new city might appear. Virtually no one but Harris. He had thought about it a lot—all through the Taku winds, the signature gathering, the days beyond the vote. "The capital should sit overlooking a lake," he said. "The lake should be large enough for float planes. You dock and walk to the Capitol. It is a rustic Capitol that fits the setting of the country. It is a state capital and a sports capital—winter and summer sports. From it you can see Mount McKinley. There is no big gold dome. That's of the past. It should be built of concrete and natural rock—something that will blend in with wilderness. Industry and farming will be all around it. It should be west of the Susitna, on the projected road to McGrath."

❬ Willie Hensley, west of the Susitna, and high on the tundra of Little Peters Hills, looked down across the valley and said quietly that he hoped the work he was doing as chairman of the Capital Site Selection Committee would count for something, hoped the group was not wasting its time. Somehow, he made himself heard without raising his voice, despite the big helicopter standing by, shaking and muttering, a hundred yards away. "One wants to think that one's energy is concentrated on something worth doing," he went on. If the people insisted on a new capital in a wild site, at least he meant to find a good one. Six possible sites were visible from the hill—six "footprints"—including one on Blair Lake (in the low ground between the Chulitna and the Susitna), one along Deep Creek (below the Peters Hills), and one on Peters Creek (among swales of open spruce) right before him. Favorably impressed by this hill-and-river, rolling, forested land, he said as much, and added that, for all his travels, he had never been in this part of Alaska.

To borrow a term used by some Alaskans, Willie Hensley is a Brooks Brothers native. In recent years, a class of native has developed, or has at least increased, that has seen and experienced a much wider segment of the world than nearly everyone else in, say, Kivalina, Kotzebue, or Unalakleet. In an old military barracks below Mount Edgecumbe, across the harbor from Sitka, is a high school staffed by the Bureau of Indian Affairs, and that is where in Willie's time the qualified Eskimo children of Kotzebue would ordinarily be sent. That was far enough from home—eleven hundred miles—but Willie went off on an educational odyssey a great deal more exotic than that. Straight out of the sod houses and the riverine tent sites of Eskimo Arctic Alaska, Willie went to high school in Tennessee. To prepare him for the experience, he was indoctrinated—age fourteen, just off the plane from Kotzebue—in Myrtle, Mississippi. If he did not previously have what has become his outreaching sense of the absurd, he surely acquired it then. A town too small to be a crossroads, Myrtle was somewhere between Corinth and Oxford—in the northeastern corner of Yoknapatawpha. The first thing that struck him, of course, was the heat—the amazing, breath-stopping heat—and he wondered who could long endure such a climate. But before he had a chance to suffocate in that way he was smothered in another. He was given what he described years later as "a hell of a dose of Southern Baptist rural religious outlook." It was a Baptist preacher in Kotzebue who had arranged Willie's travels. The preacher's parents lived in Myrtle. They had agreed to take care of this fine young Eskimo and show him the ways of America. Anxious to please, Willie became, in his own phrase, "a temporary Southern white." "It was 1956. There was hardly a ripple of change yet—of desegregation. I knew no history of the black problem. I knew nothing about slavery. I couldn't understand the situation. I couldn't believe that people would work for three dollars a day in a field. I wanted to talk to them, but I got the impression I should not." Instead, he was exposed to a battery of preachers. Myrtle was "a preachin' center," and foremost among its congested clergy was the celebrated Brother Ray, who went around in a Cadillac and wore overalls. Brother Ray's fundamentalism overwhelmed Willie, and in a religious sense he has never recovered. He does not customarily go to church. "No." He grins. "But some of my best friends are preachers."

He went to Harrison-Chilhowee Baptist Academy, in eastern Tennessee. ("It was in the foothills of the Smokies and it was very beautiful. I couldn't believe such sculptured hills.") He saw Alaska—Kotzebue—only once in those four years. Then, in 1960, he entered the University of Alaska, in Fairbanks. Halfway through, he transferred to George Washington, in the District of Columbia, where he studied Russian (and managed to see Poland and Russia on a trip sponsored by the Experiment in International Living) and got his B.A. in political science. Doing summer work in Washington for the Bureau of Indian Affairs, he "met a lot of Lower Forty-eight Indians," and became interested in their legal relationship to their aboriginal land. It was a subject that had already been much on his mind in regard to Kotzebue. In the nineteen-fifties, the federal government had ruled off land there in lots and sold it at auction. Eskimos did not have enough money or understand auctions. Doctors, nurses, teachers, and Civil Aeronautics Administration personnel bought the property. "Eskimos had owned the property communally for ten thousand years. Now the C.A.A. types owned lots. That is how I got interested. Everybody had a way to get property but the native people." Missionaries, using church land, rented lots to the natives. "You are responsible for the hereafter, not profits," Hensley said to them. "Turn the land over to the natives." The missionaries had not acted on the suggestion.

Hensley did graduate work in business and took a course in Constitutional law at the University of Alaska. For the law course he wrote an extensive paper on who owned Alaskan land. Specifically, it was called "What Rights To Land Have The Alaska Natives?" and it traced from the Alaska purchase onward the uncertain title and unrealized claims of his people. The root question was, do the Alaskan natives, by dint of aboriginal use and occupancy, have special claim to Alaskan land, and, if so, how much land, and in how wide a range around their established villages? The 1867 purchase treaty and subsequent acts of the United States Congress did not ignore the point but left it in shadow. Now, in 1966, the Eskimos, Aleuts, and Indians of Alaska were increasingly demanding a settlement. Hensley wrote his paper in May of that year, and, drawn more than ever to the subject, inevitably became drawn into politics. He helped form the Alaska Federation of Natives, a group whose efforts were dedicated to a settlement of native claims. And that fall—age twenty-four—he ran for the state legislature and was elected.

Stewart Udall, Secretary of the Interior, reacted to the native-claims situation by suspending until the question was settled all transactions in land that was under his control. He controlled nearly all of Alaska. The U.S. Constitution and several hundred treaties made with natives elsewhere in the country tended to suggest that Congress was liable if native property was abridged. In order to be free of liability, Congress would have to extinguish native title, specifically and consciously. In days gone by, the way to do that was to extinguish the native. The treatment of Indians in the Lower Forty-eight was hardly forgotten, and among the factors that were gaining momentum in the Alaska natives' favor white guilt was not the least. Other points intensified, too. The State of Alaska, having been promised a hundred and three million acres of land in the act that made Alaska a state, needed the money that would be derivable from the land. The state wished to get on with the process of selection, but what land could it select with the native claims unsettled? Oil companies, pending native-claims settlement, had nine hundred million dollars' worth of questionable leases, cloudily titled. Moreover, to protect the native interest a court granted an injunction against the building of the Trans-Alaska Pipeline pending a settlement of native claims. Pressure for settlement then came from labor unions looking toward pipeline jobs. Conservationists got into it, too, because the matter of preservation of lands in Alaska was so close in nature to the native-claims question that it more or less had to be dealt with at the same time. These combined pressures, kept at the highest levels possible by the maneuvering of Willie Hensley and his native colleagues, yielded the Alaska Native Claims Settlement Act of 1971.

When the natives settled for one billion dollars and forty million acres of land—much of it likely to contain gold, silver, and other minerals, and oil and gas—their claims were thus extinguished. This was perhaps the great, final, and retributive payment for all of American history's native claims—an attempt to extinguish something more than title. The settlement suggests not only principal but interest as well on twenty decades of national guilt. The natives of Alaska were suddenly, collectively rich. Along tribal and cultural lines, the state was divided into twelve aboriginal regions, and in each a native corporation was established to hold and invest the new wealth. The Sealaska Corporation, for example, would handle the share of the Tlingit-Haida tribes, in the southeastern archipelago. Doyon, Ltd., would be the holding company for the Athapaskan interior. NANA Regional Corporation, which grew out of the Northwest Alaska Native Association, would direct the funds of the people of Kotzebue and of ten other villages in the Kobuk Valley. In the Alaska lexicon, a new synonym for "native" was "stockholder," and NANA's five thousand stockholders would receive in incremental payments sixty-two million dollars and 2.3 million acres of land. The jets of Alaska Airlines and Wien Air Alaska were soon a third to half full of natives zipping around the state on business—for nothing, of course, prevented one corporation from investing or operating in another's region. The corporations were, as Hensley put it, "mini-conglomerates." NANA, for example, set up a development corporation that started, among other things, a protection agency and a construction firm. They won a contract for all pipeline security north of the Yukon, another to supply labor to pipeline pumping stations, another to build a high school in Kivalina (on the coast of northwest Alaska), another to build a new control tower at Anchorage International Airport. Willie Hensley, it seems almost needless to say, became a founding member of the NANA board of directors, a member of the executive committee, and president of two of NANA's principal companies. That is what is meant by Brooks Brothers native. John Sackett, of Doyon. Roy Huhndorf, of Cook Inlet. They do not travel just in Alaska. They are often in San Francisco, New York, the District of Columbia. Needing expertise beyond the attorneys of Anchorage, they use the finest and dearest of Wall Street and Washington law firms to construct and straighten their affairs.

Jade Mountain, in the Kobuk Valley, belongs to NANA. Jade Mountain is a mountain of jade. One day in Anchorage, Hensley had strewn some before me on his desk in NANA's offices. It was exquisite stone (the state gem), polished, viridian, in blocks and wafers, from the NANA Jade Products Division. "I hope that this jade will be used liberally in the new capital," he said, and he added, with a subtle smile, "because it is so beautiful, not just because we own it." And now, as he stood on the hilltop looking east toward Talkeetna and places where his Alaskan jade city might rise, it occurred to me that Willie Hensley—sooner or later—might live in the new capital, in a jade-columned mansion near the center of the town.

❲ If you order a glass of beer in Alaska, it is likely to be modest in all ways but cost, which can run upward from a dollar. If you

order a couple of eggs with toast, the bill may be three dollars
and fifty cents. If you order a new capital, just the choosing of
a site for it will run you a million and a half dollars, but the
price is in line with the beer and the eggs, and seems on the
whole accepted. Words are what the money has bought, in the
main—words by the troy ounce, delivered in Consultaspeak.

"East of Talkeetna, the cost impact will be impacted."

"The planning aspects are far more important than whatever the megastructure may turn out to be."

The prime consultant was CCC/HOK, an international
planning and architectural firm, whose planners and architects
—Ed Crittenden, Anne Kriken, Barry Quinn, Dan Gale—
came from the company's Anchorage and San Francisco offices
but had about them a certain quality of Eastern tweed. They,
in turn, reached out for help to engineers, hydrologists, econo-
mists, botanists, biologists, meteorologists, geologists (notably
Dames & Moore); and the general procedure was set up and
coördinated by Leonard Lane, the Capital Site Selection Committee's full-time executive director.

"With McHargian geophysical determinants, we factor in
the transportation and utility infrastructure."

"The approach, overall, is essentially McHargian."

Ian McHarg, the absent master, is a landscape architect and
regional planner who teaches at the University of Pennsylvania
and developed some years ago a technique for selecting the best
new site or alignment for anything from a doghouse to a city
of ten million. McHarg's method, in crude summary, was to
take all relevant information—developed by his own research
and that of his staff and consultants—and express it in the form
of markings and shadings on clear plastic overlays that could
be placed upon a map. One overlay might deal with, say,
drainage, ground water, and additional hydrological considerations; another would shade in the extent of vegetation. Each
criterion could be individually considered, then literally piled
atop the others until an expert, peering down through the

layers of plastic, could see on the map the best and worst sites for construction. McHarg had presented this to the world in a fountainhead treatise called "Design with Nature." McHarg was not connected with CCC/HOK, but when his name was mentioned its people tended to swivel and face Philadelphia.

They had buried the map of central Alaska under layers of acetate, and had eventually eliminated everything on it but the Susitna Valley. Under more overlays, the valley itself was graphically analyzed. The Land Status Acetate showed, in various colors, state ownership, borough ownership, federal ownership, and private ownership. The Natural Limitations Acetate showed, in various patterns and colors, floodplains, bogs, muskeg pockets, swamps, steep slopes, alpine tundra, moose habitats, bear habitats, salmon spawning areas. "To develop our extensive sensitivity to wildlife," Leonard Lane reported, "we talked to thirty-one people in the Department of Fish and Game." The Existing Transportation Acetate showed two-lane roads, gravel roads, dirt roads, airstrips, railroad, airport sites. The Elevation Acetate included twelve altitudes. The Capital City Footprint Areas Acetate presented the regions of the valley that had shown up best under earlier fathoms of acetate. Within each footprint, or generally buildable area, was a "centroid"—the spot where buildings would most likely rise. Following this came more plastic, neatly sketched upon, plotted, shaded—criterion after criterion, layer upon layer: the View Aspect Acetate, the Degree of View Acetate, the Water Features Acetate, the Vegetation Types Acetate, the Landscape Features Acetate, the Background Features Acetate. The committee had to develop a talent for peering down through the plastic. The committee was like a crane standing on one leg staring into a pond.

Meanwhile, to make new photographic mosaics of the valley, the consultants ordered and the committee paid for twelve thousand dollars' worth of aerial pictures. Dames & Moore defended the need for this by pointing out—to some people's astonishment—that certain features of the topographic maps of the United States Geological Survey were only about sixty per cent accurate. Stream courses, for example, were often out of date. A stream course in Alaska, writhing like a firehose, can rapidly put a map out of date.

The consultants had been hired to envision a setting, not a city. The design of the community was specifically excluded from their procedure. They could not help but consider it, though, in the light of the question that was always with them: Is it possible to create an unsterile community that has only government there?

"I sure hope so," Barry Quinn said one day. "The capital has a lot going against it. Its economic base is government. There will not be much secondary employment. And diversity makes a community healthy." Quinn, from East Rochester, New York, had been working in Alaska off and on for nine years. He was young, with dark longish hair parted in the middle, his manner gentle, engaging. "It is difficult to initiate the incentives that create diversity," he went on. "They tend to evolve naturally. And industry is simply not going to spring up here. It's cheaper to process oil and timber elsewhere. The town's overall development will depend on the development of Alaska. It may not work for this generation but for the next. You can't create a Friday-night spot in a brand-new town."

Ed Crittenden, president of CCC/HOK, is an architect and city planner, trained at Yale and M.I.T., who has been in Alaska twenty-six years. Five of his six children were born in Alaska. His hair is graying and as long as the times. There is a pipe, a sports jacket, a blue button-down shirt, a knitted tie. I asked him one day how he saw the new city, and he said he deliberately tried to avoid thinking of that in order to play his role as written. Crittenden had done the new Federal Building, the BP Building, the Union Oil Building—some of the high-rising glass of Anchorage. Pressed to describe the new capital as it might appear in his private thought, he finally said, "Well, to tell you the truth, I would reverse all of the things that people come to Alaska to get away from. I would not go along with the I'll-build-my-cabin-where-I-damned-well-want-to syndrome. I would apply ideas from the Eastern United States—a central core, a central walking mall, a controlled environment. Living structures would be concentrated, and in modules of enclosed space. There would be modules for state and local government, and commercial modules, all concentrated, with plenty of open space around them—plenty of undisturbed, or almost undisturbed, Alaska." So saying, and in a cloud of pipe smoke, Crittenden departed for Siberia. An honored figure in the field of Arctic construction and Arctic community development, he was going there to participate in the first Soviet-American exchange on human environment in the north.

❨ In recent years, certain construction has enhanced the weight of Juneau. Along Gastineau Channel, for example, runs a four-lane divided highway, engineered with the breadth and grandeur of an interstate—implying New York at one end, Chicago at the other. The road cost sixteen million dollars, and runs from Juneau out to Juneau Municipal Airport, and back —there being nowhere else to go. The new State Office Building, edificial focus of the town, has been complemented by a new courthouse and a multilevel parking garage. It is not a coincidence that so much construction came about at a time when Juneau was threatened by the movement to move the capital, and no one will argue about the fact that all this effort can be traced to one man. His name is Bill Ray. Nearly forty years ago, he turned up in Juneau after sleeping in his own blankets in the hold of the S. S. Baranof. From Wallace, Idaho, he had been driven north by the Depression, and had come to Juneau with his father to look for work. He began as a longshoreman, and, moving from job to job, he did about all there was to do in southeastern Alaska. He worked in canneries, on fishing boats, and as a deckhand on a canning tender. After the Second World War, he bought a liquor store in Juneau. He helped defeat the capital-move initiatives of 1960 and 1962. In 1964, he was elected to the Alaska House of Representatives, and eventually became chairman of its Finance Committee. In 1970 and 1974, he was elected to the Senate, where he also became chairman of the Finance Committee. As one of his constituents has said of him, "Hands down, Bill Ray brings home more bacon than anyone else in the legislature."

"They call me the lovable bandit," Ray told me one day, in his office in the Capitol. "I take everything that isn't nailed down. I admit it. Aren't you supposed to do what you can for your district? They say I have the guts of a second-story man and the brains of a Mafia chieftain." The second-story-man part was protruding under the hem of a jade-green polo shirt. Life had been good in Juneau. Ray appeared to be in his middle fifties. He had heavy eyelids, and was a little figgy in the jowls. Through his office window he gazed contemplatively at the State Office Building, whose eleven stories of airy glass were more than framed by ponderous abutments of sandstone, turreted and crenellated so that it looked something like a greenhouse prepared for war.

"That's my building there," he said. "They call that Fort Ray. It's no secret—it cost fifteen million dollars. We have thirty-five hundred government employees. That means more than ten thousand people—well over half the town—depend directly on the government. And now powerful forces are at play to kill us, all set in motion by a little clique in Anchorage."

"Clique?"

"Atwood, at heart. Atwood was here once, in Juneau, and didn't make it. Atwood has had gubernatorial ambitions, senatorial ambitions. When he looks in the mirror, he sees God. He's a brilliant man, but he has insulated his mind against reality. He misrepresents the truth. What they really want to do—the little clique that has been forcing this issue—is to put a legislative hall thirty miles outside of Anchorage, and that would be the head of the state government, but the heart and guts would be in Anchorage. What they sold the people was that the head, guts, and feathers—everything—would be in one place, and you can't do that thirty miles from Anchorage. They've done nothing but sell it on a lie. Lie No. 2: It won't hurt Juneau. They say Juneau has its cruise boats, and so on. Cruise boats? People get off the boat, look around, take a bus out to the glacier, and go back to the boat. They're visitors, not tourists. A tourist stays a week and drops four hundred dollars. A visitor comes with a shirt and a twenty-dollar bill and doesn't change either one."

"Shouldn't the state capital be near the population center?" I asked him.

"That argument doesn't hold. The spectrum of public pressure is larger where the people are. Can you imagine a march of *welfare* people? In Juneau, you don't have pressures like that. You can sit with a clear head and do your work."

I mentioned that Jan Koslosky, of Palmer, had told me that during his six years in the legislature he only went home once during a session. He said he had been a pilot for thirty years but did not like the flight into Juneau. He had had too many close calls trying to get in.

"Koslosky is a cautious man. I'll tell you this. You are safer coming into Juneau than elsewhere, because when you come into Juneau the pilot is flying the plane. The *captain* is flying the plane. He wants to be sure he gets here."

As an aircraft feels its way down toward an airport in weather, the pilot reads an instrument-approach chart, which indicates the distance and altitude from which the runway should be visible or the approach has been missed and the plane must climb out and perhaps have another try. For most airports, the missed-approach point is close to the runway, or even just above it. For Juneau Municipal, the missed-approach point is three and a half miles from the runway and fourteen hundred feet in the air. If you can't fly in visually from there, you immediately turn and rapidly climb. In all directions from the airport are mountains, and certain ones are close. As the Juneau approach chart presents the situation, "Any go-around commenced after passing the published missed-approach point will not provide standard obstruction clearance." In the legislature, quorums can erode when flights approach Juneau, fail to see the runway, and go off and land somewhere else.

An Alaskan pilot once advised me never to fly to Juneau. "It's a one-way shot," he said. "Once you get lined up on final, you're looking right at the rocks. Mountain goes straight up and down in back of it. The weather is notoriously poor. You have to have supreme confidence in all your instruments and in the F.A.A.'s instruments. The approach is relatively steep. You go from five thousand feet to sea level in fourteen-point-seven nautical miles. If you miss, you do a very steep, sharp climbing turn to avoid hitting something. An airplane is most inefficient when making a sharp turn and climbing. A mile from the runway you go over a five-hundred-foot hill, and the top has been cleared of trees so that planes will not hit them. Now, is that or is that not a little hairy? After crossing the hill, you have to make a dogleg to the right before touching down."

In September, 1971, a Boeing 727 of Alaska Airlines, with seven crew members and a hundred and four passengers, was coming in toward Juneau at an altitude considerably below the approach-chart minimum. Investigators are sure there was an error in the navigational equipment—either in the plane or on the ground. The pilot apparently thought he had passed a checkpoint he had not yet reached, and thought he was over Auke Bay. He was still in the Chilkat Range. In cloud, the aircraft flew among mountains, feeling its way down—forty-five hundred, thirty-five hundred, twenty-five hundred feet. The height of the last ridge—before the terrain would fall away to low ground and open water—was thirty-five hundred and nine feet.

Ray said he flew out to see the accident. "It was a terrible, terrible thing. The plane had split. It had been peeled like a banana, spewing people out both sides. But that is the only major accident we have had here. There are more accidents in Anchorage—more air traffic and more danger. And how many people get killed in Anchorage in car wrecks? What are the chances of getting *shot* in Anchorage—by some drug-crazed son of a bitch? Or getting acid thrown in your face? Compare *that* with Juneau. I can't even *remember* a murder in Juneau. I wonder if *anybody* remembers a murder here."

He got up, stuck his head out the door, and asked if anyone out there remembered a murder. Zero.

"I can tell you when the last one in Anchorage was," he went on, sitting down again. "It was last weekend."

"What do you suppose the new capital will look like?" I asked him.

"Personally, I think the capital's going to look like Juneau. Because it's going to *remain* in Juneau. But if there ever were a new capital, I'd want them to have a collection of buildings Alaska could be proud of, I'll tell you that—not a boxworks, not an Anchorage, not a glorified privy. Anchorage looks like Poppincorn, Iowa. There is nothing Alaskan about it. A new capital should look like Alaska."

"What sort of look is that?"

"I don't know. All I know is Anchorage stinks. The Anchorage strategy will be to piecemeal the capital. They'll peddle a temporary, functional capital to keep the cost-appearance down, and then they'll sock it to 'em, baby. At least a billion dollars. Oh, they're making a big effort, these Anchorage people, and to keep people trying that hard there's got to be, someplace, a dollar in the ground."

"So you built Fort Ray as an immovable object, a defense against the move?"

"Right."

"And the highway, too?"

"Right. God-damned right."

"And the courthouse?"

"Exactly!"

"And the garage?"

"You've got it!"

"All to turn millions into masonry that could never leave Juneau, all to stop the move?"

"That's it! That's what I did! With all that built, how *could* they move it?"

"What will you do when the capital moves?"

The Senator fell suddenly quiet, and for at least two minutes stared out his window and down the street to Fort Ray. "What *is* there to do?" he said, at last. "Just sit here and look at it, that's all. Juneau. Wiped out. With more than half of the work force gone, the city will fall dead. There won't be anything left. While the state squanders money on a new capital, Juneau will fall dead. And what will we gain? We don't—in Alaska—have money to run our schools."

He paused a moment, then went on, "Oh, we're steadily building up the University of Alaska's Southeast Branch here. We're building the fisheries-research program. There are some tourists. But, frankly, what are you going to do for tourists in the wintertime when the god-damned Taku wind is blowing fifty miles an hour and the windchill factor is sixty below?"

"Not to mention the rain."

"People make too much of the god-damned rain. There's more than average, but you kind of like it. It keeps you alert."

The Senator stood up, shook hands warmly, said he was sorry he had to go but he had a plane to catch, put on his coat, went to the airport, and flew to an apartment he maintains in Torremolinos, on the Costa del Sol, of Spain.

In Florida, in the nineteen-sixties, a movement stirred to have the capital shifted from eccentric Tallahassee to the center of the state, to Orlando. The legislature's direct response was to appropriate ten million dollars for new House and Senate office buildings and forty million for a new Capitol—in Tallahassee.

Seven per cent of Juneau's voters voted for the capital move. Some of these were government employees who had lived "up north" (as they say in Juneau) and were hoping to go back. Others were people who thought the state government had inflated the local economy. And another was Fishpole John. John Klett, from Meriden, Connecticut, was considerably more Alaskan than most Alaskans, in that he had been there more than forty years when he died not long ago. In an old shop on South Franklin, he meticulously fashioned salmon rods, and he sent them on order as far as Europe. He was a big man with stiff white bristles, a red knitted cap—and before anyone who cared to listen he would fulminate as he worked. "I voted to move it. I'm glad they're going to move the son of a bitch. Jesus Christ. It costs too much to keep the capital here. If the state government was out of here, this would be a better town. No matter where you've got a capital, you've got crime. This town is a rip-off town in a rip-off state. The dirty dozen —the people that runs Juneau— want to keep all the money to themselves, but a lot of people who don't have money get nothing and would like to see the capital go. The legislature voted themselves a raise this year—to fourteen thousand seven hundred dollars. What the hell do they do up there? Nothing. Everybody wants the legislature out of here. They're the biggest bunch of chisellers. They leave stores holding their personal checks. Sitka was the capital seventy-five years ago. Sitka is better off than we are now."

The mayor of Sitka happened to stop off in Juneau while I was there, and he did not disagree with Fishpole John. "We lost the capital, and nobody in Sitka regrets it," he said. "The government makes Juneau a rat race, where strangers come and go." The mayor of Sitka, John Dapcevich, had grown up in

Juneau, had become an accountant, and had once been the state budget analyst. "Sitka is a bad place for the capital," he continued. "And so is Juneau. But it's stupid to move it. It's just a matter of economics. We can't afford this new utopia. The Boeing report was ridiculous—not even close to the picture."

Boeing—the aircraft company—has a computer-services subsidiary that will study just about anything for anybody, and in 1974 it analyzed for the government of Alaska the cost of moving the capital from Juneau. The cost turned out to be modest, according to Boeing. Some fifteen years in the future, the cost of having relocated the capital would exceed by only a hundred and ten million dollars the cost of the capital should it stay in Juneau, in part because the state would be spared the expense of refurbishing its older buildings there. Boeing also decided that so much matériel and manpower would be on hand as a result of the pipeline project that the new capital's building costs would be significantly reduced. The Boeing report could not help but influence the fate of the initiative on the ballot, and the report left Juneau particularly bitter. Juneau attorneys were quick to say that while the report depreciated the buildings of the old capital it did not depreciate the new buildings in the new location. Juneau rumbled about a lawsuit.

One of Juneau's responses to approaching catastrophe has been to suggest that people need not actually travel to the capital to watch, or even confer with, the legislature. In Alaska, in fact, the difficulty of bringing people together to make (and to influence the making of) laws is only one of countless problems in weaving an economic, political, and cultural fabric across a third of a billion acres of land. Alaska is attempting to solve the problem with RCA earth stations that are trained on satellites and patterned so that telecommunications and closed-circuit TV can tie any part of Alaska to any other. An earth station is functioning now in Talkeetna. Others are in place as well. The goal is a hundred and twenty-nine, all over the state.

Using them, doctors in Anchorage are already treating patients lying in infirmaries in the bush. Juneau has pointed out that people in Bettles, Barrow, or Nome could go into a room in a state office building and watch, say, the House Resources Committee at work in Juneau. They could talk to the committee. They could even testify.

Rhode Island used to worry about its great size, too. In an area so large, one capital site could not serve all the people. So the legislature travelled from Newport to Bristol to East Greenwich to South Kingstown to Providence, and did not settle exclusively in Providence until 1901. Vermont's legislature travelled, too. Delaware, which is smaller than quite a few islands in Alaska, moved its capital from New Castle to Dover in order to have a central location. On the other hand, there have been capitals even more out of the way than Juneau. Of the three capitals in the history of Wisconsin, one was Burlington, Iowa. The Vermont state legislature once convened in Charlestown, New Hampshire.

Some of the people I met in Juneau were cultivating the hope that after the new capital site was chosen environmental-impact statements would show intolerable costs. The Trans-Alaska Pipeline had been projected in 1969 as a nine-hundred-million-dollar project. Now the guess was that the pipeline would cost, in the end, something like eight billion.

Meanwhile, the dissident seven per cent still wanted the capital to go. Some people in Juneau felt that Juneau was more attractive as an old mining town than it would ever be with the development that would continue if the capital stayed. They had voted for the initiative. So had commercial fishermen, irritated by a boat harbor full of pleasure-fishing cruisers owned by state employees, by a clutter of sport fishermen, while the commercial catch declined. In the Juneau Cold Storage Company, in a big room full of running water and silver salmon in iced hampers, I watched rubber-booted men and women slicing the salmon clean. As he worked, a tall, strong, unreserved young man, a big man in thick wool trousers and two wool shirts, said, "I know a girl who works in the State Office Building, and she knits a sweater there every month. I hate those bureaucrats with a purple passion—the god-damned parasites, walking around doing nothing, sitting on their butts. They're wrecking the fishing for the commercials. I'd like to see them go. I'd like to see mosquitoes eat them. I'd like to see them up in the bush."

❪ The big helicopter, in the air again with the Capital Site Selection Committee, moved generally southward in a loose, truffle-sniffing zigzag. In haze to the east we could barely discern the corridor line of the Anchorage-Fairbanks Highway. Someone remarked that the Matanuska-Susitna Borough had announced that it was going to put several dozen parcels of land on the market—land spaced through the valley from Willow to Talkeetna.

"Somebody's out for a land grab," said Louise Kellogg, and she volunteered to look into it and see what she could do to discourage feverish speculation. This was her district, her borough. She had come to it nearly thirty years before, and had long had a dairy farm near Palmer. The farm—a hundred and twenty-five cows—had been leased to a younger farmer. With a partner, she was now running an antique shop, whose contents discouraged her, she said, because so many items familiar to her when she was young had now become negotiable as antiques. When she was young, she had gone to Vassar. She had recently been to her fiftieth reunion there. She had been a member of the South Central District Republican Committee and a trustee of Alaska Methodist University. Small, gentle, white-haired, wearing trifocals, she may not have appeared to be particularly forceful, but no one seemed to doubt that she could deal with the borough. Its freeholders, like any number of other people, apparently wanted to test and sample the capital-engendered increase in the price of land. ("The capital has been located; located against the wish of the great majority of the people—located for the pecuniary and personal benefit of Tom Cuming and his brother bribers—located at a place without any natural advantages, and one totally barren of anything save whisky shops and drunken politicians . . . a place having no historic interest—simply because they could make a better bargain with the speculators," wrote the Nebraska *Palladium,* in 1855.)

Along the road near Talkeetna, some years ago, the state sold off ground for something like a hundred and twenty-five dollars an acre. Five thousand dollars will buy such an acre now. Under the aspens and birches by the roadside, fresh signs appear beside the unbuilt gates of unbuilt subdivisions—SPORTSMAN ACRES, RUSTIC WILDERNESS, TIMBER PARK—and into the woods run new roads with earth plowed up to either side like banks of brown snow. Parka Parkway. Lichen Drive. Grizzly Way. The new capital is not the only fetal town in the Susitna Valley. Where the committee hovers, speculation hovers as well.

It can be worth your life to visit such a place. Nose a car in under the cottonwoods, have a look around. Before you can back out, a salesman has appeared from behind a tree and placed you under house arrest. He has a contract in his hand, and the lots are going fast. "No" is a word he does not comprehend. He tells you—erroneously—that the man who owned the computer firm in Anchorage that did the feasibility study for the Capital Site Selection Committee sold the computer firm and bought lots in this beautiful subdivision, and so did eight others in the same office. Hurry, buy a lot, you may be too late. This little beauty is almost two-thirds of an acre, and the price is fourteen thousand dollars. The distance to Anchorage is eighty miles, but the distance to the capital of Alaska will be a great deal less than that. Meanwhile, consider the view. The lot is on a high escarpment above the Susitna, and beyond the river are broad spruce and muskeg barrens and beyond them the white mountains. That big one on the right is McKinley. The Indians called it Denali, which meant "You'll be sorry if you don't sign now." Would you like to see some wildlife? Let's go down to the airstrip. Take you up and show you a moose.

The salesman whose trap line I had happened onto one summer evening was named John Leifer. He had lived until recently in Juneau, he said, but had left because Juneau had had it. Juneau was dead. This was where things were happening now—up here in the Susitna Valley, where the capital would be. He had flown an air taxi in Juneau. "Just like a taxi-driver, but in a plane—under six-hundred-foot ceilings, two-hundred-foot ceilings. In Juneau, you fly them or starve. You get to know every curve in the shoreline." At full throttle, in a Stationair, he jumped off the airstrip and across the Susitna, and began to search its sloughs and its tributary streams for moose. Skimming trees, banking at such steep angles that his stall-warning horn was constantly sounding, he swooped and circled in the hunt for wildlife. Printed on his company's brochures were moose, beavers, bears, and wolverines, but there were none in sight beneath the plane. In wider and wider arcs, he expanded the search, diving, climbing, and repeatedly saying, "I can't understand it, I can't understand it. Where *are* all the moose?" Finally, in the arriving dusk, we flew over a black bear. Turning, making a tight one-eighty, he lined up the Stationair for a second view. He throttled back, and we glided silently down on the bear, which stood still, in nearsighted perplexity, wondering where the sound had gone. Then, suddenly, Leifer advanced the throttle and buzzed the astounded animal, which ran across the muskeg in a kind of rolling cringe as we passed over and then gained enough altitude to clear the trees.

I was to learn, much later, that John Leifer crashed and was killed close by the Susitna on the same autumn day that the Capital Site Selection Committee was crisscrossing the skies above.

Earl Cook spotted a moose from the committee helicopter. It did not so much as lift its head—just stood there in its muskeg pocket like a horse in a pasture. We circled low over Amber Lake, a site under consideration, and then turned west and crossed wide stands of balsam poplar and broad muskeg meadows, beyond which, on a clear stream, were a couple of homesteads—one a crude assemblage of shacks, the other a tidy collection of small cabins, with a rectangle of timothy and an airstrip so short it looked more like a driveway. Homesteaders—with their big (hundred-and-sixty-acre) blocks of land—stood to make or lose the most if the capital should settle near them. They could lose their remoteness, with nowhere comparable to go; new homesteading in Alaska was shut off indefinitely in March, 1974. On the other hand, homesteaders in the Anchorage Bowl had sold out for many hundreds of thousands of dollars, and analogous deals might be offered in the Susitna Valley. Meanwhile, some homesteaders who had "proved up" on their land—that is, had lived on it for three years, built a habitable dwelling, and grown a crop on an eighth of the acreage—were already selling at prices that guessed the future. Only a few weeks before, a Susitna Valley homestead had sold for a hundred and forty-eight thousand dollars, and, like the ones we were flying over, it was many miles from the road.

A homestead on the highway system would be worth a great deal more than that. I had visited one, some miles south of Talkeetna, where a young couple, Don and Patty Bender, had moved onto the land in 1974 and had lived in a camper while they mixed concrete, poured a foundation, and, together, built a house. It was a small, handsome place, with a steel-drum wood stove and big windows of insulated glass. Mount McKinley was framed in one window. Sometimes bears were too. Don Bender had a .300 Magnum but had not yet used it on a bear.

He used it for his annual moose, and through the winter he and his wife ate mooseburgers, moose sausage, moose steak. They had eggs, too, and bacon coming. Near the house was an A-frame combination coop and sty. A pig lived in one end, chickens in the other. On cold nights, the chickens found a way to get near the pig. The Benders were in favor of the capital move. "Juneau is too inaccessible," he said. "Therefore, many of our politicians have hidden from their constituents." They did not want to lose their homestead, though, no matter how much its value might appreciate. They said they hoped the new capital would "not destroy our personal place of life." Their property, theirs for living on it, would probably be worth half a million dollars by the time it was proved up. If the capital came near, that sum could multiply, and the Benders would feel some pressure to change their minds.

They had so far cleared ten acres, in conformity with the rules—dense, closed-forest acres of spruce, birch, aspen—and had planted timothy and oats. Although the homestead was in the Susitna Valley, the terrain was rough with sheer-sided hillocks, and the Benders' ten acres under cultivation looked less like a field than a bald lumpy spot on a high mountainside, the crops clinging to serpentine contours. The appearance of it all tended to suggest mockery of the Homestead Act, which was written to offer farmland to an expanding nation, and this minimal "farm" had been hacked absurdly from a steep subarctic forest. The Homestead Act, though, had a venerable history of mocking itself. It had worked well only east of the hundredth meridian, where there was enough rain to serve a farm, and homesteads in the range country and semideserts of the West had made, if anything, less sense than the homesteads of Alaska. In general, the Alaskan climate is not much more severe than the climate of, say, Montana, and the soil under Alaskan cottonwoods could be richly supportive of crops. The growing season is not prohibitively short—roughly mid-May to the first of September—and in various fruits and vegetables sugar content will build up to unusual levels in the cool air and the long northern light. A potato developed by Curtis Dearborn, at the University of Alaska's experimental farm in the Matanuska Valley, is eleven per cent sugar and can be eaten like an apple. Dearborn also developed the Alaska Frostless Potato, which survives frosting at twenty-seven degrees. Potatoes could be farmed very successfully as far north as the Yukon, and may be someday, if the idea ever takes hold. Agriculture, though, is among Alaska's foremost undeveloped assets. There is a so-called "farm loop" north of Fairbanks, with broad cleared fields and haystacks under tarps—a Pennsylvanian scene, reminiscent of the mother country. Rampant subdivisions, of late, have been eating it up. The Trans-Alaska Pipeline winds among the farms. In the Matanuska Valley, which forms a V with the Susitna Valley around the Talkeetna Mountains, the soil—loess soil—has the color and consistency of Hershey's cocoa and is rockless two feet down. Farmers from the Middle West were brought to the Matanuska Valley during the Depression and, after a disorganized beginning, established successful farms. In many parts of the valley are fields and gambrel-roofed barns, with the Chugach Mountains rising to alpine snowfields beyond—a phenomenal sight from a farm. Matanuska notwithstanding, of arable Alaska not much is plowed—far too little to be expressed as a percentage. As Alaskan land, in huge segments, is divided up for various purposes, agriculture fails to make the list. But the strawberries are delicious enough to make you drunk—Susitnas, Talkeetnas, Matareds. You can grow carrots, beets, spinach, broccoli, rhubarb, cauliflower, Brussels sprouts, zucchini—all in the heart of Alaska—and wheat, barley, alfalfa, oats, and white sweet clover eight feet high. Peas are particularly sweet and aromatic. There is virtually no need for pesticides. Cabbages grow to be two feet in diameter and can weigh seventy pounds. They look like medicine balls. If Alaska would get up off its past (the boom philosophy), it could be the world center of sauerkraut-cabbage production. That sounds laughable, but the state might come out of it economically sound. The new capital city could be sterile and governmental and given to one purpose, or it could be an island in a sea of farms—the state of Alaska, from one end to the other, being green about half the year.

Exceptions are glaciers, but they are only three per cent of Alaska—the big ones close to the gulf coastline, which reaches down and east from Anchorage toward Cordova, Yakutat, Haines, and Juneau. Something like seventeen thousand square miles are permanently under ice, while the rest of Alaska melts. Ninety-seven per cent—half a million square miles—melts. Even the great ice sheets of the glacial ages did not cover Alaska. An arm of the Laurentide covered the Brooks Range. The Cordilleran Glacier Complex, which covered the Canadian Rockies and the chains of the Pacific coast, reached out over the Alaska Range and across all the land between the mountains and the gulf. But the Interior and the Arctic Slope and all the west coast were bare. While much of New Jersey was covered with ice, most of Alaska was not.

The truly immense glaciers might be down in the southeast, but the glacier that was off to our right just now was in no sense modest. The helicopter had crossed Shulin Lake, and had circled it, tilting far over so the committee members could hang by their seat belts for a plan view, its big rotor blades biting the air with the sound of a working axe. Level again, it was proceeding west toward the Kahiltna River, the source of which, off to the north, was almost as preëminent as the mountains above. It came down out of the Alaska Range like a great white tongue. It came—the Kahiltna Glacier—from eleven thousand feet, from a high saddle between the peaks of Foraker and McKinley. And two, three, four miles wide all the way, it flowed fifty miles south into the valley, where it finally turned into river at an altitude of scarcely a thousand feet. This was the big glacier the climbers land on—and the fact that they land at the seven-thousand-foot contour has nothing to do with the strategies of the sport. They do so because airplanes are not permitted to land in Mount McKinley National Park, and the park boundary happens to cross the glacier at that level. The river below us was the product of the sun, and even in autumn and from the helicopter's high perspective it was awesome to see. Most fast rivers are white, smooth, white, smooth—alternating pools and rapids. This one was white all the way, bank to bank, tumultuous, torrential, great rushing outwash of the Alaska Range. With so many standing waves, so much white water, it appeared to be filled with running sheep. The color of the water, where it was flat enough to show, was actually greenish-gray, and its clarity was nil. It carried so much of what had been mountains. Glacier milk, as it is called, contains a high proportion of powdered rock, from pieces broken off and then ground by the ice. The colors of outwash rivers are determined by the diets of the glaciers—schist, gneiss, limestone, shale.

Glacial erratics were all over the valley, and there was one below us now. The ice in the past had nosed southward these huge monoliths—supermagnified boulders—which had rafted along on the advancing terminus and had not become caught and ground. The one beneath us appeared to be as large as a three-story building, weirdly standing in the forest. It was so big that soil had formed on its upper surface, and trees grew from it like hair.

We crossed Lake Creek, which was not a glacial stream and was running so clear we could see its gravels. Ahead was Mount Yenlo, a four-thousand-foot rise in the western Susitna Valley, and the helicopter set down there, on a southerly slope of the mountain, to release the committee. Just below, and beside the clear stream, was the most remote site under consideration for the capital—thirty-five miles from the highway and undeniably as beautiful a setting as could possibly exist in the valley. It was high grassland—under, but approaching, a thousand feet— with white birches and white spruce scattered through it, big

trees for this part of the world, almost a foot in diameter. The
mean January temperature was ten degrees, July fifty-six. The
summit of Yenlo was above the site, to the immediate northwest, and due north, close across fifty miles, was the palpable
McKinley. The committee spread out through berry fields,
these laced with stands of fern. There was sign of moose and
caribou. There were depressions in the grass where bears had
slept.

In Alaska, when you ask people if they know a certain place
—a river, a lake, a hill, a valley—they often say, "I've flown it,
but I've never been on the ground there." Alaska is too big to
be broadly inspected in other ways, but looking at something
from the air is nonetheless an inadequate perspective. Dimensions tend to be removed. There is no substitute for being on
the ground, for experiencing a landscape close at hand, for
feeling the earth underfoot. And this was frustratingly apparent now, for the helicopter had spilled us suddenly into a
three-dimensional wilderness world—for a ration of tangibility,
to last fifteen minutes. Its lights blinking, its engine guttural,
it sent out signals of impatience. Waiting to take us away, it
took away something of what it had brought us to see.

Arliss Sturgulewski, offering berries from her hand, said as
much, and shook her head, and looked long at the splendid
landscape—the city site—sloping down to the stream. "We
need the right kind of planning before Dollar One is spent on
the ground," she said. "We need to take advantage of views
—of the uniqueness of the setting—and then see to it that the
capital is not just another place. You've got to take everything
that you've learned and absorbed and make something out of
it. You can't just quantify it. You need a gut feeling, and at
least we get something of that standing here. I'm wondering
who, in the end, will run this capital. What will the land use
be, the zoning, the planning? Government is the catalyst at the
beginning, but then may lose control."

Loose flakes of gold hung in a clear amulet around her neck.
Over her blouse was a Levi jacket. She was tall, large-boned,

attractive, blond. She came from the mountains of northern Washington and had been in Alaska—in Anchorage—almost twenty-five years. Her husband had died in an F-27 propjet on its way to King Salmon, and, in the seven years since, she had immersed herself in civic affairs, most notably as a member of the Greater Anchorage Area Planning and Zoning Commission. Like the Mrs. Partington who tried to fight the Atlantic Ocean with a mop, she had watched, and she had fought, the splurge of Anchorage.

Control had been lame as it followed development, she said. "Lots were ruled off on paper that for one reason or another could never be developed. Soil testing, the presence of adequate utilities were not required. For a long time, there was no control. When efforts at control came, they lacked force and lagged behind. There were no building codes. We finally got some codes, but not until 1972. There was no floodplain ordinance until 1975. There are sixty streams and rivers in the Anchorage Bowl. Before this year, there was development in the floodplains, and even in the floodways! Authorities had to approve development that was already built. The planning commission had no power. We were only advisory. We did get some positive things. We got bike trails. But in a boom situation your development really gets away from you. Twelve thousand new people have come to Anchorage in the past year. The streets are falling apart. We were unprepared for the impact of the pipeline. When a boom comes along, you don't have strong enough rules. You can't keep up. Now look at this place —how beautiful it is. Can you imagine what could happen out here? Alaskans don't see the value of order, don't see the value of looking to the future."

⟨ We were about forty-five minutes from Anchorage, and the helicopter had forty minutes of remaining fuel—a condition that would hardly arouse the interest of many Alaskan pilots, but ours was particularly careful, and he landed again at Skwentna, where he had a cache of fifty-five-gallon drums. The bloody moosemeat we had seen there earlier was gone. The gravel airstrip was as silent as it had been before. Out of a stand of fireweed, the pilot, Bill Brandt, rolled two drums. He set them on end by the helicopter. He knocked out a bung and smelled the contents. Never knew what might get into these barrels, he remarked, and he inserted a high-vacuum hand pump and began to work. He pumped hard. With beavery sideburns and a billowing glory of a mustache, he looked like an antique Alaskan, and all the more incongruous there pumping Chevron Jet Fuel into a big chopper. He grew tired, and Willie Hensley took over, pumping in an easy rhythm and half as hard.

In the air again, we flew southeast and soon over Bulchitna Lake, a capital-site possibility, its water so clear that we could see, in places, its white sand bottom, and blue-green fathoms where the sand was below the reach of light.

"Is that Bulchitna?" said Arliss Sturgulewski.

"Bulchitna, Alaska," said Willie Hensley. "I propose that as the name of the capital."

It was a lovely lake in a closed spruce-hardwood forest, and I would much have liked to see it from its shore, but the helicopter did not set down by it, or even give up altitude. C. B. Bettisworth said he thought the surrounding terrain too flat, and Earl Cook said he agreed. A pair of eagles flew out from the shoreline trees.

We flew on over a water-dispersed country of ponds and beaver houses, bogs, muskeg fairways, and across the big rivers —Kahiltna, Susitna—to an even greater spread of lakes. These, near Willow, had become a summering world for people from Anchorage—ice out in May and swimming by July—many of whom were now experiencing their own private spasms of the Alaskan paradox, the Dallas scenario versus the Sierra Club syndrome. They worried about their country retreats while they watched the values rise. For beyond Willow, on the upland toward Hatcher Pass, in spruce-and-birch forest that gives way in a dramatic treeline to moors of alpine tundra, was a capital site perhaps more likely than all others to be the ultimate choice of voters. Its temperatures and altitude were much the same as they were at remote Mount Yenlo. Its views—of the valley and of the Alaska Range to the north—were almost as good. The railroad and highway were close. A five-thousand-foot gravel airstrip, built for B-29s, stood ready for facilities and tarmac. And—point of points—Anchorage was scarcely thirty miles away.

Willow is still a hamlet—three hundred people—with potatoes growing in surrounding clearings and tomato vines five feet high: the sort of place where it is not unknown, in the dead of winter, for an old moose hunter to die in his cabin and be brought into town frozen solid. I had stayed in Willow for a night or two, in a cabin that had no windows. Wadded paper filled the gaps in the logs. Twenty dollars a night, with heat. In the Willow Trading Post one morning, a man in a baseball suit was tending bar, and people sitting on stools there were talking about the five acres they had bought for two thousand dollars and how they had recently been offered fifty thousand dollars but were waiting for seventy-five. "OUR COW IS DEAD," said a sign above them. "WE DON'T NEED YOUR BULL." Just up the track was another, somewhat newer sign: "WILLOW BROOK ESTATES, A QUALITY DEVELOPMENT BY LANDAK, INC."

In its meetings in following weeks, the committee would finally reduce its list to three sites that would appear on Alaskan ballots, and the three it would choose would be Larson Lake, near Talkeetna; Mount Yenlo, in the western valley; and the heights to the east of Willow. The site attracting the most votes would be the site of the new capital of Alaska, and when the election came, the emphatic preference of the voters would prove to be Willow. By the terms of the initiative, the move was to begin by 1980. Opponents of the move would go on clinging to the hope that, come groundbreaking day, the money would not be there. Meanwhile, the big helicopter flew on into rain and falling darkness, down the short run to Alaska's principal city—over Knik Arm, into the Bowl. The rain blurred the windows. Through them, the streets and buildings below appeared to be lying under ten layers of acetate. The chopper touched down. Earl Cook, who had left his home in Fairbanks at six in the morning, unbuckled his seat belt with a terminal sigh. "That . . ." he said. "That's a hell of a way to get to Anchorage."

COMING

INTO THE

COUNTRY

———————

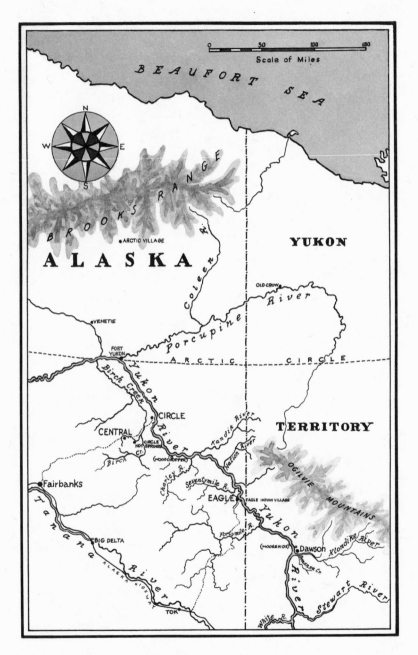

❲ With a clannish sense of place characteristic of the bush, people in the region of the upper Yukon refer to their part of Alaska as "the country." A stranger appearing among them is said to have "come into the country."

Donna Kneeland came into the country in April, 1975. Energetically, she undertook to learn, and before long she had an enviable reputation for certain of her skills, notably her way with fur. Knowledgeable people can look at a pelt and say that Donna tanned it. In part to save money, she hopes to give up commercial chemicals and use instead the brains of animals—to "Indian tan," as she puts it—and she has found a teacher or two among the Indian women of the region, a few of whom remember how it was done. The fur is mainly for sale, and it is the principal source of support for her and her companion, whose name is Dick Cook. (He is not related to Earl Cook, of the Capital Site Selection Committee.) A marten might bring fifty dollars. Lynx, about three hundred. Wolf, two hundred and fifty. They live in a cabin half a dozen miles up a tributary stream, at least forty and perhaps sixty miles from the point on the border meridian where the Yukon River leaves Yukon

Territory and flows on into Alaska. The numbers are deliberately vague, because Cook and Kneeland do not want people
to know exactly where the cabin is. Their nearest neighbors,
a couple who also live by hunting and trapping, are something
like twenty miles from them. To pick up supplies, they travel
a good bit farther than that. They make a journey of a couple
of days, by canoe or dog team, to Eagle, a bush community not
far from the Canadian boundary whose population has expanded in recent years and now exceeds a hundred. For three-
quarters of a century, Eagle has been an incorporated Alaskan
city, and it is the largest sign of human material progress in
twenty thousand square miles of rugged, riverine land. From
big bluffs above the Yukon—five hundred, a thousand, fifteen
hundred feet high—the country reaches back in mountains,
which, locally, are styled as hills. The Tanana Hills. The tops
of the hills are much the same height as New Hampshire's Mt.
Washington, Maine's Mt. Katahdin, and North Carolina's Mt.
Mitchell. Pebble-clear streams trellis the mountains, descending toward the opaque, glacier-fed Yukon, and each tributary
drainage is suitable terrain for a trapper or two, and for miners
where there is gold.

For Donna Kneeland, as many as five months have gone by
without a visit to Eagle, and much of the time she is alone in
the cabin, while her man is out on the trail. She cooks and cans
things. She grinds wheat berries and bakes bread. She breaks
damp skins with an old gun barrel and works them with a metal
scraper. A roommate she once had at the University of Alaska
went off to "the other states" and left her a hundred-and-fifty-
dollar Canadian Pioneer parka. She has never worn it, because
—although her cabin is in the coldest part of Alaska—winter
temperatures have yet to go low enough to make her feel a need
to put it on. "We've had some cool weather," she admits. "I
don't know how cold, exactly. Our thermometer only goes to
fifty-eight." When she goes out at such temperatures to saw or

to split the wood she survives on—with the air at sixty and more below zero—she wears a down sweater. It is all she needs as long as her limbs are active. Her copy of "The Joy of Cooking" previously belonged to a trapper's wife who froze to death. Donna's father, a state policeman, was sent in to collect the corpse.

Donna is something rare among Alaskans—a white who is Alaska-born. She was born in Juneau, and as her father was biennially transferred from post to post, she grew up all over Alaska—Barrow, Tok, Fairbanks. In girlhood summers, she worked in a mining camp at Livengood, cooking for the crew. At the university, which is in Fairbanks, she majored in anthropology. In 1974, she fell in love with a student from the University of Alberta, and she went off to Edmonton to be with him. Edmonton is Canada's fourth-largest city and is the size of Nashville. "In Edmonton, every place I went I could see nothing but civilization. I never felt I could ever get out. I wanted to see something with no civilization in it. I wanted to see even two or three miles of just nothing. I missed this very much. In a big city, I can't find my way out of a paper bag. I was scared to death of the traffic. I was in many ways unhappy. One day I thought, I know what I want to do—I want to go live in the woods. I left the same day for Alaska."

In Alaska, where "the woods" are wildernesses beyond the general understanding of the word, one does not prudently just wander off—as Donna's whole life had taught her. She may have lived in various pinpoints of Alaskan civilization, but she had never lived out on her own. She went to Fairbanks first. She took a job—white dress and all—as a dental assistant. She asked around about trappers who came to town. She went to a meeting of the Interior Alaska Trappers Association and studied the membership with assessive eyes. When the time came for a choice, she would probably have no difficulty, for she was a beautiful young woman, twenty-eight at the time, with a criterion figure, dark-blond hair, and slate-blue, striking eyes.

(Richard Okey Cook came into the country in 1964, and put up a log lean-to not far from the site where he would build his present cabin. Trained in aspects of geophysics, he did some free-lance prospecting that first summer near the head of the Seventymile River, which goes into the Yukon a few bends below Eagle. His larger purpose, though, was to stay in the country and to change himself thoroughly "from a professional into a bum"—to learn to trap, to handle dogs and sleds, to net fish in quantities sufficient to feed the dogs. "And that isn't easy," he is quick to say, claiming that to lower his income and raise his independence he has worked twice as hard as most people. Born and brought up in Ohio, he was a real-estate appraiser there before he left for Alaska. He had also been to the Colorado School of Mines and had run potentiometer surveys for Kennecott Copper in Arizona. Like many Alaskans, he came north to repudiate one kind of life and to try another. "I wanted to get away from paying taxes to support something I didn't believe in, to get away from big business, to get away from a place where you can't be sure of anything you hear or anything you read. Doctors rip you off down there. There's not an honest lawyer in the Lower Forty-eight. The only honest people left are in jail." Toward those who had held power over him in various situations his reactions had sometimes been emphatic. He took a poke at his high-school principal, in Lynd-hurst, Ohio, and was expelled from school. In the Marine Corps, he became a corporal twice and a private first class three times. His demotions resulted from fistfights—on several occasions with sergeants, once with a lieutenant. Now he has tens of thousands of acres around him and no authorities ordinarily proximitous enough to threaten him—except nature, which he regards as God. While he was assembling his wilderness dexterity, he spent much of the year in Eagle, and he became, for a while, its mayor. A single face, a single vote, counts for a lot in Alaska, and especially in the bush.

The traplines Cook has established for himself are along several streams, across the divides between their headwaters and on both banks of the Yukon—upward of a hundred miles in all, in several loops. He runs them mainly in November and December. He does not use a snow machine, as many trappers in Alaska do. He says, "The two worst things that ever happened to this country are the airplane and the snow machine." His traplines traverse steep terrain, rocky gullies—places where he could not use a machine anyway. To get through, he requires sleds and dogs. Generally, he has to camp out at least one night to complete a circuit. If the temperature is colder than thirty below, he stays in his cabin and waits for the snap to pass. As soon as the air warms up, he hits the trail. He has built lean-tos in a few places, but often enough he sleeps where he gets tired—under an orange canvas tarp. It is ten feet by ten, and weighs two and a half pounds, and is all the shelter he needs at, say, twenty below zero. Picking out a tree, he ties one corner of the tarp to the trunk, as high as he can reach. He stakes down the far corner, then stakes down the two sides. Sometimes, he will loft the center by tying a cord to a branch above. He builds a lasting fire between the tree and himself, gets into his sleeping bag, and drifts away. Most nights are calm. Snow is light in the upper Yukon. The tarp's configuration is not so much for protection as to reflect the heat of the fire. He could make a closed tent with the tarp, if necessary. His ground cloth, or bed pad, laid out on the snow beneath him, is the hide of a caribou.

He carries dried chum salmon for his dogs, and his own food is dried moose or bear meat and pinole—ground parched corn, to which he adds brown sugar. In the Algonquin language, pinole was "rockahominy." "It kept Daniel Boone and Davy Crockett going. It keeps me going, too." He carries no flour. "Flour will go rancid on you unless you buy white flour, but you can't live and work on that. I had a friend who died of a heart attack from eating that crap. It's not news that the American people are killing themselves with white flour, white sugar, and soda pop. If you get out and trap thirty miles a day behind dogs, you can damned well tell what lets you work and what doesn't." From a supplier in Seattle he orders hundred-pound sacks of corn, pinto beans, unground wheat. He buys cases of vinegar, tomato paste, and tea. Forty pounds of butter in one-pound cans. A hundred pounds of dried milk, sixty-five of dried fruit. Twenty-five pounds of cashews. Twenty-five pounds of oats. A forty-pound can of peanut butter. He carries it all down the Yukon from Eagle by sled or canoe. He uses a couple of moose a year, and a few bear, which are easier to handle in summer. "A moose has too much meat. The waste up here you wouldn't believe. Hunters that come through here leave a third of the moose. Indians don't waste, but with rifles they are overexcitable. They shoot into herds of caribou and wound some. I utilize everything, though. Stomach. Intestines. Head. I feed the carcasses of wolverine, marten, and fox to the dogs. Lynx is another matter. It's exceptionally good, something like chicken or pork."

With no trouble at all, Dick Cook remembers where every trap is on his lines. He uses several hundred traps. His annual food cost is somewhere under a thousand dollars. He uses less than a hundred gallons of fuel—for his chain saws, his small outboards, his gasoline lamps. The furs bring him a little more than his basic needs—about fifteen hundred dollars a year. He plants a big garden. He says, "One of the points I live by is not to make any more money than is absolutely necessary." His prospecting activity has in recent years fallen toward nil. He says he now looks for rocks not for the money but "just for the joy of it—a lot of things fall apart if you are not after money, and prospecting is one of them."

In winter on the trail, he wears a hooded cotton sweatshirt, no hat. He does use an earband. He has a low opinion of wool. "First off, it's too expensive. Second off, you don't have the moisture problem up here you have in the States." He wears Sears' thermal long johns under cotton coveralls, and his feet are kept warm by Indian-made mukluks with Bean's felt insoles and a pair of wool socks. He rarely puts on his parka. "You have to worry up here more about overdressing than about under-dressing. The problem is getting overheated." Gradually, his clothes have become rags, with so many shreds, holes, and rips that they seem to cling to him only through loyalty. Everything is patched, and loose bits flap as he walks. His red chamois-cloth shirt has holes in the front, the back, and the sides. His green overalls are torn open at both knees. Half a leg is gone from his corduroy pants. His khaki down jacket is quilted with patches and has a long rip under one arm. His hooded sweat-shirt hangs from him in tatters, spreads over him like the thrums of a mop. "I'll tell you one thing about this country," he says. "This country is hard on clothes."

Cook is somewhat below the threshold of slender. He is fatless. His figure is a little stooped, unprepossessing, but his legs and arms are strong beyond the mere requirements of the athlete. He looks like a scarecrow made of cables. All his fea-tures are feral—his chin, his nose, his dark eyes. His hair, which is nearly black, has gone far from his forehead. His scalp is bare all the way back to, more or less, his north pole. The growth beyond—dense, streaked with gray—cantilevers to the sides in unbarbered profusion, so that his own hair appears to be a parka ruff. His voice is soft, gentle—his words polite. When he is being pedagogical, the voice goes up several registers, and becomes hortative and sharp. He is not infrequently pedagogi-cal.

A decade and more can bring deep seniority in Alaska. People arrive steadily. And people go. They go from Anchorage and Fairbanks—let alone the more exacting wild. Some, of course, are interested only in a year or two's work, then to return with saved high wages to the Lower Forty-eight. Others, though, mean to adapt to Alaska, hoping to find a sense of frontier, a fresh and different kind of life. They come continually to Eagle, and to Circle, the next settlement below Eagle down the Yukon. The two communities are about a hundred and sixty river miles apart, and in all the land between them live perhaps thirty people. The state of New Jersey, where I happen to live, could fit between Eagle and Circle. New Jersey has seven and a half million people. Small wonder that the Alaskan wild has at least a conceptual appeal to certain people from a place like New Jersey. Beyond Circle are the vast savannas of the Yukon Flats—another world. Upstream from Circle are the bluffs, the mountains, the steep-falling streams—the country. Eagle and Circle are connected only by river, but each of them is reachable, about half the year, over narrow gravel roads (built for gold mines) that twist through the forest and are chipped out of cliffsides in high mountain passes. If you get into your car in Hackensack, Circle is about as far north as you can go on North America's network of roads. Eagle, with its montane setting, seems to attract more people who intend to stay. In they come—young people in ones and twos—from all over the Lower Forty-eight. With general trapping catalogues under their arms, they walk around wondering what to do next. The climate and the raw Alaskan wild will quickly sort them out. Some will not flinch. Others will go back. Others will stay on but will never get past the clustered cabins and gravel streets of Eagle. These young people, for the most part, are half Cook's age. He is in his middle forties. He is their exemplar —the one who has done it and stuck. So the newcomers turn to him, when he is in town, as sage and mentor. He tells them that it's a big but hungry country out there, good enough for trapping, maybe, but not for too much trapping, and they are to stay the hell off his traplines. He does not otherwise discourage people. He wants to help them. If, in effect, they are wearing a skin and carrying a stone-headed club, he suggests that technology, while it can be kept at a distance, is inescap-

able. "The question," he will say, "is how far do you want to
go? I buy wheat. I use axes, knives. I have windows. There's
a few things we've been trained to need and can't give up. You
can't forget the culture you were raised in. You have to satisfy
needs created in you. Almost everyone needs music, for in-
stance. Cabins may be out of food, but they've all got books
in them. Indian trappers used deadfalls once—propped-up
logs. I wouldn't want to live without my rifle and steel traps.
I don't want to have to live on a bow and arrow and a deadfall.
Somewhere, you have to make some sort of compromise. There
is a line that has to be drawn. Most people feel around for it.
Those that try to be too Spartan generally back off. Those who
want to be too luxurious end up in Eagle—or in Fairbanks, or
New York. So far as I know, people who have tried to get away
from technology completely have always failed. Meanwhile,
what this place has to offer is wildness that is nowhere else."

A favorite aphorism of Cook's is that a farmer can learn to
live in a city in six months but a city person in a lifetime cannot
learn to live on a farm. He says of newcomers, "A lot of them
say they're going to 'live off the land.' They go hungry. They
have ideas about everything—on arrival. And they've got no
problems. But they're diving off too high a bridge. Soon they
run into problems, so they come visiting. They have too much
gear and their sleeping bags are too heavy to carry around.
They are wondering where to get meat, where and how to
catch fish, how to protect their gear from bears. You can't tell
them directly. If you tell them to do something, they do the
opposite. But there are ways to let them know."

Cook seems to deserve his reputation. In all the terrain that
is more or less focussed on the post office at Eagle, he is the
most experienced, the best person to be sought out by anyone
determined to live much beyond the outermost tip of the set
society. He knows the woods, the animals, sleds, traps, furs,
dogs, frozen rivers, and swift water. He is the sachem figure.
And he had long since achieved this status when a day arrived
in which a tooth began to give him great pain. He lay down

in his cabin and waited for the nuisance to pass. But the pain increased and was apparently not going to go away. It became so intense he could barely stand it. He was a couple of hundred miles from the most accessible dentist. So he took a pair of channel-lock pliers and wrapped them with tape, put the pliers into his mouth, and clamped them over the hostile tooth. He levered it, worked it awhile, and passed out. When he came to, he picked up the pliers and went back to work on the tooth. It wouldn't give. He passed out again. Each time he attacked the tooth with the pliers, he passed out. Finally, his hand would not move. He could not make his arm lift the pliers toward his mouth. So he set them down, left the cabin, and—by dogsled and mail plane—headed for the dentist, in Fairbanks.

⟨ John Borg came into the country in 1966. He was a mailman, on vacation, and he pitched his tent by American Creek a mile out of Eagle. The Army had brought him to Alaska in the nineteen-fifties—just before Alaska became a state—and (in his phrase) "plain opportunity" was what had caused him to stay. He carried letters around Anchorage for a number of years while opportunity in other forms withheld itself. And then he found Eagle. From birth he had been at home among low populations in open settings. He had grown up in Spirit Township, in the hills of northern Wisconsin, and had gone to Rib Lake High School, thirteen miles away. Now here was a town smaller by far than any he had known—some log cabins and a few frame buildings aggregated on a high bank above a monumental river. It seemed to him beautiful in several respects. "The quality of the people who lived here at the time is what made it particularly attractive." In 1968, he and his wife, Betty, took over the Eagle Roadhouse, providing bunks and board for exploration geologists, forest-fire fighters, and anyone else who might happen into Eagle. Before long, they had the propane franchise; and Borg became, as well, the regional Selective Service registrar, and president of the Eagle Historical Society, and the local reporter for the National Weather Service, and the sole officer (at this river port of entry) representing the United States Customs Service, and—on the payroll of the United States Geological Survey—the official observer of the Yukon. Borg had left Anchorage because half of the people of Alaska lived there and that was "just too many." Now, hundreds of miles distant in the bush, he was on his way to becoming a one-man city. Inevitably, with his postal background, he also became the postmaster—of Eagle, Alaska 99738—and, as such, he is the central figure in the town. He is a slim, fairly tall man, who looks ten years younger in a hat. He was born in 1937. He has a narrow-brimmed cap made from camouflage cloth that, once on his head, is unlikely to come off, indoors or out, and gives him a boyish, jaunty air as he cancels stamps, weighs packages, and exercises his quick, ironic wit. There is a lightness about him, of manner, appearance, and style, that saves him from the weight of his almost numberless responsibilities. One place where the hat comes off is in the small log cabin called Eagle City Hall. Inside are a big iron stove, benches for interested observers, and a long table, where Borg sits with the Eagle Common Council. His bared forehead is a high one—an inch or two higher than it once was. His eyes seem lower beneath it. His regard is uncommonly stern. Shadows come into his mustache, which turns into an iron brush. The youth in the post office has been returned to sender. Behind the heavier demeanor at the head of the Council table is John Borg the Mayor.

The post office is in a small cabin about a hundred yards from the riverbank at an intersection of unpaved streets—the heart of town. Borg owns the building and rents it to the United States. He arrives there by eight in the morning, after checking the height of the river (when the river is liquid). Because this is where the Yukon enters Alaska, its condition at Eagle is of considerable interest to the two dozen villages in the thirteen hundred river miles between the Canadian boundary and the Bering Sea. Borg also reads instruments that react to the weather, and he turns on the Weather Service's single-side-band radio to attempt to send facts to Anchorage. Eagle is not in perfect touch with the rest of the world. Signals get lost. Fairbanks, urban center of the northern bush, would be the more appropriate place to call, because, among others, the bush pilots of Fairbanks want the information. But the radio gets through to Fairbanks only about one time in five. Success in reaching Anchorage is about eighty per cent. So Borg calls Anchorage, toward four hundred miles away, and the word— of the river, of the weather, of an emergency—is relayed back north to Fairbanks.

"KCI 96 Anchorage. KEC 27 Eagle. Clouds now, six to eight thousand feet. Visibility, fifteen miles. Winds, calm. River, thirty-eight and falling. Water temperature, thirty-six degrees." The air in the night went down to twenty-eight. Yesterday's high was fifty. Right now, the air is at forty-five on an uncertain morning under volatile skies—May 13, 1976. It is mail day, the country's substitute for organized entertainment, but there is no guarantee that the plane will come through. It comes two, three, occasionally four times a week. The weather is inconstant, mutable. Squalls of snow may be shoved aside by thunderheads that are soon on the rims of open skies. Borg's records show that on a July day in the nineteen-sixties the thermometer reached ninety-six. During a night in January, 1975, the column went down to seventy-two degrees below zero. Borg says the air was even colder by the river. While this is the coldest part of Alaska, it is also the hottest and among the driest. Less than four feet of snow will fall in all of a winter, and about a foot of total precipitation (a figure comparable to New Mexico's) across the year. There is a dusting of new snow, Borg comments, on the mountains down the river.

The foyer stirs. The post office has a miniature lobby, a

loitering center, with a small grid of combination boxes, public notices, and a wicketless window framing Borg himself. Camouflage hat. Faded plaid shirt. "What can I do for you?"

Lilly Allen (in her twenties) has a cartful of textbooks to ship back to the University of Nebraska. High school in Eagle is by correspondence, and is controlled from filing cabinets in Lincoln. The teachers are in Nebraska. Lilly is the resident supervisor.

Jim Dungan comes in, slowly, hands Borg a letter, and makes no move to go. He leans forward on his crutches and draws on his pipe. Dungan has more time even than his fellow-townsmen do this year, as a result of an accident. He says, often, "I'll be off these crutches soon. I won't be wearing them all my life, that's for sure." There are lead weights on the crutches today. Borg asks about them, and Dungan says they are divers' weights, and that when his leg gets better he will slip them into pockets in his wet-suit when he dives for gold. One on each crutch, the weights total fifty pounds. They are not there to create a vanity of muscles but to build his stamina, to keep him in condition.

"It's easy to get out of condition," Borg remarks. "All you have to do is nothing."

Bertha Ulvi and Ethel Beck, Indian sisters, come in to mail raingear to Ethel's husband, who is working in the Arctic for the Alyeska pipeline consortium.

A plane goes overhead. Borg, busy at the scales, says it's not the mail plane—just Jim Layman in his Taylorcraft. A few minutes later, he hears another plane, and says, "No. That's not it. That's Warbelow, coming up from Tok." Borg doesn't have to go out for a look. From the sound alone, he can usually say where an aircraft is coming from, what kind it is, and who is flying it.

Eagle is a dry community. Its leading bootlegger comes in and posts a letter, followed by his closest competitor. They, in turn, are followed by Elva Scott, Sage Cass, Horace Biederman, Sarge Waller (an alumnus of the Marine Corps), and Jack Boone. With dark furry hair and a dark furry beard, Boone appears to be part bear and part wolf. "You've got a bunch of weird individuals in this town," he observes. And he adds, "Me included."

On one wall of the post-office lobby is a thick sheaf of notices about fugitives all over the United States who are "WANTED BY FBI." They include descriptions, fingerprints, and pictures of people who appear to have arrived long since in Eagle.

Roy Miettunen comes in with a letter—a rare public appearance. He likes to talk, but he stays in his cabin; you have to go to him. In the warmer weeks of the year (a short season), he works his claim on Alder Creek, far out in the mountains, sluicing gold. He once prematurely used up his food, and he walked out in eleven days, eating squirrels. It takes more than squirrels to keep Roy Miettunen in form. He lost more than sixty pounds, and came out of the woods weighing two thirteen. He speaks slowly, firmly, attractively. With his great frame and his big head, his unfrivolous jaw, he looks more sergeant than Sarge. He was, long ago, of the Seattle police. In his cabin he has eighteen rifles, thirty-four pistols, and two swords.

A visitor from the state Department of Highways, concerned about the condition of a stretch of local road, comes in and speaks with Borg about the use of his Cat. The term Cat derives, of course, from the Caterpillar Tractor Company, of Peoria, Illinois, and, in the synecdochical way that snow machines in Canada are generally called Ski-Doos and snow machines in the Alaskan upper Yukon are called sno-gos, all bulldozers of any make or size are called Cats. John Borg's Cat is a forty-two-horse John Deere, with a seven-foot blade. Borg mentions forty dollars an hour as the asking price for his Cat —at work with him on it. The State of Alaska hems but does not completely haw. Borg nods at thirty-eight.

Anton Merly appears, and Jack Greene, followed by Ralph

Helmer, who now runs the roadhouse. He has a letter for his grandmother near Spokane. She is in her eighties, and the letter is in acknowledgement of her birthday. He tells Borg that he lived for three years on her farm after his parents were divorced. "That was a very beneficial thing in my life, although I didn't realize it at the time." Helmer, about a dozen others, and the central buildings of the city of Eagle are supplied with electricity at thirty-five cents a kilowatt-hour by a private power company consisting of Charlie Ostrander and John Borg. They have two diesel generators, which can put out twelve kilowatts over an effective radius of a thousand yards. Borg sells power to the post office. But his home cabin, in the woods far back from the river, is out of range. He has a small generator there to run the washing machine and power tools, but the cabin does not use electric light.

Kay Christensen comes in. She has no letter. She wants to speak to Borg about plowing up her garden with his Rototiller. Borg accepts the job. In the eighteen-nineties, Jack McQuesten, a storekeeper celebrated in the country, used to plow his garden with a moose.

The sky was clear at 7 A.M. Then cumulus built up, and some rain fell, and now, at eleven, comes the dinning sound of hail. Dan Kees, a relative newcomer, talks about the hail in West Virginia, where he is from, and Borg listens. Borg is a member of the Bible Chapel, politically the strongest unit in Eagle, and Kees is his pastor. Kees wears a cowboy-style hat, so wide-brimmed it could be looked upon as a stunted sombrero. He is technically a missionary here. That is, the church headquarters at Glennallen, Alaska, pays him. His parishioners are referred to locally as "the bloc," "the group," "the Christians," "the fundamentalists." They also include the families of Ralph Helmer, Ron Ivy, the Ostrander brothers, and Roger Whitaker, the regional constable. In the spectrum of Eagle society, the fundamentalists are all the way over in the ultraviolet, beyond the threshold of visible light. Dick Cook and the young people of the river (the wheat grinders, meat hunters, trappers—liberal, certainly, and in some ways lawless) are at the opposite end, deep into the infrared. A few whites are married to Indians. The Indians number less than fifty, and almost all live three miles upriver, outside the plat of the town. Philosophically, they are as close to the river people as they are to anyone else. Across the middle span of the society are— among others—drifters, merchants, visionaries, fugitives, miners, suburbanites, and practitioners of early retirement. There is something of the rebel in everyone here, and a varying ratio between what attracts them to this country and what repels them in places behind. "Never put restrictions on an individual" is probably page 1, line 1 of the code of the bush. But people here encounter restrictions from governments state and federal, from laws to which they do not all subscribe, and— perhaps to an extent just as great—from one another. Compressed, minute, Eagle is something like a bathysphere, lowered deep into a world so remote it is analogous to the basins of the sea. The people within look out at the country. John Borg remembers regretfully when there was more room to move around inside.

He takes from a wall a photograph of someone in Eagle holding a gold pan full of hailstones the size of eggs, and shows the picture to Kees, possibly to imply that hail like that could destroy a place like West Virginia. The stones falling now are scarcely half an inch thick. Their clatter is considerable, but is not enough to kill the sound of a Cessna 207, up there in the storm with the incoming mail. Borg loads up a van and drives out to the airstrip, which is halfway between the town and the Indian Village. The strip, for the moment, is white as winter. The hail continues, but the skies are broken, and around the gray clouds are wide bays of blue. Borg has collected mail here at sixty below zero, coming out from town on a snow machine for half a ton of Christmas cards arriving one month late. The 207 flares, lands, and taxis up, its wings like snare drums under the pounding stones. The pilot gets out, catches some hail, and examines it. The stones, in shape, resemble Hershey's Kisses. He looks back into the storm and sees seven geese fighting their way through the same airspace he was in moments before. "How would you like to get *that* in the eyeballs?" he says, with feeling for the geese. The pilot, new in Alaska, is from New Jersey. There is a passenger or two. A small roll of chain-link fence comes off the plane. An Indian family is expecting it, and is on hand to pick it up. Borg stuffs the van with mailbags and cardboard cartons. The wing of the 207 is now coated with slush. "That will raise hell with the airfoil," says the pilot, and Borg produces a broom. He sweeps three hundred pounds of slush off the airplane, and the pilot returns to the air.

People throng the post office like seagulls around a piling, like trout at the mouth of a brook. Many, of both races, wear sweatshirts and windbreakers on which are stencilled the words "Eagle, Alaska." Make what they will of the country, they seem to yearn for contact with the outside world. On days when the mail plane does not come, the human atmosphere is notably calmer than it is now. With a sheet of plywood against his postal window, Borg blocks himself away while he and his wife, whose head tops out at his shoulder blades, do the sorting. As letters go into the boxes, the doors open and slap shut. The babble declines. Many stand and read without dispersing to their cabins. Viola Goggans is baffled by something to do with wheel bearings. Borg gives her a short lesson in their function and potential flaws. Almost gingerly, he hands Lilly Allen a package that—as he knows from her many inquiries—contains a beautifully crafted dulcimer. He is obviously relieved that it has come at last. Sara Biederman, an Indian who lives in the town, is having trouble with the legal phraseology of a letter from Fairbanks. She comes to the window and hands the letter to Borg. "It says there's fourteen hundred and ninety-eight dollars due on your truck and if the money is not paid they will come and get the truck," he tells her. Michael David collects mail and packages, for himself and others in the Indian Village. He is young, slim, without expression. A headband holds his long black hair. Michael David is the Indian Village Chief. "He's got an awful uphill grade in front of him," remarks his counterpart, the Mayor.

⟨ Steve Ulvi wants to know if a fourth crate of bees, shipped from Navasota, Texas, has arrived for Dick Cook—and possibly a queen bee as well, due in from Louisiana. Borg shakes his head. The post office is, for the moment, innocent of bees.

Three crates arrived about a week ago, and Cook was here waiting for them, having travelled up the frozen river with his dog team to fetch them. While he waited, breakup came. It was early, and took him by surprise. He had intended to collect the bees and mush back down the Yukon to Donna and the cabin well before the ice would run. But then, one Sunday afternoon, the silent river began to move. Bank to bank fifteen hundred feet, the ice subdivided itself without particular spectacle, and, like an ore in motion on a giant belt, departed for the Bering Sea. The Yukon is a practical thoroughfare in summer and in winter, but during its times of transition it becomes almost unapproachably inimical. Great floes coming on from upriver roll, heave, compile; sound and surface like whales. Many hundreds of millions of tons of ice, riding a water discharge of two hundred thousand cubic feet per second, go by Eagle at a speed approaching ten miles an hour. Looking at the river, you cannot help but recoil. In water that cold, a human being couldn't live much more than a few minutes—a benevolent brevity, the struggle being hopeless anyway against the current and the ice. The river's edges are lined with ice that is stationary—"shelf ice," "shore ice," the first to freeze at the start of winter and the last to go in spring. It is four feet thick, but will break apart under a stamping foot, shattering into columnar palisades, untapered icicles known as "needle ice" or "candle ice." The shore ice rests on rock and gravel, while only a step or two away is the riverborne ice, big masses pounding into one another with a sound like faraway thunder, or, often, like faraway surf. These are muted sounds. For all its weight and speed, the ice moves softly much of the time, fizzing like ginger ale.

The ice run will thin out now and again, nearly disappear. The river becomes clear of all but isolated floes. In another hour, or day, heavy ice is running again—wall to wall, crunching, jamming, lethal as ever. The ice comes segmentally from upriver and from the tributary rivers. The Yukon, even above Eagle, has tributaries four hundred miles long. When ice of the Yukon, ice of the tributaries comes free and begins to run, it does so in big units. People watch for ice from Dawson—which is about a hundred miles away, in Yukon Territory—and whenever barrels, garbage, foul debris go hurtling by on soiled floes, someone will grunt knowledgeably and say, "Dawson ice." The White, the Klondike, the Stewart, the Pelly, the Nordenskiöld, the Teslin, the Fortymile let go their ice arrhythmically and give it into the Yukon. Pelly ice. Stewart ice. Teslin ice. Fortymile ice. It takes two or three weeks for it all to go by a single point like Eagle. In weeks thereafter, it forms a temporary, bobbing delta spread miles out to sea.

With the ice comes wood. The breakup flushes out of Alaskan and Canadian uplands many millions of cords of forest debris. Trunks go by that are sixty and seventy feet long. Some ride just beneath the surface. They are called sleepers. The big logs rarely retain their branches, but many still have their root structures, and those that do are sometimes called preachers, because the roots ride down in the water while the upper trunk breaks through the surface at an angle, and bows and rises, bows and rises, as it glides by. Once in a while a big trunk will nosedive and stick like a javelin into the bed of the river. Then a following ice floe snaps it in half with the sound of a battle-ship gun. Sometimes the wood in the river seems as voluminous as the ice. The people of Eagle collect logs that have paused in eddies or have otherwise come near enough to shore. Fire-wood is worth sixty dollars a cord, and twice that in winter. People have to travel considerable distances—to forest burn areas, for example—to get it legally. So it is not just wood but a great deal of cash that is bobbing by on the Yukon. For the most part, the people can't do much, however, but wistfully watch it go. The big river delivers the wood to the Yupik Eskimos of the western coast, where there is no timber to speak of and where for ten millennia—before missionaries, books, schools, and visual aids—fires were made with fuel from a forest-mountain landscape that the Eskimos had never seen and could scarcely have imagined.

Cook was anxious to get back to Donna. So, less than a week after breakup, with ice running heavy, he borrowed a canoe and started for the river with his dogs. He might have used the quiet eddy at Eagle's boat landing, a short distance upstream, but that would have meant taking the dogs through town, and Cook did not wish to create a disturbance. Several dozen dogs are chained to stakes beside cabins throughout Eagle, and Cook's loose ones, running amok, could be counted on to start fights and drive the tied ones berserk. So Cook, whose base in Eagle is a shack on some land he owns, led his dogs through woods and down to the river just below the town. He met Steve Ulvi there, who meant to go downriver with him. Slipping, falling into crevices, they slid the canoe over high shelf ice and lowered it into a small indentation of water, a petty cove. This was at an outside bend, where current runs fast in a river. Flying ice chunks in tumbling hundreds pounded by. Big flat discs, called pan ice, their edges worn round, spun among the chunks. The canoe was a nineteen-foot Grumman aluminum freighter. Cook and Ulvi loaded it—three crates of bees, two hundred and fifty pounds of gasoline, an old outboard motor, the corpse of a great gray owl, a big wooden box of supplies, two rifles, a shotgun, a sixty-pound sack of sugar, and the five sled dogs (about four hundred pounds of dog). Steve sat in the bow. Cook, in the stern, made a few shifts for balance. Then he shoved the canoe out into the stream. The ice was so heavy and concentrated that the mean free path for anything attempting to move through to a safer part of the river would inevitably be extremely short. The canoe travelled about ten feet. It was on the current for perhaps two seconds when it was hit from behind and driven like a nail into the stationary ice. It might as easily have been upended, or pressed down into the water, or, most probable event of all, rolled over. But luck was running with the ice. Wedged there, stuck, protruding backward into the river, the canoe was at least upright. Blood ran out of Cook's face. His skin became as pale as the floes in the river. If more ice were to strike the canoe now, it could crumple it up like an aluminum can. Ulvi wrenched the bow free and shoved the canoe backward. Once more it floated among the ice. He and Cook, prying hard to get the bow around, were nudged but not hit. They tried an angling path toward the slower side of the river. Ahead of them to the end of the view was a thousand acres of ice-filled water. Beyond sight, it was impossible to guess the level of danger, for ice can jam at bends, entrapping with it anything that floats, while the weight of the river builds up behind until the force is sufficient to explode the ice free.

Sarge Waller—who is, among other things, a professional riverman—later commented on Cook and Ulvi's journey and described them as "yahoos." Sarge said, "Them ice floes could knock the boat over and wipe it out. They could get wiped out ten miles down. They could be dead now. Who would know?" And no one did know for a number of days—or think much about it, truth be told. Then Ulvi and the canoe reappeared in town. He looked tired, cold, gaunt, but, withal, intact.

Ulvi is a young, cinematically handsome man, with blond

curls and blue eyes and a nineteenth-century drooping gold
mustache. He came into the country when he was twenty-
three, and has been here two years. He followed his brother
Dana, who first encountered Eagle as a stop on a Yukon raft
trip, and who is now married to Bertha Paul, of the Eagle
Indian Village. Harold Ulvi, an uncle, was the Northern Commercial Company's storekeeper here in Eagle twenty-five years
ago. After growing up in California, Steve went to college
briefly in Oregon. He backpacked all over the Western mountains. When he moved to the Alaskan bush (with his wife,
Lynette Roberts), he had in advance some of the skills he
would need. He had rebuilt every car and motorcycle he had
owned. He knew cooking, carpentry, and more than a little
about edible wild plants. Lynette and Steve, who expect a baby,
have a cabin upriver near the international boundary and live
there as much as they do in Eagle. "Dick Cook and I both hold
in highest regard not the intellectual but the man of maximum
practical application. Like Dick, I'm trying to be self-sufficient
on this earth, to live successfully without altering the environment. Cook is not sucking on fossil fuels, and I don't want to,
either. People say, 'If you feel that way, why don't you make
candles out of bear fat?' But I'm not prepared to do that. It's
all relative, of course. I do burn ten or fifteen gallons of kerosene a year for light, some white gas for my Coleman stove,
some fuel for my kicker. But if everybody else did no more than
that we would not have an energy problem. I learn things when
I visit Dick. I go see him about his garden, for example. The
most returns for the least effort—Dick is definitely interested
in that. He has great perspective, a good body of working
knowledge. He remembers when caribou were really running
around here. He's been here long enough to cover a couple of
the natural cycles. He knows a lot about guns. He hand-loads.
I hand-load. He carries a 6.5 × 55 Swede military carbine. I
carry a 7 × 57 Mauser. Some people like a high-speed bullet.
Some like a big, slow bullet. They all kill. Dick goes for a long

bullet at a moderate recoil. He believes that placing the shot is what matters most."

When the conversation in Eagle—outside the post office, inside the general store—concentrates, as it does sometimes, on Cook, not everyone is so admiring. In fact, as Lilly Allen's husband, Brad Snow, once said to me, "You will find it impossible here to say anything nice about anybody without considerable disagreement."

"Cook is a romanticist, fancies himself a latter-day Henry David Thoreau. There's not a hell of a lot of depth there."

"He's a patient hunter. He will sit half the night waiting for a beaver to come out of his house."

"He is a pontifical, messianic guru. He's no dummy. He likes all these young river buckos sitting at his feet while Donna works her tail off tanning a moosehide."

"It takes Cook two years to develop an idea."

"It took him *six* years to get himself together and get out to his cabin downriver. Ann, his second wife, was not a bush woman, and—like some other women in the country—was not willing to compromise."

"He's a wealth of information. If he's going to do something, he does it right. Build a sled. Snowshoes. Rifles. Gardens. Dogs. He's an excellent musher—as good at dogs as anybody."

"His dogs are no better than mine."

"He *is* self-sufficient. He is the closest to attaining the goals of all of the people of the river. He is the old man of the business, and he is making it work pretty well."

"He manages to suggest he knows the country, but he has never even seen the Charley River."

"Cook is not good at one-to-one relationships. So he's here in Alaska, here in the bush. We are all here for similar reasons. My mother would say we're all failures. That's not so. We are seeking alternatives."

"Cook does not want anyone else doing his thinking for him. He also does not want to let other people think. Donna is now

learning and following. When Donna starts thinking for herself, there will be trouble."

(Viola Goggans and her family came drifting into the country
in a school bus a couple of years ago, with purpose ignited by
the presence of gold. They stayed first in the drainage of the
Fortymile River, and then shifted to Eagle. Because Communists would before long take over the nation as a whole, they
reasoned, there could be "no future for the kids." Money
would be "worthless," and "the only thing that will buy anything is gold." Tom and Vi Goggans were not in a position to
hoard commercial bullion. They had entered Alaska some years
before with a baby and a dime, and only the baby had substan-
tially grown. If they wanted gold, they would have to separate
it from placer ground.

The school bus was their mobile home. For its future they
had imaginative plans. It was full size, yellow, the standard
model, and they were going to convert it into a boat. They
would then launch the bus on the Yukon and navigate downstream to a tributary river and up that to high creeks with
promise of gold. To scoffers who cared to listen Vi was not
reluctant to give details. ("They thought we was crazy. They
thought we was going to drive out on the water. They was
about ready to send a straitjacket down. We had 'em all confused.") People seemed to think that the Gogganses were going
to seal the body, drive off the bank, and let the wheels spin in
the river. Actually, they meant to slice the bus in half—the
long way, under the windows and around the ends—and then
flip over the top part and make it into a barge. The lower half
would float upright on eight evenly spaced steel barrels, and,
barge in tow, would be powered by the bus engine, with a
propeller on the drive shaft. Old Cap Reynolds, long gone from

Eagle now, once built his own miniature stern-wheeler. He took it down the Yukon a couple of hundred miles, and far up the Porcupine River. The school bus, for its part, never had a chance to prove itself one way or the other. The Gogganses had two partners, who got into money trouble and withdrew. Vi and Tom could not fund the adventure on their own. So Tom is off working on someone else's claim, and for months at a time Vi is alone with her children in a rented cabin in Eagle—a gold widow, showing visitors the few flakes and small nuggets that are the beginnings of the family's defense fund against the second coming of Russian America.

She is a small woman, not five feet tall, with a touching, uncalculating friendliness that would win her more friends almost anywhere than it has in Eagle. She says, "I'll play you a tune on this here, if you'd like it," and she picks up her Hohner accordion. Beth and Jimmy, seven and five, look on. She plays "You Are My Sunshine." It is the only tune she knows on both the piano and the chord sides. She plays it again. Intently, she tilts her head toward the keyboard. Her hair is tallowy blond. She has a narrow face, and many missing teeth, a prominent nose. She wears a red headband above blue denim. She is thirty-nine. Before Alaska, she lived all her life, and went for a time to grade school, in Havre, Montana. Asked for more, she plays "Roll Out the Barrel," apologizing for its incompleteness, for without the support of chords, she suggests, a barrel will not roll. Carrying a thermos of coffee, she goes to the Common Council meetings, where she is sure she has identified at least one pure Communist, albeit he is just an observer like herself and not a member of the Council. "I got a family now. I like to find out what's going to happen when they get older. I never been to a council meeting before I came to Eagle."

Jess Knight, thirty years ago, made a log raft, draped a car over the raft with paddle wheels in place of tires, and drove on the river a hundred and sixty miles to Circle. The school bus is still beside the Yukon but is hardly ready to go anywhere. It is beyond hope for road or river. It has no wheels, no motor, no seats—items sold to pay for food. The bus interior is utterly stripped out, and all the windows have been shattered—random targets of random bullets.

"I like Eagle, but not the people. They are either Bible thumpers or alcoholics. They try to rub the Bible on you. They don't like it that I won't go up in front of them and confess. If you confess, you confess in silence, before God, and not broadcastin' it. Leanin' on the Bible there, they can't stand up on their own two feet. They talk nice to you, and what they say about you hurts when they think you won't know."

❴ At home, I spend much of my time looking out of windows, and in the cabin I am occupying here nothing changes the habit. Outside is First Avenue: mud and dust, pocked and gravelled, the principal thoroughfare of the city, where children go by in wagons harnessed to dogs, and old-timers in pickups cruise slowly back and forth—"trolling," as someone has put it, for conversation. The cabin is tight, comfortable, heated by an Ashley. It is said of a fine stove like this one that it "will drive you out of here at seventy below," a promise enhanced by bush architecture. Cabins are generally small, so the stove can retain command. My wife was here for a time. We slept in a loft just above the Ashley. Routines developed. Every other day, we sawed and split some wood, but, with the ice petering out on the river and the sun shining eighteen hours a day, we were soon using the stove for little more than to get our blood moving in freezing temperatures as the day began.

All water must be lugged from the community well house, which is up past the post office, in the center of town—drinking water, dishwater, bathwater. I prefer my scent. Under the eaves of the cabin, however, are barrels, buckets, tubs, which will occasionally catch enough water to wash and rinse a moose. In the rainwater, lather swells and crowns, forms pillows on the skin. The lather is a particular luxury in Eagle, where rain is fairly scarce and the well water is so hard it turns soap into stone. Eagle is directly over an old inactive fault, and its water rises through a fracture from an exceptionally deep source, bearing a taste of soda. There is a stream not far away called Champagne Creek. The ground that lies between the cabin and the outhouse is unvegetated glacial flour—fine-ground soil, soft as powdered talc, brought down by the Yukon from the ice fields of the high Wrangells and left here for aeons past. It sticks to shoes and is tracked in. Clothes become stiff with it, so they are washed in leftover bathwater—and, after that, in goes the odd pot or pan. Finally, the water washes the floor, where its arc of utility ends. What is left is carried to the riverbank and dumped over. A block of shore ice, at the same time, is chipped out with an axe in order to refill an insulated cooler.

A quart of milk in the cooler cost $1.36. It came from Visalia, California. It is neither condensed nor evaporated but "sterilized" whole milk, in a can, without preservatives. It is fine milk, but too expensive. Condensed milk, appropriately diluted, works out at 60¢ a quart, and powdered milk at half of that. Frozen steak costs $4.20 a pound, bacon $2.07, chicken $1.15, hamburger $2.10, cheddar cheese $2.35, butter $1.85— all this in Eagle's only store. Grapefruit cost 55¢ apiece, a cucumber 75¢, tomatoes and lettuce about $1.15 a pound. Fresh food, after travelling upward of two thousand miles, for the most part has jet lag. Campbell's soup is 51¢ a can, a dozen eggs $1.30. A standard box of Morton's salt costs 62¢. Much is said about the high cost of things in Alaska, but what seems remarkable is that prices are not much higher than these, since virtually everything arrives by truck, plane, or boat from the rest of the United States. The supply lines to Anchorage and

Fairbanks are long and costly enough, but these prices—
roughly half again as high as they would be in New Jersey—
are set in Eagle, where nearly everything has been brought in
light planes another two hundred miles over mountains. Dave
McCall, the pilot-storekeeper, charges 19¢ a pound for flying
things in. Hence the especially costly salt.

Outside the cabin window, a robin is hopping around with
feathers fluffed up against the cold. The ice goes out. The birds
come in. Transition is almost instant from winter to spring. It
is curious to see these robins—big, tough robins—so far up
here, so near the Arctic Circle, near the top of their range.
They seem miserable, fluffing themselves up into balls in an
attempt to make down jackets of their own feathers. Dozens
of Lapland longspurs are jumping, pecking, jumping, pecking
in the dust near the robins, and looking immeasurably more at
home. We have seen warblers, juncos, blackbirds, gyrfalcons,
a pair of golden plovers, an Arctic tern. A seagull sits on the
outhouse, thirteen hundred miles upriver from the sea.

Twilight holds through the night now, and darkness has
gone for the summer. There is little need of lamps, but when
I want them to read or write by I fiddle with mantles and pump
up pressures for intense white-gasoline light.

The dogs staked out all over town set up a chorus wail. They
seem to be responding to direction from the sky, because their
arioso howls begin with a simultaneity that has no explanation.
There is a hint of wolf in some of these dogs, and the part that
is wolf seems to be their voices. The wailing stops the way it
starts—all at once there is silence, and no saying why.

In woods across from the cabin window, the remains are
visible of two or three older cabins—moldering away, so far
gone now they are barely discernible and have almost disappeared. A little to the right of them is Elmer and Margaret
Nelson's new place, wood still shining from the saw. The
neighborhood represents the rise and fall and rise of Eagle. The
Nelsons have come here to retire, like one or two other couples

in the town, which, as retirement centers go, is about as far as you can get from Sun City. Margaret Nelson is grandmotherly, with whitening hair, and Elmer is wiry, spare, and gray. She came to Alaska from the state of Washington in the thirties, worked for the Northern Commercial Company, and, during the war, wrapped parachutes in Fairbanks. He grew up on a homestead in Montana and has lived in Alaska fifty years. He built roads and he trapped. Deep among the mountains off the left bank of the Yukon, Nelson and a partner had a chartered airplane fly them around while they dropped packages. Eventually, they landed at a hand-dug airstrip. This would be in September most years. They would ask the pilot to return a day or two before Christmas. Then—without machines of any kind, without dogs—they would separate and cover country as rapidly as they could in an attempt to get to their dropped supplies in advance of foraging bears. They laid out patterned traplines—loops, cloverleafs. Every five days, they rendezvoused—each to see that the other was all right, and to pass on information. This was total wilderness. They were something over a hundred miles from Circle and eighty from Eagle and eighty from Big Delta, where the Nelsons lived at the time. In any kind of need, there was nowhere else to go. In discrete valleys were a few cabins, and they stayed in them or siwashed (camped on the trail). When they were picked up—after three months in there, generally apart and alone—they had collected a good share of their income for the following year.

❙ The Nelsons' place is landscaped only by its woods. Neat, odd, it lacks the expectable outdoor furnishings of an Alaskan cabin. My side of the road makes up for that. A few feet away from me, in the direction of the center of town, is the cabin of Dale and Gloria Richert, who sell used snow machines, washing machines, sleds—examples of which are strewn about the space between the cabin and the road. The cabin is roofed with slit and flattened fuel cans. Richert had a store in Michigan not long ago. It was firebombed by hoodlums. This helped him decide that an appropriate community in which to seek a new life might be somewhere near the Arctic Circle. A sign among the used machines says "Eagle Sports Shop." Richert has lures, flashlights, tents, boots—a little L. L. Bean going on inside the cabin. In their regard for his goods, the river people call him Taiwan.

Close by me the other way are the yard and cabin of Louise and Sarge Waller. The remarkable propinquity of these dwellings is characteristic of nearly all settlements, large and small, in Alaska. In three hundred and seventy-five million acres—a sixth of the whole United States—so little property is available for purchase that conditions are as crowded as they are in Yonkers. A window of my cabin frames a postcard view of Sarge's yard, which, in no discernible geometric arrangement, contains boxes, tarps, stove parts, cans, buckets, Swede saws, washtubs, tires, sawhorses, fourteen fifty-five-gallon drums, and five snow machines in different stages of dismantlement. When you drive along an old back road in the Lower Forty-eight and come upon a yard full of manufactured debris, where auto engines hang from oak limbs over dark tarry spots on the ground and fuel drums lean up against iron bathtubs near vine-covered glassless automobiles that are rusting down into the soil, you have come upon a fragment of Alaska. The people inside are Alaskans who have not yet left for the north. An architect I know, who prefers to style himself an "environmental psychologist," once remarked to me, "Aesthetics are not compatible with survival." In any case, Sarge Waller's place is by no means atypical of the world he has taken for his own. He is out in his yard now, surviving. He is piling up wood. On his pickup—which has three spare tires, a gun rack, and a searchlight—is a load of driftwood he has collected from the boat-landing eddy. To get his cabin through a winter, he needs at least five cords. His cabin, exhaling smoke, is angular and miscellaneous. Sarge himself is less vulnerable to heat loss. He is a big man, with a girth approximating four feet. His arms are legs of lamb. His large, ovoid head is covered with Marine brush. In all this magnitude, his eyes, which are dark, seem small. Sarge is amiable, garrulous. In his house is a framed photograph of the younger Sarge, dimensions the same. He is dressed for battle, but not in his staff sergeant's uniform of the United States Marines. Instead, he wears the white robes of karate, cinctured with black. Sarge was tough. He has dragons on his skin, and snakes, and skulls—eleven tattoos, from as many parts of the world. He survived the battle of the Chosin reservoir, in Korea. He liked the Marine Corps as he found it in 1949 but not as he left it a decade later. He was a junior in high school when he joined up, and what the Marines had then, he says, was "spirit de corps." In the aftermath of Korea, the U.S. Marines, in his view, "turned into a Girl Scout troop." If a private first class became troublesome, a sergeant could no longer "punch him in the mouth." An increasing number of officers, at any rate, would not encourage or support such gestures. One day at Camp Lejeune, in North Carolina, a corporal in Sarge's unit had trouble with a private and the private was locked up in the brig. Sarge took justice literally into his own hands. He went to the brig, reached through the bars, grabbed the offending Marine private, and pulled him forward with such force that his face crashed into the bars and blood ran from his nose. Sarge explained why he had come, and left. In short order, his phone "jumped a foot off the desk." The chaplain wanted to see him. "This is no longer the old Marine Corps," the chaplain informed him, and warned him that a repetition of such behavior could cost him his stripes. He remained a sergeant, but such a disappointed, disillusioned one that he planned on quitting, and wondered what on earth he would do.

He had grown up in Massillon, Ohio. (His father was a conductor, brakeman, trainman on the Nickel Plate.) In Mas-

sillon, there was an old man with fur clothes and nuggets in his
pockets—a living mothball from the far-northern rush for gold.
He liked to talk to kids, and every Saturday he told them
stories. He showed Sarge pictures of the wild north. Sarge took
to trapping, hunting, and fishing until the truant officer was
sent in search of him. When he was nine, he got his first rifle,
and decided he would live someday in Alaska. All this came
back to him as a depressed Marine—in 1959, the year the
territory became a state. Sarge quit the Corps and moved
north. It was another eleven years before he came into the
upper-Yukon country. He lived meanwhile in Slana, on the
"Nigger Highway"—that is to say, on a road that had been
built by a black regiment of the Army Engineers. He married
Louise there, a somewhat metropolitan woman, touched with
glamour. She was an outback restaurateur. She had a daughter,
and they had two more, and Sarge, all the while, had a vision.
He was a riverman whose time had not yet come, and one day
he would live, utterly on his own, on a big river in a big
wilderness. To fulfill these requirements, he need not go far—
not two hundred miles away. He arrived in Eagle in 1970 with
two boats, a thousand feet of lumber, corrugated roofing, and
what he estimated to be a year's supply of food. It was a place
"where a guy could branch out into the country." With his
three daughters and his wife, he went fifty miles down the
Yukon and built a cabin. Sixteen by twenty feet, with log walls,
it was two stories high, and was thus unusual. Its upper level
was a sleeping loft. Food ran low, and Sarge's hunting, much
of the time, failed to make it up. On rabbit tacos, his waist
shrank and shrank to a low of thirty-four. He trapped with
some success. Meanwhile, his "womenfolks," as he lumps
them, were not affectionate toward the cabin. They were lone-
some, for one thing—miles from the nearest human being—
and, for another, the cabin had not been designed by a heating
engineer. The warmth of the wood stove collected against the
roof, and the overall insulation was not adequate to keep much

heat on the ground floor. The family was in the cabin all winter, 1970–71, and spent much of it up in the loft. There were times—too many times for the womenfolks—when the stove could not raise the temperature of the ground floor any higher than forty degrees below zero. In this situation, Sarge's vision, the dream of his life, froze solid. He saw himself as a man of the wild, but his family did not. Whatever else might happen to him, though, he was not about to lose his spirit de corps—and the corps, now, was his family. He retreated from the deep wild and settled with them back in Eagle. Louise, more at home, became the clerk of the city and in some ways its leading politician. Gracefully, she will still say of her husband, "He does not have blood in his veins—he has Yukon River water." Sarge has set himself up as a charter boatman, taking hunters and geologists downriver. He has established traplines near town. For the most part, though, he seems to enjoy himself talking; and he likes to say, "I did not come up here to work anyway. I don't work. And my family is happy."

⟨ Jim Dungan comes swinging up the road on his way from his cabin to the urn of coffee at the store, where he can sit on a stool and use up a part of his day. When he leaves, he will go down by the river and stare, leaning forward on his crutches, for as much as an hour at the flamelike, firelike movement of ice. Meanwhile, he greets Sarge. He waves in my direction, too. "Just call me Hopalong," he says. Visiting Jim's cabin now and again, I will have a drink of Postum or coffee and be let into his present and all but disoriented world, which has no walls of time. "I'll be off these crutches soon," he says, as if I had not previously heard him say it. "I won't be wearing them all my life, that's for sure."

When the crutches go, he wants to get out again into the

wild with a suction dredge. Like Sarge Waller, Jim Dungan has
dreamed of a life beyond community, a cabin somewhere up
a faraway stream, an existence financed (in his case) not with
furs but with gold. "Just to get out and live the way I figure
a guy should. I didn't buy land here in Eagle because I like the
town. I like the country. The dredge gives me a purpose out
there. If you're not gettin' good color, you can shut down the
dredge, take a pan, and go off prospecting for a couple of weeks.
Set up a little lean-to. Find a better place. Get the dredge and
work the better place."

Suction dredges are a modern vogue, and, if any comparison
is valid, are miniature versions of the old gold dredges—the
shiplike, company-owned floating units that elsewhere in
Alaska still eat whole streams. Suction dredges are portable,
cheap, irresistible to a certain class of lone, adventuring miner.
They are floating units, using inner tubes or Styrofoam blocks.
Typically, they will have a seven-horsepower engine and a
short, narrow sluice box. The whole unit can be dragged about
by someone in a wet-suit, holding a long hose that sucks up
stream-bed gravel. *Alaska* magazine advertises a "high-impact
Jet Age plastic" sluice box that sells for $39.95, a Gold-Vac
dredge for $295. Dungan prefers somewhat better gear, and
figures that thirteen hundred dollars would equip him. Generally, the miner kneels in the river, its riffles driving at his chest,
but he can go down eight, ten feet, if he knows what he is
doing, and draw gravels from crevices in rock. The hoses are
usually about four inches in diameter, and can swallow stones
almost as large. Rocks, sand, gold, and gravel go into a hopper,
then on through the sluice box, which catches the gold. That
is what Jim Dungan came into the country to do—in 1968,
with a partner called Polack Joe. Dungan was an experienced
diver. ("I used to be able to hit sixty feet free-diving with no
air.") The partners first worked the Bottom Dollar, a small
tributary in the Birch Creek mining district, upward of a hundred miles west of Eagle. In one six-day period, they got forty-
seven ounces of gold, worth about two thousand dollars. They

left Alaska, but came back for good in 1970 and worked the Fortymile River, near Eagle. "We were living all over the Fortymile. We'd find an old cabin, and dry off, and then get back on the river. We caught grayling, shot rabbits. Me and Joe. It's a different way of life, not the rat race you got down there. That's all it is down there that I can see. Up here, a person is as good as he's going to make it. A guy's freer in this country. Down there, you're so restricted. Up here, they ain't gettin' you for spittin' on the sidewalk."

A flood on the Fortymile for the time being killed the good life. It might have killed the partners. It utterly destroyed their suction dredge. The partnership broke up; Dungan went to Fairbanks and took a job. He planned to work until he had bought a truck, a cabin in Eagle, and a new dredge. First as a cook and later as a jug-hustler, chain man, and shooter, he worked for Geophysical Service, Inc., using seismic instruments in the search for oil. From the air, six months of the year, large parts of the green surface of Alaska appear sutured with seismic trails. A jug is a geophone, and as many as two thousand may be set in the ground, usually in straight lines, to monitor the waves from dynamite blasts as they reflect from underground formations. After each blast, jugs from the rear are moved to the front. Day after day—usually in winter, to reduce damage to the terrain—the procession moves cross-country. Dungan worked on seismic crews from the North Slope to southeastern Alaska—walking a hundred and ten miles once in the Arctic in winter, calling in helicopters to drive off grizzlies in summer, and saving the money he earned. He once worked a line down the Susitna Valley, and on winter nights could see the lights of Anchorage. He went no closer. "Jesus Christ, you go in there and there goes your winter's paycheck. I just stayed in camp." He saved enough to buy his cabin in Eagle and, later, a three-quarter-ton green Ford pickup. He was about ready to buy his new suction dredge when he came back to Eagle on leave from a job in the Brooks Range, May 14, 1974.

He got drunk that night with a celebrational friend, and the next morning, feeling drier than the town itself, he decided to take a ride over the mountains to a roadhouse where he could see some friends, drink a beer or two, and buy some booze for fresh reunions. The pickup spat and sputtered. It was just a year old and in powerful shape, but had been idle all through the winter. He reasoned that its engine was full of carbon, so he went into the hills burning it out with speed. He was found two hours later. The truck had rolled three times. He had broken all his left ribs and both legs. The right leg was not so much broken as shattered. Pieces of the bone were never found. Eagle's satellite radio called for help. Thirteen hours after the accident, Dungan reached the hospital in Fairbanks, two hundred miles away. In the years since, he has been given skin grafts, bone grafts, a steel plate, and seven pins that look like wood screws. "They said I didn't have much chance of keeping my leg after the bone graft and the plate, but I fooled 'em. I still have the leg." The plate is to come out when the bone graft is solid, but the plan is not working well, because a hole will not close in the leg above the plate. "Sometime next winter, I should be working. After the cast comes off, I can walk with a shoepac and a cane. I'll be off these crutches soon. I won't be wearing them forever."

His cabin, where he does most of his waiting, is eight feet by twelve—not quite three steps by four. He sits at a table, and I sit on his bunk. The stove fills the rest of the room. The previous owners were a family named Waite—trappers, now gone from the country. Four of them—two girls and their parents—lived in the cabin two years. With a tar roof and board siding, it is lined with aluminum foil and looks like a baked potato experienced from the inside. There is one small window, with two panes, presenting a view of stacked cordwood—birch and spruce. When I first called on Dungan, in the course of a trip through the country in 1975, he said he was disturbed about his wood stove, because it was not airtight and had been hard to control. When the temperature outside was sixty below zero, the stove had driven the temperature up to a hundred and thirty degrees, and Dungan was besaunaed in his own steam. He has since replaced the stove. I remember, too, that he had a glass jar full of king salmon preserved in rock salt. He said he was saving it for his Christmas dinner.

I ask him now about the salmon, and he tells me that it spoiled. He spent Christmas in the hospital. He still has the bad salmon. "When my leg heals, I'll use it for bear bait."

His green pickup, its roof crushed down, now sits in front of Dan Kees' house, next door. Kees bought it for parts, and the hulk is there for Dungan to stare at, which he often does. Dungan is thirty-nine. His dark hair is receding. He has a quietly modulated voice, and the wide stare of a wounded creature. He grew up mostly in Wisconsin, stepson of a railroad switchman, and went to Cudahy High School, in Milwaukee, and straight into the U.S. Marines. He worked for eight years on the assembly line at American Motors. "That's enough to drive a man completely insane." It drove him, at any rate, to Vietnam—as a reënlisted Marine. "That's one place I'd rather forget, to tell you the truth. I hear all this petty-ante bitching around here, and I think, They should really have something to bitch about. This town is divided between the outlaws and the do-gooders. I don't give a damn about their stories about each other. I try to stay out of it. This is just like every other bush town. If I could be, I'd be in the high country, or on the Yukon River."

A quiver of arrows hangs from a rafter. Tacked to another rafter is an emblem that says "GSI ARCTIC OPERATION 1969–70." A note on a wall calendar under January 17th says "SUN—frist time since Nov. 21." There are pictures on the table and the windowsill. One is of his stepfather, recently dead, others of a child or two. There are six pictures in all, of the family of his only, and older, brother. "My brother, Bob, was killed in 1972 in a light airplane in the Lower Forty-eight. That's him. That's his little girl there. She got run over by a car."

"Have you ever been married?"

"No. I've always been just kind of a bum."

Joseph Hajec, Polack Joe, also worked for American Motors. Dungan tried decking on car ferries and driving spikes in the railroad yard before the two of them left for Alaska. "We were working the whole god-damned year to get two weeks' vacation. Then we'd head for open country. Then back to work for eleven and a half months to get back to the country. Some people get a good job at American Motors and think they've got it made. If you can go out and enjoy the country—to me, that's the life. My reason for being up here is basically a guy can be an individual. In Milwaukee, we had armed robberies, murders, rapes. There's no crime in Eagle. I didn't feel safe walking a country road in Wisconsin. I feel safe going down here to the store."

In Dungan's cabin are two pistols, two shotguns, and three rifles. He keeps a pistol and a shotgun always loaded. "Bears come right into town here. You never know. The first night I ever spent in Eagle, I was sleeping in a tent. I had two Eskimo women with me and a case of booze. When I was sleepin', I had a four-hundred-pound black bear lookin' me in the face. Dave Crump, who was there, shot him under the chin with a .30–'06. You never know. Besides, I've got a philosophy. I let the people know the guns are loaded. I've always kept a gun. I kept a .38 in Wisconsin. There are no bears there. But there are jealous husbands. I'm not exactly an angel."

He lights his pipe. It is long and low and looks somewhat Sherlockian and even more like a toilet bowl. He wears a cotton sweatshirt, corduroy trousers. His toes look like dead wizened tubers protruding from the cast. "I'm hopeful that in a matter of weeks they'll cut this cast off and say, 'Dungan, put on a shoe.' That damned life goes by too quick. You look back and say, 'Where'd that go to?' If this hole's healed up by summer, I'm going to go for gold. Everybody says a suction dredge is just a god-damned toy. But I'm going up there as a way of being independent, as a way of making a winter's grub. These guys who go out trapping—Cook, Edwards, Potts—they could make five times as much on the pipeline. But they're independent. I'll use all the proceeds from dredging first to buy a snow machine to take food and equipment in winter to the dredging sites—spare parts, gasoline, case lots of bacon, beans, and rice. Up in the Fortymile country, I got a couple of places picked out. It's high country, closer to bedrock. I'll stake no claims. I'll just go for the gold."

"What would you do if you got a hundred thousand dollars' worth of gold?"

"Put it in the bank."

"How would it change your life?"

"It wouldn't."

⟪ Wyman Fritsch, a conventional placer miner, has a nugget larger than his thumb. He found it in the Discovery Fork of American Creek, some ten miles out of Eagle, and he says it is by no means the largest one he has taken from that stream. He has been mining there for fifty years. He was a boy when he came into the country. He is currently known as The Man with the Big Nugget. He showed it to me the other day, so that I could hold it in my hand and rub the genius of the gold. It was lumpy, pitted, pocked, rough, ugly—an apparent filling from the tooth of a Sasquatch. The marvel of it—as the earth's elements go—is that when Fritsch came to it with his mining equipment, scraping up the deep gravels of American Creek, it was there as nearly pure metal. Gold is not merely rare. It can be said to love itself. In the idiom of science, it is, with platinum, the noblest of the noble metals—those which resist combination with other elements. It wants to be free. In cool crust rock, it generally is free. At very high temperatures, however, it will go into compounds; and the gold that is among the magmatic fluids of interior earth may be combined, for example, with chlorine. Gold chloride is "modestly" soluble, and will dissolve in water that comes down and circulates in the magma. The water picks up many other elements, too: potassium, sodium, silicon. Heated, the solution rises into fissures in hard crust rock, where the cooling gold breaks away from the chlorine and—in sizes ranging from specks to the eggs of geese —falls out of the water as metal. Silicon precipitates, too, filling up the fissures and enveloping the gold with veins of silicon dioxide, which is quartz.

Gold can be taken from such veins with dynamite blasts, pneumatic drills. But that requires the funds and efforts of a large corporation. The deepest mine in the Western Hemisphere—the Homestake gold mine, in Lead, South Dakota— goes down into the earth more than a mile and a half. Its capital cost to date has been upward of a billion dollars. Alaskan lone miners—people who have, or who have had, names like Pete the Pig, Pistolgrip Jim, Groundsluice Bill, Coolgardie Smith, Codfish Tom, Doc La Booze, the Evaporated Kid, Fisty McDonald, John the Baptist, Cheeseham Sam, The Man with the Big Nugget—prefer to wait for God to break open the rock, to lift up and expose something like the Sierra Nevada and with epochal weathers blast it and spall it and tear it apart until the gold rolls out into the rubble of the streams. Placer mining— separating gold from stream gravels—is difficult work, but beside any other method it is comparatively easy. *"Placer,"* in Spanish, means "pleasure."

This is the country that Arthur Harper came into in 1873. The journey itself—two thousand miles, a large part of it on scarcely charted Arctic rivers—was an accomplishment in exploration, but to Harper that was incidental. A native of Ireland—intelligent, intense—he was a big bull-shouldered man with an H-beam jaw and a look so glazed it correctly suggested a quest. He had spent a lot of time in American goldfields, and he had what the geologist Alfred Hulse Brooks later described as "a conception of the broader orographic features of the western cordillera." That is to say, Harper had noticed that the important gold discoveries of North America had occurred in the Western mountains, and that the mountains went a great deal farther north than did—at that time—the discoveries. This suggested to him that as the highlands traced their way around the basin of the Yukon River, in Canada and in Alaska, their contributive streams in all likelihood contained undiscovered deposits of gold. Always confident that this was true, he searched with only modest results for upward of twenty years. Elusive stories were already in the air. An itinerant missionary named Robert McDonald, eleven years ahead of Harper, was said to have found a stream in the country where gold was so concentrated he picked it up with a spoon. There was no saying where, except that it was probably a tributary of Birch Creek. The strike in 1880 at what became Juneau was far to the south but was nonetheless encouraging. It was the northernmost discovery in North America to date. Harper tried Birch Creek, the Fortymile, the White, the Stewart, the Tanana, and myriad branching streams. He went to some of the right rivers and looked in all the wrong places. The luck of the Irish he had left at home. He killed and ate game along streams near the mouth of the Tron-diuck, missing the gold below. Here and there, with his pan, he did find enough color to support his conviction. With Leroy Napoleon (Jack) McQuesten, who came into the country by the same route in the same year, he sent back the word that drew prospectors northward in numbers sufficient to favor a find. And so—in a broad orographic way—he was the discoverer of the gold of the Yukon.

McQuesten, from Maine, was no less a believer than Harper, but it was McQuesten's way to support the search rather than pursue it. He took furs downriver and returned with goods. Representing the Alaska Commercial Company, he set up trading posts—for example, Fort Reliance (1874), forty miles up the Yukon from what came to be known as the Fortymile

River. The posts were served by stern-wheeled steamers arriving from the Bering Sea. McQuesten grubstaked prospectors
—in many cases, for penniless year after penniless year—with
a generosity that would have bordered on charity were it not
for his merchant's instinct that when the dust at last came out
of the streams it would settle in the merchant's safe. The first
major strike in the region was made on the Fortymile in 1886,
when prospectors named Harry Madison and Howard Franklin
—acting on suggestions made by Harper—went twenty-five
miles up the river, dug to bedrock, and found coarse gold. Just
before freeze-up, they emerged with the news. After volunteer-
ing to relay it to the outside world, an Alaska Commercial
Company river pilot named George Williams made an overland trip and raced the coming winter. He almost survived the
trip. Of exhaustion and cold, he died like Pheidippides deliver-
ing his message. McQuesten, who was in San Francisco buying
supplies, bought more supplies. He need hardly bother to help
spread the word. Along the two thousand miles of the Yukon,
a dozen whites had lived before. They would now be coming
in many hundreds, and soon in many thousands. Harper and
McQuesten had spent thirteen years preparing the way—developing transportation, gathering detailed geographical and
geological information. Needless to say, they readily established a trading center where the Fortymile goes into the
Yukon. Shovels and flour, picks and pans were for sale there.
Advice was plentiful and free.

For seven years, the Fortymile—yielding as much as eight
hundred thousand dollars in a season—was the focus of attraction in the mining of Yukon gold. The drainage was almost
wholly in Alaska but ran a few miles into Canada—dissecting
a high plateau immediately to the south of what is now Eagle.
In 1893, excitement shifted to a relatively distant part of the
country. McQuesten grubstaked two prospectors named Pitka
and Syroska, sending them downriver and into the hills to have
another look for the Reverend Mr. McDonald's legendary

spoonfuls of gold. Pitka and Syroska made their strike at a fork of small streams some fifty miles from the Yukon, in a world of mica schists and quartz intrusions, of sharp-peaked ridges, dendritic drainages, steep-walled valleys, flat spurs, and high, isolated mountains locally known as domes. While find followed find, small brooks acquired their ultimately storied names—Mammoth Creek, Mastodon Creek—and since all of them drained into Birch Creek, the area became known as the Birch Creek mining district. Hundreds of miners left the Fortymile to rush to the new discoveries. McQuesten, of course, followed, and built a store. Because miners were so scattered in the hills, McQuesten established his trading post at the river port that supplied them, which had been named Circle City in the mistaken belief that it was on—and not, as it was in fact, fifty miles below—the Arctic Circle. Quickly becoming the foremost settlement on the Yukon, it proclaimed itself "the largest log-cabin city in the world." By 1896, there were ten thousand miners in the district. The resident population of Circle was twelve hundred. Works of Shakespeare were produced in its opera house. It had a several-thousand-volume library, a clinic, a school, churches, music and dance halls, and so many whorehouses they may have outnumbered the saloons. Then certain fresh information came floating down the river from the half-abandoned settlement at the mouth of the Fortymile.

Two men known for their low credibility had walked into Big Bill McPhee's Caribou Saloon, at Fortymile, and announced a new find upriver. Scarcely an eyelid moved. One of the men, Tagish Charlie, was an Indian. The other was Lying George Carmack. Lying George said they had found pay on a small stream off the Tron-diuck, where a third member of their party, an Indian named Skookum Jim, had remained to guard their claims. The saloon was full of miners. No one was much impressed. For every worthwhile tip that might ever come along there were dozens upon dozens of meretricious leads to feverish diggings and dismal disappointment. Moreover, Carmack had a reputation for tall tales and short accomplishments. He was also the victim of their prejudice, for he was the white husband of a Tagish squaw. He had gone so native he actually wished to be chief. He encouraged himself with a double dram of whiskey. It mattered a great deal to Carmack that these skeptics believe him. He felt, he said later, as if he had dealt himself "a royal flush in the game of life." He and his companions had staked all the ground the law allowed them, and now he earnestly sought the respect that might come to him if he made these beggars rich. He finished his whiskey, and he took a used rifle cartridge from his pocket and turned it upside down. Gold is characteristic of the stream it comes from—the shape of the nugget, the rustlike shadings of the flake. Flat, rough, oblong, tear-shaped, round, smooth—bits of gold are the consistent signatures of the source placer. An experienced miner can look at a nugget and name the stream. A crowd drew in around Carmack's gold. Only a small amount was there, but no miner in the saloon had seen its like before. They fell silent. The surveyor William Ogilvie, who was working out of Fortymile at the time, made the quiet observation that, in effect, the gold could not have fallen from the sky. Faking nonchalance, miners melted away. The claims of George Washington Carmack, Skookum Jim, and Tagish Charlie were recorded, and soon the stream where they had staked them was named Bonanza Creek. It is the richest placer stream that has ever been found in the world. The discovery claim was ten miles above the Tron-diuck—an Athapaskan phrase meaning "hammer water." (Fish traps made of stakes had been driven into its bed.) Tron-diuck, alchemized into English, became Klondike.

   I cannot resist a digression into the fate of Big Bill McPhee, who was apparently generous with his cache in a way that any number of his clansmen are not. One person who asked for his help after Carmack's visit to the saloon was Clarence Berry, a young man from California who was eager to stake his own claims and who had all the determination and physical strength required in a miner but had come to Fortymile with no money, no food, no supplies of any kind. McPhee told Berry to go out to the cache and take whatever he needed. Berry's claims, as things proved out, were among the richest on Bonanza Creek, and they led to the development of a widespread mining conglomerate and, later, to added fortunes in California oil. Big Bill, for his part, settled in Fairbanks. One day his home and saloon there burned to the ground, destroying all of his assets in the world. Berry, in California, heard of this through his company and at once sent a message north: Rebuild, restock, restore everything; have all accounts sent to me.

The fact that a hundred and fifty million dollars was awash in the drainages of the Klondike diminished but did not extinguish the goldfields of the Alaskan Yukon. Circle City declined by eighty per cent but did not ghost out. Enough miners remained in the Birch Creek district to remove half a million dollars' worth of gold in the season after the Klondike strike. The Fortymile region was drained of talent, but not necessarily of the best talent. Established miners continued to work its streams. For the majority, certainly, the years around the turn of the century were ones of rushing to and fro, impelled by the brightness of news. Miners of the Alaskan gold country went into the Klondike with the advantages of propinquity and experience over the green multitudes coming up from the United States, most of whom found every stream that showed any color completely staked. The Klondike was in Canada. Ninety per cent of the miners were American. The Crown imposed a heavy tax on wealth drawn from Her Majesty's placers. The Royal Canadian Mounted Police, understaffed and apprehensive, sent a letter to Ottawa setting forth the possibility that the Americans might by force attempt to move the international boundary far enough east to comprehend the Klondike. But, without violence, many of them just went qui-

etly "home," crossing the line to Alaska, to settle in places—
and to work streams—that often flaunted remarkably patriotic
names: Eagle, Star City, Nation, American Creek, Washington Creek, Fourth of July Creek. In 1900 came the rush to the
beaches of Nome. Eight thousand left Dawson, the instant city
where the Klondike meets the Yukon, and conspicuous among
them all was Ed Jesson, who came walking into Eagle carrying
a bicycle. Riding down the frozen river, he had thirteen hundred more miles to go, but for the time being he was going
nowhere; his bearings were cold and stiff. When the temperature went up enough, he rode away. Meanwhile, someone else
on his way to Nome went by on ice skates. Populations halved
in Eagle and Circle, but, as before, miners by no means disappeared from the country. Nor have they ever. Birch Creek and
the Fortymile, where the Yukon mining began, have always
since discovery had miners on their creeks.

The principal technique of placer mining is to wash gravel
through a long, narrow sluice box, its bottom ribbed with
partitions that simulate the riffles of a stream. Gold and heavy
sands settle among the riffles, while stones and boulders move
on through the box and out the far end as "tailings." The
pioneers, with their picks and shovels, could move about five
cubic yards of gravel a day. Before long, these individual pros-
pector-miners were outdone by small groups who could collectively move more stone—for example, with mechanical scrap-
ers—and who could greatly increase available water by building
elaborate wooden flumes. Giant, high-pressure hoses were developed as well, with dug reservoirs feeding mountainside
ditches from which water would fall through pipe to emerge
from nozzles with power enough to excavate gravels to bedrock.
Inevitably, big dredges were built, too—by companies that
bought up claims and worked entire streams. The dredges
floated on ponds of their own making and on capital from cities
months away.

Notwithstanding all this, the individual miner persevered.

Quite apart from the major strikes, a kind of life had been discovered that to some—to Axel Johnson, for example—was no less alluring than the gold. Johnson was a Swedish fisherman who came into the country in 1898 and built a cabin, dug a garden at the falls of the Seventymile River. He worked Big Granite Creek, Alder Creek. He "sniped" a lot of his gold— just took it from likely spots without settling down to the formalities of a claim. He would go to the deep holes of stream rapids and periodically clean them out with a large instrument that resembled a spoon. Or he might take, say, eighteen hundred dollars out of a little bench of gravel, working it by hand. When he came into Eagle for mail and supplies, he sniped as he travelled, and once picked up sixty-seven ounces on the way. He trapped; and below his falls he caught Arctic grayling in such quantities that he had enough to dry and keep for winter. He lived well. He died in his cabin, in 1933. The life that attracted him, with its great liabilities and its great possibilities, has gone right on attracting others, and has been enhanced occasionally by a fresh sense of boom. There have, in fact, been three boom eras in the gold streams of Alaska. The second came in the nineteen-thirties, when the price of gold doubled. During the rushes of the eighteen-nineties, the price had been around seventeen dollars an ounce—a figure that remained essentially steady until 1934, when the government raised it to thirty-five. Lonely miners out on the creeks were suddenly less lonely. Fresh activity was encouraged as well by the almost simultaneous advent of the bulldozer, which could push around roughly four hundred times as much gravel per day as an old-timer with a pick and a shovel. The third Alaskan gold boom began in the early nineteen-seventies, when the United States allowed the price to float with the world market and announced that American citizens, for the first time in forty years, would be allowed to buy gold and save it. The price giddied. It approached two hundred dollars an ounce. Then it settled back to present levels—below a hundred and fifty.

New miners come into the country every year—from Nevada, Montana, Oregon, wherever. They look around, and hear stories. They hear how Singin' Sam, on Harrison Creek, "hit an enrichment and took out nuggets you wouldn't believe." They hear about "wedge-shaped three-quarter-inch nuggets just lying there where water drips on bedrock." They hear about a miner in the Birch Creek district pulling nuggets from the side of a hill.

"I have always been mining, always preparing ground. I'm not telling you how much money I've got ready to dig up. She's in the bank. Trouble is, there's too much gravel with it."

In tailing piles left behind by dredges, people hunt for nuggets that were *too big* to get stopped in the sluice boxes and went on through the dredge with the boulders. People reach into their shirt pockets and show you phials that are full of material resembling ground chicken feed and are heavier than paperweights. Man says he saw a nugget big as a cruller tumbling end over end in the blast from a giant hose. It sank from view. He's been looking for it since. Man on Sourdough Creek, working for someone else, confessed he had seen a nugget, and reached to pick it up, and found it was connected by a strand of wire gold to something much larger and deeper. He broke off the nugget and reported nothing. He could hardly mark the spot. Later, he went back to try to find what was there—he knew not where.

❪ To stories of such nature Stanley and Ed Gelvin have not always been immune. Son and father, deep-rooted in the country (the one by birth, the other since long before statehood), they live in Central, a community with a Zip Code and a population of sixteen, so named because it was the point on the Birch Creek supply trail from which the miners fanned out to the gulches. Some went surprisingly far. Both Stanley and Ed Gelvin are, among other things, pilots, familiar with the country from the air; and some years ago they became more than a little interested in certain conjunctive stream courses in high remote terrain, where they saw aging evidence of the presence of miners. The site is—they request that I not be too specific —somewhere in the hundred-plus miles of mountain country that lies between Eagle and Central. Along a piece of valley floor more than three thousand feet high they noticed, among other things, a wooden sluice box weathered silver-gray, a roofless cabin, a long-since toppled cache. The old-timers did not build cabins, caches, and sluice boxes just in hopes of finding worthwhile concentrations of gold. Having found it, however, they lacked the means to remove anything like the whole of what was evidently there, even when they dug down in winter into places where flooding would stop them in warmer weather —thawing frozen deep gravels with fires and hoisting it up in buckets for sluicing in the spring. Under the stream beds were soaked unfrozen depths known as live ground, where the old-timers could not have worked at all. While some Alaskan streams freeze solid, most continue to run all winter under phenomenally increasing layers of ice and snow. The phenomenon is overflow, which has so often been lethal to people travelling streams on foot—soaking themselves, freezing to death. Water builds up pressure below the ice until it breaks through a crack and spreads out above. When the pressure is relieved, the flow stops and the water becomes a layer of ice. Before long, snow falls, and compacts. More pressure builds, and water again flows out on top. Through a winter, these alternating layers of snow and ice, white and blue, can build up to great confectionery thicknesses—but the stream below remains liquid to bedrock. With appropriate earthmoving equipment, Stanley pointed out, a guy could go into that live ground and scrape up what lay on the rock. No such machine had ever reached these alpine streams, as a glance at their

unaltered state confirmed. They were much too far from the
mining road and the dredged and bulldozed creeks of the
district. It was almost too bizarre to imagine—a bulldozer in
the roadless, trail-less wilderness of those mountains. The price
of gold, on the other hand, had lately quintupled. Maybe going
in there was worth a try. Over the Gelvins' kitchen table, father
and son kept talking, and a program gradually evolved. Attention became focussed on the family backhoe. The first neces-
sity would be to sample the deep gravels and see what was
there. That long steel arm and big steel bucket could reach
many feet into the bottom of a stream. If a guy wanted to have
a look at what was lying on the bedrock, that backhoe would
be the thing. Maybe a guy could fly it up there. The backhoe
was a modified tractor that had once belonged to the United
States Air Force and had hauled bombers around in Fairbanks.
It weighed five thousand seven hundred pounds. A guy could
take it apart. Reduce it to many pieces. Fly it, in the family
airplanes, like birds carrying straws, nut by bolt in fragments
into the hills.

When I first met the Gelvins, in the early fall of 1975, pieces
of backhoe were strewn all over the ground beside the airstrip
behind their cabin. The machine itself was still recognizable
but was fast melting away under the influence of the wrench.
The airstrip looked like a dirt driveway scarcely ten feet wide,
with weeds upgrown on either side almost to the level of a
Cessna's wings. The runway had a dogleg. Every so often,
Stanley or Ed would stuff some parts into an airplane, roll off
in a plume of dust, disappear around the bend, and reappear
eventually, rising, to clear a backdrop wall of spruce. Stanley
—tall, lanky, still in his middle twenties—being of the country,
was a gold miner almost by nature. His father, Ed Gelvin, was
more diversified. Over the years, he had become, it seems safe
to say, as much as anyone in Alaska an example of what Steve
Ulvi has in mind when he speaks so admiringly of "the man
of maximum practical application." Mining, as it happened,

was what first drew Ed and his wife, Ginny, into the country. In the early nineteen-fifties, he worked some claims on Squaw Creek, near Central. He moved a lot of gravel but not a lot of gold. They liked the country, turned to other things, and stayed. Trapper, sawyer, pilot, plumber, licensed big-game guide, welder, ironworker, mechanic, carpenter, builder of boats and sleds, he suffered no lack of occupation. I once asked him if there was anything that could go wrong around his place that would cause him to seek help from elsewhere. He looked off into the distance and carefully thought over the question —this compact and gracefully built man of fifty or so with thick quizzical bifocals, a shy smile, a quiet voice. Finally, he said no, he guessed there wasn't. Ginny hunted with him, and ran the traplines as well. They raised a son and three daughters, who were so fond of moose and caribou they never much cared for beef. Over all the years, meanwhile, and despite the multifarious activities which followed that first attempt at mining, Ed had more trouble getting gold out of his mind than he had had getting it out of Squaw Creek. He had contracted gold fever, the local malaria; and he passed it on to Stanley.

If they were teased by the sight of the old relics they saw in that high nameless valley, there were stories around that were stimulating, too. Old miners in the district said they had always heard it was shallow ground up there, with good colors near the surface—and not much developed by the real old-timers. It had been the valley of, among others, Pete the Pig. That would be his cache lying on its side. Pete the Pig Frisk was a savvy prospector, an efficient miner, not one to waste his time where there was no pay. He found a good pay streak there, and not a few bears. He was a clean, attractive man, Pete the Pig—but he grunted while he worked, while he rooted for gold. When he opened his mouth to speak, he grunted first. When he got old, he went to the Sitka Pioneers' Home. From time to time, the miners out in the country saw a published list of who was there. One year, Pete Frisk's name was gone from the list. In

1962, a man named Brown—from Oregon or "somewhere down near there"—had had himself flown to Pete Frisk's valley in a helicopter. He had a partner with him, two pet Airedales, and a set of miniature sluice boxes that were innovative and effective as tools for prospecting. He also had a .357 Magnum for grizzlies, of which he killed three. When the partners left, they attempted to walk out, by crossing mountains to the Yukon. Because the creeks and streams of Alaska have a geminate quality that can fool even people who know them well, the two men thought they were on Coal Creek headed for the big river when in fact they were on Hanna Creek headed somewhere else. Brown's partner came out weeks later, with an injured leg, floating on a raft he had made on the Charley River. Brown, for his part, "stayed" in the high country; that is, he apparently died there. He was never heard from again. His partner said they had separated after the injury, as Brown went on for help. All that was ever found was the carcass of an Airedale, butchered out as for the table, but uneaten. Possibly, a bear ate Brown. His widow suspected something worse. She thought there had been more than just colors found up there in Pete Frisk's valley.

A dozen years later, Stanley Gelvin, in his Aeronca Champ with its dunebuggy tundra tires, flew so low he skimmed the dwarf willows, hunting the valley for a place to land. Thirteen treeless summits, each about the height of the high Adirondacks, surrounded the three confluent streams there, and down from this nippled coronet ran sweeping tundra fells deceptive to view. They appeared to be as smooth as fairways, but with their sedge tussocks and fissured soils they were in fact as rough as boulderfields. Flying near stallout speed, Stanley followed one creek and another, studying the ground. Finally, he saw a place he thought he could get out of if he were to set the plane down. The walk would be long if he couldn't—not to mention what to do about the plane. Rising, circling, returning, he gingerly put his wheels on the ground and jumped back at once into the air. Felt pretty good. He circled again. He rolled his wheels on the tundra twice more. It was thumping rough, but it seemed negotiable. He set the Aeronca down.

Taking off successfully, he went home and told his father, and they began to advance their plans. First, they should improve the landing place. They had a little Ranger—a diminutive tractor, like a Cub Cadet—which they had used to like purpose when they built a cabin on the Charley River years before. Ed cut the Ranger in half. They flew it to the mountains, and he welded it back together. The backhoe before long followed, and when it was at last reassembled they scooped into the center of a stream. Bedrock was eight feet down. Even at six, they panned the colors they had hoped to see.

They had intended to spend the whole of the following season ranging with the backhoe around the claims they had made, trying out pieces of seven miles of streams, but early results were so encouraging that they sharply foreshortened the tests. To put it conservatively, a pay streak appeared to be there, and what was needed now—since the backhoe was just a fifty-seven-hundred-pound shovel—was a means of moving gravel in a major way. The Caterpillar Tractor Company produces the eponymous Cat in seven sizes—styled D3, D4, and so on to D9. Most gold miners use something less than the largest, but the Gelvins—forming a partnership with two friends in Fairbanks—decided to go all the way. The supreme Cat, twenty-seven feet long, eleven feet high, with a blade of fourteen feet, could sweep forty yards of gravel before it— possibly a hundred dollars a shove. Ed Gelvin went to Los Angeles to shop for a used D9.

With his partners in Fairbanks putting up the money in return for a half interest in the claims, he paid forty-seven thousand five hundred dollars for a ten-year-old machine—D9, Series G. In the fleets of general contractors, it had spent its lifetime ripping raw California land, making freeways, and preparing building sites on beaches and deserts. Who, watch-

ing it there—clanking, dozing, wheezing, roaring, grunting like
Pete the Pig—could ever in farthest-fetched imaginings have
guessed where it would go? It went to Seattle by train, and by
barge to Whittier, in Prince William Sound. There the Alaska
Railroad picked it up and took it to Fairbanks, where, in early
April, a lowboy hauled it up the dirt road north. Forty miles
from Central, the haul stopped—blocked by the still unbroken
winter snows. The road had been smothered since October. Ed
Gelvin, who was observing from the air, landed on the road and
with Stanley put the blade on the Cat. The weather in a
general way was warming. Snow was melting. Ice was beginning to rot. If the D9 was going to move up frozen stream beds
and climb into the mountains, it had to keep going now. If the
road was closed, the Cat would open it.

When Stanley Gelvin was a small boy and did his elemen-
tary-school work by correspondence from the kitchen table in
Central, he was from time to time required to draw a picture.
When the choice of subject was his to make, he always drew
a Cat. He operated one before he drove anything else. Now,
with a Cat all around him, he knew where things were. He
sensed like an athlete the rhythm of the parts—the tilt cylin-
ders, the blade-lift arms. A good Cat skinner is a Cat mechanic,
and, from the torque converter to the sun-and-planet gears, he
knew what was making the moves. "I know what's inside the
thing—everything—and what makes it work. My father knows
how the stuff goes together, too. If the thing needs work, we
do it."

The snow-obscured road leading on toward Central was—
even at its best, in summer—a tortuous trail. In several high
places, it traversed the flanks of mountains as a fifteen-foot
shelf with no rail of any kind and a precipitous plunge on the
outboard side. On the last of these mountain passes, twenty
miles from home, Stanley encountered drifts that were thirty
feet deep. To keep going, he had to bite into the snow, doze
some to the brink, send it avalanching down, then turn and

bite some more—all the while feeling for the road, feeling with his corner bits (the low tips of the blade) for the buried edge where the road stopped and the plunge began. A D9 is in some ways the most difficult Cat to operate. "You've got so much iron in front of you you can't see what you're doing." It is also his favorite size, because it is so big it does not bounce around. This one weighed a hundred and ten thousand pounds. Its balance point was ten feet back of the blade. Repeatedly, Stanley moved the blade eight feet over the edge. He knew where it was. If he had gone off the mountain, he would have raised one fantastic cloud of snow. Instead, he trimly dismantled the prodigious drifts and dozed on down to Central.

To the pads of the track Ed Gelvin welded ice grousers. They would keep the Cat from sliding. They were small pieces of steel, protruding like hyphens from the tracks. Ed and Stanley had built a steel slick plate and a steel sluice box, and Ed had rearranged them as a huge loaded sled—eight feet wide and twenty-four feet long: I-beams, H-beams, three-sixteenths-inch plate. He had made a thousand-gallon fuel tank. It was full and on the sled. Here and there, he slipped in snowshoes, gold pans, a two-hundred-amp generator, a welding tank and torch. Finally, he secured to the top of the load a plywood wanigan—that is, a small hut, with three bunks, propane, and a cupboard full of food. The rig, composed, weighed about twelve tons. When it was hooked to the D9, Stanley left for the mountains.

He crossed low terrain at first. His mother rode with him. His father hovered in the air. Then he changed passengers, taking on a friend named Gary Powers, and they began to move up Woodchopper Creek. His altitude at the start was nine hundred feet. The highest point on the trip was well above four thousand. They travelled five days, fourteen hours a day. There was plenty of wind. The highest temperature they experienced was zero. They stopped to cut their way through trees with a chain saw (fearing to doze them because the wanigan might be

crushed). The Cat fell twice through rotting ice. With no
difficulty, it climbed out of the water. There was some luck in
the conditions, but not much. With less ice in Woodchopper
Canyon, Stanley might have been stopped. But successive over-
flows on the creek had built the ice thickness in places to thirty
feet. Nearing the head of Woodchopper, he moved the Cat
slowly up a steep slope of ice, slid back, crept again, slid back,
and thought for a while he wouldn't make it. Without the
grousers, the big rig would have been stopped, but they held
just enough, and gradually he crawled out of the head of the
creek—only to move into snow so deep the D9's steel tracks
spun out. Stanley thought it wise to stop for the night. For one
thing, all this was happening in a blizzard. Next day, the sky
was clear, the air colder, and Stanley moved on a contour
through the deep snow until he found an uphill route. Steadily,
he climbed ridges, sometimes in little snow, sometimes in
seven-foot drifts. At one point, the going was so steep that he
disengaged the sled and tried first to clear a trail. "I knew that
ridge was too steep to go over, because it was almost vertical.
So I went around to the right. Without them ice grousers, the
machine would have slid sideways and straight to the bottom
as if it was on skates. Gary was scared to death. I went real slow
now, and slipped some, and then went down to a dead crawl.
I had it idled as low as it would go. I went on a half a mile or
so. When I saw it was possible, I went back for the sled."

Landing on skis, his father would fly him out, and the D9
would sit idle in the mountains until summer. Meanwhile,
there was one last ridge to cross. "One side was sheer, and the
other had deep snow and was very steep. It must have been
forty-five degrees. A guy could have maybe gone around one
side—if you'd left the wanigan, dug the snow, and plowed a
road. But I didn't want to make a horrible-looking mess. I
moved slowly up. The track did spin a bit. I couldn't go straight
up. It was too steep. I couldn't go sideways too well. I couldn't
go back, because I had the sled. I'd have been afraid to back

down. You can cut a road into the side of a mountain if you
want to with a Cat like that, but I just inched up the thing,
and over. I didn't want to dig up the country."

❲ Brad Snow and Lilly Allen came into the country in 1974.
They were twenty-six and twenty-one. Their route had begun
in New Hampshire and had included Anchorage, where they
took jobs to collect enough money to venture into the bush.
Like many other young couples who wished to get past the
turnstiles of urban Alaska, they studied the map and guessed
at the merits of this or that possible destination. Many people
they encountered seemed to be headed for McGrath and
Bethel and points between on the Kuskokwim River. Allen and
Snow therefore looked the other way. "None of those people
even knew where Eagle *was*. We figured it was the place to go."

They arrived in a pickup—with their axes and hammers, drill
bits and drawknife, whipsaw; their new, lovely, seventeen-foot
Chestnut Prospector canoe. They were exploring in more ways
than the geographical. They were looking for a milieu—and a
manner of developing their lives. For necessary money, they
could work from time to time in Fairbanks—and, possibly, in
Eagle. But they hoped to live much of the year apart from any
community. "I reject suburbia," Snow was not shy to explain.
"I reject crowds. I do not want a new car, a fancy house. They
are not worth working for. In the Lower Forty-eight, economic
pressure made it impossible for me to have the land and space
I would like to have without spending twenty years to get it and
then being surrounded by box houses. In order to get anything
like what I wanted, in New Hampshire, I would have had to
deal in large figures. I was unwilling to complicate my life to
get those figures."

What he and Lilly sought was terrain where the individual

spirit might be confined only by the metes and bounds and rules of nature. They meant to go down the Yukon, whose banks were just the beginnings of millions of acres of wilderness. They asked around—of others, like Dick Cook, who had pursued the same idea—and they discovered the country's code of seniority right. Tributary rivers were prime locations. There was someone already living on each incoming stream for a considerable distance below Eagle. The first vacancy was the Nation River, forty-six miles away—a little far, but it would do. Snow had brought with him a sense of impending catastrophe, in large part because he had staked his plans on the character of the Yukon without even knowing if it was safely navigable or a boiling flume of rapids. When he had become assured that for all its great power the big river ran smooth, his confidence improved. He felt expansive as he loaded the canoe with seven hundred pounds of grain.

He was an electrician by trade—a fact of no value on the Nation. He was good at carpentry, though, and he was a sharpshooter—skills enough for a beginning. Seven miles up the Nation, he and Lilly built a ten-by-fourteen-foot cabin of unpeeled, saddle-notched logs. It had two windows, paned with soft clear plastic. It was chinked with moss. Its roof consisted of layers of sod, moss, and plastic. It was a tight, well-made, neatly made cabin. Its door, for some months, was nothing more than a hanging blanket, but even on nights at thirty-five below zero the cabin was so warm that the blanket was kept to one side. They had an airtight heat stove ("a poor man's Ashley"), and their cookstove was a sheepherder's unit, its firebox scarcely a cubic foot. With the whipsaw, Snow made boards for a bench and a table. From dry spruce he made dowels, which he tapped into holes drilled in the wall logs, and on these he set shelves for their pinto beans and bulgur, their whole-wheat-soy ribbon noodles, their cherry butter and corn-germ oil, rolled oats, popcorn, brown rice, and wheat berries. He killed a moose, and they hung strips of the meat from the ridgepole to dry. They preserved blueberries, cranberries, rose hips. In the clear Nation, they fished for grayling and northern pike.

They had only two dogs with them, and one night Miki, a Siberian husky, was off scenting the neighborhood when Snow and Allen heard the nearby howl of a wolf. Snow took a shotgun and walked in the direction of the sound. He came back with Miki on a stick. The wolf had ripped the dog's throat. The winter was otherwise safely uneventful, with the exception that Snow one day decided he had appendicitis and took off for Fairbanks, leaving Lilly Allen behind. For five weeks, she was there alone, more than fifty miles from Eagle, with no idea if he was dead or alive. In the end, it was Snow's woman, and not his appendix, that was inflamed.

Not many months before, they had made a trip to Basking Ridge, New Jersey, to be married. The bride's father wore lilies of the valley. He is an Exxon exxecutive. Lilly went to Ridge High School and for one semester to the University of Arizona. She was working as a waitress on Route 16 outside Conway, New Hampshire, when Snow came into her life. She wanted someday to own fields of sheep, she told him, because she was "into spinning and weaving." He wanted to go where even fleece would freeze. He was from Reading, Massachusetts, had studied some at the Universities of Massachusetts and Hawaii, and had been to trade school, but he had found a deeper interest working in New Hampshire forests for the Appalachian Mountain Club. A lithe man of middle height, he has a big brown beard, a tumble of shining brown hair, a serious turn of mind. Lilly Allen—handsome, unadornedly feminine— is facially Puritan, sober, with a touch of anachronism about her, as if on Sundays somehow she occupies a front pew, listening to Cotton Mather.

"We came here to get away from lots of people, lots of machines, and into a simpler way of life," she will say. "Everybody in Eagle says they came here 'to get away from it all.' We

found 'it all' in Eagle. We came here to do without unnecessary things, to live out, to deal with the land in a more natural
way."

In the vernacular of the river people, hunting moose, caribou, porcupine, duck, bear, rabbit is known as "getting your
meat," and for Snow the task was complicated from the beginning by more than the problems of stalking and marksmanship.
He had trouble, sometimes, pulling the trigger on a wild creature. "I hunt for meat, but I don't really enjoy hunting," he
confesses. "It comes down to having or not having a spirit of
predatorship. If Dick Cook or Charlie Edwards sees a goose,
he doesn't hesitate. Bang. But I stop and admire the goose, and
then I think of the gun. When I shoot a moose, I walk up to
it with profound reverence—this beautiful beast that I, a
scrawny little thing, am destroying. The last time I shot my
moose, I cried. I really sympathized with him. I don't know
how to put it. Having shot the animal—and seeing it lying
there, dying—shakes me up."

In their search for ways to make a living in the country,
Snow and Allen avoided trapping altogether. "I would do that
if I had no other way to get money," he explains. "But I don't
want to kill animals up here to clothe fat whores in New York.
I don't mind wearing furs, but I prefer not to sell them."
Meanwhile, there was money to be made fighting fires—in a
smoking forest with a water bag on his back—and from two
such experiences he earned a thousand dollars, or more than
half of what they needed for a year.

They were still tasting their new and more natural life when
Lilly's parents arrived for a visit in Eagle. In two canoes, the
four went down the Yukon for a few days, just to have a look
at the cabin on the Nation. The journey was more than Lilly's
mother could complete, but Snow and his father-in-law left the
women camped behind and tracked the Chestnut up the
stream. It was a laborious effort, and they had been at it several

hours when a helicopter suddenly came over the trees and passed them. Just the sight of it angered Snow, because—fifty miles from civilization—it ruined the wild scene. The two men tracked on, forgot the chopper, and finally arrived at the cabin. It had a door now, and an ingenious Oriental-puzzle sort of lock, which Snow had devised. Scarcely had he brought out some gear to air when the helicopter returned. It circled, landed on a gravel bar. "Let me do the talking," said Snow.

The pilot got out, and so did a man with a federal patch on his shirt. He was a short, slight, briefcase of a man. "Hello," he said. "I'm Dave Williams, of the Bureau of Land Management. You're on a canoe trip. I'm very sorry to disturb your wilderness experience. We're just checking here. Do you mind if we look around? This isn't your place, is it?"

Snow was noncommittal, but he became increasingly irritated as Williams went into the cabin and rummaged among its goods. The pilot said, "Really nice place here—nice, well-built cabin. This your place?"

Brad and Lilly own a framed copy of a celebrated photograph made by Dorothea Lange in Kern County, California, in the nineteen-thirties, which shows a compressed-air pump at a rundown rural filling station and two prominent signs— one saying "AIR," the other saying "This is your country. Don't let the big men take it away from you."

"Yes, it's *my* place," Snow blurted.

Williams reappeared like a genie. "Did you say *your* place?" he asked.

"Those are my things in the cabin," Snow said. "I'd rather you didn't go through my things."

"I said, 'Is this your place?' "

"You seem to think it's yours."

As he left, Williams said, "The cabin is in trespass. Very likely you'll be hearing from me in a short while. This is now the twentieth century. You can't just do what you want to do. You cannot play with the wilderness."

❨ Snow was shortly given written notice that the cabin was on federal ground, that its presence conflicted with "the necessary and appropriate use of said land," and that if he left his personal property there it would be removed and stored at his expense. Lilly Allen was mentioned only as "any and all other persons." Alaska had attracted them. The United States had rebuffed them. Sarge Waller got a notice, too, about his cabin at the Kandik. Other notices went down the river. In the hundred and sixty miles between Eagle and Circle, the exact small number of people living on or near the Yukon had always been indeterminate, and as the scrutiny of the Bureau of Land Management drew closer the number became even less determinate than before. Under blue wisps of smoke separated by pieces of land the size of Eastern counties, people did what they could to remain invisible, knowing they were in trespass on federal land.

From time immemorial until the nineteen-seventies, anyone who had the drive and spirit to build a cabin in this northern wilderness was not restrained from doing so. For a long time, gold was the almost exclusive draw, and, as Lieutenant Frederick Schwatka had observed when he was sent to scout the region in 1883, "the discovery of gold in paying quantities is probably the only incentive for men to enter the country, and were it not that indications are seen all along the river, white men would probably never venture in." In more recent times, though, as the pressure of population in the Lower Forty-eight increased toward critical levels, a quite different incentive presented itself as well. Some of the hardiest people in the society were drawn to bush Alaska in search of a sense of release—of a life that remembered the past. The Alaskan wild was, as advertised, the last frontier—where people willing to combat its cold and run its risks could live an existence free from supererogatory rules as long as they did no harm to one another. The government did not interfere, and through the Homestead Act and other legislative provisions it even assisted this dream; but, with the discovery of oil at Prudhoe Bay on the edge of the Arctic Ocean, events began to occur that would change, apparently forever, the use and demarcation of Alaskan land. Meanwhile, certain long-established forms of freedom would disappear—the sort of freedom that drew a family like the Gelvins a generation earlier into the country, the sort of freedom envisioned by young people who set off to live in the wild of the upper Yukon. If the oil had never been discovered, there would not have been an eviction notice prepared for Brad Snow.

The discovery of the oil was in 1968, and after it became clear that there would be no pipeline until the land claims of the natives were satisfactorily extinguished, the United States Congress (attempting to satisfy not only the natives but at the same time the conflicting ambitions of conservationists and developers; attempting to promote the economy, protect the ecology, and respond multifariously to the sudden demand for this long-ignored but now prime segment of American national real estate) got together in a single bill the mighty ziggurat of legislation within which the catalytic pipeline would seem, while important, almost minor. Long after the publicity had receded and the pipeline had become as little discussed as the Big Inch, the social and political effects of its progenitive congressional bill would still be poignantly felt. Everyone of any race in all Alaska would be affected by the Alaska Native Claims Settlement Act. In elemental respects, the character of Alaska would change.

The natives would be afforded some variety in the choosing of their forty million acres of land, but much of it would be close to established villages. Included, meanwhile, among the epic consolations given the conservationists—the big pieces of land that were to be set aside for consideration as national parks, forests, rivers, wildlife refuges—were more than two million acres along the Yukon between Eagle and Circle. Many millions of additional acres—including the valley where the Gelvins legally staked gold claims—were to be closed to all but those in pursuit of "metalliferous minerals." Meanwhile, the State of Alaska was still choosing the hundred and three million acres awarded to it in the Statehood Act. It had until 1984 to complete the selection, and for the time being the land under scrutiny would remain—to the individual—beyond reach. When one adds in the existing parks, government forests, and wildlife refuges and a vast federal petroleum reserve in the north, not much remains, so it is one of the ironies of Alaska that in the midst of this tremendous wilderness people consider themselves fortunate to have (anywhere at all) a fifty-by-a-hundred-foot lot they can call their own.

Meanwhile, down below, outside, people who sit on sidewalks wearing Italian hiking boots and machine-faded jeans imply an extremity somewhere else. Surely, some of them will stand up and leave town, and when they leave they will go toward the wild—probably to the nearest mountain. Some will keep going to an even wilder place. Some will go farther than that. The logical inevitability for this chain of beings is that the ultimates will appear in Eagle (or Circle or Central or somewhere else in Alaska)—where civilization stops. And a very few will then jump free, going deep into the roadless world. By the time they reach Eagle, their momentum is too great to be interrupted by an act of Congress, even if they know of it and understand what it says. What the law now calls for is the removal of the last place in the United States where the pioneer impulse can leap from confinement. It is in the character of the impulse that the impulse will leap anyway—so the Bureau of Land Management, custodian of all the huge acreages under shift and selection, is charged with driving the trespassers away. Whites feel sold out and shoved under by the settlement of the native claims. Reticence has never been a characteristic of people attracted to this kind of terrain. They howl their upset, its focus the B.L.M.

"You can't go out and build a cabin and live in the goddamned woods, which people have been doing since the country was founded. Nobody argues with a few parks, but such a big percentage of the land is too much."

"It's not as if we're building fifty-thousand-dollar houses with asphalt driveways and stinking cesspools."

"Our cabins are more like tents than like most people's homes. They are made with native materials—white spruce, earth, moss. They are biodegradable. When they are abandoned, trees thirty feet high grow up out of the sod on their roofs. Eventually, the cabin collapses and disappears into the ground."

"Most people felt if we became a state we'd get rid of some of this federal control, and actually it's got worse."

"Alaska's ruined by this native-land deal that's went through. You could build a cabin anywhere, and mine anywhere, when I came. Now Alaska is going to be just like every other state."

"What bugs me is that when decisions are made about Alaska, people from Texas and Ohio, California and New York carry more weight than people from Alaska."

"Why should people be hassled for building cabins out here? What harm are they doing? Why should they be bothered? Why destroy a life simply because it exists? Slap a mosquito, yes. But if a life is not harming, why destroy it? Every species of animal has a wide genetic base, or they don't exist. Our living out here is a widening of the genetic base. I think the government people are fools to wipe us out."

"It's public land. We're the public."

"Down at the North Fork are twelve cabins. Mostly, the sites have been in use since the turn of the century, maintained and repaired by trappers and prospectors. Now the B.L.M.

wants to kick these people out. It tells them they can never go to those cabins."

"Why should they drive us away? They ought to pay us to be out here—just to keep these places in good shape and well supplied."

"There are emergencies in this country, and when they happen sometimes cabins are needed."

"More than one life has been saved when someone in trouble has come upon a cabin."

⟨ The country is full of stories of unusual deaths—old Nimrod Robertson lying down on a creek in overflow and letting it build around him a sarcophagus of ice; the trapper on the Kandik who apparently knocked himself out when he tripped and fell on his own firewood and froze to death before he came to—and of stories also of deaths postponed. There are fewer of the second. I would like to add one back—an account that in essence remains in the country but in detail has largely disappeared.

On a high promontory in the montane ruggedness around the upper Charley River lies the wreckage of an aircraft that is readily identifiable as a B-24. This was the so-called Liberator, a medium-range bomber built for the Second World War. The wreckage is in the dead center of the country, and I happened over it in a Cessna early in the fall of 1975, during a long and extremely digressive flight that began in Eagle and ended many hours later in Circle. The pilot of the Cessna said he understood that the crew of the Liberator had bailed out, in winter, and that only one man had survived. I asked around to learn who might know more than that—querying, among others, the Air Force in Fairbanks, the Gelvins, various old-timers in Circle and Central, some of the river people, and Margaret Nelson, in Eagle, who had packed parachutes at

Ladd Field, in Fairbanks, during the war. There had been one survivor—everyone agreed. No one knew his name. He had become a symbol in the country, though, and was not about to be forgotten. It was said that he alone had come out—long after all had been assumed dead—because he alone, of the widely scattered crew, was experienced in wilderness, knew how to live off the land, and was prepared to deal with the hostile cold. Above all, he had found a cabin, during his exodus, without which he would have died for sure.

"And the government bastards try to stop us from building them now."

"Guy jumped out of an airplane, and he would have died but he found a cabin."

If the survivor had gone on surviving for what was now approaching thirty-five years, he would in all likelihood be somewhere in the Lower Forty-eight. When I was home, I made a try to find him. Phone calls ricocheted around Washington for some days, yielding only additional phone numbers. The story was just too sketchy. Did I know how many bombers had been lost in that war? At length, I was given the name of Gerard Hasselwander, a historian at the Albert F. Simpson Historical Research Center, Maxwell Air Force Base, Alabama. I called him, and he said that if I did not even know the year of the crash he doubted he could help me. Scarcely two hours later, though, he called back to say that he had had a free moment or two at the end of his lunch hour and had browsed through some microfilm. To his own considerable surprise, he had found the survivor's name, which was Leon Crane. Crane's home when he entered the Army Air Forces had been in Philadelphia, but Hasselwander had looked in a Philadelphia directory and there was no Leon Crane in it now. However, he said, Leon Crane had had two brothers who were also in service—in the Army Medical Corps—during the Second World War. One of them was named Morris. In the Philadelphia directory, there was a Dr. Morris Crane.

When I called the number, someone answered and said Dr. Crane was not there.

I asked when he would return.

"I don't know" was the reply. "He went to Leon's."

The Liberator, making cold-weather propeller tests above twenty thousand feet, went into a spin, dived toward the earth, and, pulling out, snapped its elevator controls. It then went into another spin, and the pilot gave the order to abandon ship. There were five aboard. Leon Crane was the co-pilot. He was twenty-four and he had been in Alaska less than two months. Since the plane was falling like a swirling leaf, he had to drag himself against heavy centrifugal force toward the open bomb bay. He had never used a parachute. The outside air temperature was at least thirty degrees below zero. When he jumped, he forgot his mittens. The day was December 21st.

The plane fiercely burned, not far away from where he landed, and he stood watching it, up to his thighs in snow. He was wearing a hooded down jacket, a sweater, winter underwear, two pairs of trousers, two pairs of socks, and felt-lined military mukluks. He scanned the mountainsides but could see nothing of the others. He thought he had been the second one to go out of the plane, and as he fell he thought he saw a parachute open in the air above him. He shouted into the winter silence. Silence answered. Months later, he would learn that there had been two corpses in the aircraft. Of the two other fliers no track or trace was ever found. "Sergeant Pompeo, the crew chief, had a hell of a thick set of glasses. He must have lost them as soon as he hit the airstream. Without them, he really couldn't see. What was he going to do when he got down there?"

For that matter, what was Crane going to do? He had no food, no gun, no sleeping bag, no mittens. The plane had been meandering in search of suitable skies for the tests. Within two or three hundred miles, he had no idea where he was.

Two thousand feet below him, and a couple of miles east, was a river. He made his way down to it. Waiting for rescue, he stayed beside it. He had two books of matches, a Boy Scout knife. He started a fire with a letter from his father, and for the first eight days he did not sleep more than two hours at a time in his vigilance to keep the fire burning. The cold awakened him anyway. Water fountained from a gap in the river ice, and that is what he lived on. His hands, which he to some extent protected with parachute cloth or in the pockets of his jacket, became cut and abraded from tearing at spruce boughs. When he spread his fingers, the skin between them would split. Temperatures were probably ranging between a high of thirty below zero and a low around fifty. The parachute, as much as anything, kept him alive. It was twenty-eight feet in diameter, and he wound it around him so that he was at the center of a great cocoon. Still, he said, his back would grow cold while his face roasted, and sparks kept igniting the chute.

He was telling me some of this on a sidewalk in Philadelphia when I asked him how he had dealt with fear.

He stopped in surprise, and looked contemplatively up the street toward Independence Hall, his graying hair wisping out to the sides. He wore a business suit and a topcoat, and he had bright, penetrating eyes. He leaned forward when he walked. "Fear," he repeated. "I wouldn't have used that word. Think about it: there was not a hell of a lot I could do if I were to panic. Besides, I was sure that someone was going to come and get me."

All that the search-and-rescue missions had to go on was that the Liberator had last been heard from above Big Delta, so the search area could not be reduced much below forty thousand square miles. Needless to say, they would not come near finding him. He thought once that he heard the sound of an airplane, but eventually he realized that it was a chorus of wolves. In his hunger, he tried to kill squirrels. He made a spear, and threw it awkwardly as they jumped and chattered in the spruce boughs. He made a bow and arrow, using a shroud line from his parachute, but when he released the arrow it shot off at angles ridiculously oblique to the screeching, maddening squirrels. There was some rubber involved in the parachute assembly, and he used that to make a slingshot, which was worse than the bow and arrow. When he fell asleep by the fire, he dreamed of milkshakes, dripping beefsteaks, mashed potatoes, and lamb chops, with lamb fat running down his hands. Awake, he kicked aside the snow and found green moss. He put it in his mouth and chewed, and chewed some more, but scarcely swallowed any. Incidentally, he was camped almost exactly where, some twenty-five years later, Ed and Virginia Gelvin would build a cabin from which to trap and hunt.

Crane is a thoroughly urban man. He grew up in the neighborhood of Independence Hall, where he lives now, with an unlisted number. That part of the city has undergone extensive refurbishment in recent years, and Crane's sons, who are residential builders and construction engineers, have had a part in the process. Crane, more or less retired, works for them, and when I visited him I followed him from building to building as he checked on the needs and efforts of carpenters, bricklayers, plumbers. He professed to have no appetite for wild country, least of all for the expanses of the north. As a boy, he had joined a city Scout troop, and had become a First Class Scout, but that was not to suggest a particular knowledge of wilderness. When he flew out of Fairbanks that morning in 1943, his lifetime camping experience consisted of one night on the ground—with his troop, in Valley Forge.

He decided on the ninth day that no help was coming. Gathering up his parachute, he began to slog his way downriver, in snow sometimes up to his waist. It crossed his mind that the situation might be hopeless, but he put down the thought as he moved from bend to bend by telling himself to keep going because "right around that curve is what you're looking for." In fact, he was about sixty miles from the nearest human being, almost a hundred from the nearest group of buildings large enough to be called a settlement. Around the next bend, he saw more mountains, more bare jagged rock, more snow-covered sweeps of alpine tundra, contoured toward another river bend. "Right around that curve is what you're looking for," he told himself again. Suddenly, something was there. First, he saw a cache, high on legs in the air, and then a small cabin, with a door only three feet high. It was like the lamb chops, with the grease on his fingers, but when he pushed at the door it was wood and real. The room inside was nine by ten: earth floor, low ceiling, a bunk made of spruce. It was Alaskan custom always to leave a cabin open and stocked for anyone in need. Split firewood was there, and matches, and a pile of prepared shavings. On a table were sacks of dried raisins, sugar, cocoa, and powdered milk. There was a barrel stove, frying pans on the wall. He made some cocoa, and, after so long a time without food, seemed full after a couple of sips. Then he climbed a ladder and looked in the cache, lifting a tarp to discover hammers, saws, picks, drills, coiled rope, and two tents. No one, he reasoned, would leave such equipment far off in the wilderness. "I figured civilization was right around the corner. I was home free."

So he stayed just a night and went on down the river, anxious to get back to Ladd Field. The moon came up after the brief light of day, and he kept going. He grew weak in the deep cold of the night, and when the moon went below the mountains he began to wander off the stream course, hitting boulders. He had been around many corners, but no civilization was there. Now he was sinking into a dream-hazy sleepwalking numbed-out oblivion; but fear, fortunately, struck through and turned him, upriver. He had not retraced his way very far when he stopped and tried to build a fire. He scraped together some twigs, but his cut and bare hands were shaking so—at roughly fifty below zero—that he failed repeatedly to ignite a match. He abandoned the effort, and moved on through the snow. He kept hitting boulders. He had difficulty following his own tracks. He knew now that he would die if he did not get back to the cabin, and the detached observer within him decided he was finished. Left foot, right foot—there was no point in quitting, even so. About noon, he reached the cabin. With his entire body shaking, he worked at a fire until he had one going. Then he rolled up in his parachute and slept almost continuously for three full days.

In his excitement at being "right around the corner from civilization," he had scarcely looked in the cache, and now he found rice, flour, beans, powdered eggs, dried vegetables, and beef—enough for many weeks, possibly months. He found mittens. He found snowshoes. He found long johns, socks, mukluks. He found candles, tea, tobacco, and a corncob pipe. He found ammunition, a .22. In the cabin, he mixed flour, peas, beans, sugar, and snow, and set it on the stove. That would be his basic gruel—and he became enduringly fond of it. Sometimes he threw in eggs and vegetables. He covered his hands with melted candle wax, and the bandage was amazingly effective. He developed a routine, with meals twice a day, a time for hunting, a fresh well chopped daily through the four-foot river ice. He slept eighteen hours a day, like a wintering bear—not truly hibernating, just lying there in his den. He felt a need to hear a voice, so he talked to himself. The day's high moment was a pipeful of tobacco puffed while he looked through ten-year-old copies of *The Saturday Evening Post*. He ransacked the magazines for insights into the woods lore he did not know. He learned a thing or two. In a wind, it said somewhere in the *Post,* build your fire in a hole. He shot and ate a ptarmigan, and had the presence of mind to look in its stomach. He found some overwintering berries there, went to the sort of bushes they had come from, and shot more ptarmigan. Cardboard boxes, the magazines, and other items in the cabin were addressed to "Phil Berail, Woodchopper, Alaska." Contemplating these labels, Crane decided that Alaska was a fantastic place—where someone's name and occupation were a sufficient address. One day, an old calendar fell off the wall and flipped over on its way to the floor. On the back was a map of Alaska. He stared at it all day. He found Woodchopper, on the Yukon, and smiled at his foolishness. From the terrain around him, the northward flow of the stream, the relative positions of Fairbanks and Big Delta, he decided—just right—that he was far up the Charley River. The smile went back where it came from.

He decided to wait for breakup, build a raft, and in late May float on down to the Yukon. After five or six weeks, though, he realized that his food was going to give out in March. There was little ammunition with which to get meat, and he had no confidence anyway in his chances with the rifle. If he stayed, he would starve. He felt panic now, but not enough to spill the care with which he was making his plans. He had set off willy-nilly once before and did not want to repeat the mistake. He patched his clothes with parachute cloth, sewing them with shroud lines. He made a sled from some boards and a galvanized tub. He figured closely what the maximum might be that he could drag and carry. On February 12th, he left. The sled would scarcely budge at first, and snow bunched up before it. Wearing a harness he had made, he dragged the sled slowly downriver. Berail's snowshoes had Indian ties. Try as he would, he could not understand how to secure them to his feet. The snowshoes were useless. Up to his knees, and sometimes to his hips, he walked from dawn until an hour before dark each day. He slept beside bonfires that burned all night. Blizzards came up the river some days, and driving williwaws—winds of a force that could literally stop him in his tracks. He leaned against the wind. When he could, he stepped forward. Once, at the end of a day's hard walking, he looked behind him—on the twisting mountain river—and saw where he had started at dawn. The Charley in summer—clear-flowing within its canyon walls, with grizzlies fishing its riffles, Dall sheep on the bluffs, and peregrines above it in the air—is an extremely beautiful Alaskan river (it has been called the loveliest of all), but for Leon Crane it was little more than brutal. He came to a lead one day, a patch of open water, and, trying to use some boulders as stepping stones, he fell in up to his armpits. Coming out, barging through snowdrifts, he was the center of a fast-forming block of ice. His matches were dry. Shaking as before, he managed this time to build a fire. All day, he sat steaming beside it, removing this or that item of clothing, drying it a piece at a time.

After a couple of weeks on the river, he found another cabin, with a modest but welcome food cache—cornmeal, canned vegetables, Vienna sausage. He sewed himself a backpack and abandoned his cumbersome sled. Some seven or eight days on down the river, he came around a bend at dusk and found cut spruce tops in parallel rows stuck in the river snow. His aloneness, he sensed, was all but over. It was the second week of March, and he was eighty days out of the sky. The arrangement of treetops, obviously, marked a place where a plane on skis might land supplies. He looked around in near darkness and found a toboggan trail. He camped, and next day followed the trail to a cabin—under smoke. He shouted toward it. Al Ames, a trapper, and his wife, Neena, and their children appeared in the doorway. "I am Lieutenant Leon Crane, of the United States Army Air Forces," he called out. "I've been in a little trouble." Ames took a picture, which hangs on a wall in Philadelphia.

Crane remembers thinking, Somebody must be saving me for something, but I don't know what it is. His six children, who owe themselves to that trip and to Phil Berail's fully stocked Charley River cabin, are—in addition to his three sons in the construction business—Mimi, who is studying engineering at Barnard; Rebecca, who is in the master's program in architecture at Columbia; and Ruth, a recent graduate of the Harvard Medical School. Crane himself went on to earn an advanced degree in aeronautical engineering at the Massachusetts Institute of Technology, and spent his career developing helicopters for Boeing Vertol.

"It's a little surprising to me that people exist who are interested in living on that ground up there," he told me.

"Why would anyone want to take someone who wanted to *be* there and throw them out? Who the hell could *care?*"

Al Ames, who had built his cabin only two years before, harnessed his dogs and mushed Crane down the Yukon to Woodchopper, where a plane soon came along and flew him out.

Crane met Phil Berail at Woodchopper, and struggled shyly to express to him his inexpressible gratitude. Berail, sixty-five, was a temporary postmaster and worked for the gold miners there. He had trapped from his Charley River cabin. He was pleased that it had been useful, he said. For his part, he had no intention of ever going there again. He had abandoned the cabin four years before.

❴ The river people refer to seasons of their year with names like "ducks" and "fish."

"We'll be in Eagle soon after fish."

"There's not a lot to do before ducks."

They hunt ducks in May, and work on things that are needed for the coming winter—a new toboggan, for example, so it will age all summer and be slippery and hard in the fall. New cabins are started, and repairs are made on others. In July, nets are put out for king salmon. There is some use of fish wheels—postcard symbols of the Yukon. A fish wheel is a revolving trap that was invented by a white man but is generally associated with Indians. The big kings weigh as much as sled dogs. Their dense ruddy flesh—baked, smoked, or canned —is one of the supreme gifts of nature. The river people are less interested in kings than in the chum salmon that follow, for while king salmon may be luxuries on the human palate, chum—dried or frozen—are year-round staples for dogs. They are, in effect, gasoline. A team consumes at least a thousand a year. The river people believe that the health of a sled dog can be measured by the proportion of fish in its diet. When they happen to do odd jobs for one another or engage in barter, they like to be paid in dog salmon. Lilly Allen has given fifty salmon for a quarter of a bear. You try to get your meat around the first week of October, hunting moose and bear while they are still fat. "This is a fat-starved country. This is not the coast. You'll look a long while before you'll see a seal in the river." You see ice instead, coming down in the middle of the month. At the sight of it, harnesses are brought out and repaired. The ice is light at first, and goes tinkling by, but with advancing cold the floes increase, harden, crash, thunder—until one day a startling silence replaces the sound. Trapping begins, and lasts off and on until April. The Indians used to follow this cycle more than they do now. The river people have taken up where the Indians left off. April is a lag month—not a lot to do before ducks. April is a good time to go out of the country and work on the pipeline, or on something else that yields money for wheat berries, ammunition, and fuel.

Spread out they may be, but the river people are social and gregarious. News moves quickly of a reason to convene. Dick Cook shot a wolf near Eagle not long ago and stewed it in a twenty-one-quart pressure cooker. His ilk in eager numbers gathered around the pot and ate twenty-one quarts of wolf. Not all gatherings are impromptu. To celebrate the 1976 vernal equinox, for example, the river people held a tribal convention just below the mouth of the Nation. It was planned many months in advance and went on for nearly a week. To them, the vernal equinox is a more important date than Easter, just as December 21st is a more important date than Christmas, and in each case by a factor so large it tends to dismiss the comparison. The vernal equinox is the fulcrum of light and dark which holds the promise of warmth to come, of the summer fish runs and garden harvests, the growth of Brussels sprouts and Mary Jane. Nearly everyone grows the latter. The law does not frown upon the practice in Alaska. In the long northern light, the compound serrate leaves will rise on tall stems to the height of a man, and as whole stands come together, enmeshing, interdigitating, they form colonies of such spiky luxuriance that small segments of the banks of the Yukon appear to have been painted there by Henri (le Douanier) Rousseau.

The specific site of the river people's equinoctial gathering was the abandoned camp of Jim Taylor, who went out of the country in 1933 to die of cancer. By the evidence of what he left behind, he was a far-northern Crusoe. He could have earned an advanced degree in log architecture. He failed at mining, working the gold-bearing placers off the left bank of the Yukon, but he loved the country so much he stayed on, and he paid off his debts trapping. On the right bank near the Nation, he built a cabin that included a dumbwaiter, which served as a refrigerator when it was lowered into a spring. There were two rooms, full of period "Alaska furniture" made from orange crates, Blazo boxes, and egg crates. He built other cabins for shopwork and storage. Where most people chain their dogs to trees or to stakes in the ground, separating them in short-radius confinement, Taylor built long, palisaded, individual dog runs, each including a log kennel and a fragment of a running brook. For times of severe weather, he built an entire cabin exclusively for dogs. It has six rooms, three on either side of a central corridor, and appears to be a small, comfortable jail. Taylor could pull a lever from outside and release simultaneously six chattering huskies. Taylor had the first radio in the country, and miners would come down their streams and cross the Yukon to visit him and hear it. He was a big man, and is remembered as a "good guy." Surely he would have been flattered that his like in the nineteen-seventies chose to gather in his compound. The main cabin burned some time ago, but the rest is there, intact, the sod roofs shaggy with growing spruce.

It was a council of war and a party, too—a time of talk and music, no booze—a way to keep contacts, to exchange opinions and information.

"The economy's got to go eventually, because they're into using minerals and resources way too heavy."

"Keep a cache of ammunition. You can't survive without a rifle."

The ground was white, the brooks and rivers frozen. The people slept for the most part in tents. They strategized about the federal bureaucracy—how to oppose it, how to melt out of its way. They planned a network of cabins for winter travel. They tried, with no success, to agree on a communal bulk food order, and on a way to administer common ownership of a truck for use in Eagle. Their desire to be "tribal" does not approach in strength their need to be self-reliant. For all their garrulity, they are not compact. As they always do, they talked in loops without end about hunting, fishing, trapping, and dogs; knives, axes, the kerf-width of saws; mortises, tenons; steel-cut oats; oars, poles; sleds, toboggans; aluminum boats; trail sets, visuals, tracks on the pan; single trees, spreaders; the collars of stoves; what sort of pups a certain bitch might throw; shelter, clothing, death, and marten bait (grouse wings versus salmon skins versus strawberry jam); and as the talk curved through its long ellipses it turned and returned, as always, to the Yukon, to every gravel bar, rock, rip, eddy, and bend—free or under ice. They baked pies. They argued ethics. Is it wasteful to feed moose to dogs? They tacked up a moosehide. The girth alone covered thirteen cabin logs. There was a common hunt across the Yukon in the Fourth of July flats, and a common mush—a dog Olympiad—far up the Nation River. Competition, open or subtle, is in everything they say and do. Who —figuratively, physically—goes deepest into the wilderness? Who is the most established, the most "dug in"? Who takes the highest percentage of his food from the land? Who has been caught in the deepest overflow? Who has the oldest whipsaw, the oldest bench screw? Who has the best woman?

A good woman is a subservient woman, or so it seems to the alien eye. As Brad Snow has explained to me, "Women's lib doesn't survive very well in the bush. There's a bunch to do—and responsibility has to be delineated where it fits. The meal has got to get cooked. The meat has got to get found." Snow, nonetheless, prepares about half of the meals he shares with Lilly Allen. Charlie Edwards, while a star of a hunter, grinds grain and bakes bread at home. But those are exceptions. Cook cooks nothing. By and large, the men seem to be waited upon to an extent that even our forefathers might not have known.

In a good fish year, two moose, two hundred ducks, and seventy-five quarts of king salmon will be plenty for one river couple. The upper Yukon now is considered "full," saturated with settlers, all space reserved—roughly one person for every five miles. Not everyone on the river gathers for the equinox. Some are not tribally inclined. I was in the Yukon Trading Post in Circle one time when a man about forty came up over the riverbank and bought six bottles of Worcestershire sauce, twelve packets of yeast, a case of matches, some Spam, sardines, hot dogs, three pounds of tea, a hundred and fifty pounds of sugar, a hundred and fifty pounds of rice, fifty pounds of cornmeal, and two cigars. He counted out three hundred and forty-four dollars cash, laid it on the counter, and went back to the river without so much as a word about the weather. Frank Warren—pilot, trapper, keeper of the Trading Post—remarked that he had happened by that man's cabin one day and had thought to pay a visit. It was a small cabin, eight by ten, without windows. As Warren approached, he heard a voice. The man was telling himself a joke. Reaching the punch line, he erupted in laughter. Warren tiptoed away.

Of Cook's mentees, Charlie Edwards seems to be the most wild, in the extent that he prospers away in the woods. As energetic as he is successful, he lives on his rifle for months at a time. "I get so high being out in the woods it's like doing acid," he says. "I get high just being straight. I'm happy. I never wanted to work for anybody but myself. I wanted a country big enough so I could move into the woods. I can live good in the woods here on two thousand dollars a year." He makes that much trapping. His wife, Cheryl, brings back fifteen hundred dollars more from seasonal work in Fairbanks. He saves money by assembling his own ammunition. They live at a creek mouth under twenty miles from Eagle because Cheryl is less comfortable farther away, and, as Charlie elaborates, "It's a hell of a lot nicer when you got an old lady than when you ain't." They make candles from the wax of their own bees. When they take a moose, they use everything. Cheryl sews Charlie's clothes. He wears moosehide trousers, mukluks of moosehide and fur, a marmot vest, a patchwork parka of beaver, caribou, wolverine, and wolf. "If I get myself another bear, I'm going to have fur pants," he told me once, and the next time I saw him his pants were hairy and black. He is twenty-five or so and comes from a well-to-do family in Fairfield, Connecticut. He went for a time to Suffield Academy, in Connecticut, where he is remembered (by a faculty member) as "a renegade of tremendous aggressive energy—really into the music of the time. He baked his hash in those little ovens, you know. He was into philosophy, as I recall. He left of his own accord." Cheryl is dark and slight, and also from Connecticut. Edwards is of middle height, strong, with missing teeth, and a golden ponytail flying behind. They are well dug in. They have a good cabin, a log sauna, and impressive caches, impressively filled. "I couldn't ask for any more out of life," he says. "I don't care if there's a life after life. I'm having an awful good time in this one."

From Eagle, Circle, Central—the communities of the country—the river people are watched with absorption, not to mention awe and envy, admiration, contempt, and fear. They are widely looked upon with high esteem, and the reverse, too, since almost no one in the country is shy to put the slam on any being that heaves into sight, let alone the people of the river. That is to say, some who would not advance a toe into the wilderness will travel any distance by tongue.

"Alaska was one of the few places left where you could do this sort of thing. There is room enough in Alaska. What harm have they done to the country? They trap a little. They put up fish. They're not hurting anything."

"They're a generation too late."

"They are unrealistic romanticists, and some are just plain stupid. They are devoid of values—materialistic, selfish people. We are constituents of a society grounded in law. They flout the law to live their romantic life style. They harvest moose, bear, fish—whatever they can get their hands on that they can fit into a pot—without regard for seasons or for sex, or for the law. Anything that walks, crawls, flies, or swims is fair game to them. They are interlopers. Every time they kill a moose or bear and toss it into the pot to feed their dogs, they deprive me of the opportunity to see that moose or bear. When I see something, I leave it to the person after me to see. Frankly, it just tees me off. I consider them to be a goddamned curse."

"They're a public nuisance."

"English common law used the term 'public nuisance' to refer to, for example, a slaughterhouse upwind. The people had the right to abate such a public nuisance. These people on the river are not a public nuisance. Hell, no. If I were twenty-one, I'd build there, and if the United States marshal came after me I would kill him. People should not have to live in ghettolike shacks they can control you in. The prime urge of all life is for an exclusive domain. Each human being needs that. These kids are trying to get away to a place of their own."

"I've got a .357 Magnum. If someone tried to kick me out of my cabin, there'd be a murder in defense of my home. Instead of landing in that helicopter and driving Brad Snow off his place, the government should have given him patent to five acres of land and said, 'You've done a good job. You're not a god-damned parasite living on others.' "

"That helicopter. If I was Snow, I'd have set her afire."

"These river people couldn't make it if it weren't for the present accident of the high price of fur. Some hapless lynx comes along and stumbles into their trap. The three hundred dollars you can get from a lynx is what is keeping them alive."

"I can't stand them—they're so sociable."

"I don't believe—and I don't think any other Indian believes—that these young people down the river are harming anyone. But I don't believe they have a right to be there. They don't own the land. Really, they got no home. They got nothing. They live pretty tough. They learn fast, but I don't think they are as well prepared as older pioneers. One man up in the Seventymile last winter lost his toes. He got caught in overflow."

"They come and they go. It takes a peculiar type person to live in this country. The winter usually weeds them out."

"Several who came in last spring went out again in the fall, satisfied in their own minds that this is no country for them, and we are of the same opinion," wrote Gordon Bettles the better part of a century ago. "When we old prospectors jump off, there won't be any tough fellows to go in there and go through the hardships we went through. There's a future in Alaska for the young man with the right kind of stuff."

"A blue column of smoke, faintly rising from the spruces of some lonely gulch, guides one to the lonely camp of some pioneer who has been in Alaska since the first discovery of gold," said a United States government bulletin describing this country in 1905. "Over a cup of coffee, prepared in an old baking powder can, one is made to understand the important part these men have played in the development of this portion of our possessions and their reasons for having learned to call it home . . . men who have labored hard in a quiet way to satisfy the craving for individual independence and have gained through hardship something that is worthwhile even if their hopes are not yet realized."

❲ Dick Cook, in his generosity, lifts from his plate a small gob of muskrat fat and gives it to me. The fat is savory, a delicacy. The lean of the "rat" could be taken for dark, strong chicken.

He is saying, "There's a pride to doing something other people can't do. My life style is what so many people dream about. What they don't dream is that it took six or eight years of hard work to get it. A lot of these people who keep coming into the country don't belong here. They have fallen in love with a calendar photo and they want to live under a beautiful mountain. When they arrive, the reality doesn't match the dream. It's too much for them. They don't want to work hard enough; they don't want to spread out—to go far enough up the streams. This is relatively poor trapping country. You need a twenty-mile radius. But they won't move away from the Yukon. My cabin is the farthest off the river. Have another cup of tea."

Tea strong enough to blacken tin. Hanging over the campfire is a No. 10 can, coated with carbon from the fire, and even blacker within, its bottom a swamp of leaves. To use his own term for what he is doing here, Cook is on vacation. In cool spring weather toward the end of ducks, we are close by three lakes near the Yukon, far downriver from Eagle. He is here to hunt. The vacation is from the weight of tasks at home, which is ten miles away. His shelter is only his orange canvas tarp, one side strung between spruce, the opposite staked in the sphagnum. He finishes his duck-and-muskrat stew, and stretches out under the tarp, head propped up, taking his ease. He remarks that Nessmuk could not stand the confinement of an A-shaped or wall-sided tent and neither can he.

Cook's knowledge of wood lore is encyclopedic. Impromptu,

he can, and readily will, give a thirty-minute lecture on just
about any aspect of it from wolf dens to whetstones, so it is no
surprise—except in a geographical way, far off in the Alaskan
bush—to hear him invoke the pen name of the nineteenth-
century Eastern writer George Sears, called Nessmuk, whose
"Woodcraft," published in 1884, was the first American book
on forest camping, and is written with so much wisdom, wit,
and insight that it makes Henry David Thoreau seem alien,
humorless, and French. Donna Kneeland is beside the fire, her
legs folded straight beneath her. She adds wood. She is attempting to dry, possibly repair, a boot that has a two-inch rip
near the sole. A parabola of wire crosses the top of the No. 10
can. She lifts it. With a short stick in her other hand, she tilts
the bottom, pouring tea into my cup. I welcome it, to defray
the chill, which neither Dick nor Donna seems to notice.
Staked out in the woods around us are seven sled dogs. They,
too, are on holiday.

When new people come in, Cook continues, he recom-
mends that they rent a cabin in or near Eagle, somewhere close
to civilization, and spend a winter there first—with the wilderness a quarter of a mile away. "That leaves some unburned
bridges. Try trapping, hunting meat, getting some skills together—setting yourself up. Money will not accomplish it, but
money is important. You need axes, splitting mauls, rifles, saws,
winter clothing. The average person brings—or buys within a
couple of years—at least ten thousand dollars' worth of gear.
It helps to have a truck at the post-office town. A small boat
with a kicker costs twelve hundred dollars. Bring a two-year
supply of food. You won't learn enough in a year."

Donna, looking up from her boot, says, "Steve Ulvi, when
he was here last week, wanted to know what traps to buy, and
he—"

"He asked a lot of things, but that is his business," Cook
says, with such sharpness that Donna falls silent.

"Why do people live in Eagle?" I ask him.

"I don't know," he says. "I've always wondered. Some of

them came with the intention of going on into the bush and have never carried it out. One person in Eagle has tried three times. But a lot of people come with a desire not to work— just to be there and not to work. I've never understood that. The country and the weather are too hard just to sit."

He draws an analogy between what he has done and what the early Western settlers did. They dug makeshift houses into the dirt while concentrating on the clearing of fields and the construction of barns. That was the way settlement had to take place. "If you built a nice house first, your livestock would die." Dogs, in Cook's case, were his livestock, so fishnets came first. Then he planted a garden. Then he set traplines. He learned sleds and mushing from Indians. "There were several of the old ones around who knew what they were doing and were still sober enough to talk about it." He has continued to learn, he says, just by observing other people along the river. "Charlie Edwards *does* things. I sit and think them out. I've learned more from his mistakes than I've learned from my own. I feel at home now, after twelve years—at home on water, in the woods, in summer, in winter. I feel a part of what is here. The bush is so far beyond what anybody has been taught. The religious power here is beyond all training. There are forces here that a lot of people don't know exist."

"What are they?"

"They can't be articulated. You're out of the realm of words. You are close to the land here, to nature, to what the Indians called Mother and I call Momma. Momma decides everything. The concept is still here, but the Indians have given it up. They say the Indians now have rights to land in which to do their subsistence hunting and trapping. That is ridiculous. It is about time the whites got it equally. There is just no land, no legal place to go, in Alaska. If they wipe out the white people who are living in the bush, they wipe out the native culture."

He shifts his weight, and for a moment I can see his arm. There is a chamois-cloth shirt under his cotton pullover, but both are so shredded and rent with holes that the arm is visible

behind its curtain of rags. The skin is as white as paper. A skull
and crossbones is tattooed there. A dagger sunk into the skull
from above protrudes from the chin like an iron Vandyke. It
is flanked by the letters US and MC. "I grew up in Lyndhurst,
Ohio. My father was in the commercial-industrial air-condi-
tioning business. I helped pay my bills at the Colorado School
of Mines by going into the mountains with dynamite, blasting
open pegmatite dikes and selling the crystals. Students then all
had dynamite in the trunks of their cars—like nowadays they
all wear Vibram soles and carry sheath knives." Cook's first
wife was a model. She left him, and for a time he looked after
his two infant children. When she divorced him, he lost in
court a case for custody. "Since then, I have never understood
trees," he says. "They put down roots." He has not seen his
children in a great many years. One is eighteen, and has a child
of her own.

There is a small, square-ended aluminum boat—dragged in
here over riverine muskeg and rammed through hells of willow.
In it now is an armory of guns, one of which belonged to Dick's
father and grandfather. The lakes are small. Quietly, we paddle
across one of them, leave the boat, and creep through the
woods. We avoid a mound of bear scat—fairly, but not acutely,
fresh. It glistens but has stopped smoking. Approaching the
shore of the next lake, Dick motions us to get down, and we
crawl toward the water without damaging the silence. The
forest cover extends to the edge. We lie there, behind trees,
looking out. Dick lifts a shotgun. In the beginnings of the
twilight, a pair of loons are cruising. They are beyond range.
Their heads are up. Their bodies float high. They sense no
danger. Their course is obliquely toward the gun. Now we can
distinguish the black-and-white shingling on their necks. Silently swimming, they come nearer still. Loons. They are quick.
Diving, they can suddenly be gone. He fires. He fires again.
The loons elect to sprint down the surface—cacophonous,
flailing—their splayfeet spading the water. A pellet or two may
have touched them, but it seems unlikely.

Dick hands one of the guns to Donna and says that he is going to skirt the lake. If the loons return, she is to fire. Silently, he is gone. We hear nothing of his movements among the trees. He is gone an hour. Donna, whispering, asks me if I know much about this gun.

"Nothing," I tell her.

"Nothing?"

"Nothing."

"Neither do I. Those loons will have to come pretty close before I'll try to hit them."

A single loon now tests that distance. It comes swimming around a peninsula of sedge and adopts a path that leads directly toward the muzzle of the gun. Serene in its ignorance, it glides steadily onward without even a slight change of course until, with the distance nearly closed, its breast seems a yard wide. Still it has not seen us. The gun is aimed and ready. If the bird swims any farther, it will hit the shore. Donna blasts. The loon's move is too quick to be called a dive. It is a complete and instant disappearance. There is no commotion, no blood in the water, no loon.

We whisper through the time. At length, more shots ring out, down the lake. It is the sound of Cook, missing. Eventually, he comes back. We now try another lake—creeping the final dozen yards through the forest to its shore. "Wait here," Cook says, and he leaves the .22. "Kill a rat if one goes by." Meanwhile, he will circle the shoreline. This lake has rats for sure, and there—he points to a far cove and a barely visible line of darning-egg heads—are ducks. In the unending twilight, another hour passes. At various distances and times, we hear half a dozen sharp reports. "You can be active in a job in town, but it doesn't seem as important," Donna whispers. "Here the important thing is—well, getting your meat." She mentions that she was a stewardess once for Reeve Aleutian. A muskrat rounds a clump of sedge, swimming before us, left to right. Donna follows it with the rifle and fires. The water jumps a foot. We cannot see the spent bullet, sinking like a pebble toward the bottom of the lake, but the muskrat probably can. There was something she particularly liked about Reeve Aleutian. The airline was always ready to ignore its schedules and serve as an emergency ambulance service for the entire island chain. And so the work was, as she phrases it, "more interesting than just coffee, tea, or me." Winds blew seventy miles an hour over the islands sometimes. A DC-3 would try to touch on a runway and have trouble setting down because its wings wished to stay in the air. In an Electra once, she was approaching Adak, winds in the seventies. Suddenly the turbulence increased and the Electra overturned. It was not just steeply banked—it was flying upside down. Donna noted with interest the silence of the passengers. She had thought that in such a situation people would scream. Objects fell to the ceiling. Toilets spilled. The plane crossed the island, and slowly rolled upright. Its second approach was successful. On the ground, after thanking the passengers for flying Reeve and wishing them a pleasant stay on Adak, Donna suggested to the other stewardess that they have a drink. "That is the only time in my life I have ever done that," she whispers now—"taken a drink, you know, in order to relax." Intense firing breaks out far down the shore, a Boone and Crockett sonata. When Cook appears again beside us, he has nothing in hand and nothing to retrieve. He says, "One trouble with this type of life is you can go hungry when you screw up." This is true in two ways, for cartridges cost a few cents apiece and shotgun shells a quarter. In effect, he has been firing grocery money into the lake. We return to the sled dogs and the lean-to, but soon Cook, frustrated, says, "If we don't get something, we're not going to eat," and, cursing Momma, he takes off once more, for a final walking circuit of the shore.

By the fire, Donna sews a patch on a pair of Dick's trousers, and remarks to me that for an Easterner I seem to be surprisingly dressed, in that my boots and vest and general gear are the sorts of things she associates with Alaska. I explain to her about the Wild East, and how I like to go out when I can, and that I always have. "But I'll tell you the difference, Donna. The difference is that pile of bear sign back there, and the absence of trails, and . . ." My thoughts race ahead of what I am trying to say. The difference is also in the winter silence, a silence that can be as wide as the country, and the dreamy, sifting slowness of the descent of the dry snow. If there were only twenty-five people in the state of New Jersey, they would then sense the paramount difference, which is in the unpeopled reach of this country. I may have liked places that are wild and been quickened all my days just by the sound of the word, but I see now I never knew what it could mean. I can see why people who come to Alaska are unprepared. In four decades of times beyond some sort of road, I never set foot in a place like this. It is in no way an extension of what I've known before. The constructions I have lived by ought not, and do not, apply here. Left on my own here, I would have to change in a hurry, and learn in a hurry, or I'd never last a year.

For a time, the only sound is the fire. The dogs are asleep. There's no wind. The forest is as quiet as it was, a month before, under snow. Donna tightens the thread. She says, finally, "I know what you mean. When I first came out here, I felt the same way. I saw what it was like and I thought, I'll never survive."

What would she do in a medical emergency, like a simple case of appendicitis?

"I hope this doesn't sound corny," she answers, "but things are living and dying out here all the time. If I got appendicitis, I would just die."

Cook, in half an hour's absence, fires one shot. When he comes back, he drops a muskrat on the ground with a hole above its ear. Donna says, "They're hard to skin when they've been shot in the head." She skins it out neatly, and covers the pelt with salt. The inner rat goes into the pot.

We roll out our sleeping bags side by side, remove our boots, settle in. I have before now lacked the courage to reach into my pack and take out a thing for which I feel a great need.

Antithetical forces are in strife within me. What I want is my pillow. Its capacity to soften the coming sleep is perhaps not as great as its capacity to humiliate me before these rugged pioneers. Shame at last loses out to comfort. My hand goes into the pack. The pillow is small and white. The slip is homemade, with snaps at one end, so that it can contain a down jacket, which it does. I mumble an explanation of this, saying that nonetheless I feel a touch ridiculous—in their company, in this country—reaching into my gear for a pillow.

"Don't apologize," says Cook, getting up on one elbow to admire the pillow. "As Nessmuk said, we're not out here to rough it. We're here to smooth it. Things are rough enough in town."

◖ Rich Corazza came into the country in 1974. In Wyoming and Colorado, he had worked in the open, and the attraction held for him by the upper Yukon was unarguably succinct: "There ain't no barbed wire up here." Trapping in winter, gold-mining in summer—he would try whatever the country might offer, but not to take and go. He did not seek a living so much as a life. He was twenty-three, and he was in love with a woman named Sara, but she was thousands of miles away—outside—and, while he fervently hoped she would join him, she was, for the time being, less appealing than the Yukon. In the fall of 1975, he learned of a cabin where he might spend the approaching winter. It had been built by Sarge Waller, who had used it one winter and decided not to do so again. Waller's cabin is just upstream of where the Kandik River, coming in from Canada, gives itself up to the Yukon. Corazza would be alone there, but he would not be entirely without neighbors. There were three occupied cabins within a quarter of a million surrounding acres.

After hitching a boat ride or two, he finished his journey on foot. Walking upriver, he came to the Kandik on the seventh of October, late in the day. The Kandik surprised him—too big and fast to ford. So he slept where he was, his dog, Molly, beside him. When he woke, his bag was covered with an inch of snow. He built a raft and crossed the river.

For several months, he kept company with a journal, written on loose sheets of ruled yellow paper.

> *Thursday, Oct 9 . . . Seen a white weazel right outside the cabin, his nest is in the dog house. Plan to cut wood tomorrow, seems like Molly and I are just waiting for winter. Things are pretty well straightened up at the cabin and damn it sure feels like home. Wish we had a moose! Good night, Sara.*

The writing atrophied when perhaps he felt even more at home. The seasons changed, and he went elsewhere in the country to mine gold. Behind him he left only two signs of his occupancy: beaver castors hanging from a beam, and, up on one wall, the record of his novice days.

> *Friday, Oct 10 . . . I have 3 Swede saws here and the biggest works the best, it is a 5 footer. After a hardy breakfast, I will now attempt to secure the winter's wood.*

One day in June, I stopped in at the cabin, on my way by canoe downriver. The mouth of the Kandik is roughly halfway between Eagle and Circle, the upper and lower gateways of the country. The mountainous land between them comes to an end with a final bluff near Circle. Beyond that bluff is another world, an almost oceanic peneplain known as the Yukon Flats. Brad Snow had never been near this natural boundary, and was interested in expanding his knowledge of the river. He had the canoe. For my part, I was on my way to a lengthy visit with Ed and Virginia Gelvin, in Central, and with miners of the Birch Creek district, and was only too pleased to be able to make the journey in Snow's nineteen-foot Grumman freighter. We left Eagle in what was locally termed a heat wave—seventy degrees. Steve Casto, standing on the high bank watching us go, said it was too hot a day to drink coffee.

> . . . *Sure is nice to come into a warm cabin. As Sally once wrote, "It's never too cold to cut wood when you're out of fire."*

> *Saturday, Oct 11 . . . Just a skiff of snow on the ground, the Yukon isn't flowing ice yet, but I think maybe she will shortly. Driftwood really burns good and there is a load of it about 100 yards from the cabin. It's rough cutting but I'll get after it today. Good morning, Sara!*

> *Sunday, Oct 12. Cut wood & hauled it for 5 hours yesterday, good thing too on account that the ground is white this morning and still snowing, good day to set by the stove. 37° and windy on the Yukon.*
> *Didn't get much accomplished today. It snowed off and on again, dropped to about 30° and is hanging there. I went hunting near a lake about a mile from here. No sign of anything except squirrel, of which I shot one and boiled it up for Molly, she's looking awful thin. It would be nice to throw her a moose bone (me too).*

Just as the country ends with an isolated bluff, it was thought once to begin with one—a high, mansarded prominence that looms above Eagle. When Lieutenant Frederick Schwatka, U.S. Army, was sent to look over the area in 1883, he was instructed to determine, roughly, where the Yukon came into Alaska. Rafting hundreds of miles through Canadian mountains down the giant bending river, he noted shifts in its direction, guessed distances, guessed current velocities, ran the data through his mind, and what is now named Eagle Bluff he called Boundary Butte. It was some guess—like a sailor's fixing his position by the feel of it—for the hundred-and-forty-first (boundary) meridian was scarcely twelve miles upstream, and, by air line, six miles away. William Ogilvie, sent by Ottawa, surveyed the border four years later. Eagle, Alaska, looking east from a bend in the river, has all before it a sweep of boundary ridgelines, and behind them rise the Ogilvie Mountains, Yukon Territory. The international boundary is now absurdly shaved. Trees are levelled and brush kept cut in a thirty-foot swath.

> *Monday, Oct 13. 28° and wintery at 8 this morning. My wood supply looks meager for the weeks of cold weather ahead. (So does my meat supply.) Keeps me on the ball.*

When Brad Snow's canoe went out past Eagle Bluff, the buildings of the town diminished behind until the white ones looked like dentils against the pale green of birch and aspen that were just coming into their leaves. There were blocks of shelf ice still along the shore. Belle Isle, in the river at Eagle, was a dark loaf of spruce. American Summit, the southern backdrop, and the Ogilvies, to the east, were dusted white. I was wearing a T-shirt in the bright June sun, but I soon put on a sweater. The temperature of the river was forty-six, and the air close above it was cool. Six miles downstream, I had added a down vest, a 60/40 windbreaker, and a rain suit, hood to heel. Brad Snow was in a rain suit, too. We were driving into a head-on squall, and there were whitecaps on the river. Another bend and there was sun again; another bend, more rain.

> *. . . Met Harold today, he is Fred's partner. They're pretty much "hippies" it seems to me but real nice fellas. Found out he is the one who came down on the raft with all the supplies for he and his new found gal from Kentucky. Strange world, but I remember the time I resorted to offering a gal life in the woods. How can an adventurous young thing resist?*

Some of the people who live together in remote settings along the river refer to themselves not as couples but as units. It happens at times that two half-its will decide to form a new unit. Or one might go out to Fairbanks and come back with someone new. The country is not without its citadels of right-eousness, wherein certain burghers seem to look with disdain upon what they refer to as "river people's morals." They have possibly forgotten that this river is not the St. Mary, the Ste. Anne, the St. Croix, and does not flow uphill or in any sense suggest detachment from the functions of the earth. In their disdain, they overlook tradition. Beside the Yukon, a young woman of indisputable appeal once presented herself to a sa-loonful of miners and auctioned herself to the highest bidder. She offered fair terms. If she were to back out at any time within six months, he would get a complete refund. If he backed out, she would keep the money. All right, now, get up your pokes, boys. Who's the first bidder? There were bidders enough, and she brought down the gavel for a pretty sum. So far as is known, she stayed with the winner forever.

When people seeking gold first came across the high south-eastern passes to the headwater lakes of the river, they hewed boats out of the forest and took them down the Yukon in small, inexperienced navies. One young wife fell out of a boat and appeared on her way to drowning. She thrashed and bobbed and went under at least twice, while her husband anxiously watched. At length, another man in another boat saved her. When her husband rowed over to pick her up, she demanded instead her duffel. Then and there, she formed a new unit.

Tuesday, Oct 14. 21°... Walked through the spruce and hit the Kandik about 1 1/2 miles up. It's pretty well froze in places. A guy couldn't even line a canoe up for the ice. ... Still no ice on the Yukon ... I only been wearing longhandles and a wool shirt and I've been sweating at times.

Wednesday, Oct 15. 28°. Sunny. Prettyful.

Thursday, October 16. Fred came down yesterday, left a dog here overnight, and said that some people on the river will be meeting for the spring equinox at Nation (the old Taylor place).

Sun. Oct 19 . . . Beaver is one of the best tasting meats I've ever had—fatty and kinda naturally sweet. I got the castors and am soaking the oil glands in water for scent.

Sun Oct 26. 20°. Windy. Still snowing. About 6–8 inches on the level. This morning big sheets of ice were flowing on the sides of the river, and by now (11:45 A.M.) there is ICE all the way ACROST. BIG sheets 40–50 ft long and they just keep packin' together, fusing to the sides (banks) or just keep flowing downstream, quite a site.

Brad Snow said that if the canoe were to tip over, it would have to be abandoned, because the river, even now, in June, was too cold to allow the usual procedure of staying with the boat and kicking it to shore. "Keep your clothes on in the river. They provide some insulation, and you will need them later on. It's a good idea to have some matches tucked away in a dry container. We would need a drying fire." With luck, and fair probability, the canoe would go into an eddy, he said, and might be recovered there.

Nothing much was going to turn us over, though. Only at one or two points in a hundred and sixty miles did we see anything that remotely suggested rapids, and these were mere drapefolds of white in the otherwise broad, flat river. Sleepers were in the water—big logs flushing down out of Canada and floating beneath the surface—but they were going in our direction and were much less dangerous than they would have been had we been heading upstream. The great power of the Yukon —six and more fathoms of water, sometimes half a mile wide, moving at seven knots—was unostentatiously displayed. The surface was deceptively calm—it was only when you looked to the side that you saw how fast you were flying.

From the hull, meanwhile, came the steady sound of sandpaper, of sliding stones, of rain on a metal roof—the sound of the rock in the river, put there by alpine glaciers. Dip a cupful of water and the powdered rock settled quickly to the bottom. At the height of the melting season, something near two hundred tons of solid material will flow past a given point on the riverbank in one minute. Bubbling boils, like the tops of high fountains, bloomed everywhere on the surface but did not rough it up enough to make any sort of threat to the canoe. They stemmed from the crash of fast water on boulders and ledges far below. Bend to bend, the river presented itself in large segments—two, three, six miles at a stretch, now smooth, now capped white under the nervously changeable sky. We picked our way through flights of wooded islands. We shivered in the deep shadows of bluffs a thousand feet high—Calico Bluff, Montauk Bluff, Biederman Bluff, Takoma Bluff—which day after day intermittently walled the river. Between them— in downpourings of sunshine, as often as not—long vistas reached back across spruce-forested hills to the rough gray faces and freshly whitened summits of mountains. Some of the walls of the bluffs were of dark igneous rock that had cracked into bricks and appeared to have been set there by masons. Calico Bluff—a sedimentary fudge, folded, convoluted in whorls and ampersands—was black and white and yellow-tan. Up close it smelled of oil. It was sombre as we passed it, standing in its own shadow. Peregrine falcons nest there, and—fantastic fliers— will come over the Yukon at ballistic speeds, clench their talons, tuck them in, and strike a flying duck hard enough (in the neck) to kill it in midair. End over end the duck falls, and the falcon catches it before it hits the river. As we passed the mouth of the Tatonduk, fifteen ducks flew directly over us. Brad Snow reached for his shotgun, and quickly fired twice.

Fifteen ducks went up the Tatonduk. Above the Nation, steep burgundy mountainsides reached up from the bright-green edges of the river, then fell away before tiers of higher mountains, dark with spruce and pale with aspen, quilted with sunlight and shadow. Ahead, long points of land and descending ridgelines reached toward one another into the immensity of the river, roughed now under a stiff wind. Filmy downspouts dropped from the clouds. Behind the next bend, five miles away, a mountain was partly covered with sliding mist. The scene resembled Lake Maggiore and might have been the Hardanger Fjord, but it was just a fragment of this river, an emphatic implication of all the two thousand miles, and of the dozens of tributaries that in themselves were major rivers—proof and reminder that with its rampart bluffs and circumvallate mountains it was not only a great river of the far northwestern continent but a river of preëminence among the rivers of the world. The ring of its name gave nothing away to the name of any river. Sunlight was bright on the mountains to both sides, and a driving summer rain came up the middle. The wind tore up the waves and flung pieces of them through the air. It was not the wind, though, but the river itself that took the breath away.

Mon Oct 27. Good morning, Sara! 6°. . . The water froze in the water buckets and I slept good. . . . The river is really flowin' a lot of ice, but it is still moving—ripping and tearing at the shelf ice on the banks.

Wed Oct 29. —20° this morning, clear as a church bell and feels good. Got a ruffed grouse and a squirrel yesterday, also set some rabbit snares.

Rain gone, and in sun again we could hear the consumption of an island. Large pieces of the bank fell thunderously into the water, because the Yukon had decided to yaw. We passed a deep fresh indentation in the shore where a dozen tall spruce had plopped at once. They were sixty-foot trees, and so much of the ground that held them had fallen with them that they now stood almost vertically in thirty feet of river. Ordinarily, as a river works its way into cut-bank soil the trees of the bank gradually lose their balance and become "sweepers"—their trunks slanting downward, their branches spread into the water. The islands of the Yukon have so many sweepers that from a distance they look like triremes. The river roars through the crowns of the trees with a sound of heavy rapids.

Fri Oct 31. −32° & clear. Thank God for wood!

Sat Nov 1. −33°. It sure got to cracking and buckin' last night. She is really still out this morning. It took 8 days to freeze since the ice started flowing. The Yukon is froze solid.

Often, after the general freeze-up, there is a lead in the left-bank bend beside Eagle—the current keeping open a patch of river long after the rest is ice. It can stay open for more than two months. A cold snap—reaching, say, seventy below zero—will finally close it.

Barney Hansen, who came into the country fifty years ago to mine gold, says he once watched a file of thirteen caribou pick their way down Eagle Bluff to drown in the river lead. The bluff approaches sheer, and its face is rough with crags and ledges and plunging tight ravines. Slowly, surely, the thirteen creatures descended, almost every move a feat of balance and decision. Poised there, each avoiding a fall to destruction, they gave Hansen and whoever else may have been watching plenty of time to wonder why they had chosen that route. They could readily have swung wide of both the town and the bluff. Finally, they reached the ice and started across the river. Everywhere around the lead, the ice was solid to the farther shore. Yet the thirteen caribou one after another jumped into the open water. The current drew them to the downstream end, where it sucked them under the ice.

In May, when big floes begin to move downriver like ships, caribou have been observed upon them. Caught crossing the river when the ice moved, they now stand in huddled helplessness, riding to certain death as the support beneath them crashes, cracks, diminishes in size, and ultimately rolls over.

> *Sun Nov. 2. −35°. . . . Beautiful, clear day. Still no moose sign. Lots of overflow on the Yukon. I set out some traps and snares tonight, feels good to be runnin through the woods lookin for them little critters.*

> *Mon Nov 3. −38°. Still and clear.*

> *Wed Nov 5. −31°, still clear and I still love Sara a bunch. Today is woodchoppin day, so I et 3 lbs. of taters, a pound of spam, and a gallon of coffee. I'm not full, but it'll have to do.*

> *Thur Nov 6. −30 . . . Seen a fresh cat track today where the lynx had bedded down right beside a rabbit run. Twice he had picked himself a good spot to lay in readiness for a meal.*

> *Sun Nov 9. −24°. Reset some traps. Got a lynx comin to one of 'em. Put some squirrels in a couple for marten bait. Did a lot of snowshoeing & breakin trail and am tuckered out.*

> *Mon Nov 10. −12° cloudy and may snow. Today is the anniversary of being in Alaska for exactly one year now. Quite a lot has happened and if I had Sara now it would be the end of a near perfect year. Still, it was the best decision I ever did make, and am very glad things worked out. If I was religious, I might say, "Thank you, Lord." Amen.*

Approaching the mouth of the Kandik, Snow and I maneuvered among shoals and heavy driftwood in an attempt to get

to shore, going in for an assessive look at our friend Sarge
Waller's cabin. We went up the bank. Snow gave the cabin a
long, professional sniff—a construction worker's frank inspection. "This," he said finally—and paused a moment to mortise
the words—"this is the most poorly built cabin you ever will
see." The walls were convex. The foundation was not banked.
The roof was virtually without insulation. The corners were
mail slots for the wind. The loose sheets of Corazza's journal
were held by a metal clip hanging on a wall. I took them down
and riffled through them.

The journal was roughly four thousand words. (Only fragments are here.) The author's name was nowhere on it so far
as I could see. It had been left in an empty cabin, in near-
absolute wilderness, on land that belonged to the people of the
United States, of whom I was one. If ever a piece of writing
was born in the public domain, surely this was it. Yes—but it
seemed private. It wasn't like food in a cache, to take and later
replace. I returned it to the wall.

A few weeks later, I was sitting in the roadhouse in Central
talking with a man who was down from the mining claims on
Porcupine Creek. He was young, dark-haired, strongly built.
Like most bush Alaskans, however new to the bush they might
be, he had greeting in his face. In the course of a second beer,
he mentioned that he had spent the winter in a cabin near the
mouth of the Kandik.

I surprised him by telling him I had glanced at his journal,
and had wished I could someday read it. He said he had a little
time off and had been thinking of going up there anyway; he
would see me again in a few days. He went eighty miles up the
river and brought back the journal.

> *Wed Nov 12. —3° cloudy & snowing. Molly of the North,
> great Alaskan cat hound, says she likes this turn in the
> weather. She has put on considerable weight and looks real
> strong.*

Saw a gyrfalcon today. Flew right over my head clippin along at a pace so fast it sounded like a jet. Almost white bird. Could have been a female, it was pretty good size. Also saw a bird killed hare yesterday near the cabin. Bet it's that gyr's meal. This country is neat.

We carried mail with us downriver, and now and again Brad would, in effect, toss it into the woods. There were people in there who would read it. The names on the packages and envelopes were not familiar to me. Snow said, "There are those on the river who are discreet and those who are not. People like Dick Cook and Charlie Edwards need to talk and be chatty in Eagle. Others come into town rarely, say nothing much, and leave."

We stopped one morning in a hidden slough with letters for Jan Waldron. She was slender, lankily built, with long blond hair, a quick and friendly smile. She ran down the bank and fairly jumped into the canoe. "Gosh, it's so good to see you." Her husband, Seymour Abel, had been away many days. Their home was a wall tent on supporting courses of logs, with a door that was more like a window. We crawled in. She and Seymour were just camping in this tent, she explained, and opened some beer she had brewed there. She pointed proudly to a cavity in the earth at her feet. To surprise and please Seymour, she had passed the time removing a stump. I remembered meeting Seymour, briefly, in Eagle, where we had talked about bears, and the pros and cons of carrying a protective gun. "If you're going to get et, you're going to get et," he had said, conclusively, and, repeating himself, "If you're going to get et, you're going to get et, whether you have a rifle or not." Seymour came into the country from Tennessee. Jan is a born Alaskan. "I'm so glad to see you," she said again, and opened another beer. The top of the tent was lined with Styrofoam. In the gable was a shelf of books. There was a plank table, a Singer sewing

machine, a banjo, a guitar, a violin. There was a barrel stove.
The chimney, where it poked through the tent, was flashed
with a two-gallon can. Dark-haired sled dogs were staked outside. A day or so before, they had raised a great clamor. To Jan,
it signalled the nearness of a bear. Carrying clothes for washing
to a small clear stream, she took along a gun because of the
bear. "Are you sure you have to go?" she said as we stood up.
"It's so good to see you. Why go?"

Around the turn of the century, when dog teams travelled
more frequently on the river, there was an isolated roadhouse
not far from where Jan lives now. The woman who ran it would
shoot at people who tried to go by without stopping.

*Fri Nov 14. −28°. Clear. I have become pretty well used
to the cold now and can get a roarin fire going awful quick
these days. Caught a hare and one beautiful red fox today.
The fox had been caught in a trail-set about a mile from where
I crossed his tracks. She had broken the wire I had tied to the
trap chain. I followed her to the river and then ran up to
within shooting distance. She was moving pretty good with
a #3 double spring on her front paw. I shot her right below
the eye at 100 ft. with the pistol (Ruger). She sure is pretty
and would make Sara a nice hat.*

*Sun Nov 16. Full moon, and the Yukon is in party dress.
Everything is lit up just prettiful. . . . I jumped a bunch of
grouse (ruffed) roosting. Got 5 with the pistol and about 18
shots. Could have got more but I run plumb out of shells. I
sure do love that grouse meat.*

*The moon cycle is funny up here. It starts waxing in a small
arc through the southern sky, then day by day it gets brighter
and the arc gets higher and longer till it's full moon almost
overhead and stay light all night. Just magnificent!*

*2 of them grouse I got at 40 yds with that little Ruger
(makes a guy proud). Wish Sara would fix em up for us.*

We passed fish camps all down the river, for the most part established by Indians and abandoned now—places that once netted as much as thirty tons of salmon a year. At one fish camp stood the biggest cache I have seen in Alaska, virtually a full-size cabin in the air, resting on columnar stilts. All it contained was a beaver's forepaw.

Tues Nov 18. −22°. The other day when I got them grouse, a funny thing happened. The last grouse was perched in the top of an alder about 30 ft high. I shot at it twice from about 35 yds and thought I'd missed it. But it stayed up there. I snuck up to about 20 yds from it and emptied the pistol. It still sat there. It was gettin dark and I was out of shells. I figured that that grouse wouldn't be a meal for me. Then all of a sudden I got MAD, went over to the tree, shook it, and yelled, "Get outa there you son of a bitch." Well, down comes a blanket of snow on my head—but also Mister Grouse, who is only winged. He scooted along the ground for awhile and then just disappeared! By God, he was gone just like that. Then I flashed to a memory that Dad had told me a story of a grouse he had winged and the dog pointed at a bunch of leaves. Finally he seen a feather stickin out of the leaves, took off his hat and caught him a grouse in it. Well, I seen where he last was and used my mitten (it was 20 below and didn't want to take off my hat) to clamp down on the snow and by Jesus if I didn't come up with another supper in my hands. Made me laugh just a bit to think that my anger had been changed so fast into a memory. Had some grouse gumbo last night. Ummm!

The brilliance of this north country under the full moon is dazzling to say the least. At midnight the sky is still a deep blue with the twinkling of many bright stars. Moon shadows of the tall spruce are everywhere and the Yukon River lays quiet and white. This moon seems to stand guard on this country.

There has long been talk of a tourist road connecting Eagle and Circle. Running for the most part beside the river, it would "open up" what is generally regarded as the handsomest stretch of the Yukon in Alaska. The longest piece of road along the Yukon now runs three miles upriver from Eagle to Eagle Indian Village. On the river near that road, I have paddled more than once in dust that was thicker than smoke.

> *Mon Nov 24. −6°. Plan to go upriver.*

> *Tues Nov 25. −4°. On the way up, Bob's lead dog got caught in one of Fred's Conibears. Boy it was a mad scramble for Bob and I to get to the front of 9 dogs and prise the jaws apart on that trap. The dog acted like nothing had ever happened and went right on again. Could have been tragic but it turned out funny. . . . Found out that Thanksgiving is on the 27th. . . . It was fun to run them 9 dogs all strung out single. Bob and I took turns as it was a rough run over the muskeg and the sled was loaded heavy (probably 500 lbs +). It tipped over 5 or 6 times but things went smooth. Both of us were wore plumb out. . . . I fell through the ice 2 or 3 times yesterday, & ran around with wet pacs. Feels like I frosted the ends of my big toes a bit, but they're far from my heart, so I'll keep on truckin.*

We stopped one night at an abandoned cabin, containing so much clutter of junk debris that we decided to sleep outside. Mosquitoes were dense there but tolerable—not yet coming in clouds. In the Yukon Flats, beyond the mountains, were thirty-six thousand lakes and ponds, with geese, canvasbacks, scaup, cranes, swans, teal, and widgeons in millions, and mosquitoes in numbers a physicist would understand. But we were still upriver, and only five or six thousand of them were now close around us. I asked Brad if he would like to share my netted tent. Inside it moments later, he told me how his wife plays what she calls Revenge. In the security of a tent, she places near the netting an example of her flesh until it drives to frenzy the singers in the night. A truly ambitious mosquito will soon thrust its proboscis through the net. She then seizes the proboscis and yanks the bugger inside. For my part, I mentioned that when mosquitoes seek human blood they are fulfilling their sexual cycle, doing what nature is instructing them to do, and therefore an authentic conservationist will never react unfavorably to the attentions of a mosquito. This simple test—a way of telling the phonies from the truly committed—I had first come upon long ago in the Lower Forty-eight. Gradually in Alaska, however, I had come to realize that an Alaska mosquito is not a Lower Forty-eight mosquito that has moved north. Before getting into the tent, I had slapped my leg, turned the palm up, and counted seventeen corpses in my hand.

Sat Dec 13 . . . The weather has been −50 or lower (−60 was the lowest) for 12 days but this morning the wind started blowing and the weather warmed up some 40° to −8. I ran the dogs down across the river to get a load of fish yesterday. Saw fresh moose sign and Errol & I spent all day today hunting. Lots of sign but no luck. I haven't checked my line since the new moon and it's already past half. Tomorrow will be the day. There seems to be more cat around since it got cold.

Sun Dec 21 . . . Errol and I were hunting cause the 2 moose were staying in this area. Errol ran into them and got us both of them, by God! We eatin high nowadays. Moose liver and steak for breakfast. Hmm! We had a real chinook for a few days and the temp went up to 39° above. Couldn't believe it.

Mon Dec. 22. Zero. Oboy! Biscuits gravy & moose steak this fine day. Yepper, sure wish Sara were back home where she belongs.

> *Tues Dec 23. Zero and clear . . . Made a few more cat sets today in the slough. Missed a cat in one of my cubbies.*

A "cat" is a lynx. A "lynk" is also a lynx. Nine times out of ten, people who say "lynk" are trying to sound like trappers.

> *Mon Dec 29. +15° . . . Walked up to 3 Mile today with Molly on a lead rope (she was leading me). We didn't hit a fresh track till after dark on the way back. She struck out on the cat's trail but didn't run it very far, it was in thick alders. She sure wanted to though.*

> *Jan 7. −40. I've had some bad luck. Molly run off about 3 days ago at 25 below. I could hear her howling bloody murder from the cabin here. I'd just got a fire started after a 6 mile hike down river. Well, I figured, she got herself in a trap, so I went to looking for her. Found her 3 hours later, almost to Errol's cabin with her right front paw in a number 4 doublespring. It was frozen solid. My lantern had run out of fuel and there was no moon. We ran to Errol's cabin where I soaked her paw in lukewarm water for about an hour. It swelled plumb up as big as a cat track, but today it started to blister and I think it may heal. The swelling's gone down a bit. Poor ole Molly Blue!*

> *Jan 8. −40. Red is the color of my barrel stove when it's 40 below, when it's 40 below! A bit nippy these last few days, but it's nice to set by a roarin stove.*

Snow and I lingered at the mouths of tributary streams, and went miles up the Charley, the river of Leon Crane. Logs cruised toward us like alligators, and with the same stately glide. We surprised ravens, geese, a bald eagle, which lumbered into flight. It slowly achieved altitude, its wings barely recovering from flap to awkward flap. Peregrines, which nest on bluffs above the Charley, can pin down one of these eagles and keep it where it is indefinitely—the falcons diving, pecking, strafing, dominating, while the symbol of national grandeur cowers on the ground, a screaming eagle. After nine or ten miles, the Charley, with riffles, increased its gradient rise, and the immense, confining forest began to open to big, long-distance views. Far up the corridor of the river were white-patched mountains, and far behind them more and higher mountains totally covered with newly fallen snow. We tied up in an island slough and climbed the steep face of a bluff—loose, flaky shale; no trees; not much to hang on to—and when we had worked our way upward five hundred vertical feet I looked back at what seemed a straight plunge to the river. It was a bluff of swallows and lupine, blueberries and bears. We saw only sign of the bears. Brad was carrying his rifle. He remarked that his friend David Evans, who has been in the country about as long as he has, apparently rejoices in a nearly perfect state of "anestrophic anticipation." Asked to explain what that is, Snow said, "You have no sense of catastrophe. You walk through the valley of the shadow of death and you fear no evil—not because you are fearless but because you have no awareness of what may happen. David walks miles and miles, unarmed, and doesn't seem to understand that there's a chance of being mauled."

We sat down and ate berries, looking up frequently at many hundreds of square miles of dark broadloom forests curling at the edges into rising tundra fells, which ended in mountain rock. Through the mountains came the clear river, often deep within its peregrine bluffs, which were pinpointed white with visible Dall sheep and darkened by invisible bears. It was landscape uncompromised, under small white cumulus by the tens of dozens evenly spaced to the corners of the sky. I remembered Frank Warren, in Circle, talking about the Park Service's yen for the Charley, and saying, "What can you do to improve an area that is perfect? What possible satisfaction could a hiker ever get walking on a man-made trail?" We descended the bluff and descended the stream, stopping at the

cabin built by Al Ames, where the government had posted a
sign beside the door forbidding habitation.

We drifted down the Yukon through a windless afternoon.
The fast-flowing water was placid and—with its ring boils—
resembled antique glass. Down one long straightaway, framed
in white mountains, we saw ten full miles to the wall of the
coming bend.

> *Fri Feb 6. Been traveling this ole Yukon from Sam Creek*
> *(at times to Coal Creek) all the way to 20 miles this side of*
> *Eagle. Not much cat sign anywhere . . . Molly is healed up*
> *pretty good.*

> *Sat Feb. 7. −37° before sunrise, now an hour later it's*
> *−40 and droppin fast, looks like another snapper! Beautiful*
> *light show last night . . . Sara, where are you?*

❲ Stanley Gelvin grew up in the country, and therefore has no
capacity to see it as exotic. He has sampled other worlds, which
have failed to attract him—Fairbanks, mainly, and a visit or
two outside. He has spent most of the nights of his life in
sleeping bags. When he sleeps in a bed with sheets and blankets, he turns, tosses, and flips until the bedding is out of tuck
and is composed in mummy shape around him. While Stanley
was growing up, Central, Alaska, with its population under
twenty, did not offer him a large reserve of playmates. Instead,
he had engines. Getting to know them, he acquired a primary
skill of the country, and now has almost a maker's sense of their
design and function. In mining, hunting, trapping, ice fishing,
he and his family used everything from rasping little two-cycle
chain-saw engines to the turbocharged diesel of the D9 Cat.
They have pumps, generators, airplanes, snow machines, wash-

ing machines, automobiles, pickups—and when you are well over a hundred miles from the corner garage you do not go there to have someone listen to what seems to be wrong. Stanley, in his middle twenties, has never known that sort of dependence. Like his father, Ed Gelvin, he routinely works on the pumps, the saws, the cars, the planes. "Living in the bush, you have to," he says. "I don't know anything different. You just have to be a good mechanic. You have to modify machinery until you get the imperfections out. I never found nothing I couldn't fix."

From early youth onward, Stanley's gold fever has been chronic, running along steadily a few degrees above normal. As a child, he made little rocker boxes and took them out to Deadwood Creek to separate from its gravels its cereal flakes of color. As he moved through the boxes small heaps of pebbles and sand, the point was not lost on him that a guy could move a whole stream bed with a big machine, and when that day came a guy would have to be able to maintain the machine. For ten dollars, he bought from a neighbor a pre-Second World War Chevrolet. It was long since dead on the road. He sent off for piston rings and gaskets from Sears in Philadelphia. The bearings were babbitted and could not be replaced, so he took out the shims and adjusted them for proper clearance. He was seven years old. He had a book on auto mechanics. He did a valve job. He installed the new gaskets and rings. The engine sat up in its coffin.

Ed and Ginny Gelvin ran the Central roadhouse for a time. To drivers who had made the long trip from Fairbanks up the dusty seasonal road Stanley was generous with alarming advice. "Why don't you turn that bearing over? If you don't, you'll be sorry." A truck driver came in once, hauling supplies to Circle, and before he could fairly sip his coffee he was confronted by this little kid telling him his differential was in bad trouble. "Don't worry about it, son. It always sounds like that," the driver said, departing. Thirty miles up the road, the truck went around a curve, and the wheels tried to turn—as they are wont to on curves—at varying rates of spin. The differential failed to see the difference anymore. The breakdown was complete.

The mining season ordinarily is short. It can be even shorter when a stream remains "glaciered" until the middle of July. A bush Alaskan—miner, trapper, whatever his interests may be —is particularly secure if he carries a union card and can go out part of the year for extra money. Stanley belongs to 302 —the Fairbanks local of the Operating Engineers' union. In Fairbanks, in the cabs of cranes, he sometimes sets steel for ironworkers—an extremely delicate job. "One slip and you can kill someone. You work in fractions of an inch, making bolt holes line up. You're swinging all the time. It's harder to operate equipment than to fly." After growing up on the seats of Cats—plowing snow, skidding logs—he went out to work on the Chandalar Shelf, the Dietrich River, Galbraith Lake, running his first D9s, building the pipeline road. He prefers to be in Central. In 1975, in Greenhorn Gulch, ten miles up a creek from home, he set up a twenty-four-foot wooden sluice box that took in nearly a hundred and fifty dollars' worth of gold in every hour it ran. Unfortunately, it ran only twenty-four hours (an aggregate of short bursts), because water was scarce in the gulch. The experience, however, was anything but discouraging. Thirty-five hundred dollars will fuel a fair amount of living in the bush. With his infant son, Jimmy, and wife, Andrea, who is the daughter of a Fairbanks contractor, Stanley lives in a new cabin on his parents' property. He would have liked to build somewhere else, off in the hills or out near the Yukon, in an unneighbored place he could call his own, but, in the vastness of all the surrounding country, land was not available. That, for Stanley, has been a bewildering disappointment. When he was born, in 1950, the country was open and free. Expectations were that when he grew up he could live where he pleased. Then Alaska became a state. Oil was discovered. Homesteading ended. In the great reapportionment of Alaskan land, the squares seemed to be moving as well as the checkers. Stanley, who had always been at ease with all aspects of this place and latitude, now found himself feeling more than uneasy. A government many thousands of miles away had "frozen" the land with printed words. It was settling forty million acres on Eskimos, Aleuts, and Indians, but for his future it offered little more than atrophy, a narrowing of what he once might have looked upon as his birthright opportunities. He could not comprehend this. He was a native, too.

When Stanley's mother was a girl, she lived in urban Pittsburgh, and she often said, "When I grow up, I'm going to live in a log cabin with a wolf hide on the wall." She read Louise Dickinson Rich ("We Took to the Woods"), Willa Cather ("O Pioneers!"), Jack London ("White Fang"), and works of Peary and Byrd. Her father, a carpenter, had a cottage about ninety miles north of the city. He took her there to fish for bass, perch, and bullheads, and to hunt rabbits, squirrels, and ducks. Driving home, she could smell Pittsburgh long before its stacks came into view, and she would begin thinking of the next trip to the cottage.

Ed Gelvin grew up on a small dairy farm a mile and a half out of Hartstown, Pennsylvania, in the northwestern corner of the state. There were eighteen cows, a hundred and some acres. Four generations of Gelvins had lived there. Ed's father, Stanley Gelvin, liked horses so much he did not buy a tractor until 1939, when Ed was fifteen. As a twelve-year-old, Ed plowed behind a team, and planted corn, wheat, and hay "in a little valley of real rich sandy loam." He milked, he fed the stock, and when his chores were done he hunted and he trapped. A skunk pelt was worth eight dollars, a muskrat three. He mailed them to Sears, Roebuck in Philadelphia, who sent him a check or credited the furs against items he ordered from their catalogue. He got to know Ginny when he was still in his teens. "Her Dad had this little cottage in a swamp, about a mile from our farm."

Ginny talked of "going somewhere"—a place where "you could make your own life." The Second World War interrupted the conversation. Ed apprenticed himself as an ironworker, helped build a defense plant near his home, and went into the Navy, which trained him as a shipfitter in Newport News. She joined the Women's Army Corps. They were married in 1946, and he went back to "putting up iron," while Ginny went back to thinking of a place where they could be more on their own. "I noticed a lot about this keeping up with the Joneses. Look-alike houses were starting. I couldn't see living like that. I couldn't see straining and striving to make a better can opener when all it does is open a can." She wrote a letter, and Ed signed it. "Department of the Interior, Washington, D.C. Dear Sirs: Would you please mail me any information you have on the Territory of Alaska."

They bought a new sedan (a naïve beginning) and started out in June, 1949. Neither of them had ever been west of the Mississippi. In Montana, they saw, for the first time, high mountains topped with snow. In Alberta, they began seeing moose racks on barns and houses. In British Columbia and Yukon Territory, they saw mud, and rain, and spruce. On the nineteenth of June, they crossed the hundred-and-forty-first meridian, and now "the roads were like crick beds, the rocks were like grapefruit"—Alaska! Not that they needed further proof of where they were, but they got it forthwith when they stopped at a roadhouse, three in the afternoon, and everyone in it was drunk. In Fairbanks, hungry, they cruised around looking for a place to eat, but all they could afford was soup and coffee, for two dollars and fifty cents. There were no hotel rooms. They slept in the car. Of the many hundreds of people they would come to know whose arrivals were similar to theirs, most—within days, a month, a year—would turn and go. The Gelvins sold the car and bought a pickup. Ed got a job in the railroad yard, and before long was building a school. One day in July, they went up the long dust trail to Central, to the domes of the Tanana Hills. Their purpose was to see caribou, and they stood on high passes and swept with their eyes the tundra fells. The nearest caribou was somewhere else. All they saw was the country.

If gold first drew them to settle here, the country itself is what kept them—the rivers, the mountains, this immense wild range lying open to anyone who could meet its climatic terms. In their first mining season on Squaw Creek, they made expenses and then some. After that, because of slow-melting stream ice, they barely made expenses. That is when they would have left if gold had been all they wanted, but they had chosen the country in the way that someone else would choose a career. Sense of place registered higher with them than a sense of accumulating wealth. They went to work at almost anything that might support them, and tried to stay where they were. They first lived in Circle Hot Springs, a clump of buildings around a natural phenomenon that fogged the winter air with warm steam and coated the spruce with ice. Central was eight miles away. It appealed to them because it was "less junky than most Alaskan towns." It was scarcely a town at all, had never had a school or a church—just a few cabins around the T in the road where a spur went off to the Springs. They took on the local mail run. They cut and sold cordwood and lumber. They ran the roadhouse for a year and a half. They shot wolves for the bounty, which was fifty dollars. The price of fur was too low at first to make other animals worth trapping, but as the price went up their lines went out, and fur eventually became their primary source of money. Meanwhile, Ed went off to construction jobs—a month here, six weeks there. In Arctic Alaska, in winter, he helped build stations of the DEW line. He built oil-drilling platforms in Cook Inlet and rigs on the North Slope. He was gone, in aggregate, no more than three months a year. Since 1970, the family has lived almost wholly on the possibilities of the country, and Ed has gone out for work only twice.

Stanley and then Betsy went to grammar school at the kitchen table. The material came by mail from Baltimore, and in the season when the sun was gone for upward of a month the children worked by kerosene light (or gasoline-generated electric light), while their mother watched over them and licked the stamps. When Stanley reached junior high, he went to school in Fairbanks, and was ahead of his peers by a couple of levels. Education as a whole, though, was a patchwork affair, a hazard of the bush—correspondence, boarding homes, shuttlings to an apartment in Fairbanks. The Gelvins' twins, Carol and Colleen, six years younger than Stanley, went to grade school in Fairbanks and high school by correspondence from Central—under the program run by the University of Nebraska. The course was "cattle-oriented," according to Ginny. While they might better have been studying, say, aviation and geology in addition to fundamental subjects, they sat at the table in their log cabin at fifty degrees below zero in the penarctic twilight studying animal husbandry. Colleen stayed the course, but Carol went off to Colorado to finish high school from the home of an uncle. Stanley matriculated at the University of Alaska, intending to become a mining engineer. He stayed two weeks, leaving when he discovered that he had to study English, too. Only Betsy, the middle child, went on through college. There was no television in Central. The children could watch it in Fairbanks if they wanted to—and, in their mother's words, "see the foolishness of it." But Ginny always felt relieved that Central was, as it still is, beyond TV's frontier. She had seen TV in a bar in Ohio in 1949 and had sensed what it could do to children.

For years, she kept a diary of the meals the family ate. Grouse, which she hunted with a .22, occasionally appeared in it, and beaver, lynx, mountain sheep, grayling, and pike, not to mention king salmon. But the main staple of the house was always moose, as a flip of the pages reveals. These were the features of consecutive winter nights:

> *Spaghetti with mooseburger.*
> *Moose steak.*
> *Omelet.*
> *Moose steak.*
> *Moose roast.*
> *Pinto beans and cabbage.*
> *Toasted cheese sandwiches.*
> *Moose stew.*
> *Moose meatloaf.*
> *Leftover moose.*
> *Leftover moose.*
> *Sandwiches.*
> *Spaghetti with mooseburger.*
> *Swiss moosesteak.*
> *Leftover moose.*
> *Roast moose.*
> *Moose steak.*
> *Moose sandwiches and soup.*
> *Mooseburgers.*
> *Mooseburgers.*
> *Clam chowder.*
> *Fried moose liver.*
> *Swiss moosesteak.*
> *Ground moose in Spanish rice.*

Looking up from this list when I read it, I asked her, "What are we having tonight?"

"Swiss caribou," she said.

With fair regularity, the family would listen—as they still do —to programs like "Tundra Topics" on KFAR, "Pipeline of the North" on KIAK, and "Trapline Chatter" on KJNP (King Jesus North Pole). As a public service in the absence of telephones, Alaskan radio stations spray messages around the bush. "To Brenda Carter. I'll be in late tomorrow night. I love you. John." "To Mr. O at Eagle from J.R. at Fairbanks. Please clean the snow off my roof." "To Martha Malcolm in Eagle. Angela Harper is in Fairbanks and O.K." "Passed police exam. Love, Jim." "Planning to have baby born at Lynette's cabin. Ellen and Jim Frazier. Eagle." "To Jan and Seymour on the Yukon from Mom in Anchorage. Are you there?" "To all my brothers and sisters in Anaktuvuk Pass . . ." "Please, Isaac, don't drink. We'll be getting married next week." "Chris is still hoping to make it out before breakup." These one-way communications are the only device to beat the mail. In recent times, the Gelvins' daughters have been working as bookkeepers and bull cooks on the Trans-Alaska Pipeline, and when they go out of Fairbanks to a new assignment or are coming home on leave they let their parents know by "Trapline Chatter." "Even when there's no message for us," their mother says, "it's a good way to keep up with what is going on around the bush."

The Gelvins bought their cabin from an old-timer who had once worked claims on Mastodon Creek. Gradually—as they added a room, razed a woodshed, built a porch—a new cabin evolved. It ate up and spit out its predecessor. In their sawmill, they cut their own lumber. Ed designed a gravity-feed system featuring the first flush toilet in the history of Central. It works much of the time. There is a supportive outhouse that is not always redundant. He dug Central's first year-round well. The kitchen sink is fed by a hand-cranked iron pump. Dishwater is heated on the stove. Ed designed and built the all-metal shop-garage, the one-plane hangar. He works with sheet metal like a tailor handling flannel, and has been called the best welder in Alaska. There are beautiful sleds in the shop and on the ground outside—Yukon sleds, basket sleds, racing sleds, freight sleds, bobsleds. He built them. He is the author of a laconically written booklet called "How to Build an Alaskan Dog Sled." The team is staked near the cabin. His lead dog, Tara, is fifty-per-cent wolf.

Gelvin is soft-spoken, clean-shaven. His construction shoes, his dark poplin work clothes, his visored cap do not suggest the extent to which he stands out against the landscape. Had he remained in the Lower Forty-eight, he would have gone on being an ironworker of the highest ability, but the geometry of his life, which in the far-northern bush is an ever-changing set of interlocking polygons, would have been less discernible—more like a faint straight line. Shy, quiet, admirably unassuming—whatever else he is up here, he is not anonymous.

"I worked with him on the Colville River. He knew what he was doing. Everything he did he did well and quickly. He is the most efficient man I've ever met."

"A lot of these bush Jacks-of-all-trades just want things to work out. Ed wants them right."

"He is the most capable man I've ever known. Every move he made he was doing something. There were no dead moves."

"The Gelvins are here thirty years and they attack any project with the enthusiasm of a newcomer."

"They leave a situation better than they found it."

"They are modern-type pioneers. They do things the old way, they do things the new way. They are the kind that built the country."

Ginny Gelvin is of middle height, with dark hair, dark quick eyes, and a skeptical corner-mouth grin. She wears jeans, usually with a wool shirt. She is comfortable in her surroundings, and is made nervous if she has to visit a populous place—even Fairbanks, a hundred and twenty-seven miles away, which she calls "town." She does not like, among other things, being dependent for water and power on sources outside her family's control. She has endured a flood in town, and the threat of earthquakes. At such times, she yearns for home. "Out here, anything can happen and it doesn't bother you. We have our own power system, our own well. We have double systems generally. We have kerosene and propane light when we don't want to run the generator." With temperatures that snap toward seventy below, they also have snows that close the road six months a year and bears that visit in summer. She looks up sometimes and sees wolves in the yard. She says, "In town, I always feel insecure."

Operating a sewing machine, her husband is, if anything, more able than she, at least when tailoring moosehide. With a rifle, she is the better shot. In two big gardens and a greenhouse, they grow most of their vegetables—tomatoes, peppers, cabbages, lettuce, kohlrabi, beans, cauliflower, celery, rhubarb, blood-red turnips a foot in diameter that resemble the hearts of bulls. They smoke salmon. They fly to Arctic lakes, drill holes in the ice with an auger attached to a chain saw, and pull out northern pike. Hunting game not just for food but for profit as well, Ed is the region's only registered big-game guide. For sums upward of two thousand dollars, he will take some cheechako up into the hills and glass and glass until he shows him a full-curl Dall ram or a grizzly big enough to carpet a hall.

The Gelvins have ten acres of land, an extraordinary spread for a family to own up here in ironic Alaska. A stream, Crooked Creek, runs along one side. Their compound has grown to sixteen buildings, nearly all of which are extremely small by any but local standards. Considerable safety is in these numbers— always somewhere to go, at fifty below zero, in the event of fire. There is a guest cabin, an eight-by-fourteen-foot wanigan (which is a habitable cabin in itself), a meat cache, a smokehouse, a toolshed. A "warehouse" contains sugar, flour, cornmeal, paper goods, coffee (things that can ignore the cold). Even the family's "attic" is a small freestanding building. Most of these structures are made from logs, and the scene might suggest an Eric Sloane book on Early American cabins were it not that the compound is for the most part arranged around one end of an airstrip. Your eye also rests on the fibre-glass greenhouse, not to mention the hangar and workshop. There are no anachronisms. All of it meshes in this place and time. The main cabin is L-shaped, and its long sides are eighteen and thirty-two feet. Floor to ceiling, its height inside is ten courses of logs. There are many dozens of books, a core sample of which would be "Scotty Allan, King of the Dog Team Drivers," "Mining Engineers' Handbook," "Developing Gold Properties with Airplane Placer Drills," "The Home Physician and Guide to Health," "Yukon Women," "Fifty Years Below Zero," "Ancient Men of the Arctic," "The Call of the Wild," "The Wilderness Trapper," "The Trail Eater," "Grizzly Country," "Notorious Grizzly Bears," and "Return of the Alaskan." A waist-high bookshelf separates the kitchen area from the living room, where a couch and a couple of chairs— the walls, too—are draped and decorated with the long soft pelts of timber wolves. A full basement is below. There are five rooms in all. The wolf bitch Tara was not named for this house, but there is more analogy than meets the eye, for it is as handsome a cabin as there is in the country, and could be a setting to remember if the life here were to vanish with the wind.

(When I have stayed with the Gelvins, I have for the most part occupied a cabin toward the far end of the airstrip—a place they acquired not long ago from an old-timer named Curly Allain, who was in his seventies and went south. He had no intention of returning, but he left his cabin well stocked with utensils, food, and linen—a tin of coffee close to the pot, fifty pounds of flour, five pounds of Danish bacon, firewood in three sizes stacked beside the door. Outside, some paces away, I have stood at a form of parade rest and in the broad light of a June midnight been penetrated in the most inconvenient place by a swarm of indecent mosquitoes, and on the same spot in winter, in a similar posture at the same hour, have stared up in darkness from squeaky snow at a green arch of the aurora, green streamers streaming from it all across the sky. At home, when I look up at the North Star I lift my eyes but don't really

have to move my head. Here, I crane back, lift my chin almost
as far as it will go, and look up at the polestar flirting with the
zenith. The cabin is long and low, and its roof is loaded white
—mantled eighteen inches deep. Its windows are brown-gold
from the light of burning lamps. The air is so still I can hear
the rising smoke. Twenty-two degrees below zero. Balls of ice
are forming in the beard. I go back inside and comb it off, and
jump into a bag of down.

The spruce in their millions are thick with snow, but not
heavy snow—a light dry loaf on every bough, with frost as well,
in chain crystals. Just touch one of these trees and all of its
burden falls, makes craters in the snow of the ground. The load
is so delicately poised a breath can break it, a mild breeze
denude the forest. Day after day, the great northern stillness
will preserve this Damoclean scene, while the first appearance
of each February dawn shoots pink light into the trees, and
colors all the blanketed roofs, the mushroom caps on barrels
and posts. Overhead, sometimes, a few hundred feet above the
ground stillness, the wind is audibly blowing.

I have flown with Ed in winter to this place and that, in his
Bellanca Citabria, landing on frozen rivers and sloughs. The
first time he set down, I did not know the plane had landed.
The snow was so deep and so dry there was no feel of the skis
touching. When we ran into some unseasonably warm air one
day—a williwaw blowing over the mountains from the south
—the Citabria's oil temperature began to climb toward an
unacceptable level. He landed on the Yukon, got out, opened
the engine cowling with a Phillips screwdriver, and removed a
sheet of cardboard. He had put it there to block off the oil
cooler, to keep it from doing too good a job. "When you bring
an airplane into this country, you have to modify it in various
ways," he said. "You prepare it for our kind of cold. Block off
the oil cooler. Cut a bigger hole in the breather tube so it won't
freeze up and blow your nose seal. Partly cover the bugeyes—
the air intakes—on the cowling. You adapt for summer, too.

When a new plane comes into the country, people say, 'It's still in wheel pants,' because wheel pants are the first things to come off. You put on tundra tires, and a big Scott tail wheel." The Citabria is built for short takeoffs, but, even so, when he bought it he replaced its fixed prop with a constant-speed prop, and he drooped the ailerons and adjusted the gap seals so he could get off the ground in two hundred feet (unloaded). "That's the way it is out here—you adapt things to the country. If something breaks down, you tear it apart and learn that way. Stanley is way better than I on airplanes. He built the new bungee-cord landing gear for his Champ. It originally had a sixty-five-horsepower engine. He took a ninety-five-horse engine from a wrecked 140, rebuilt it, replaced parts, put it in the Champ, and took off. Stanley can listen to an airplane from a distance and tell its horsepower, and with one glance he knows if it has a PA18 rudder, a PA11 horizontal stabilizer. I'd rather have him working on my airplane than just about any licensed mechanic I know." We got back into the Citabria and prepared to lift off from the river, but the snow was soft, the skis stuck, and the plane at full power plowed along well below takeoff speed. We were glued to the Yukon. Ed, though, had had this possibility in mind and had therefore chosen to land on a smoothly frozen segment of the river many miles long. He turned around and taxied back to where he had started, completing a large oval imprint, which suggested a race track. Then he went around and around it, packing and smoothing the surface until the plane began to move with increased speed and the skis at last came off the snow.

Ed did not know how to fly when he came into the country but inevitably took it up as an important skill of the bush. Since there are so few people in all Alaska, the coincidence is more commonplace than remarkable that he was taught by Don Jonz. Jonz, whose name had once been Jones, instructed in Fairbanks, and Ed remembers him as "a flippant, cocky sort of guy." He was the pilot of the Cessna 310 that disappeared on its way to Juneau in 1972 with Alaska's Representative Nick Begich and his Louisiana colleague Hale Boggs. The plane apparently iced up and fell into the Gulf of Alaska. As it happened, the issue of *Flying* magazine that was on newsstands at that time contained an article called "Ice Without Fear," by Don Jonz. "The thought of inflight structural icing inspires the crazies in a lot of airmen," he wrote. "In my opinion, most of it is a crock. . . . It's hard to convince some people that the sun is always shining on top. . . . If your bid for blue sky is unsuccessful, you have a monkey on your back. The trip down won't be pleasant. . . . Ice can be, and is, consistently deadly. An aircraft under severe ice loads suffers on both ends of its speed range. Stall goes up. Cruise goes down. When the two meet, the world comes to an end."

The Gelvins never fly anywhere without leaving a note on the kitchen table saying where they have gone and at what time, and giving a flight plan. They are known as people who will go out of their way to fly over someone's remote cabin to be sure that smoke is visible there, but the cabin will be in their flight plan. On long trips, if something of surprising interest attracts their attention—some digression they would like to make—they resist the temptation. They stay with their plan, because if searchers had to look for them they might look in the wrong place. Their planes have emergency-locator beacons, and each contains survival gear—an axe, a week's food, flares, a tent, two sleeping bags. Snowshoes are strapped to the wing struts. They haven't had much trouble. Stanley once had a rough landing at the family's cabin on the Charley River. The "airstrip" there is so short it looks like a helicopter pad, with a surface of grapefruit gravel. The plane came down short and hard, bending a strut to the point of fracture. The propeller was bent, too. Stanley and his father cut a spruce and wired it, as a splint, to the damaged strut. They removed the propeller and laid it across two big logs. With a third log, they pounded the prop until its gross disfigurement essentially disappeared. They put it back on the airplane, revved up, and flew away.

Ginny worries now and again about her husband and son. I remember her pacing around one day when they were two hours overdue from the mountains, where they had gone to work on the airstrip that would service the development of their gold claims. They were using Stanley's Champ. She kept watching the dogs outside, waiting for them to herald the plane, for they always hear it long before she does. She spoke of going to Circle, thirty-five miles away, to ask Frank Warren to fly reconnaissance with his plane to see if there was trouble, but first we would wait a bit longer, with a glass of MacNaughton's Canadian. "I'm not really worried," she said. "But I always get to thinking about it when they don't come home when they say they're going to." Tara at last delivered an annunciating howl. The other dogs joined in.

After the plane arrived, Stanley opened the cowling with a penny, poured in some oil, gassed up from a gravity-feed tank, got a towel and some soap, spun the prop with one hand to start the engine, ducked under a wing, climbed aboard, and flew eight miles to the Springs to take a shower. The planes are used more than the VW and the pickup. Flying is the talk of the table, when the talk is not about gold. Weather, parts, loads, structures—Stanley flips through aviation magazines and tells his father about stall-spin accident rates in various aircraft per thousand hours. Stanley was once cruising in the mountains looking for a place to fish, Ed has told me. He saw a gravel bar that looked negotiable, so he set the plane down, but the bar was rougher and shorter than he had thought. It was Mistake No. 1 to risk landing there. Now he made Mistake No. 2: he went fishing. The sun came out. The day warmed up. Warm air is less dense than cold air, and provides less lift. The warmer the air, the longer the run for takeoff. When Stanley tried to leave the gravel bar, he went off the end of it and almost into the river. The tail of the plane dragged in the water as he barely lifted away. "His legs were shaking," said his father. "He learned judgment there."

Ed is a careful and skillful pilot unendangered by bravado,

and I would rest on his judgment wherever he thought he could go—all of which, I feel, is an essential preamble to going on to say that on the day I arrived from upriver, by canoe from Eagle, he cracked up the Citabria. The word the family used was "dinged." He dinged the airplane. Patricia Oakes, down the road, said "pranged." In a place where flying is in many situations the only means of travel, people are careful how they land certain words. Whatever happened, no one said that the plane had crashed. He had been up in the gold-claim valley, where still there was unmelted snow, on which he landed (with wheels). Rolling to a stop, he set the hand brake, so the plane would not slide in the breeze. When eventually he took off, he forgot the hand brake. Like skis, his oversize tundra tires, locked and rigid, slid along the snow. The Citabria got up all the speed it needed to lift into the air. Ed flew home with the brake still on. At the lower altitude of Central, the gravel runway was bare and dry. He came in on final, flared, and made a three-point full-stall landing. When the wheels touched, they grabbed the ground. The Citabria did a forward flip. Ed hung there for a moment in a ganglion of straps. Then he disengaged himself and finished his trip on foot. The extent of his physical injury was a cut on one hand, but his pilot's pride was pranged. For the plane's part, the prop was bent, the windshield was smashed, a wing member was cracked, a strut was gone, the fuselage was dented, the tail was crumpled. Ed got out his Buck knife, his welding torch, his hacksaw. He cut away fabric. Carrying parts into the shop, he repaired the plane. He figured the job would cost at least six thousand dollars in Fairbanks, so clearly he was making money. A guy seizes an opportunity when it comes, in the bush. "Drive a car long enough and you'll have both minor and major scrapes," he said, straightening with force of muscle the rudder's tubular steel.

"That's the sort of thing they say in Eagle," I told him. "They say about the pilots there, 'You can't learn to ski without falling.' "

On a wall of the shop is a museum of traps—a catalogued collection of about a hundred and fifty, of various types and ages. Hanging opposite are some dozens of furs—wolf, fox, wolverine, lynx. Most will go to markets outside, but Ed and Ginny also sell quantities of wolf ruffs to regional Indians. Their snow machine—Ski-Doo Alpine—rests on the floor below the furs. It goes ten miles an hour on the trail, and the two of them ride it. Ed took me out with him once, and as we chugged along among the laden spruce at least a thousand trees thanked us for coming by dumping on our heads a tumult of snow. We collected a marten that had climbed up a pole-set for a grouse wing and was now hanging by a leg in a lifelike pose, frozen stiffer than taxidermy, its forepaws stretched as if leaping for prey, its eyes, at fifteen below zero, like white chick-peas. The coat was toast brown. We saw the scant remains of a wolf-killed moose, and a bowl in the snow full of feathers of grouse. A springing lynx had killed and eaten it. Amazingly, for a cat of such size—big as an ocelot, thirty pounds, with long dangling legs—its tracks were shallow in the deep dry snow. The pads of a lynx are like pancakes.

Ginny wears a one-piece snow-machine suit with a sewed-on wolf ruff, Ed a down parka with a wolf ruff and an Eddie Bauer down cap that he has trimmed with mink. Both wear mukluks with felt liners and felt insoles inside the liners and more felt between the liners and the soles. (Mukluks, with their soft moosehide bottoms, thin leggings, and layered contents of felt, are the lightest, driest, warmest, most comfortable things I have ever had on my feet. Water is their nemesis, so they function only in cold snow.) The Gelvins make their sets for the most part near lakes east of Central. They use single and double long-springs—the sort of trap that has a "pan" held by a "dog" (trigger), which releases snapping jaws. They use coil-spring traps and jump traps. They use Conibears—traps made of rectangles of heavy steel rods that are brought together with enough force to destroy vertebrae. The Gelvins might cut a

hole in lake ice and dangle a snare that is baited with cottonwood. A beaver, caught in the snare, drowns. Most of their trap
sets are cubbies, though—contrived shelters of cut boughs—
with a grouse wing or a piece of lynx or beaver inside. They
make rounds every three days. When they find, say, a lynx in
a trap, the cat is generally just sitting there, patiently waiting
for another surprise. They choke it with rope or wire. If a fox
is alive, they rap the snout with a stick. The fox loses conscious-
ness. Standing on its chest will cause its heart to stop. Mink
and marten ordinarily freeze, but if one is alive it is taken in
hand and squeezed. Caught in a Conibear, a wolverine or a fox
is usually dead. If not, it is shot with a .22. (Some trappers shoot
everything.) Wolves, standing in their double long-springs, are
shot in the ear. Owls, hawks, and ravens occasionally get into
the traps. Ginny tried to trap a bear once, within a few feet
of their cabin in Central. She strewed grouse carcasses in a
tempting circle. The bear sat on the trap, leaped six feet in the
air, and ran off defecating cranberries. Despite such failures,
the take of a typical recent season has been ten thousand
dollars' worth of fur.

Ginny looks through *Alaska* magazine, where her attention
is arrested by letters from the Lower Forty-eight. " 'There was
a time when man was justified in taking wildlife,' " she reads
aloud, " 'for then man's survival was at stake, but that time is
long gone. What is left of wildlife now belongs to all of us, and
not to a few.'

" 'The Kodiak bear is brought back to the Lower Forty-eight
to be mounted as lifeless trophies on rich men's walls.'

" 'There is absolutely no defensible position for trapping.'

" 'I would hope the day will come when men no longer want
to kill everything that moves.' "

She slaps the magazine down on the table. "They don't
understand," she says. "Trophy hunters go for big boars. That
gives younger grizzlies a chance to breed, and makes for better
breeding stock. These people who write these letters are not

even rational. They say we're out to kill everything. People in the Lower Forty-eight do not understand Alaska."

"They have everything wrong," Ed inserts. "They think it's all ice and snow and igloos here."

Ginny continues: "They wonder how Alaskans get their mail, and what they do in winter. They can't believe anything can grow here. They're amazed we can't buy any land. They think Indians are Eskimos. They know nothing about Alaska, and yet they've been manipulating us for years. We thought statehood would put an end to that."

"They don't understand trapping. They don't understand the harvesting of animals," Ed says. "And they say that Alaska is 'fragile.' All this delicate-ecology business just kills me. How could it be so delicate if it has survived all these Siberian winters? Alaska would be O.K. as a state if the feds hadn't kept two-thirds of it. Now, under the native-land-claims act, they want to make eighty million acres into parks. My contention is that nothing stays the same in this earth. Everything changes. You can't keep anything. Even the vegetation changes. So all this preserving things—it doesn't work."

Ginny is still fuming at the magazine. "Oh well," she says, shoving it aside again. "The bad image of trapping has at least raised the price of furs. People down there are afraid they won't be able to get them."

Moose racks protrude from under the gables of buildings in the compound. It is important to the Gelvins, as to Alaskans generally, that this custom be seen as a symbol of respect— respect for the moose and for the needs of the people who use moose to sustain their lives. "If people had to buy meat and raise a family, it would be pretty rough," Ginny says. "It is a serious thing to get that meat. During the season, in the fall, people don't say 'Hello,' they say 'Did you get your moose yet?' We help each other out. People who don't get their moose will be given a quarter here, a quarter there, by others."

"The best way to shoot a moose is to be doing something

else when he walks up to you," Ed says. "The best thing in the world to call a moose is to chop wood. When one comes near, I grunt like another bull, and he comes nearer."

The four dressed quarters of a good-size bull moose will weigh maybe seven hundred pounds. Deduct a little over a third for trim and bones, and what is left is upward of four hundred pounds of meat, or nearly enough in itself to see a family of six through a winter. Meanwhile, the competition for the meat moves in packs through the nearby terrain—the Preacher Creek pack, the Porcupine Creek pack, the pack near Medicine Lake, the pack between Central and Circle. Ed remembers a time when he was off working on a drilling rig somewhere and saw a copy of *Not Man Apart*, the journal of the conservation organization called Friends of the Earth. It contained an article on Alaskan wolves. "I couldn't believe the misconceptions. Some of the things it said were outright lies. It said wolves live on weak, sick, and crippled moose and caribou. That is not true at all. Do you think a moose that has run hard for many miles and has been encircled four or five times is weak, sick, or crippled? Sometimes you see a moose standing up with blood pouring out of it and big hunks of meat torn from its body. Would a sick moose be standing? There aren't that many sick moose in the country. Wolves seem to know when calves are coming. They hang around and grab them when they drop. Are the calves sick? They are certainly weak. People like the Friends of the Earth and the Sierra Club have the idea that we want to kill *all* the wolves up here. We like wolves. They're a part of everything else. People need their fur for ruffs. But they also have to be controlled if we are going to harvest game."

"I see a lot of women writing these articles," Ginny comments. "Seems kind of strange."

The State of Alaska has been auctioning the skins of wolves killed by the state in a program of wolf control. The program annoys the Gelvins. Wolves, they say, belong to the people, not to some government agency. For the state to—in effect—get into the fur business is a bad precedent. Hunters at present can shoot two wolves a year, and trappers can take all they want, but that does not keep the numbers sufficiently down. "In the forties, there was a situation like now," Ed Gelvin says. "Wolf were up. Caribou, moose, and sheep were down. A big poison and bounty-shooting program followed. By the sixties, things were just about right. There were plenty of wolves and moose and caribou and sheep. The bounty was still on, and we could hunt from planes. Then all these wolf-loving outfits came along. The outside pressure stopped aerial hunting. Wolves are high now and game is low."

Even Ginny's brother is sometimes "one of them that don't understand." In the same mail with the *Alaska* magazine was a letter from him saying that nature has its balance and advising her, "Don't fool with it."

"But it's not a balance," she says. "It's feast or famine. The cycles go up and down. Some years there are rabbits all over the road to Circle. Some years there are none. Nature can't cope with itself. Enough wolves should be shot to keep things even."

From the air, the Gelvins see the wolf-moose story in all its phases—the chase, the standoff, the kill, the sign. They see a ring of wolf tracks where a pack first encircled a moose, and a while later another ring, and then another, another. Each time, the moose fended off the wolves, recovered its wind, broke out, and ran on. Now the plane goes over the resting pack, perhaps five wolves. Not far away, the Gelvins will see the moose, its forelegs spread like an A-frame, its head down, its blood bright red on the snow. Returning later on, they see nothing where the moose was but a hoof and some hair, within a tracked circle. A sticker on the rear bumper of their Chevrolet pickup says "EAT MOOSE—10,000 WOLVES CAN'T BE WRONG."

A number of times a day, as I walk back and forth between

Curly's cabin and the main one, I pass Tara, in her pen. Not only is she fenced in, she is also chained to a stake—a double precaution. I have spoken in a soft soothing voice in her direction for weeks on end, but I remain a stranger, and whenever I come near her she races around her stake in the tight circles it prescribes, while from her throat comes a threat so guttural and wild that it calls into question the strength of the chain and the fence. Her mother was pure wolf, from Anaktuvuk Pass, dug out of a den by Eskimos. Tara—pale, silken, a flowing runner when she pulls a sled—has the long legs of the timber wolf, and they fairly whirl her around the stake, a flying blur, but, as fast as they move her, her eyes are always on mine. Her eyes are ochre. She once got out, and slit the throat of Andrea's pet dog, Lazarus. Lazarus survived. But I have no doubt that if Tara were to come off that chain and out of that pen as I am passing by, there would be nothing much left of me but a rubber hoof and a little hair on the unencircled ground.

One summer day, Ed and I made a two-hundred-and-fifty mile run in the pickup to collect a shipment of dog food in Fairbanks. Not far from town, we came to the Trans-Alaska Pipeline, which descended a long incline like a pneumatic message system in an as yet incomplete department store. We pulled off the road to contemplate this wonder; and as we sat there Ed mentioned an oil-drilling rig he had helped assemble in the far north, years ago. It had a jackknife mast. "You do the work on the ground, and then the thing stands up—a hundred and fifty-seven feet high." He had done all of the welding, in winter, with temperatures at forty and fifty below.

"How was that?"

"Pretty cold, most of the time."

The rig drilled a dry hole, and then was moved sixty miles to try again. The second drilling found oil. It was the discovery well of the 1968 oil strike in Arctic Alaska, and was called Prudhoe Bay State No. 1.

Across a sea of fresh dirt, a D9 Cat with a side boom was

holding a section of pipe in a sling. Welders, with their pinpoint fires, were beading away, making a butt-weld joint. We
walked over for a closer look. With their face masks, their
heavy suiting (against cold that did not happen to be there),
they looked like astronauts. Ed said they had six passes to make,
six revolutions of the pipe—the first bead, the hot pass, the
filler (three times), and the cap. The pipe was no wider than
the spread of a child's arms, but nonetheless the work seemed
to me long and tedious. "To me it's not," Ed said. "You have
to pay attention to see that the metal's going in there right."
He spoke with the welders. He said he was surprised they
weren't using low-hydrogen rods. The welders looked up with
interest, and talked tensile strengths in Oklatexan accents.
Unused rods were lying around in profusion on the ground. As
we left, Ed picked up some, like a figure gathering flowers. One
of the pipe welders—a big man in cowboy boots—called out,
"Hey there, y'all don't need to do that. Y'all just back your
truck up here and we'll give you some." Ed responded to the
suggestion. Into the back of the pickup the welders set several
cylindrical cans full of high-tensile rods. Driving away, Ed said
the hourly wage those men got was no more than it would
be in a place like New York. What attracted them was the
overtime—ten- to fourteen-hour days, time and a half Satur-
days and Sundays. Some miles up the road, we stopped and
looked at another pipeline, of larger diameter, built many years
ago on an eighty-three-mile route to carry water to float gold
dredges. Ed said he resented the long struggle carried on by
environmentalists telling Alaskans they should not build their
oil pipeline. The delays caused by the great battle had injured
the state. "The pipeline is using resources," he said. "It's a way
the state can pay their bills. It doesn't spoil the appearance of
Alaska."

An hour later, we were looking from a summit pass long
distances across the peaks of the country. We paused, taking
it in, and he told me another story remembered from the North

Slope. He and the others would now and again see a lone raven, flying over the flat tundra. It would fly on and on, close to the ground. Below the raven, almost always, was a running fox. Mile upon mile, the fox stayed under the raven. If the raven sped up a bit and settled to the ground, the fox then stalked the raven. When the fox sprang for the capture, the raven—at the last moment—would jump into the air, and fly on across the tundra, with the fox running below. The relationship was apparently static, a ritual equilibrium, a possible pantomime. One day, such a pair came flying and running almost into camp. The raven set down. The fox went into its assassin creep—one crafted step after another—and then made a sudden dash. The raven jumped into the air. After a short flight, it came down, and was again stalked and rushed by the fox. Again it made a short flight, and settled down, even closer to the crew. The fox renewed its subtle glide, this historically futile contest with the raven's eye. Once more came the move, the rush, the leap. The fox caught the raven, ate it on the spot, and left a pile of black feathers on the ground.

❲ Joe Vogler came into the country in 1944. He was from Barnes, Kansas, near the Little Blue River, where he grew up on a farm that had been homesteaded by his grandfather. On a boyhood day that stands particularly fresh in his mind, he saw a guinea hen running around the farm in agitation and dismay. "I mean, she was a-talkin'. She was raising hell." Near her nest was a large bull snake, awkwardly out of streamline, with bulges below its neck. He feared serpents, but he killed this one with his corn knife, and cut off its head. "My goal in life is to serve a good purpose." From its tubular body he gently squeezed twenty-one eggs. He wiped each one with his handkerchief and returned it to the nest. The guinea hen eventually hatched twenty-one chicks. Joe had come along before the snake had a chance to crush the eggs.

He went to a one-room school. He bucked his teacher. He swam in the Little Blue, fished for bullheads and carp, and put out trotlines for channel cats. "We planted a hundred and eighty acres of corn one year and we didn't raise a cob as big as my finger. When it's dry, it's bad there. My mother and father are dead now. This is my country up here." As a result of the dry weather and agricultural depression of 1921, a number of neighbors had to give up their homes, and Joe formed a boyhood wish for enough gold dust to pay his taxes as long as he lived. He went to the University of Kansas and earned a law degree, and was admitted to the bar in the same year. It was 1934. There were no jobs, so he went home and put up the harvest. The Great Depression kept him on the farm, and he never really practiced. He was not much interested in the law anyway, but the general absence of opportunity embittered him. A few years later, he had a job with Dow Chemical in Texas, and he lost it—in large measure because he referred to Franklin Roosevelt as "a dirty rotten son of a bitch of a Communist traitor." It was an era of intense patriotism. It was the height of the Second World War. Vogler's remarks were not looked upon favorably by his superiors. His animosity toward President Roosevelt was grounded in the view that Roosevelt "put the government into the business of providing security instead of opportunity," and it seemed just a matter of time before a good part of the creative vitality of the American people would disappear into an absorption with security, a craven and self-defeating need. The Dow people told him he was unfit to work for Dow Chemical, unfit to get along in the American society. This was clear enough to him, and he left for Alaska. "The only two things I have ever been afraid of are snakes and claustrophobia," he likes to say. So he chose to live in a country where he had nothing to fear.

Vogler is a friend of the Gelvins, and I met him when he

stopped by and exploded with pleasure at the sight of their infant grandson. I have seen a fair amount of ground with him since. He is a roamer, a garrulous companion, perhaps the most active prospector in the country, and least active miner, although he owns several patented claims, including Woodchopper, two hundred and thirty-three acres close to the Yukon. If the Gelvins, in their quiet and straightforward way, exemplify the versatility of people who are long established in the bush, Joe Vogler is a sort of cartoon Alaskan, self-drawn: a part-time politician with strong attitudes and a stronger, not to say incendiary, way of expressing them. In recent years, he has become a figure of some significance not only in the upper Yukon but all across the state—as an advocate of independence for Alaska.

"A colony is any people or territory separated from a ruling power but subject to that power," he says. "The United States has made a colony of Alaska. When they want something, they come and get it. We are their oyster. They open us when they need us. Under the flag, you've got to have uniformity of laws. They have laws in the Lower Forty-eight that protect their environment, their resources. They need those laws. The laws unfortunately apply to us, and we do not need them. They hinder us. We are a developing nation, like any developing nation in the world, and we cannot develop under American laws. They can take their Fourth of July and go to hell with it. They have their independence from Britain. We do not have our independence from them."

He is tall, weathered, rangy—now in his middle sixties—his features strong and handsome. His hair is sandy, and his clear blue eyes seem set in a permanent squint. His voice is husky, its register high. He wears khaki work clothes, and a dark visored cap, and on his hip, bouncing in rhythm as he hikes along, is a holstered Smith & Wesson .44 Magnum revolver, which he refers to as "the hog leg." One day when we were resting from the exertion of climbing a granite-pinnacled hill above his claims on Ketchem Creek, he leaned against a boulder, wiped his forehead with his cap, and said, "If we ever get a revolution going, I want to import a bunch of guillotines. Lots of black currants up here. If you're dying of thirst, you can get water out of those mossberries. My government is my worst enemy. I'm going to fight them with any means at hand."

"What are you going to do when the feds take away your hog leg?" I asked him.

"Ever see one of these little fellas?" he said, and he dug down deep in a trouser pocket for a derringer .22 Magnum. It was as small as the palm of his hand but had two barrels, one above the other. "When the bureaucrats come after me," he went on, "I suggest they wear red coats. They make better targets. In the federal government are the biggest liars in the United States, and I hate them with passion. They think they own this country. There comes a time when people will choose to die with honor rather than live with dishonor. That time may be coming here. Our goal is ultimate independence by peaceful means under a minimal government fully responsive to the people. I hope we don't have to take human life, but if they go on tramping on our property rights, look out, we're ready to die." (Vogler does not avoid confrontations. For example, he once said to the mayor of Fairbanks, "You son of a bitch, get ready to look at this town for the last time, because I'm going to close your left eye with one fist and your right eye with the other." Joe's violence was entirely in his rhetoric, though. His difficulty with the mayor led to a courtroom, where the mayor paid a fine.) "The czars exiled misfits to Siberia," he said. "The Soviets do that, too. The Siberian exiles will eventually break away. Alaska is the place for misfits from the Lower Forty-eight. And we will eventually break away. Alaskans are inheritors of determinative genes that took people out of Europe to the New World. Alaska attracts construction workers who are wild hairs, willing to take a chance. The Gelvins would be misfits somewhere else. They're doers. They don't destroy. They build. They preserve. They are conservationists in the true sense of the word. They have killed wolves right and left. They are responsible for many moose being alive today. That Ginny—she's a hell of a gunner. She can take a Browning and shoot the hell out of wolves."

His voice lowering a bit, he said, "Ed is fortunate that Ginny likes it here. This is a hard country on women. That makes or breaks a man here—a woman." His own wife had left him, and gone outside, some thirty years before. "She did not like this country." His children were one and three when he put them on a plane with their mother and saw them for the last time. "My daughter, I think, is married to a professor in Manhattan. I would not know my children if I saw them right here on the trail."

The granite pinnacles were an enlofted Stonehenge, an alpine garden of standing rock. The views were of the local domes and the middle-distant bluffs of the Yukon. There were dwarf spruce and lupine. There were lovely young aspen, their leaves spinning like coins. "What do you think of my little private park? Isn't it nice?" Vogler said, and he called attention to the unusual size of the feldspar crystals in the granite, which could not have become so large unless they had cooled very slowly, so there had once been at least a mile of rock above the place where we stood, of which the pinnacles, with their big crystals, were a slowly uncovered vestige. "To me," he said, "that is the writing of God."

He had bulldozed the trail to the summit, on federal land —a mile and a half from his gold claim. He said, "God, I like to move dirt with a Cat. I may make another road up here from one set of pinnacles to another, just for my private use. I could level the top with dynamite, and build a cabin. Wouldn't that be a crow's roost? Parks should not be federal—that's where my bitch comes in. The federal government should have nothing to say. I'd like to have seen the natives get a hundred million acres—anything to get the land away from the federal government. They tie it up. They just set on it, making jobs for bureaucrats. They're going to destroy private ownership in Alaska."

He picked up and tossed idly in his hand a piece of dry wolf feces with so many moose hairs in it that it looked like a big caterpillar. "Greedy gut-ripping son of a bitch," he said. "Stinking dirty cowardly predator. I'd kill the last pregnant wolf on earth right in front of the President at high noon. People who are against killing wolves are sentimental idiots who don't live up here. If they came and lived here, I'd listen to them. If the majority here did not want to kill wolves, I would not want them killed. But the meat the wolves take is needed. I believe in my own kind. I believe in gold, I believe in yellow scrap iron, and I believe in my own kind."

"Yellow scrap iron?"

"Bulldozers. Cats. Earthmoving equipment."

Vogler travels the mining district in a big three-axle truck so much the worse for wear it appears to have been recently salvaged after a very long stay at the bottom of the Yukon. He drives it on what roads there are and, where roads do not exist, directly up the beds of rushing streams. Lurching, ungainly, it is a collage of vehicular components—running gear from one source, transmission from another—that Vogler selected and assembled to be "good in the brush." The front wheels are directly under the cab, and the engine mount (high off the ground) is cantilevered a full eight feet forward to become a projecting snout, probing the way toward gold. The cab and engine are military fragments, artifacts of the Second World War. The frame was taken from a twenty-five-year-old tractor trailer. A long flatbed reaches out behind and is towered over by a winch and boom. There are no fenders. Much of the engine's cowling is gone. The headlights, far out front by themselves, suggest coleopteran eyes. Enfeebled as the rig looks, it has six-wheel drive and, thunking up ledges and over boulders, is much at home in a stream.

With his colleague Wayne Peppler, Joe has been using the

truck to transfer from one claim to another steel pipe to be used in hydraulic mining, and they have taken me with them on their long working days. There is no muffler system in Joe's truck, and most of the bulkhead is missing between the engine and the cab, so the full detonations of the engine come directly to the ears, enough to mask the sound of any roaring stream, to blot out everything but Joe, shouting, as he did one day, "Jefferson got away with the purchase of Louisiana. Seward did the same thing here. The purchase of Alaska was unconstitutional. There are only two clauses whereby Congress can purchase lands—for a seat of government, or for military forts, docks, arsenals, and magazines—unless you go to the common defense and general welfare, which is the trash bin of the Constitution. Since the Congress had no authority to buy Alaska, they in effect held the land in trust for the first legally constituted government to come along. The federal government should now, therefore, yield all the lands of Alaska to the state."

Since it seems unlikely that the United States will pursue such a course, Vogler would like to advance his cause by suing the federal government for violation of the statehood contract. In the Statehood Act of 1958, Alaska was given twenty-five years to select a hundred and three million acres, he pointed out, but thirteen years later, to clear the path for the removal of oil, Congress passed the Alaska Native Claims Settlement Act and gave forty million acres to the natives, while setting aside eighty million more as proposed federal wildlife and recreational reserves. The State of Alaska had by that time chosen only a small fraction of its promised land. Now, suddenly, its latitude of choice had been drastically narrowed, and he meant to sue. He would ask the court to set aside the statehood contract for substantive violation. After the case was decided, he said, he would like to see certain choices on the next Alaska ballot: (1) a return to territorial status; (2) reaffirmation of statehood, with appropriate damages; (3) commonwealth status; (4) independence.

Generous by habit, Joe brought lunch for the three of us in a brown paper bag, and as we gathered convivially he spilled the lunch onto the bed of the truck—Hershey bars, Butterfingers, Mounds, Bit-O-Honey. These candy bars were all we ate in seventeen working hours. Tearing off a Bit-O-Honey wrapper, he released it into the wind, saying, "We are totally controlled. We can't even kill our own wolves. The posy-sniffers yelp too loud. With statehood, we were supposedly given management of our game. Now they won't even let us do that. Our sole desire is, we'd like to run the show."

When I felt myself becoming sick on Butterfingers, I ate an antidotal Hershey bar, while Joe stayed with the Bit-O-Honey —agglutinated, Pre-Cambrian corn syrup that seemed peculiarly appropriate to the effort it was serving, which was, after all, the removal of gold.

"This ain't part of America. This is a foreign country," Wayne Peppler said.

"Just as removed as the Colonies were three hundred years ago," said Joe.

"People up here are running scared and bewildered," Peppler said. "They're afraid they ain't going to be free anymore."

Peppler is a lean, sinewy young man with dark, swept-back hair and a face that makes an angular silhouette. He came to Alaska more or less directly from a Los Angeles high school, because—as he remembers imagining—"the little guy could count for something here." In Alaska's 1974 gubernatorial election, he was the Alaskan Independence Party's candidate for lieutenant governor, a nominee by petition. The Party's candidate for governor was Joe Vogler, and his name appeared on the ballot with those of William Egan, the Democratic incumbent, and Jay Hammond, a Republican. In implication and influence, the results of Vogler's campaign were more sizable than anyone might have guessed. All told, just under a hundred thousand votes were cast. The number by which Hammond defeated Egan was only two hundred and eighty-seven. Almost five thousand people voted for Joe Vogler and his declarations of independence.

❨ Vogler and I stopped by one morning, some fifteen miles up the road from Central, to say hello to Fred Wilkinson, a soft-spoken and retiring bachelor, whom Joe described as "a working fool." Wilkinson's grandfather staked claims to four miles of Miller Creek in 1903. His father and uncle also mined there, and Fred now works the same claims, living alone in isolation, with five pieces of heavy equipment, including two D8 bulldozers and a D9, with which he moves not only the gravels of the stream bed but also the gravels wherever the stream, in the shifting courses of its geologic history, has been. In a process analogous to the separation of isotopes, he goes through roughly forty thousand cubic yards of pay dirt a season and from it removes a handful of beautiful teardrop nuggets and several pints of flaky dust worth tens of thousands of dollars.

For a man who works in the summer sun, he looked remarkably pale this day, and in his rubber boots and torn brown denims seemed to have come out of a coal mine and not from a stream of placer gold. Solidly built, rugged, attractive, he seemed above all else grim. He soon told us he was feeling lonely and scared. Vogler, out of sheer good nature, had brought along some sandwiches and pie, and Wilkinson, as he sat at his table and ate, said that an International Scout belonging to the federal government had appeared there yesterday, with four men in it, one of whom had handed him some papers, which he now shoved across the table past the pie. They were from the Region X headquarters of the United States Environmental Protection Agency, in Seattle, and were titled "In the Matter of Fred Wilkinson, Alaska. Findings of Violation and Compliance Order."

"Somebody's got to go, Fred," said Joe.

Although Wilkinson had been advised nearly a year before of the requirements of the Federal Water Pollution Control Act, he had not applied for a National Pollutant Discharge Elimination System permit, the documents said, and he was forthwith to apply for one or incur fines up to ten thousand dollars a day. He was to dig settling ponds for all the mud stirred up on his claims. If the water five hundred feet downstream at any time contained more than twenty-five Jackson Turbidity Units above normal background levels, he was subject to penalties also at the rate of ten thousand dollars a day. If he had questions, he should call Area Code 206, in western Washington, 442–1275, and speak with an attorney there. The nearest telephone—not that Wilkinson would have hurried to pick it up—was more than a hundred miles away.

"The government swine," said Joe. "Hate 'em, hate 'em, hate 'em, Fred."

"Three of them were from the state," Fred went on quietly. "The federal man's name was Lamoreaux. He told Del Ackels, up Gold Dust Creek, that sulphides uncovered by his Cat were polluting the stream."

"I wonder what Lamoreaux is going to do when I jab him in the belly with my .357."

"He was just the man the government happened to send," Wilkinson said.

"If you step on a rattlesnake, does the rattlesnake go for you or for the man who sent you?" said Joe. "I am a rattlesnake, and I will sink my fangs into the ones that come. They're taking our country away from us, Fred. They're taking our country away. They're taking private property without due process of law."

Nearly all mining claims are on public land, but under the Mining Law of 1872, which remains in force, miners not only own a hundred per cent of the gold they extract but have traditionally been able to do almost anything they wished on the land, just as if they, and not the people of the United States, were the owners of the property. The pick-and-shovel miners of the gold-rush days started out with that understanding. Across the decades, hydraulic miners, dredgers, and Cat miners have all had a sense of uninhibited franchise, too. And now, after more than a century, Bill Lamoreaux, of the United States Environmental Protection Agency, Jeff Mach and Lance Elphic, of the Alaska Department of Environmental Conservation, and Bob Fedeler, of the Alaska Department of Fish and Game, had come to say that things had changed. Fedeler was worried about the grayling in the stream. The fish could not spawn up a tongue of mud. Wilkinson was ordered to "ensure that the receiving stream is not blocked to fish passage," or risk heavy fines for that, too.

"Ten thousand dollars a day," Vogler repeated. "You've got to kill for that."

(Vogler has actually taken a shot at a man only once in his life, but that was long ago in Texas and he missed.)

To Wilkinson's considerable surprise, there was a stir of arrival outside, and Bob Littlefield appeared in the door. Gold miners work backbreaking hours, seven days a week, and it is most unusual for one—let alone two—to appear on another's claim in the middle of a day. Littlefield is a short, pleasant, round-faced man with a beard and tortoiseshell glasses and a ready smile that was not ready just now. He had come over from his claim on Harrison Creek, about eight miles away, because he wondered if some government people had been to see Fred.

Wilkinson had thought he was alone—singled out by the government as an example to other miners. He felt some relief, he said, and his pallor began to recede. "What did you say to them?" he asked.

"I said, 'I ought to shoot the four of you and bury you with your car,'" Littlefield told him. "The fed, Lamoreaux, bragged that he was going to close down all miners who do not comply."

Vogler said, "I'm going to run over him with a Cat and turn mosquitoes loose on him while he dies."

"We're not polluting," Littlefield went on. "We're creating turbidity with what is already present—with rock, mud, and dirt. We don't do more than what Mother Nature does in spring or after a rain."

"It's the nationalization of gold."

"The mining law says the man below you has to put up with what comes down from above. Settling ponds won't work. They'll silt up in a week's time. Wildlife will get mired in them. The E.P.A. says we have to push the silt out, but that is unreasonable, expensive, hard on the equipment. In five feet of silt, most Cats would sink out of sight."

"It's a tragedy that we must live by their laws."

And now another figure appeared in the door (Joe Green, of Mammoth Creek), and another (Bob Sherwood), and another. Miners' meetings, at the turn of the century, were the courts of the country. They heard cases of every kind, and decided the fate of the accused. Whether they "blue-ticketed" an offender, exiling him or her forever, or merely levied a fine, it was a system of justice that worked. In Fred's place now, there was an iteration of the old way, and as the miners presented their cases to each other they made up in spirit what they had come to lack in authority.

"We're just trying to make a decent living, and the government won't let us."

"The reason they're after us is because they've received complaints from canoers on Birch Creek. They complain that the fish can't see the hook. Canoers stay a week and contribute nothing to the economy."

"They got a package, they throw it in the creek. They're here today, gone tomorrow. We're here. It's our way of life."

"Thomas Jefferson said you need a revolution every twenty years to keep the country in balance."

"These government people coming around amounts to harassment."

"I said to them, 'I'm going to go on mining—and mining here. Meanwhile, get your ass off this claim.' "

"Murder! Kill! Burn! Torture!"

"I've been working the same creek fifty years, and when I shut down for the day I always caught grayling for dinner until tourists started coming and fished out the stream."

"Settling ponds have to hold a full day's run through the box, which is impossible."

"They say miners resist change."

"Anyone's going to resist getting his head bashed in."

"They can't really pinpoint what damage we're doing."

"We're not damaging anything."

"We're not dumping acids—we're only stirring up what's there. The same laws that apply to Homestake and Kennecott apply to us."

"The posy-sniffers are behind all this."

"When John Seiberling, the congressman, came to the country, he saw the tailings at Woodchopper and Coal Creek, and he said, 'What a mess.' He's the same one that would ban all handguns in the United States. His family is from Akron, Ohio, and makes tires. His family has probably released more pollutants than have ever been released in all Alaska."

"He probably feels guilty about that."

"We are *improving* the creeks from the standpoint of game. After the bulldozer has cleared the overburden, redtop grasses grow up that harbor mice and small rodents. Ermines and foxes come in to eat the rodents. Then comes your willow brush, and that brings in your moose. Before, there were alders, which moose don't eat. So I say we are improving the creek."

"Kill!"

"It's an independent life. We keep our bills paid. We make a little money. We hurt no one—except maybe finer sensibilities who don't like to look at our tailing piles."

"We've left some passable road. We've left something to make up for the 'destruction' of the creeks."

"Henry Speaker has a lawyer in Portland. He's up in years, but he's good. He specializes in mining laws and defends small miners."

"I'll put in a thousand dollars for a lawyer," Wilkinson volunteered. "I'll go along with the rest of you. I'll do what the lawyer says, and I'll hope he's on the right side of the law."

When the others, including Vogler, prepared to disperse, Wilkinson, still far from relaxed, decided to go over to the North Fork of Harrison Creek for an audience with Henry Speaker—the richest and oldest working miner in the district. I asked if I could go with him, and Wilkinson said he would be glad to have the company.

At speeds as low as five miles an hour, we moved south through the mountains in Wilkinson's pickup on a road roughly scraped into the tundra. It led first up Mammoth Creek to Independence Creek and Mastodon Creek, past huge hills of tailing gravel, where the C. J. Berry Dredging Company had mined in the nineteen-twenties and thirties. Wilkinson pointed up Mastodon as we went by its mouth, and said that the 1893 discovery, first in the district, had been just up there —"only one reef away." He noted, too, that wherever a creek would "rib in" to another the names of both tended to change. In the early days, miners could stake only one claim per creek, so they divided the waters with semantic abandon. Mammoth Creek was actually Independence below Mastodon; Crooked Creek was actually Mammoth below Porcupine; and the whole lot of them emptied into Birch Creek. We followed Independence Creek until it was a rivulet, and then moved up into high terrain and crossed a dome of alpine tundra that gave panoptic views of higher domes and more tundra, yellow and purple with avens and saxifrage. "Once you scrape it, it takes aeons to grow back," Wilkinson said. The tundra was in places moving on its own. Down the steep treeless mountainsides the surface soils

were creeping—wet now in summer, heavy-liddedly sliding
over the permafrost, forming semicircular folds like bunting on
a bandstand. Solifluction. We crossed a divide and descended
steeply to the North Fork of Harrison Creek, still another
Birch Creek tributary, which had been evaluated by some
professor, Fred said, at a million and a half dollars a mile.
Henry Speaker was down there now, proving the professor
right. Unhindered by the constant upkeep of bulldozers, unen-
cumbered by a need to stockpile many drums of fuel, moving
just as much gravel per season as the Cat miners and with a
cost overhead ninety-seven per cent lower than theirs, he is a
hydraulic miner, one of the last in the country of his kind. The
drawback of the method is the need for ample water, which is
not always there. Speaker had begun his operation by building
a reservoir a mile and a half upstream. Then, with a little Cat,
he had cut a beautifully engineered minutely inclined ditch
along one steep side of the V-shaped valley of the stream. The
ditch, being almost on a contour with the reservoir, would carry
water to a point some three hundred feet of altitude above the
segment of the North Fork that he meant to mine. The water
would then plunge down the mountainside from the ditch
through iron pipe of decreasing diameter and come out
through a giant nozzle with such force that from one established hosing position it could tear to bedrock more than a
hundred thousand square feet of land. The giant, as such nozzles are in fact called, has the appearance of a naval cannon,
is attached to the pipe with a ball socket, and is counter-
balanced with a "jockey box" full of small boulders, the result
being that, for all its power, it can be controlled with one hand.
Speaker, a hand on the giant, stood almost literally astride the
stream. Behind him, in the direction of the reservoir, open
spruce forest ran down the steep slopes and across the valley
floor, all but concealing the as yet unmined, meandering
stream. The banks were still shelved with thick blue ice. In the
other direction, in the range of the working giant, the valley

had been torn apart from wall to wall. Every vestige of what had been there before—forest, tundra, soil, gravel—had been driven asunder, washed over, piled high, and completely changed. It was an exposed boulderfield, all its overburden flushed away. The nozzle opening was five inches, less than the spread of a hand. At a hundred and twenty-five pounds of pressure per square inch, though, the column of water shooting out of it had the hard, compact appearance of marble. Its great arc of power, as it trajectoried over the stream, seemed to subdivide into braided pulse units hypnotic to the eye. And where it crashed at the end of its parabola it sounded like a storm sea hammering a beach.

Henry Speaker is a little over five feet tall. Clear-eyed, firmly put together, in his seventies and obviously in fine condition, he appeared to have figured out how to extend beyond previous limits the so-called prime of life. The skin of his face was hickory brown—tight skin, across sharp peregrine features, wrinkled only with a welcoming grin. He wore hip boots, overalls, and gold-colored monkey-fist gloves. On his watchband were rubies embedded in an egglike field of placer gold. On his head was a brown Stetson—the only Stetson I've ever seen that was made of hard plastic. It had a crack in it that was patched with grout.

He said the horsepower of a D9 Cat was about half the horsepower he had coming out of that hose—look out, you could burn your fingers on the water. To be burned by water seemed irresistible. I put my fingers on the solid ice-cold projectiling cylinder a few inches out from the nozzle tip, and pulled them away in an instant, burned. Speaker suggested that I toss a rock into the water jet to see what would happen. I lobbed up a big one. It intersected the jet about a foot from the nozzle, shot through the air like a discharged ballistic shell, and smashed into a pile of tailing boulders several hundred feet away. There was an eternal rainbow under the jet. The air around it swirled with mist and spray. Speaker said he had been operating giants for sixty years—in Oregon before Alaska—and he had once seen a jet of water (out of control) go straight through the body of a distant grazing cow.

Nearly three hundred feet from the nozzle was a sluice box with wide wooden "wings" that helped funnel the gravels through. The art of the giant, Speaker said, was to clean all the gravel off the bedrock without digging into it holes that could entomb the gold. With only a slight miscalculation, an error of timing and the eye, the jet could destroy the wooden sluice box, which was forty-eight feet long and five feet wide. To build up water for the sluicing, he drove gravels before the hose, causing them to heap up and dam the stream. He waited twenty minutes for a pond to fill. Then he aimed the giant at the dam, played the jet up and down, and cut a deep aperture directly in front of the box. Water and gravels roared through —a roiling brown inferno.

Speaker soon built another dam, swishing the jet carefully from side to side, piling up gravel and rocks. Certain small boulders struck by the jet leaped ten feet into the air. While he waited for the pond to fill again, he went up his pipe to check his ditch. The whole mountainside system consisted of four thousand feet of steel pipe, eleven inches in diameter at the lower end, increasing up the slope to twenty-two inches at the top, where it came out of the ditch. "Notice how much harder it is underfoot near the bottom," he said as he briskly walked up the pipe in perfect balance, his voice as pantless as if he were sitting in a chair. I had to run to hear him— struggling the while not to fall. Near the top, he said, "The pipe is not quite full up here, you can feel it jumpin' yet." It was studded with pressure valves and ringed with slip joints. Without the valves, he said, changes in pressure could "suck the pipe flat." Without the slip joints—sleeves made from fifty-five-gallon drums—the pipe could expand and buckle in the sun. He had taught himself to weld, and had built the system alone, for less than twenty thousand dollars. At the top, he checked the level of the water in the ditch, the rate of its flow into the orifice of the pipe. "This ditch is seven thousand six hundred feet long, and I built it in eight days," he said. "How's that for bulldozin'? I guess that's the record, ain't it? See the grass here. Moose and caribou come to this ditch and graze here, the full length of it. This ditch is just a flower garden when the flowers are in bloom."

Speaker had crawled across the mountains with his wife, Lora, in a twenty-thousand-dollar Winnebago—his cabin. He winters in Oregon. Rejoining Fred Wilkinson, we went into the Winnebago for a cup of coffee. On the door was a decal that said "Sheriff's Posse Comitatus," and one with a sketch of a Colt .45 over the message "Warning. Intruders and Trespassers Beware. This Property Protected by Armed Citizen." Speaker sat Wilkinson down and told him not to worry about the government invaders, with all their compliance orders and threats of fines, because what they were doing was unconstitutional. "The Constitution protects you and I," he said. "Our forefathers saw to it that our government, just like the King of England, can't harass the citizens. The government cannot harass the individual. I've been studying the Constitution now for two years. The people is the master, Fred. The government thinks they are. They've just turned that right around and they've made the people believe it. The Bureau of Land Management and the Office of Environmental Quality say they are concerned here, but two branches of government enforcing the same law is unconstitutional. In fact, government agencies are unconstitutional, because they infringe on your constitutional rights. They're trying to kill private enterprise, but don't worry. Your livelihood is guaranteed by the Constitution."

Wilkinson wanted to know what Speaker had said when the four men in the government Scout appeared on his claim. "I said to them, 'You go harassing me and I'll be looking at you through bars. I will put you in jail.'" To back up his threat, he had handed them a printed document with big block letters that said "LEGAL NOTICE: To federal officers of the IRS, HEW, HUD, Environmental, Health, and other unconstitutional agencies . . .WARNING! If two or more persons conspire to injure, oppress, threaten, or intimidate any citizen in the free exercise or enjoyment of any right or privilege secured to him by the Constitution . . . they shall be fined not more than $10,000 or imprisoned not more than ten years."

"Their complexion just changed when they saw that," Speaker reported. "I told that Lamoreaux he should be ashamed of himself, for he was killing private enterprise, and when it is dead, people will accept Communism. No law is constitutional that says you're guilty before you do something. The people on their property's got the right to choose to do as they please. Now government agents are coming to tell us what we can't do, but don't worry, the laws they are going by are in violation of the Constitution and are therefore ultered virus and not law. Now, that's right in the god-damned book. That's the law." He picked up a copy of the United States Constitution and held it out for Fred and me to see. "Boy, this is exciting to read," he went on. "It's too bad when our own people wants to sell our country out. Pretty near every law in the books is unconstitutional, because they conflict with protected rights. I'm afraid we're going to have to fight now for our freedom."

Lora Speaker, who lacked her husband's lean, smiled amiably, nodded agreement, and, at a gesture from Speaker, brought out of a cupboard an economy-size Jif creamy peanut-butter jar in which was twenty-five thousand dollars' worth of gold. It was so heavy I thought it would break the glass. It was all dust and small flakes, and had with the greatest of patience been separated—most of it by Lora—from the black and ruby sands (magnetite, hematite, scheelite, garnet) that are heavy enough to stay down with the gold all through the sluicing and the cleanup. Some miners nudge the sand aside by letting the mixture fall through the wind. Some use electric fans. Most wash it free with water in a gold pan. Some gold is so fine that on the water's surface tension it will float. Wilkinson mentioned that he sprays his gold with Windex as a means of keeping it down.

Speaker said he was "ratholing" the Jif jar. He was not ready to pay the Internal Revenue Service any portion of the gold's value (his privilege until it is sold). Cradling the jar like a sixteen-pound shot, he said, "The United States government has two ships out on the ocean right now looking for new sources of gold. They got a source of gold right here, and they want to shut it down. How god-damned crazy can those god-damned guys get? According to the Constitution, our money is supposed to be gold and silver. That's the way our forefathers set it up. Paper backed by paper is worth nothing. With gold from California we paid our debts to England—gold that came from our soil. It should be like that yet."

Some days later, I met Bill Lamoreaux, of the United States Environmental Protection Agency, and I asked him about his trip in the Scout to see the recalcitrant miners. Lamoreaux seemed easygoing and calm. Sandy hair. Brown beard. Twenty-nine years old. He had degrees in sanitary engineering from San Jose State. He said he had found the miners, on the whole, an amiable and agreeable lot—not bristly and tough, as he had expected them to be. In his travels among them, there had never been a threat of violence. He had found Wilkinson confused but apparently eager to do right. Littlefield had said he would soon build settling ponds. Speaker had been friendly and polite, even while explaining to Lamoreaux that "everything since the 1872 mining act is unconstitutional" and saying that he was going to take the case to court and personally fine Lamoreaux ten thousand dollars a day for trying to enforce unconstitutional laws. Most of the miners in the country had applied for permits. "They can appeal permits. They can work within the law. They have real good attitudes generally. That Joe Vogler keeps his mind right on what he's talking about.

There's a hell of a lot of nice people out there. I enjoy them. They're some of the most straightforward people you'll ever meet. They don't beat around the bush."

(Earl Stout, who was teen-age and full-grown before Henry Speaker was born, is too old to be concerned with settling ponds or enforcement orders or turbidity units in any form. He worked Sly Creek, Fourth of July Creek—and in 1959 he retired to his cabin on Crooked Creek, in Central. He eats potatoes. They are the fundaments of his breakfasts, his lunches, and his dinners. "I ain't too heavy on the meat situation. I never was. I get my outfit in the fall of the year. Potatoes." He is in ruddy health, white-haired, of medium height, a little stooped—eighty-five years old. He smokes a pipe. In his cabin are three calendars and three clocks. He gets up at exactly five-thirty every morning. Evenings, just before he goes to bed at nine, he goes to the calendars and crosses off the day.

This is a Friday in winter, as it happens. Sometime this morning, he filled his gas lantern. That is about all he has accomplished today. "In fact, I ain't done a whole lot since I retired in '59," he says, and in the silence that follows the ticking of his clocks sounds like the puffing of locomotives. There is an iron bed, a couple of chairs, and a big galvanized tub full of melted stream ice. When he needs more, he will cut it out of Crooked Creek and haul it on a go-devil behind his old Oliver Cat. In his Bean's boots, open wool shirt, and gray trousers, he sits and sleeps and reads—*Newsweek, Popular Science, National Geographic, Prevention.* On a shelf beside him is a book called "Upper Tittabawassa Boom Towns," in a couple of which (Hope and Sanford, Michigan) he grew up. He came to the upper Yukon fifty years ago.

On Fridays now, at precisely four o'clock, he goes down the

road to collect his mail. He could run this errand at almost any time and on almost any day. In good weather, the mail plane arrives three times a week. But Earl Stout likes to gather mail in weekly units. "What's the use of getting it," he explains, "before it's all in?" Saturday nights, he used to play pool at the Central store—stick in hand, cigar in mouth, brandy on the cushion. "That was until the old Chevy went out. Now I stay home. All the years I was on the Yukon, there was no place to go. The nearest person was five miles away. You got to get used to staying home." He sorely misses Bob. A black, short-haired mongrel, Bob was for many years Earl's only companion. Five wolves running on the creek overtook Bob not long ago. They left his collar and a small piece of his tail. After finding the blood and the fragments, Earl drank a bottle of rum. It is 3:45 P.M. He gets up and pulls denim overalls over his trousers. He ties strings around the ankles. He puts on mittens and a wool cap, and he says, "I can't take the cold the way I used to." The air outside is ten below zero. I make a move to leave. "You don't have to go," he says. "It isn't time yet. There's still ten minutes." He waits until the clocks say four. "Now," he says, "it's time to go."

❨ For all its miners and trappers and conjugal units on the river, the country seems to have an even higher proportion of people who prefer to be surrounded by but not actually to be in the wilderness. To describe Eagle, for example, the last word that I would once have imagined ever coming to mind is the one that comes to mind now: Eagle, in its way, is suburban. This remote cluster on the Yukon, two hundred air miles from Fairbanks, is as good a place as any to avoid being too much on your own if you wish at the same time to draw a circle around yourself a very great distance from the rest of your life.

In all directions from Eagle are tens of thousands of square miles of deep and total wild, into which a large part of the town's population—living in dependence on supplies from cities—rarely sets foot.

Jack Boone came into the country in 1973. "Basically, I'm a square," he says, and in Eagle he has built an octagonal cabin. He makes no effort to conceal his justifiable pride in his work. The cabin is a log structure of clean lines and apt proportions —as apparently durable as it is imaginative. "I have the ability to earn my living completely with my brain, but I don't want to," Boone remarks, making an instant friend of the visiting writer.

He sits at dinner, three children around him—Margaret, Cindy, and Daniel Boone. His wife, Jean, is in Anchorage, five hundred miles away, with a fourth child, who was in need of medical attention. Lacking money to pay for the journey, Boone went down by the river to the cabin of Jim Scott, explained the situation, and sold Scott two cords of firewood as yet uncut. "I don't believe in welfare, in assistance of any kind," Boone says. "There have been times when economic circumstances have forced me to take a small amount of it. Some people here make it a way of life. The poverty level for a family of six is eight grand. I made four grand last year. I do not constitute the way I am living as poor."

He is a big man, whose woolly beard and woolly crewcut surround pale-blue penetrating eyes. There is often a bemused smile. His voice is smoothly rolling and timpanic. He seems to drive it, like a custom-built car, to play it like a slow roll of drums. "You may have noticed my speech is not perfect," he says. "That is deliberate. My language was once a distinct liability. I have had to alter it over the years to get along with the people I have worked with."

I remark that in his conversation there is an indelible aura of culture and education, whether he likes it to be there or not.

"I am putting that on for you," says Boone, opening a quart

of homemade beer. "Fifteen years ago, I spoke perfect English. I deliberately destroyed that capability. Every beer drinker in this town has drank this product, admired it, tried to duplicate it, and failed. I can still write perfectly, with no difficulty."

"Why have you come here?"

"The advantages of modern civilization do not impress me."

He grew up in Oroville, in northern California, and for a time studied electronics at Caltech, but had no desire to join the surrounding society. "I do not like the forcing of the individual toward a high-expense manner of living," he explains. "I do not like restrictions placed on one's life just because of close proximity to several million people." He is a direct descendant of Daniel Boone, on what he refers to as "the squaw side." First, he migrated to Juneau, and set up a marine-electronics business, but, as small as Juneau is, even Juneau was too restricting for him. So he chose a town on the Alaskan Yukon, where there was more elbowroom than he would ever care to explore, and not a great deal of employment opportunity. "Those who are trying to live an independent life style in the country are paying a very high price for it," he says. "Unless one's name is John Borg, it is difficult to find much of a job —indeed, any job—in Eagle." Boone eventually found one— as a seasonal laborer with the local road crew. And so did his neighbor Jack Greene. Working together all day, the two scarcely speak. It is a feud of buried origins, apparently deep, a feud not dissimilar from all the countless crosshatching cabin-fever feuds of Eagle, in some measure having to do with the general fierceness of competition for the few available jobs, in some measure with rivalry over the building of their cabins, but mainly as a casualty of place—a community deeply compressed in its own isolation, where a cup of borrowed sugar can go off like a grenade. The Boones and the Greenes live on Ninth Avenue, a euphemism for a pass a bulldozer once made through woods at the uphill end of town, about half a mile from the Yukon. Outside Boone's cabin is a sign that reads

"Welcome to Those Who Wish Us Well, and the Rest of You Can Go to Hell." Boone means what it says. "Anyone who walks past that sign is probably broadminded enough that I can get along with them," he explains. "Diana Greene will not walk past that sign."

Diana Greene is a doctor of philosophy in classical literature, her husband an electronics engineer. Their awareness of Boone's sign is in the sub-basements of subliminal. They came into the country in 1974—on a ten-thousand-mile journey in search of a place to build—to create a life exotic to the ones they had known before, and a cabin to contain it. He was from Greene, New York, she from Long Island. They had met in Boulder, where she was in graduate school and he with the National Bureau of Standards. He was her first husband, she his second wife. In the course of their quest, Eagle seemed the only choice. ("Everywhere else we went in Alaska, people were really rowdy—no couth.") By mail from Colorado, they later bought a building lot at auction, and, starting with a big wood-sided flatbed Chevrolet truck, began assembling things for Alaska. They bought a two years' supply of food—fifty pounds of rice, fifty pounds of rye, two hundred pounds of wheat, a hundred pounds of salt, and so on to twelve pounds of almonds and twenty-five pounds of black-eyed peas. They packed up their cellar of homemade wines. He built five cabin windows. Each was three panes thick, all quarter-inch glass, heavy as a desk top, set in a redwood frame. The first and third panes were sealed with synthetic rubber, while the inner one gapped an eighth of an inch from the bottom, so air could circulate to either side. This would be a tight cabin. They also piled onto the truck a double bed, a couch, chairs, a rolltop desk, two stoves, chain saws, a generator, a washing machine, a Louis Quatorze boudoir dresser with a mirror that might once have framed Marie Antoinette. With this altitudinous load, they backfired downhill into Eagle one spring day, and braked to a halt at the roadhouse. "I'm embarrassed to say this," said

Greene to Ralph Helmer, "but I've come here to build a cabin and I don't know where my land is." Helmer pointed back up the hill.

Greene is as good with his hands as Boone. Their cabins were begun at about the same time, with exchanges of beer and wine. There was a tacit race—to the ridgepole, to completion. The Greenes won, three months to seven. Between them, the two families cut upward of three hundred logs, finding them dead on an old burn forty miles down the road, where the Bureau of Land Management would permit the cutting. The Greenes' cabin is eighteen by twenty-four, with attached foyer, long-lash eaves, and big overhangs at either end supported by a ridgepole thirty-eight feet long. Greene's brother-in-law was with him at the time, and the two of them twitched the big logs out of the forest with rope and brute effort. Boone concluded that he could not do that. He decided that logs twelve feet long were all his daughters could manage. Therefore, he would build an octagonal cabin.

For ceiling poles, the two families cut and peeled an aggregate of five hundred three-to-four-inch green spruce. Each of them also set ten fifty-five-gallon drums, filled with gravel and punctured at the bottom, gingerly into the ground—twenty separate excavations, dug carefully so as not to melt or break away the permafrost. Building his floor, Greene used the ship-lapped boards from his truck body—and two kinds of insulation. Boone chinked his walls and insulated his floor and ceiling with moss collected by his children, planning to supplement it with cement and lime, while the Greenes used fibre glass between their logs. With their heating stove and cooking stove, the Greenes had powerful defenses against the coming cold, almost enough to drive them out into the snow, because if their cabin was handsome, it was ten times as snug. A lighted match could make it warm. The Greenes burn wood at the rate of four cords a winter. The Boones, with their larger cabin, use fifteen.

Jack Greene has built an efficient cistern, with an adroit

plumbing system that services a kitchen sink and a solar-heated shower. His cabin's interior, while not as soaringly airy as Boone's, is spacious and, like the Greenes themselves, is amply touched with elegance. He is blond, with a strong and handsome face that would not be out of place on an old coin, she light and slim, with brown, quick, smiling eyes. Around their table pass sparkling cherry wine, additional wines from varietal grapes, wines they have made from berries in Eagle, wild-cranberry ketchup, baked salmon, mincemeat made from moose. From under the gable at one end of the cabin protrudes a pair of moose antlers fifty-six inches tip to tip, truly a mighty rack. Greene was humming along in his orange Volkswagen bug one day when the moose stuck its nose out over the road. He has shot spruce grouse from the VW, opening the door and firing a .22. In like manner, with a .30–'06, he dropped the big moose.

"They will not live long here," Boone says of the Greenes. "You have been there. How would you describe their cabin?"

"Very nice."

"It is very fancy, I would say. They serve gourmet meals. No one in Eagle will ever appreciate that. None of us slobs will notice. She's a Ph.D. Between her and this town there's a sociocultural gulf."

Boone rolls himself a smoke while I make a trip to his outhouse. On its interior walls are a set of rules for displaying the flag of the United States. Boone's octagonal cabin, from the outside, has enough grace of line to be saved from resembling a military blockhouse. He is building an identical structure close by, as a garage and shop. The ceiling of the main cabin is eighteen feet high, and there are two balconies, with two children bunked on each balcony. A footbridge runs between. From window to window, the logs of the walls are horizontal, while above and below the windows the logs are vertical, creating an unusual and effective symmetry. "I'm kind of anti-money," Boone says. "I don't hardly believe in the stuff, but in Auke Bay, near Juneau, I built a place for two thousand dollars that was appraised when I left at forty-three. I'm an accomplished scrounger." He and his tall, sharply intelligent wife are also accomplished teachers. Their children are educated at home, and in national testing place as high as five years ahead of their ages.

He opens another quart of beer. It is brewed in a plastic garbage can, in which the Boones mix twelve gallons of water, ten pounds of sugar, a tablespoon of yeast, and forty-eight ounces of hop-flavored extra-pale malted barley syrup, yielding the equivalent of a six-pack a day, or a little over five cases every three weeks, saving themselves approximately two thousand dollars a year against the twenty-four dollars a case charged by Eagle bootleggers. Moreover, it is fine beer. One would have to bypass Milwaukee and St. Louis and scour Europe to find its peer. It may be getting to me. Boone says not to worry: "I have drank it for years and never had a hangover." Close by him is a gun rack with three rifles. He sees me looking at them and says they are loaded. "Hunting season comes in the fall, and the fall is the busiest time of year for anyone who is trying to live any kind of subsistence life style," he says, apropos of nothing much, since the season just now is spring.

"Do you hunt a lot?" I ask him.

"No. I cannot say I am a hunter. I have not hunted anything in the three years since we came to Eagle. The purpose of the rifles is protection."

"Do you fish?"

"We buy our salmon."

"Do you use the river?"

"We have a small boat and a kicker but have not yet been out on the Yukon. We have not had time."

"Have you travelled some on foot in the country?"

"Since I've been here, I've done very little that did not have a purpose. I'm not really sure that I could enjoy trekking ten miles without a goal. I don't think I would defend that position. It's probably wrong. It's how I am. I know I'm a freak. That's why I moved to Eagle." He rolls another cigarette. He lights it thoughtfully. He spreads a screen of smoke through the octagon. "If you live in this country awhile," he says at last, "you really get to appreciate a stove and four walls."

⟨[Boone's forked message of warning and welcome—the sign on the path to his cabin—is by his report an effective deterrent to virtually every member of the Eagle Bible Chapel, known to the laity as the fundamentalist bloc. "They are here for the religious climate," says Boone. "I don't go to church. I'm not a religious man. I wouldn't go to church *here* if I was. We are moving closer to anarchy now, but the bloc still controls every winter paying job but schoolmaster. Eagle is excellent for unemployment, incidentally. If you work part of the year, it's a good place to be sure of not being offered a job. On public assistance, people can live quite well here. Even members of the bloc take food stamps, unemployment, and welfare, in various combinations. They are very social. They have dinners, prayer meetings, men's Bible study and women's Bible study once a week. They have a sewing circle that is open to Indians. Indians do come. Social relationships between the bloc and the Indians are good but condescending. To the best of my knowledge, no one in the bloc touches alcohol. In Eagle, there is one lush. Also, there are five or six people who live in the town because it is dry—who go out of their tree when a bottle appears. None of these are in the bloc. Those of us who are not in the bloc are rugged individualists, and we can't get along with each other. When I was elected to the city council a couple of years ago, I had eight friends. After six months, I had two. This does not happen among the Christians. They sit down and pray about it and decide it isn't worth it. In Eagle, there are many arguments, many short-term enemies, but few permanent enemies. The bloc will forgive and forget—the day after they have screwed you."

Eagle has upward of fifty registered voters. Roughly twenty are in the bloc. Not long ago, when the population was smaller and the bloc was proportionately larger, most of the city council was of the religious group. Eagle was their town. The landscape is what lasts around here. The people huddled upon it are—in the long span of things—as rootless as the wolves. The religious bloc, already losing its political grip, has been a factor in the town for less than a decade—its existence dating to the arrival in the late nineteen-sixties of Betty and John Borg. Other couples soon moved to join them, their common affiliation being a relationship with the Central Alaskan Mission, in Glennallen, with which the Eagle group has since relaxed its ties. While the rugged individualists went on being rugged and individual, the people of the bloc helped each other in the finding and swapping of jobs, and they cornered the job market: fire-control officer, school-bus driver, school custodian (the grammar school is three miles away, in the Indian Village), teacher's aides, preschool program, and on down a list that attained to much length through the many positions—postmaster, weatherman, customs officer, and so forth—of John Arthur Borg, the mayor. The group's minister, for a time, was Roger Whitaker, who resigned to become constable. "The whole bloc is a Communist front," commented one resident observer. "First, they get to the kids. Then, when they feel the time is right, they take over the police power."

Resident observers have a great deal to say about the bloc, which has harvested in Eagle the timeless fruits of hegemony, the ripest of which is gossip:

"They feel threatened at every turn. They are frightened, terrorized."

"They came not with a sense of mission but to seek a protected enclave. Religiously, they keep to themselves. Politi-

cally, they want to control the town. They preferred it here
when everybody knew everybody—knew what everyone was up
to. Everybody let everybody else know what they were doing.
Now they see rigs going through town and they don't know
who is in them. They don't like that."

"They have dug a hole in the world and are trying to stay
in it."

"They have a map of Eagle with flags on the cabins of
sinners. They invite one sinner a week to dinner, and attempt
a conversion."

"On the school bus, their children sing hymns, recite the
Twenty-third Psalm, and tell other children, who are not
'saved,' that they are damned forever to Hell."

(On December 12, 1917, at a meeting of the Eagle Common Council, a citizen complained that Miss Owen, the
teacher, was compelling her pupils to pray in school.)

"Neither the religious people nor the river people have any
interest in seeing Eagle develop economically. In that one
respect, we see eye to eye."

"They were against the federally funded alcohol program,
because there was nothing in it for them. The money bought
a pool table, card tables—alternatives to booze."

"It was all for the natives. Alcoholism is widespread among
the whites, too. But they don't show up as well against the
snow, you see, as these buggers with the dark skin."

In 1898, in Eagle, small building lots sold for a thousand
dollars. In 1947, thirty dollars would buy an entire acre—a
price that reached two hundred by 1967 and two hundred and
fifty by 1971. By then, however, some outsiders were beginning
to ask not so much about the price of land as about the legality
of the manner in which lots were sold.

"If you went to their church and were one of their kind, you
could buy land. But if you were a drinker—that is, not one of
them—they wouldn't talk to you. You couldn't get nothing."

"They were five out of seven on the city council. It was the city council that sold the undeveloped city lots. If you were not acceptable to them, you were turned down."

"Man named Carr, from Anchorage, owned eight or ten lots here, and wanted to sell them. He arrived one day with letters he'd received from people in Eagle. He went into the road-house—some Christians were in there, and Sarge Waller—and asked where he could find Jo and David Barnett. The Barnetts were living in a tent, hoping to get land for a cabin. No one said a word. The man repeated his question. Where could he find the Barnetts? Finally, Sarge said, 'Well, God damn it, I know where they are if nobody else does.' And he went and got the Barnetts."

In the fall of 1973, a majority was elected to the city council which was—in the adroit parlance of this community—un-church. Within a year, the town held its first public-land auc-tion of modern times—and now the way was open to the Greenes, the Boones, the Vandals, the Visigoths. The invaders had to pay, of course. Here in a wilderness that reaches out beyond comprehension, two thousand dollars became a going price for less than an eighth of an acre.

"The do-gooders used to control the town, but at last they are being outvoted."

"They really blowed their cools when I got this place."

While other things erode, John Borg remains the focus of Eagle. Because of his power and positions, he is the focus of the tattle as well. In a community of palavered reputations, no one is so thoroughly discussed as Borg. First, there are the usual and expectable patterns:

"Borg is confused, conservative."

"He professes to be quite Christian, but his religion is shal-low."

"He's an opportunist."

"He hasn't missed any bets around here to date, but he is basically honest."

"He gravelled his road at the city's expense."

But even more of what is said about him is confided almost in whispers:

"I don't want you to say who said this. Do you promise not to mention my name?"

"Yes. Tell me what you like. It will not be attributed to you."

"Is that a promise?"

"So help me."

"Well, I think he's one of the finest persons in town. He's always willing to help anyone. He's friendly. He keeps his likes and dislikes to himself. His religion is his personal concern. He doesn't try and force it on anyone else. He is one of the few people in Eagle who is willing to do things. He keeps the well house going. He tills people's gardens."

"He is the one person in his group that tolerates the river people."

"In general, he has tried to help us, has tried to help the Indian community."

"He has a lot of energy, and he lives in a place where there are limited outlets for such energy, and that's why he holds so many jobs."

"He is a leader, a goer, a doer. At thirty below zero, he will get on his snow machine and go fifty miles—for a reason. At zero, he will go for no reason. During the winter we lived at Gravel Gulch, he was the only one who came to pay a visit. John could live in this country on his own. He could do it without the group. Most of the others never leave their stoves in winter."

"Even if I don't like their ways, I still talk to him. He's good."

❡ Borg insists that he has no ambition to run the town he runs. He implies that he does so by default. "I would be tickled to death if someone would take over some of these jobs—*and* do them," he told me one day when I was helping him lug cartons off the mail plane. "I'm certainly not trying to build a kingdom around me. I have accepted these responsibilities not because I think no one else can do them. I do the weather job, and the U.S.G.S. river job, and the U.S. Customs work because they interest me. People say I'm trying to build me an empire in Eagle, but I don't think they'd be breaking down the door to ask for these jobs if I were to leave."

Like Boston and Chicago, Eagle seems to foster strong central figures. Bob Steele, whose daughter Roberta still lives in town, once ran the roadhouse and the post office and was, as well, United States Commissioner and United States Deputy Marshal. Esther and Anton Merly, now for the most part retired, preceded Borg in various positions, including the weather, the customs, the roadhouse, and the post office.

"When the Merlys turned their jobs over to John, they were looking for someone they could control."

"Borg wouldn't say yea, boo, or nay without consulting the Merlys."

"In this town, they are the puppeteers, Borg the puppet."

"The Merlys began the 'right people' idea long before the Borgs came into the country. Anton once said to me, 'It used to be so good when everybody thought alike here.' I said to him, 'How dull life must be for you.'"

Anton Merly is a tall man, bald, approaching seventy at apparent full strength. Esther has a shrewd and watchful look. She is dour and apronly and has a warm smile not easily won. For all the gossip they draw in parts of the white community, it is worthy of note that they enjoy high respect—for their understanding and compassion—among the Indians. When they were children, the Merlys grew up five miles apart on homesteads in North Dakota. Their parents had arrived there in wagons. "The winters we remember in North Dakota were worse than any we have known here," Esther has told me, and

Anton explained: "In North Dakota, it blows pretty near all the time. Here, the wind doesn't blow. In North Dakota, we had thirty-five-mile winds at thirty below. Here, you go out and you can see where you're going, and there is no danger. There, if you went out and a blizzard came up you were lost, unless you had a fence or a good horse that could take you home."

They came to Alaska in 1949 and to Eagle in 1955. "We could see there was a future here, with places so cheap—as low as a hundred and fifty for a cabin and a lot." They bought seven lots and four cabins as a start. "You're crazy," an old-timer said to them. "The town is dying." In 1959, the year of statehood, the population of Eagle was nine. Almost the entire city was on the city council. The Merlys took turns as mayor. Inevitably, they all but cornered the paying jobs, and were only too glad, they say, to pass them on, when they could, to Borg.

"Borg may be independent of the Merlys by now."

"No. The Merlys are the land barons here, the manipulators of everything that goes on behind the scenes."

"When I came into the country, I asked the Merlys if they knew of a cabin for rent. They said no. We talked awhile, and discovered we had a mutual acquaintance in Tok. The Merlys suddenly remembered a cabin that was vacant. It was far out of town and had no door. We talked some more, and it turned out I knew a friend of theirs who lives somewhere near Big Delta. Anton then remembered an empty cabin close to Eagle with a door but no windows. Later, when we hit on the name of a really good friend we have in common, I ended up with a fine cabin in the heart of town."

"Make no mistake—the seat of government of Eagle, Alaska, is Esther Merly's kitchen."

It is a spotless room, a Midwestern farm kitchen with a big wood stove and, of all things, a big white refrigerator. Anton established the first generator in Eagle, and later sold it to Borg. The Merlys now buy their power from him.

Borg has no specific trade or skill, but he feels that he could support his family anywhere, because "jobs exist if you are willing to do the work." Among his constituents are those who may sit around and disagree, but no one, at least, will ever say of Borg that, given a task to do, he is not willing. He is up at 6 A.M., twiddling shortwave dials. He listens, some days, to news on the BBC. His cabin is on Third Avenue, in deep woods. A fresh black bearskin is nailed to an outside wall. Borg does not welcome the bears that come to town. He shot one not long ago on Jefferson Street, near the post office, after children came running to tell him it was there. This one was near his own door. He seldom goes out of town to hunt, and describes himself as "not much for fishing." He gets a few grayling each year. Neat as he is in person, his yard is a scavenger heap of fuel drums and machine fragments—a true Alaskan ornamental garden. He has three snow machines, a pickup, and a Mercedes-Benz, which appears to have left Germany during the Weimar Republic and to have been driven across Canada without reference to roads. There is a hutch of rabbits, which he calls his Arctic chickens—two fat bucks and a bordello of does. "This type of life style isn't all that severe," he says. "The severity of it is a state of mind. You have your basic cabin, and you need water and wood. It is easy to get wood. Certain people, that's all they do. They live on money they earned elsewhere. When I have absolutely nothing to do, I'm just driven up the wall. I don't know what I'd do if I didn't have something to get me up in the morning. So I open my mouth and get another responsibility." Some people in Eagle don't even haul wood. Borg hauls it for them—for twenty dollars an hour or fifteen per cent of the wood. He takes his Cat across the river ice, two bobsleds riding behind him, and goes three miles through the spruce to the site of an old forest burn.

A trail leads from his cabin to his post office through a beautiful grove of aspens. To keep in close touch with his home and his bloc, he has a battery-operated field-telephone system of the type that contributed to battle tactics in the Second

World War. As the resident officer of the United States Customs Service, he pretty much lets the business come to him. He is responsible for anything that comes floating or flying out of Canada, but problems are almost nil. Around the turn of the century, there was a certain amount of waltzing with customs. A boat built in Canada with Canadian trees was a "British bottom," and by the rules of U.S. Customs had to pay a handsome fee to continue downriver past Eagle. The duty on Canadian sawboards was negligible. So Canadian crews arriving in Eagle would unload their boats, unscrew the decks, totally disassemble the hulls, and pay duty on a rick of Canadian lumber. Then they would put it all together again and shove off into Alaska. Monitoring something like that kept customs men busy, but what Borg sees now are mainly homemade rafts, many of which are barely afloat, having disassembled themselves while still in the river. He examines gear, checks identification, asks people where they're from and where they are going. "I don't sit on the riverbank. The people come to me. I've never made a seizure." Occasionally, the Brainstorm arrives—a small barge that hauls fuel and building materials from Dawson, in Yukon Territory, down the Yukon into Alaska and up the Porcupine River back into Canada, to Old Crow, an aggregate five hundred miles. Borg does the customs paperwork, and says it is no less voluminous than it might have been for the Queen Mary. With regard to aircraft, "most pilots are aware of the fact that they are in bad trouble if they have not reported to customs somewhere along the way." So they seek him out, too.

("I have wondered whether the customs collection at Eagle pays for itself nowadays, or whether the salaries and other expenses of collection do not exceed the revenue," wrote Hudson Stuck, the Archdeacon of the Yukon, in 1917.)

In the small, seventy-five-year-old log-cabin city hall, Borg runs his council meetings with a skepticism (he is now the only member from the bloc) that is muffled toward his colleagues and less so toward the language of state and federal statutes. "All this government talk is so many big words," he says. Federal funds are contributing to the restoration of the courthouse, near the center of town. Wearily, Borg explains that careful archeological excavations must be performed with "magic wands and metal detectors" or the federal money will not be forthcoming. He calls it a "federal fiasco." He refers repeatedly to the Eagle Historical Society as "the Eagle Hysterical Society." He does not appear to be fond of history, but he is the president of the society. Councilman Horace Biederman, pressing for his dream of a new community center (also to rise on federal funds), mentions HUD and "what they call a block-type grant."

"Who is Hud?" asks Borg, and moves on to new business: the dumping of trash. A sign on the wall says "Get Into America."

At home in his cabin after a long complex day, the Mayor will sometimes relax with cassettes he owns of radio serials from the nineteen-thirties and forties. He leans back, presses a lever. The tape rolls. There is a sound of whistling gales. An announcer, urgent and stirred, says, "Now, as howling winds echo across the snow-covered reaches of the wild northwest, the Quaker Oats Company, makers of Quaker Puffed Wheat [sound of rifle shot] and Quaker Puffed Rice, the delicious cereals shot from guns [sound of rifle shot], in coöperation with the Mutual Broadcasting System presents 'Sergeant Preston of the Yukon' [sound of howling husky]. It's Yukon King, the swiftest and strongest lead dog of the northwest, breaking a trail for Sergeant Preston, of the Northwest Mounted Police, in his relentless pursuit of lawbreakers. [Voice of Preston: "On, King! On, you huskies!"] Gold. Gold, discovered in the Yukon, a stampede to the Klondike in the wild race for riches. Back to the days of the gold rush and the adventures of Sergeant Preston and his wonder dog, Yukon King, as they meet the challenge of the Yukon."

There is a sewing machine in the post office. Betty Borg works there when John—hauling wood, plowing gardens—is away. Dark-haired and bright-eyed, she is petite, and as trim as he. They have one child, Barbara, whose advance upon the years of secondary education has presented a dilemma to the Borgs. They feel that the supervised high-school work available to her in Eagle is more than a match for academic programs elsewhere, but they worry that she will be deprived socially, that she will suffer for lack of activities with others. Yet to leave the country in search of a high school is to give up what they have here. "I've got the most secure economic situation in Eagle," he says. "I've got it made here. To move means cashing it in, means starting all over again." A boarding school is not, apparently, in the conversation, but how about a high school in Anchorage or Fairbanks, where she might be able to live with friends?

"The life style is unacceptable there," says Borg.

"Unacceptable?"

"Too much garbage." He refers to drugs in Anchorage high schools and police having to keep order there, teachers smoking in the classroom, a grade-school teacher using *Playboy* as a textbook—an overall atmosphere "where kids' rights reign supreme."

"Politically, most of us are conservative," Borg says of the bloc. "We have a common denominator, the church. We are the largest mutual-admiration society in Eagle. There's some truth in some of the gossip about the group. But we have a basis for conversation, a common spirit about many things. Others are interested in drinking. We are not. They gripe and bellyache. The problem is, so few people here have a steady job. They complain at council meetings, and when I assign them to a committee to look into their own complaints they can't back away fast enough. If you have a solid group, outsiders will chip away at it. When people say we don't want them, it's their rationalization, not ours. We haven't closed doors to anybody, and aren't about to."

When Borg ran the roadhouse, he tried to get the Common Council to advertise Eagle on the radio. He would hardly do that now. When he had been here four years, the population was thirty-six, and—in the flux that is the way of things with the careers of white Alaskans—he and his family were by then the fifth-longest continuing residents of the town. The river people soon arrived, and the Wallers, and whatnot. In a couple of years, the population more than doubled. "I don't say they'll have to sharpen my head and plow me into the ground to get rid of me," Borg says now. "Too many people, and I would want to leave. If you double your population, you geometrically square your problems. With a thousand people, Eagle would not be the same."

"It would be like the eighteen-nineties."

"Only worse. You don't need a vacation from Eagle to get yourself together again. People are not assigned here. They live here by choice. When the road closes in the fall, we are not snowed in. Other people are snowed out."

(On the twelfth of June, 1950, there was a motion before the Common Council of Eagle, Alaska, that "a mowing machine" be acquired "to clean the streets." Seconded. Carried. As bush communities in Alaska go, Eagle is a trig town. It has a reputation for grace and beauty. This is not always evident to the eye of the outsider, which tends to alight on yards full of old tires, fencing, caribou racks, dogsleds, snowshoes, lynx pelts, pole wood, fifty-five-gallon drums, cans, kayak frames, kerosene heaters, cast-iron grain mills, tarpaper, fuel cans, six-cell batteries, corrugated roofing material, and rotting fish compost in open pits. The inhabitants have the aesthetic disadvantage of being human beings. Where people exist, things are gross. In Short Hills, New Jersey, and Greenwich, Connecticut, the lovely creatures on the combed lawns are spared their own grossness because they pay not to see it, they do not picnic at the town dump. There are community dumps in Alaska, too, but much of what might go there lingers in the yard because one day it could be needed. If, to some extent, the people of the bush array themselves in squalor, it surely does not exceed what everyone creates but most don't see.

The center of town, in fact and in function, is the well house, because few people have their own water. It is a white frame blockish structure, taller than wide or deep, with a pagoda roof, and a firebell cupola up against the sky. The windmill standing beside it has a long history of lassitude, a record expressible in revolutions per month. March 26, 1951: "Tank very low but today some wind arrived allowing an extra half-foot of water to be collected." November 26, 1917: "No wind during past month and tank dry." In present times, the windmill sings castrato. A Jacuzzi submersible pump, hidden in the well house, tops up the twenty-thousand-gallon cedar tank. Water comes out of a hose and nozzle of the type used for pumping gasoline. Firefighting equipment is piled up in the well house, and so are kerosene pots for mercy flights (for spacing around the airfield to light emergency landings). The outer door opens out, and shuts like a book with an inner door that opens in. After these two comes a small foyer, then another door, which leads to the water. All this to keep back the cold. The deep cold comes in waves, spells, snaps—and really long ones are rare. From late in December, 1917, until early in February, 1918, the air was never warmer than forty-six below. If you want to be very sure of encountering someone, know his habits and meet him at the well house. A prominent citizen of Eagle (the description will not reveal him, because in Eagle there is no other kind) recently did just that, with intent to take advantage of the complex doors. A's wife was in B's cabin. B kept a 12-gauge shotgun, loaded with rock salt, leaning by the door. A knew about the salted shotgun. He studied B's habits, and when B went to the well house A locked him in with three doors. Then A, picking B's cabin lock, recaptured his wife,

> who walked down the street with
>   him hand in hand,
> enjoyin'
>   the sportin' life.

Killing frosts can come at any time of year. Vegetable gardens will have bonfires along all four sides. Up the Yukon five miles and behind the first bend, the tributary Eagle Creek cuts a wide V into the jagged mountains. One distant peak—without a name, like the others—sits exactly in the trough of the V: a sort of gunsight mountain. Even in the floodings of solstitial light, it will turn, from time to time, pure white. If Eagle is, as it has been said to be, the best-looking town in Alaska, it is infinitely outclassed by its setting—high on its bend in ten visible miles of river, among heathery soft and purplish stands of cottonwood, stream-course white spruce, and, on the uplands, black spruce only eight inches in diameter but two and a half centuries old. Near the summit of Eagle Bluff, soaring fourteen hundred feet above the town, the flag of the United States flies eight thousand seven hundred and sixty hours a year. A huge rugged cross was hauled up there and erected, but it lacked the endurance of the flag and lies toppled on a ledge below.

The city's budget this year is thirty-seven hundred dollars. That should mow a lot of streets. There are people, as in any town, who wonder where it all could go. Its highest and best use is self-preservation, for the courthouse (1901), the well house (1903), the old log church (1900) are settling with dignity into their own foundations, and while state and federal money might help with the larger places, any number of cabins and buildings are of similar age. Eagle was the first incorporated city in interior Alaska, and Theodore Roosevelt's picture is on the courtroom wall, because he signed the papers that made it so. Eagle was a city before Fairbanks was a tent.

Anchorage was thirteen years unborn. On the bench in Eagle, James Wickersham, United States District Judge, presided over three hundred thousand square miles of land. Eagle may have an A-frame here and there, two gas pumps, and a couple of picture windows looking out past biffies at the Yukon, but in many of its essentials its appearance is long unchanged. It much resembles itself in, say, 1905.

Leaflets were tacked up around town that year showing a resolute character holding a pistol aimed at the viewer. They were titled "Western Philosophy," and said, in intimidating black-letter type, "LIVE EACH DAY SO THAT YOU CAN LOOK EVERY DAMN MAN IN THE EYE AND TELL HIM TO GO TO HELL." The intent may have been to buck up the miners, a few of whom had hearts of gold but in other respects were equally yellow and soft. "OTT & SCHEELE, General Merchandise," said a big sign over the door of what is now the Eagle Roadhouse. At the top of a post in front was a kerosene lamp. The North American Trading & Transportation Company did business out of a corrugated-tin building put up in 1899. A store of the rival Northern Commercial Company (a structure now vacant) was just up the street from the Riverside Hotel, the Coffee House, the Laundry and Baths, the Olympia Bar, and Henry Raymond's combined Saloon and Chamber of Commerce. On May 22, 1905, there was a motion before the Common Council that women be prohibited from frequenting saloons. Seconded. Carried. The women wore long dresses with full sleeves, pinned their hair up, and sometimes carried parasols. The men, with any sense of occasion, wore ties and vested dark suits. There were many sod-roofed log cabins. Three hundred people lived in the town. The Merlys' place was here, and the Ivys', the Stouts', George Beck's. The hall of the Improved Order of Red Men, which still stands on Third Avenue, was the scene of the gatherings and dances and assorted activities of "acknowledged conservators of the history, the customs, and the virtues of the original American people." The Improved Order of Red Men was dedicated to "friendship, brotherly helpfulness, fraternal love, and good fellowship," and was for whites only. Its charter purpose was that the "memory of primitive red men will be preserved to the latest period of recorded time." On November 27, 1905, an ordinance was passed by the Common Council "to restrict and regulate the disposition of intoxicating liquors within the town of Eagle." Everyone voted aye. The community had a handwritten newspaper, the *Eagle City Tribune.* The first typewriter arrived that year. Lumber was cut for the making of culverts. An ordinance forbade throwing garbage over the riverbank. (It remains, by and large, in force.) The Heath Hotel was near the Grotto Restaurant was near the United States Customs House. The customs agent is preserved in a photograph that looks very much like John Borg.

The log church, close by the river, was the purview of the Reverend and Mrs. James Woolaston Kirk, who came into the country in 1899. Their first services were held in a saloon. Their first pulpit was covered with wolfskin. They brought with them a bell cast in Albany. (It is still here.) They did not espouse the Western Philosophy. They were from Philadelphia, and they meant to put some of Rittenhouse Square down on the bank of the Yukon. Dr. Kirk was tall, with opalescent eyes under brows that lifted like spires. Mrs. Kirk was spruce and petite and from the front row of a good long history of choirs. When the couple arrived in Eagle, the miners took one look and instantly got the picture, warning each other that the "minister" and his wife were obviously professional grafters. Mrs. Kirk was forming her impressions, too. She wrote that she was "heartsick when I saw those bold, degraded persons, calling themselves women, who were in the place bent on lowering all standards of morality. I never before saw iniquity in its unblushing hideousness, for wickedness does not stalk abroad in the big city, where the law protects the safety and morality of its citizens." (In December of the following year, Margaret

Johnson was fined a hundred and fifty dollars "for the crime of keeping a Bawdy House," and put in jail until all was paid —"not to exceed eighty-five days.") Mrs. Kirk had with her a foot-pumped organ. She could swell a room with hymns. She also had the first dustpan and brush ever seen in the Interior. She had crystal and china and napkin rings. When miners came into her cabin, tears sometimes collected in their eyes. The miners were homesick. Winter and summer, life in the gold camps and on gold claims was spare and sometimes bitter. They came to her, confided in her, and asked her to play the hymns. "Once, I was worth three hundred thousand dollars, had a fine home and a noble wife," one miner told her. "All are gone and I am here to get money enough to educate my two daughters, but if the whole camp was compelled to put up ten dollars in gold dust or be shot we would all have to die." Mrs. Kirk prayed and played for him. A young man came to her once depressed and suicidal. She played the intermezzo from "Cavalleria Rusticana," and after a time he got up and went back to work feeling better. "Although the Fortymile and Birch Creek districts are among the oldest of the gold-placer producers of Alaska," Alfred H. Brooks was reporting at the time, "investigations show that they are by no means exhausted and that, with the introduction of improved methods of mining, they will continue to yield good returns." Brooks, whose name would rest in the Brooks Range, was the U.S.G.S. Geologist in Charge of the Division of Alaskan Mineral Resources, and he was quite right, of course, but the good returns did not apply to all. While Brooks was fostering new successes, the failures went off to Mrs. Kirk.

When miners and prospectors, in the eighteen-nineties, had begun appearing in the country in rush quantities, there was —on the American side of the boundary—little order and less law. The War Department, imagining a need for both, sent Captain P. H. Ray on a journey of reconnaissance in 1897. Ray travelled up the Yukon on a cargo-carrying riverboat that was hijacked when it reached Circle City. The miners took the supplies, because they were otherwise going to starve, and they scrupulously paid a price they thought fair. (The boat had been saving its goods for Dawson, in Canada, which glittered with economic inflation.) Ray continued upriver. When he wrote his report, he said there were eighteen thousand people in the region, "which on our side of the boundary is without semblance of law, civil or military." There was a need for Army installations, he said. "A turbulent element is coming into the country that will have to be controlled." He recommended, among other things, a military garrison at the mouth of Mission Creek. It was a good site—fairly level and well-wooded ground on a high bank of the Yukon—close to the international boundary. Ray had scarcely left the country when twenty-eight miners platted a townsite on the same bend of the river where he had said the fort should be. If they were not the first real-estate speculators in the Territory of Alaska, they were somewhere high on the list. They might have called the place, say, Rustic Wilderness, but they happened to glance up at the white-headed birds that lived on the river bluff that would dominate the town, and decided to name it for them.

For a hero dead in the Philippines, the Army base was called Fort Egbert. Police work became the least of its preoccupations. The Army Signal Corps wanted to extend its great web to cover all America, including the upper Yukon. Communications in Eagle were nothing to write home about. After the Eagle post office was established, in 1899, the Post Office Department, in Washington, decided to establish a winter mail route across the Alaska Range from Valdez, on Prince William Sound, to Eagle, on the Yukon. A carrier, with eleven horses and a sack of mail, set out in October for the north. Eleven horses died. The carrier kept going, of course, and in the dead of winter he finally came walking into Eagle. The trip had cost the government three thousand dollars. In the sack were three letters. The Signal Corps meant to improve on that with instantaneous messages, by overland wire, from Eagle to all the world. Laying the wire was a project weirdly analogous to the building of the Trans-Alaska Pipeline, in that it required the clearing of a tortuous route north from Valdez (now the pipeline's southern terminus), with camps set up along the way and crews working the equivalents of overtime and double time. The crews were soldiers, earning thirteen dollars a month. Their boss was Lieutenant William Mitchell, twenty-one years old. He was on his way to fame in the air, to a court-martial, to a vindicating posthumous medal, but this was two years before Kitty Hawk, and all he had on his mind was how to move men and materials through several hundred wilderness miles where men and mules carrying heavy loads sank deep into muskeg. Mitchell's solution was to transport in winter what he would build in summer—a procedure new to the Army, and requiring Mitchell to become an expert in everything from Arctic clothing to the efficacy of sled runners. To protect morale, he prohibited thermometers. Work proceeded even at forty and fifty below. Mitchell was not lacking in flair. He was a Crockett on snowshoes, a beardless Boone. Travelling the line from crew to crew, he wore fringed hide clothing trimmed with extensive beadwork. His rifle was kept in a beaded sheath. He devised a parka of stuffed mattress ticking. He wore a beaver hat.

Poles were set, and wire strung, in summer. Repair cabins were built at regular intervals, relay stations where necessary. Finally, in June of 1903, the project was complete. Mitchell before long departed. His construction was fated for brief use and long desuetude. Isolated bits of wire still hum in the wind. Cabins here and there remain intact. For the time being, though, in 1903, a town that would celebrate its nation's Bicentennial beyond the reach of television and telephone—without public utilities of any kind—had a telegraph line from which word of great moment could go in an instant around the earth.

"Have Charly Harper in custody."

"Get typewriter from clerk's office and ship to this office."

"Pawn takes pawn."

"Queen to King's Bishop Four."

"Knight to King Six. Check."

"Ascertain if Alexina Byron is a proper person to conduct a barroom. The Judge is adverse to granting liquor licenses to women."

The date of that last message was the eighth of August, 1905 —a wet summer in much of the country, very good for mining but with less rainfall locally and, in the Fortymile, consequent despair. In the desk of John Robinson—Deputy United States Marshal, Eagle, Alaska—was a letter from an agent of the White Pass & Yukon riverboat company in Dawson, Yukon Territory, that said, "Dear Sir: I have your letter of May 31 advising me of four insane persons coming up on the Lavelle Young en route to the outside. I may say that we have no regular place for the accommodation of insane people; however, we have often taken out batches of insane people for the Northwest Mounted Police here, and if they are violent or apt to annoy passengers we construct cages for them on the main deck." Robinson presumably shipped them out. After at least a dozen telegrams went up and down the country, Alexina Byron got her license to operate a barroom, although women were not to be served there. Eugene Miller was jailed that fall for indecent exposure, Frank Van Norstran for cursing and swearing and making unnecessary noise. Winter came down particularly hard. A few days after the first of December, Berber the tailor froze to death. On about the same day—at any rate, on December 5, 1905—a stranger appeared on a sled on the Yukon, came up the bank, and mushed into town. The temperature was sixty degrees below zero. He was of modest height, with a wiry spareness that was somehow evident within his abundant furs. His hair was thin and was beginning to recede. His glance was level, prosaic. He asked where he could send a telegram. His voice was accented, attracting no interest, for half the Tower of Babel was already in the goldfields. In the telegraphy office, he sat and wrote for some time. The moment did not call for a ten-word cryptogram. Nothing had been heard from him for two and a half years. He wrote, actually, a thousand words. Addressing the message to Dr. Fridtjof Nansen, in Christiania, Norway, he signed it "Amundsen." The essence of what he had to say was that he had discovered the Northwest Passage.

His sloop, Gjöa, was frozen in sea ice nearly four hundred miles north. To get from the ship to Eagle, he had travelled a great deal farther than that: over passes among mountains of nine thousand feet, then following the routes of frozen rivers —the Coleen, the Porcupine, and two hundred miles on southward up the Yukon. An Eskimo man and woman travelled with him as far as Fort Yukon, and a whaling captain whose ship was so badly damaged that he was on his way to San Francisco for another. Amundsen stayed in Eagle two months, going like everyone else to the well house for his water, and waiting for mail from home. His men were provisioned and safely encamped, and for him, meanwhile, Eagle was more comfortable than the shore of the Beaufort Sea. Neither in "The North West Passage" nor in "My Life as an Explorer" does he say what he thought of Eagle's collective cupboard, but he would have had his Alaska strawberries, his bacon, doughnuts, condensed milk, sweet chocolate. Butter cost as much as four dollars a canned pound, oranges about fifty cents apiece. A hundred pounds of sugar was thirty dollars, a hundred pounds of flour fifteen. The cost of a breakfast of ham, eggs, bread, butter, and coffee approached three dollars. At the Eagle Roadhouse all these years later, the cost of the same breakfast has gone up fifty cents. Alaska strawberries were dried beans.

The nine officers and the hundred and thirty-eight enlisted men of Fort Egbert apparently gave him an awestruck, warm reception. His tenth day in Eagle was December 14th. It would be the date, six years later, of his unprecedented arrival, with associates and dogs, at the South Pole. Meanwhile, though, he had tales enough to tell. He had determined, on his voyage, the exact location of the North Magnetic Pole—the other, and more scientific, purpose of his trip. He had spent two winters frozen in ice. He had come near burning the Gjöa to a crisp. In August, less than four months before, he had been trying to pick his way westward through shallow water that had never been sailed, and he felt such stress that he could not eat or sleep. One sounding would be more discouraging than the last. The bottom was a lethal maze. The hull barely slid above it, once with an inch to spare. The Gjöa thus crept westward, and on the western horizon one day there was a sail. "A sail!"

> It meant the end of years of hope and toil, for that vessel had come from San Francisco through Bering Strait and along the north coast of Alaska, and where its deep belly had floated, we could float, so that all doubts of our success in making the Northwest Passage were at an end. . . . Instantly, my nerve-racking strain of the last three weeks was over. And with its passing, my appetite returned. I felt ravenous. Hanging from the shrouds were carcasses of caribou. I rushed up the rigging, knife in hand. Furiously I slashed off slice after slice of the raw meat, thrusting it down my throat in chunks and ribbons, like a famished animal, until I could contain no more. Appetite demanded, but my stomach rejected, this barbarous feast. I had to "feed the fishes." But my appetite would not be denied, and again I ate my fill of raw, half-frozen meat. This time it stayed by me, and soon I was restored to a sense of calm well-being.

The sighted ship was a whaling vessel, and when the whalers met with the company of the Gjöa they guessed that Amundsen was at least fifty-nine and possibly as much as seventy-five years old. From the age of fifteen, he had had what he described as "a strange ambition" to "endure . . . sufferings" at extreme latitudes: "Perhaps the idealism of youth, which often takes a turn toward martyrdom, found its crusade in me in the form of Arctic exploration." He was thirty-three years old.

The Arctic tree line in Alaska and Canada does not even closely follow a degree of latitude but is a jagged graph made by the digital extremities of the boreal forest as they reach with varying success into Arctic river valleys. Amundsen's route from the Gjöa to Eagle happened to go up the valley of what has since proved to be the northernmost extent of trees. As he travelled southward (for the most part on skis), he was impatient to glimpse the beginnings of the forest, for he had not seen a tree in two and a half years.

> *I . . . knew that on this day we should reach the wooded district, and I was very excited at every turn in our course. When at length the first fir tree stood out against the sky up on the ridge—a very diminutive, battered little Christmas tree, hanging out of a crevice—it produced a wonderful sensation, reminding me that we were now out of the Polar regions and on more homely human ground: at that moment I could have left everything that was in my charge and scrambled up the rock to catch hold of that crooked stem and draw in the scent of the fir trees and the woods.*

Amundsen remembered his two months in Eagle as a "cherished" and "pleasant" time. The cabin he lived in belonged to Frank Smith, the manager of the Alaska Commercial Company store. It is still here. The main part is only twelve feet wide and fourteen deep, with two extensions out the back that make it long and narrow, like the Gjöa. Only the name of the street it is on has changed. The cabin is just off First Avenue, on Amundsen.

Amundsen had heroes, his own capacity for awe. He met such a person on his way back to his ship. He departed Eagle

February 3rd (leaving Fix, one of his sled dogs, behind, because Fix had gorged himself on the provender of Eagle and was a useless ball of fat). He retraced his route, rejoined his two Eskimo companions in Fort Yukon, and had gone maybe a hundred miles up the Porcupine when he saw one day a dark, solitary speck on the distant snow. It moved toward him. An hour later, the gap closed, and he met a man named Darrell, who was hauling a small toboggan by hand. Darrell worked for the Hudson's Bay Company, and he was carrying mail. He had come from the Arctic Ocean and had crossed the mountains alone, because an unusually heavy snowfall on the North Slope was too deep for dogs. "I could not believe my eyes," Amundsen wrote in one book. "Here was a man, hundreds of miles from the nearest human being, with not a soul to aid him in case of illness or accident, cheerfully trudging through the Arctic winter across an unblazed wilderness, and thinking nothing at all of his exploit. I was lost in admiration." And in another book he said, "I stood looking after him as he disappeared from view, and I thought, if you got together a few more men of his stamp, you could get to the moon."

⟨ The riverboats that stopped at the port of Eagle were stern-wheelers of the Mississippi style, with curtained saloons and decks for strolling and wood piled high on their bows. They burned a cord an hour. They ran until mid-century. "It's a dirty shame they ever stopped," says Barney Hansen, who well remembers them. "If they'd quit giving so much money to foreign countries and kept the steamboats on the river for God's people to run in, it would have been wonderful, but they didn't." The Sarah, the Yukon, the Lavelle Young—there were dozens of them, and they tied up at Eagle, their company flags and thick smoke flying, intense in their competition: Northern

Commercial versus North American Trading & Transportation. They could be heard miles away, their big pistons thumping. Al Stout, who now works claims on American Creek, came into the country working on such a vessel, and it cured him of riverboats forever. His bunk was in the stern, directly above the thump. He worked six hours on and six off, with additional duty at every wood stop and every port. He fell asleep in any slack moment, wherever on the boat he might be. His pay was two dollars a day. He got off at Eagle, and stayed off, to become a miner—a relatively easeful occupation.

One-way tickets on the steamers were blue. They were not always bought by the people who used them. They were sometimes bought by the community. In Council meeting on December 13, 1909, for example, the "matter of relieving the town of Otto Strom was generally discussed and it was arranged to start him down the river." His offense was assault and battery—obviously even a heavier crime than prostitution, for no blue ticket had been forthcoming when the Fort Egbert surgeon, earlier that year, discovered that Gertrude Carson was suffering from v.d. The commanding officer requested that the community banish Ms. Carson, because she was a menace to the health and discipline of the troops. Two months later, though, she was allowed to reopen, provided she keep "sober and clean, and a respectable place in her line." Her cabin was in the western half of Block 18 on C Street, where, in a move to clean up First Avenue, all prostitutes had been consigned a year before (and where all the cabins are gone and a grove of aspens quakes today). Those were milestone times for Eagle. The windmill was shipped in, with a bill for almost twelve hundred dollars. And a package arrived that killed Fort Egbert dead. In it was a wireless transmitter, and all the work of Billy Mitchell, five years after its completion, was in the instant obsolete.

By 1910, nothing was going out on the wire. In 1911, the War Department closed the Army post. Forty-five buildings had been built, and a water-supply line from American Creek. At intervals through the woods, this water line passed over fires that kept it fluid twenty-four hours a day. The soldiers burned three thousand cords of wood a year. When they departed forever, Eagle was balder than Kansas, and six thousand stacked cords stayed after them to rot. Regulations prohibited the departing soldiers from giving or selling materials to local people, so they ignited a pyre of coonskin coats—two hundred coonskin coats—and they threw their rifles into the Yukon.

A few years ago, Tom Scott, of Eagle, took a job in the Washington office of Alaska's Senator Mike Gravel. On a lunch hour, he happened into the Library of Congress, and could not believe what he saw—"all that material there to be used." He looked up "Fort Egbert" and was soon directed to the National Archives, where he found plats and photographs and records—a trove unknown in Eagle. Much of Fort Egbert had long since disappeared—the gymnasium, with its basketball court; the post exchange and commissariat; the veranda-bordered barracks, so odd and Southwestern—but the N.C.O. quarters were still standing, and the enormous mule barn, the quartermaster warehouse, the granary, the water-wagon shed, not to mention various ruins with outlines intact. Scott called a friend named Gerald Timmons in the Bureau of Land Management. What could be done in the way of restoration and preservation? Timmons told him to write certain letters on Gravel's stationery and ask Gravel to sign them. The first letter went to the Bureau of Land Management. As a citizen of Eagle, and without revealing his employment with Gravel, Scott went to Senator Ted Stevens, of the opposite party. The Senator asked Scott, who was twenty years old, what a hundred and fifty thousand dollars could do. "We were so naïve. With a hundred and fifty thousand, we figured we'd have a Williamsburg here." The Fort Egbert restoration was soon in the B.L.M. budget for seventy thousand dollars, to be repeated annually. To preserve buildings in the city, twenty-five thousand was provided by the state and matched by the National Park Service—a deal engineered by "Gravel." The Seabees were sent in to work on the mule barn. They were transported by the National Guard. Eagle is indeed becoming a far-northern Williamsburg, to the particular wonder of young Tom Scott, who says, "It's just amazing. I can't believe it. So many resources are *available.*"

⟨ When Jim and Elva Scott, Tom's parents, came into the country to settle, in the early nineteen-seventies, they paused on the hill above Eagle and reminded each other that they had lived in many Alaskan bush communities, and with regard to this one they wished to share a firm resolution: in its politics they would not become involved. A couple of years later, he was impeached as mayor. The tattle says "impeached." The word is a shade strong. He resigned, at any rate, in foul humor, and a majority of the Council enthusiastically approved. His initial act had been to kill the opening prayer. It was while he was on the Council that the preponderance of the religious bloc came to an end. When members of the Bible Chapel hopefully asked him if he would come to a Scripture reading, he mentioned his atheism and said he might have "little to contribute." His principal offense, though, if such it was, seems to have been the advice and support he gave his son in the effort to preserve and restore the fort and the town.

"They made deals with the government—him and Tom—regarding the designation of historic sites, which require approval by the city. None was given."

"Eagle was in the National Register of Historic Places for two years before the city found out it was."

"When Eagle was changed from a First Class to a Second Class City, he executed the papers without notifying the

Council. He did not acquaint the people with appeals procedures."

"Recently, he has said that the city should be abolished, due to excessive taxation. He says the public well should be closed and abandoned."

"He thinks the Bureau of Land Management could run Eagle better than the Council."

"I don't like his ways. He wants the town government out of here. He's a Communist."

"Show me the card. But I'll buy Socialist—and I don't think we need any in Eagle."

"He's such a wide person. He has so much of everything. But at times he does not listen to other people's ideas."

"The people of the Indian Village respect him. I respect him."

Jim Scott is a big man, angry and funny, his face alive with wit. He is a forester, now retired from long federal service. He is the salt and the pepper of Alaska. He is my neighbor, and, while I am here, my landlord. The two cabins are back to back. We split our wood against the same log. I watch from my window to encounter him there. He sets the axe down, puts a boot up, looks out over the Yukon, and says, "When I came here, I was, in effect, seeking the philosophical outlook of our Founding Fathers—you know what I mean?—here in this great and glorious community." He lifts the axe. "The town is corroded with ne'er-do-wells," he says. Chop. "It is, in effect, Forest Lawn for the living." Chop. Chop.

His eyes are owlish, because snowlight blinded him once, burned his corneas. He has a beardless, broad face, suggesting honesty—the face of an overweight hawk. I remember thinking when I first saw him that he looked a lot like George Washington—a Washington caught by a cannier Peale, with a slicing edge in his demeanor, as if someone had just put a question to him concerning his expense account. As an "administrative forester," he made patterned journeys across hundreds of miles of Territorial Alaska, by float plane, by canoe, by snowshoe. In his "idiot bag" he carried forms and applications—for homesteads, cabin sites, "headquarters sites" for bush endeavors—and he tried to educate people in the responsibilities of living on public estate, so they could stay within the rules, legalize their occupancy, prove up. He became their friend. He willingly brought them supplies—hams, snares, traps, shells, sugar, flour, medicine—when they sent him lists and asked the favor. He ate and slept in their cabins, and he always paid. He paid five or six dollars to roll out his sleeping bag, and two for any meal. There were no exceptions. "I didn't want so much as a piece of pie hanging over my head." Chop.

For a time, the family's cabin was in Homer, on Kachemak Bay. He would fly to Kenai, and walk the roadless miles home —seventy by airline, upward of a hundred on foot. One night, after snowshoeing a good distance at thirty below zero, he stopped at a cabin, tired. He said he would sleep on the floor, but the people insisted that he sleep in a bed with their children—a small boy and a small girl. The boy wet the bed all night. His sister kept warning him he was going to get spanked. Jim just lay there between them, floating on his back in a lake of urine, saying nothing. "It beggared description" is what he says now. "In effect, it was enough to pale the Pope." He uses exactly the same terms to summarize his experiences on the higher levels of bureaucracy.

When he had risen in the world, up out of the fun and into the shuffling paper—when he had become district manager, based in Anchorage, and in charge of half Alaska—he dealt regularly with, among others, people of the petroleum industry. They invited him for cocktails. "I never darkened their door. I avoided them like the bubonic plague. It made it so much easier to deal with the sons of bitches." It seems possible that if Jim Scott had ever cut down a cherry tree, he would have reported it, and would not have had to be asked.

He was born in Appleton, Minnesota, on the Pomme de Terre, commencing a lifelong passion for rivers. It culminates now with the Yukon. The river is why he is here. He has a twenty-foot Chestnut freighter canoe. He has been a canoe-man from his earliest youth—on the Pomme de Terre, the Red River of the North, the Minnesota, the Otter Tail. He was in Alaska as a bachelor before the war. Elva, just graduated from Berkeley and a registered nurse, met him when he went through California on his way—as things eventuated—to Brit-ain and France with the Army. Since his return, they have lived in Alaska.

He worked for the Bureau of Land Management, but does not adopt a B.L.M. attitude toward the river people, who are, by and large, his friends. He is, in his way, as vehement as they. He says he had hopes for the work and future of the bureau in the days of President Kennedy (the B.L.M. has caretaker responsibility for most of the land of Alaska), but things later slid in an erosive way, and now the B.L.M., by his description, "has reverted to being a national grab bag surrounded by peo-ple in sharkskin suits." Scott is nothing if not verbal. He loves, and sometimes makes, words. He rolls words on his tongue with such savor that certain ones—"gymanastics," "mythyology"— would appear to have an extra syllable; he seems to like them so much that he is reluctant to let them go without a bonus.

He despises exploitation of the mythology of Alaska. When he is in the summer Arctic and sees Eskimos hurrying in parkas and mukluks to beat drums before tourists, he wishes he had enough money to pay them all to stay home. He is a xenophile. He is interested in high-latitude peoples, and has travelled from one country to another completely around the Arctic world. The State Department has sent him abroad, exporting his knowledge of northern vegetation. He praises the way things are ordered and organized in Lapland, Iceland, Finland, Soviet Siberia. For Russian conservationists he has particularly admir-ing praise. "And they are the supposed barbarians. We are the ones who are barbaric."

"He's a Communist. He's an out-and-out Communist."

"Show me the card."

He describes the building of the Trans-Alaska Pipeline as "a frenetic exercise, reactionary in character," and explains, "Ten per cent of the world's population is using sixty per cent of the world's resources. The inevitable result of that is conflict. Whenever a society puts all its chips on depletables, it's in trouble. We should socialize base minerals and hydrocarbons. It's the only way the public interest can in truth be served."

"I'll buy Socialist."

He says that the deals and the legislation that enabled the construction of the pipeline "constitute a scandal exceeding Teapot Dome—so corrupt and immoral it beggars description." The eighty million acres of proposed parks and reserves which were a "tradeoff" for the petroleum industry's exploitation of the land are not only an example of "national vanity" but collectively a poor one at that, because "the best parts of Alaska" (from an economic as well as an aesthetic point of view) are not marked for preservation. He has in mind, among other places, sections of the Wrangells, of Wood River, of the Brooks Range. "They have been sold out, and the people of the United States sold short, to the merchants."

By the terms of the Statehood Act, Scott remembers, the hundred and three million acres that the state was to choose as its share of the land were meant to be entirely below a line formed by the Porcupine, the Yukon, and the Kuskokwim Rivers—the so-called PYK Line, a bend sinister across interior Alaska. North Alaska was to be a national-defense zone. "Anxious to please mercantile interests, the government ignored the PYK Line, but it was never revoked, and Prudhoe Bay really belongs to all the people. The merchants got the pipeline without much of a god-damned ripple, really. They'll get anything else they want, too—through cheap tradeoffs among politicians. All high-latitude areas are seen as places to be exploited. It fries my fanny." It would seem to be—chop—enough to pale the Pope.

One sometimes gets the impression that Scott lives in Eagle so he can contemplate Canada. His picture windows look east across the Yukon into Yukon Territory. "That's God's country there," he says, with a sweeping gesture over his home-caught, homegrown, homemade American dinner—his king salmon, his tomato salad, creamed corn, lowbush-wild-cranberry sauce on yogurt, cranberry brandy. In the view's right-middle ground is Eagle Creek, where he and I once fished for grayling. It is in the United States, and if it is not God's country, God should try to get it, a place so beautiful it beggars description—a clear, fast stream, which on that day was still covered on both sides and almost to the center with two or three feet of white and blue ice. The steep knobby hills above were pale green with new aspen leaves; there were occasional white birch, dark interspersed cones of isolate spruce, here and again patches of tundra. Overhead was a flotilla of gray-hulled, white-sailed clouds. Fresh snow was on the mountains in the distance. The Scotts have all that framed in their Thermopane—a window that could have been lifted from a wall in Paramus and driven here, to the end of the end of the road. The window is synecdoche, is Eagle itself—a lens, a monocular, framing the wild, holding the vision that draws people up the long trail to the edge of things to have a look and see.

Out the other way, past my place, is the town. Scott is its conscience, if no longer its mayor. He does not miss the Council meetings or any opportunity to pull the trigger of his .45-calibre principles. Tonight is not an exception. All are present: Borg, with his toothpick; Sarge Waller, hatless, his fringe of hair cut crew; Junior Biederman; Dave McCall; Taiwan Richert, with his cigarette papers, his corncob pipe; Dave Roy; Steve Casto. The Common Council of Eagle, Alaska. Louise Waller sits as city clerk. A dozen observers fill the benches by the walls: Diana Greene, crocheting; Elva Scott, doing needlepoint; Viola Goggans, with her headband and her thermos. T. J. Voithoffer calls attention to the town's bank account, which is above fifteen thousand dollars. He says that Eagle has become "a regular greedy overtaxed municipality, like all the ones we escaped." The figure has long since irritated Scott, for in the most recent tax assessment Scott's assessment proved to be a full twelfth of the town's budget. ("You can imagine how this titillated my Celtic sensitivities," Scott told me. He went to the tax-assessment-equalization meeting and made no comment about his own situation but inquired into the criteria the assessor had used. When he found that there were no criteria —except what the town thought the payer could pay—his Celtic sensitivities went critical, and his tax bill atrophied as well.) Voithoffer's complaint is noted. Scott lets it pass.

Waller takes the floor. "In the minutes, April 26, which I was not here," he begins. . . . Jim and Elva Scott had said they wanted it recorded that they saw a conflict of interest in Sarge Waller's being a Council member while Louise Waller was a city clerk, and in Sarge Waller's being a Council member and also being given a job in the courthouse restoration, where jobs are awarded by the Common Council. Just what is the problem, Waller wants to know—what do the Scotts want to prove?

"Who hires the workers on the building—the city or the B.L.M.?" Scott asks.

"The city."

"How many applications were there beyond the number hired?"

"Three."

"Therefore, Sarge voted for a job for himself, and that is conflict of interest. The state has a conflict-of-interest law. Eagle is big enough not to have a councilman whose wife is clerk, a councilman who is employed as a result of a Council vote. We wish to have that point recorded in the minutes. There are no personalities in this."

"I think there *are* personalities!" Louise Waller shouts, and delivers a statement of the devotion to the United States felt by the Wallers, with undertone implications that the Scotts are Communists.

Sarge is shouting. Scott is repeating himself, also in high throat: "The *state* has a conflict-of-interest law."

Sarge now bellows out, "You came here saying you were retired and were just going to build your house, and you have been doing nothing but stir up trouble ever since."

The debate has gone up out of the larynx and into the bulging eyeball. An Eagle mayor once died in Council meeting. Through it all, Elva Scott is as calm as a gavel. When the Wallers shout questions at her, they get polite, quiet replies, without interruption of her moving needle. She is sharp, forensic, clever—politically very able. She is a medical person, interested in the damage, not the fight. Gradually, with a few references to Scott's memorable mayoralty, the thunder recedes.

The Scotts and the Wallers are next-door neighbors. Walking home, I ask Elva how such a great and angry confrontation will affect Jim's relationship with Sarge. "Jim doesn't have a relationship with Sarge" is Elva's reply. "Therefore, it can't be affected."

Elva has long-lashed gray-blue eyes that are as smiling as they are shrewd. Her insights seem to begin where many people's bottom out. Decades ago, she was diagnosed as having Hodgkin's disease, from which her oldest son, who shared it, is dead. She does not seem to be much affected by the tumult of the world. She is above average in height and in the strength of her frame, and she has the open, handsome face, the look of reposed affection that one associates with the exemplar Scandinavian women. Her name was Nelson, and she grew up in San Fernando. She has a master's degree in education from the University of Alaska. For many years, she ran the school-district health program in Anchorage. In Eagle, she runs, in effect, a clinic in her kitchen. She does preventive work that is paid for by the state, but most of her effort is donated. With a health aide in the Indian Village, who has had six weeks' training, Elva has all of the medical experience that is available in Eagle. The hospital in Fairbanks is three hundred and eighty miles away by road, an hour and twenty minutes through the air. When Charlie Juneby, in the Indian Village, had an emergency last year that resulted in a kidney transplant in Seattle, a red signal was sent out of Eagle on the medical satellite system, interrupting an agricultural program coming in from New Zealand. Fairbanks failed to catch the signal, but someone in Hawaii did, and telephoned Alaska. In the black of night, a plane came from Fairbanks, and Eagle was ready with flares all around the landing strip and headlights at either end. Juneby was in Seattle nine hours after the signal.

People like to sit and listen to the satellite—to the medical problems of all of Alaska. Their own they take to Elva. Her couches and chairs are often filled with fundamentalists, river people, bootleggers, and Indians. Old Sarah Malcolm sits there —with moosehide in her lap, sewing—absorbing at least ten times what she pretends to understand. Louise Paul, short and solid, saying nothing, is said to be the matriarch of the Indian Village. Archie Juneby—tall, slender, handsome, with a dark ponytail—drank too much last night with his brothers and smashed up Max Beck's boat. They come to Elva. Elva goes to them. She knits her day through the Village and the City. Mental health and alcoholism are the principal problems. "In the Village, children's ears run so much the people once thought that was normal and healthy," she has told me. "People come in off the river with blood infections, red streaks up their arm. They get cystitis from not enough water. They come down from Dawson with v.d. We don't have laboratory tests. We treat on symptoms. An outboard motor chewed on a guy's legs awhile. We sewed him up. I tell everyone, 'I don't mind helping you out. Just don't use me.' We don't want to be awakened for nothing, for someone who is merely drunk. For gunshot wounds and stabbings I of course get up. Oh, we have enough of that sort of thing. Yeah. You betcha. We're getting ready to have dinner with company and they come in and bleed all over the sink. Who needs TV in Eagle? We've got action enough in the streets."

Guns blazed in Eagle a short time ago—a row at Y's, big pistols cracking in the night; no casualties.

G's first wife died giving birth to H. G married N, who died in two years. G then married W, who was half his age. H, now fourteen, became pregnant, no one knows by whom, and gave birth to Z. Z is now one year old. Her mother has gone to Fairbanks and has disappeared. W has left G. He approaches sixty. He is alone with the infant Z.

When D's cabin caught fire, D was out of the country. Half the town—Christians and drinkers alike—came out to fight the fire and loot the cabin. There were individual piles of loot, and fights over the piles. "That's my pile." "The hell it is, it's mine."

M has requested that if his cabin ever smolders in his absence people please stay away and let it burn to the ground.

C drinks gin, Listerine, rubbing alcohol, and vanilla extract.

A's wife went off with X to one of Billy Mitchell's old telegraph cabins forty or fifty miles into the mountains. Writing out a false but wholly effective message, A chartered an airplane and dropped the message near the cabin: "Your brother is dead. The funeral is on Friday. Come in."

TV.

❲ By a campfire near the boundary—the north-south Canadian boundary—Michael John David reads aloud to me and to his brother from "Lame Deer Seeker of Visions." It is one of several books he carries in his pack. Around us are tall spruce that Michael means to cut and float six or eight miles down the Yukon to become the walls of his new cabin. He is the chief of Eagle Indian Village. " 'I think white people are so afraid of the world they created that they don't want to see, feel, smell, or hear it,' " he reads. He has turned with no searching to what is obviously a favorite passage. " 'The feeling of rain and snow on your face, being numbed by an icy wind and thawing out before a smoking fire, coming out of a hot sweat bath and plunging into a cold stream, these things make you feel alive, but you don't want them anymore.' " He pauses to chuckle, to flash a grin. "Do you like this?"

I tell him he hasn't read enough of it to me. The book was written by John Fire/Lame Deer and Richard Erdoes, and is dedicated to Frank Fools Crow, Pete Catches, George Eagle Elk, Bill Schweigman, Leonard Crow Dog, Wallace Black Elk, John Strike, Raymond Hunts Horse, Charles Kills Enemy, and Godfrey Chips. Such names are as unfamiliar to Michael as they are to me, for they belong to the Minneconjou Sioux, in the Lower Forty-eight, and he is of the Hungwitchin of the Athapaskans. His family came into the country in immemorial time. Long before their settlement became known as Eagle Indian Village, it was known as David Camp. David, Juneby, Malcolm, and Paul are the four major families of the Village now. Michael throws a stick onto the fire and continues: " 'Living in boxes which shut out the heat of the summer and the chill of winter, living inside a body that no longer has a scent, hearing the noise from the hi-fi instead of listening to the sounds of nature, watching some actor on TV having a make-believe experience when you no longer experience anything for yourself, eating food without taste—that's your way. It's no good.' " He laughs aloud—a long, soft laugh. His voice is soft, too—fluid and melodic, like nearly all the voices in the Village. The contrast with my own is embarrassing. No matter how I try to modulate it, to experiment with his example, my voice in dialogue with Michael's sounds to me strident, edgy, and harsh. He is twenty-five years old. His body is light, his face narrow, his nose aquiline. His hair, black and shining, passes through a ring behind his head and plumes between his shoulder blades. He wears a khaki jacket, patched pink denim trousers, leather boots, a belt-sheathed jackknife. He may be an Indian, but he looks like a Turk. On his head is a fur hat that

has the shape of an inverted flowerpot—a long-haired fez. His
thin, Byzantine mustache droops at the wing tips. He has a
miniature beard, scarcely a quarter inch long, tufting from the
point of his chin. His brother, Minicup, teen-age, wears blue-
jeans, a red headband. Minicup is taciturn but obviously interested and even inquisitive, his eyes moving back and forth
between Michael and me. He was baptized Edward David.
Minicup is a name he gave to himself years ago.

We are finishing dinner, a common enterprise. It began,
after making camp, with a mutual presentation of what each
of us had to offer. Michael and Minicup set out Spam, Crisco,
Sanka, fresh carrots, onions, and potatoes. I set out tins of beef
stew, and corn, tea, sugar, raisins, nuts, chocolate, and cheese.
Michael, opening the Spam, said, "I remember when it cost
a dollar." Between us there has been a certain feeling out of
ways and means. It is my wish to follow Michael's lead, to see
how he will go about things in the woods. To some extent, he
seems to want to do the same with me. It was he who chose
this campsite—a couple of hundred yards into the forest and
away from the Yukon's right bank, on flat ground covered with
deep sphagnum, close to the edge of a small, clear stream.
Wicked thorns grow out of the moss on long roselike stems.
We hacked at them with our knives until we had cleared an
area big enough for my small nylon A-frame and the brothers'
wall tent—an orange Canadian affair that Michael, for privacy,
often stays in at the Village. Before building the fire, he turfed
out the moss, cutting eight inches down and removing a five-
foot square. Even so, he did not get to the bottom of the moss.
I then, automatically, without pausing to think, went off to the
river for rocks. I brought back two or three in my arms, like
loaves of bread, and dropped them on the moss. I returned to
the river. The brothers followed. We all collected rocks and
carried them back into the woods—gathering, in several trips,
more than enough for a fireplace. I was about to begin building
one but checked myself and relinquished the initiative. Why
should I build the sort of three-walled fireplace I would make

in Maine? I wanted to see what they would do. I fiddled with my pack and left the rocks alone. Michael and Minicup laid them out singly—one after another, scarcely touching—in the closest thing possible to a perfect circle. I could not see what the purpose of such a circle might be. It could not shield the fire from wind, nor could it support the utensils of cooking. Possibly it was to retain the spread of smolderings through the moss, but it seemed awfully large for that. Why had they made it, unless purely as an atavistic symbol, emplaced by what had by now become instinct?

Now Michael, finishing his dinner, has a question for me. He says, "Why did you go get the rocks?"

I mention fireplaces I have made on lakes and rivers in Maine.

"Maine?" he says. The word "Maine" seems to excite him. "Have you been to L. L. Bean? I sometimes send for shirts and pants from there, and boots similar to yours."

Through the late but barely graying evening, we walk a couple of hours beside the Yukon, going upstream at first, within sight of the shaved incongruous border, which, on the far side of the river, comes up from the south and plunges down a ridge to the water. For the most part, we walk by the river, but we make occasional penetrations through alder hells and into the woods to assess the trees. In many places we see upheavals where bears have dug roots. The ground appears to have been plowed. Bear tracks, heading upriver and down, are in sand at the edge of the water. Michael tells of a couple of tourists who were approaching Eagle not long ago when they saw a grizzly chasing a black bear. The grizzly caught the black bear, tossed it around, broke its neck, and started to eat the warm carcass. The people got out of their car with cameras and moved toward the feast. The grizzly charged them. They were lucky. They made it back to their car.

Resting on Michael's shoulder is his .30–'06. After a time, we turn around, retrace our tracks, and then go on for some miles downriver. We pass the high stump of a white birch, eight inches in diameter. Inside is nothing. The wood, over many years, has completely disintegrated and disappeared. The bark—firm, unaltered, and solid—stands like a stovepipe on its own. Michael stops, and lifts his rifle as if he is about to fire. He moves it slowly, pointing along a bend of the river. He does not intend to shoot. He is using the rifle's six-power scope as if it were a monocular. He often raises the gun just to look around, to look at anything at all—the better to examine it, through the scope. This is more than a little disconcerting when he happens to be looking at you. Lowering the gun, he says, "Is 'Robinson Crusoe' fiction?"

I tell him it is, and ask why he wants to know.

He shrugs, and says he has always wondered. A scattering of feathers attracts his eye. He picks one up, saying, "A hawk killed a robin." He says he once climbed Eagle Bluff for a peregrine chick, trained it, and later let it go. We come upon a set of amoeboid tracks ("Porcupine") and grapelike clusters with star points in the sand ("Fox"). That brown object in the brush—what is that? "A garbage bag from Dawson."

I ask Michael where he earned the money for his 1967 Oldsmobile Vista-Cruiser.

"The Slope," he says. As an apprentice heavy-equipment operator, he has two thousand hours to his credit. Operating a bulldozer, he helped build the haul road that accompanies the Trans-Alaska Pipeline.

"Thanks to you, people will drive from the Caribbean Sea to the Arctic Ocean," I remark.

"Caribbean Sea?" he says. "Where is that? Is it far from New York?"

"It would be like going from here to Adak."

"Pretty far," he says, and after a moment mentions that one of his boyhood friends in Eagle Indian Village was sent off to be raised in New York. The boy's mother and father and his Uncle Pete mixed grape juice with wood alcohol from the school duplicating machine and drank it. The father went blind. Uncle Pete and the mother died. "The kids were not fed three times daily after that. Their home was upside down." It was arranged, somehow, for one boy to go off and live with a family in New York. "When he came back, years later, he knew nothing," Michael says. "He knew white things but not Indian things. He punched holes in foil in which meat was roasting. The same with potatoes. He saw a porcupine and thought it was a raccoon. He knew nothing." Michael walks in silence for a while, and then, as if trying the words on his tongue, he repeats, "Caribbean Sea."

Beside us now is a slough. It separates the Yukon's right bank from what Michael calls Old Man Clark's Island. "We have rabbit drives there. Drive the rabbits from one end of the island to the other and kill them. Not now, though. They go through a cycle. Now there are no rabbits." He has on occasion come to this side of the river to hunt sheep. "When you can barely see a sheep," he says, "the sheep can count your fingers. That's how sharp eyes they got." We see a cottonwood that has been chewed by a beaver. We see, moments later, the beaver. Michael raises his rifle and follows it through the scope. Head up, swimming, it cuts a straight wake in the almost still water of the slough. Michael chooses not to shoot but to save the beaver. He will shoot it in time. He looks up from the gun. "This place compared to a city is—well, pretty nice," he says. "We have a little bit of everything—animals, fish, mountains, forest. Even people down the river envy what there is in this country." With a slap on the water, the beaver is gone. A light, cold rain begins to fall. We return upriver to the campsite and the tents.

❲ A few days ago, when I heard that Michael was going up the Yukon for cabin logs, I went to ask if I could join him. In a canoe, I approached the Indian Village, which sits on the left bank—twenty, thirty feet above the river. It is a linear community: cabins spaced along the river a third of a mile, facing, across the water, a six-hundred-foot bluff. In front of each cabin, the steep slope of the riverbank glitters with broken glass —micaceous flakes, the Indian midden. I kept the canoe close under the bank, sliding below the Village. When the youth above are drinking, they like to shoot over the river at the bluff —a .30-calibre declaration of joy. That is what they were doing at the time, so it was prudent to be under the bullets. Harm, of course, was not intended. In 1898, one Angus, who lived up there, organized what he hoped would be a massacre of the whites of Eagle, but, like many projects that have got started in the Village, it was not carried out, it was merely conceived. The Hungwitchin appear to be characteristically passive. When and if they do go on what Michael likes to call "the warpath," their preferred weapons are legal briefs and lobbies —supplied by the native regional corporation that stands behind them. I went up the bank and found Michael alone in a cabin, sober and disconsolate, sitting in a chair, looking straight ahead. His face seemed less alive than cast. The cabin was spotless and almost empty, with psychedelic posters on the walls. It is shared by Village bachelors, of whom he is one. He was anxious to go upriver and to get back well in advance of the next session of the Village Council, he said. It would be of great importance to him, because it would have to do with control of alcohol. When I left him there, he was still staring straight ahead, listening to the reports of the rifles.

A door or two away was the cabin in which Michael grew up. Like most cabins in the Village, it is essentially one room, twenty by twenty feet, with a storm vestibule full of dog harnesses, guns, mukluks, parkas. In the main room, all furniture is against the walls, which are insulated with carton cardboard ("Burger King Frozen Shoestring Potatoes"). There are three beds, a bench and a table, a tall oval heat stove, a propane oven and range. Cordwood, stacked waist-high, is inside the cabin as well. Yet the first two impressions the cabin gives are a sense

of neatness and a sense of space. Michael, three brothers, and
two sisters are grown and away now, if not altogether gone. So
his parents, Bessie and Harry David, have only four children
at home with them still. The beds touch like dominoes. The
three youngest sleep in one, parents in another, Minicup in the
third. Clothes are in boxes under the beds. A broom hangs by
the door. Coming inside in winter, you sweep your legs free of
snow before it melts.

No one seems to knock. People just come in and sit down
and don't say much until something occurs to be said. Harry,
on the bench by the table, may be slowly sharpening a saw,
Bessie pouring cups of tea. A radio plays rock. Charlie Juneby,
big as a bear, comes in with a frozen mop, and without explanation sits and drinks tea. He is joined later on by his brother
Isaac. Stay in one place long enough and almost the whole
Village appears and visits and goes. If consumed time is the
criterion, visiting is what the Hungwitchin mainly do. They tell
about hunting. Jacob Malcolm impressively describes himself
stalking moose on snowshoes—successfully running them
down. In the phenomenal stillness of the winter air, he lights
a match to see how the flame may bend, then he chooses his
direction of approach. Jimmy David comes in, and drops a pair
of bloody white ptarmigan on the floor, presenting them to his
mother. A fresh snowshoe hare already hangs from a wire on
the wall. Bessie wears slacks, has a ready grin. Her hair is tied
behind her head. Her oldest child is in his thirties, her youngest
is eleven. She is some years younger than Harry. Harry is as
trim as a coin. He is short and gray-haired, wears glasses. He
is intense, and is known for working hard. "I work hard, come
in, take a god-damned good shot before I eat. I like coffee, too,
soon as I get up." Harry is the kind of man who shakes Tabasco
on his beans. "At home, I'm kind of hazy like, don't feel very
good, no satisfaction with anything. I enjoy myself outside,
across the Yukon River, feel fine, feel full of hell and vinegar,

full of life, energy--lots of energy." So saying, one February day he went out of the cabin and walked seven miles in the snow. I went behind him, in his tracks. We are the same size; he has a rolling gait, a shorter stride than mine, but he made the going easier for me. He wore rubber boots, rubber trousers, a blue down jacket, a dark-brown leather hat. In his cheek he had a dip of Copenhagen snuff. When he stood still, to talk, he leaned forward. We walked some distance on the Yukon River, which, under the snow, was now smooth and now mountainously jagged where the ice floes at freeze-up had jammed. Gradually, we crossed over, and then went up a crease in the bluff—Harry without the slightest pause, as if he were ascending stairs, when in fact the snow on that precipitous ground was underlaid with ice, and a slip could mean a long fall down. He carried a stick. "This is a good place to go up from the Yukon River," he said, reaching back for me with the stick. Beyond the top, he had cut a maze of trails, miles through a forest burn. He works six and seven days a week cutting cordwood for sale. He does not use a power saw. "John Borg lost his way one time, coming to get some wood, and he said, 'God damn it, Harry, you got too many trails up here'—but he got a good trail to here, don't kick about that." We passed a large pile of whole spruce trunks—up to thirty feet long, their bark blackened— that Michael had cut and had stacked by himself. "He's a young boy. By God, he handle it," Harry said. "He's a well-liked boy. The girls are crazy for him. He is the chief. He has done his country good. By talking, you know—making everything go nice. I think he's got a little college in him. He studies the right way for his people. He like to see people get along together, make no enemy with nobody."

Fifteen years ago, Harry was the chief. "Anyone interfere with our country, we got a right to pitch in and kick like hell about it. You white people butt in, take our traplines, our fishing. That's what we try to stop."

"How do you feel about independence for Alaska, Harry?"

"That's the best way to look at it."

Making a long loop through the burn, we came out eventually at the highest part of the bluff, directly opposite the Village: a panoptic aerial view, of such height and distance, taking in so much river and mountain land, that it emphasized the isolation and the elongate symmetry of the Village by the river and—what is not apparent up close—its beauty. For Harry, this was obviously the supreme moment in the country—the sight of his village from the air. He was born, he said, far down the Yukon River, at the mouth of the Kandik, in 1913. "They kept on moving in those days. They don't stay one place. They lived off the country. They lived in tents, ten by twelve, the biggest they ever had. They just keep on moving. They don't stay in town all the time, like we do." Harry's father, Old David, died when Harry was six, and he was raised for a time by Chief Alec, at Fortymile, but when "the flu came up the river" Chief Alec died, and so did his wife, Mary Alec. Harry was returned to his mother, at Eagle, and lived with her until she died. In the same year, his stepfather drowned. Harry was by now a young man. He hauled wood for the riverboats, and he worked aboard them, too, until they stopped running, "when the Jap tried to take Alaska." At Moosehide one time, near Dawson, he met Bessie. "She is what they call a Crow, I think. One day, I bought two bottles of Hudson Bay rum— a hundred and fifty proof—and a keg of beer, and I married her." Looking across at their cabin, in miniature, in the third of a mile of cabins all touched with smoke, he said he had cut its logs by Eagle Creek and floated them down the Yukon River. For a time, he made his living as a trapper and in summer fished, with a wheel, on Goose Island. He pointed. "That is Goose Island, in the Yukon River—there." He soon went to work, seasonally, for the gold-mining operations at Woodchopper, Coal Creek, and Chicken. "For many years, my work and unemployment just connected." His and Bessie's children were born in the cabin—Michael in 1951, "clever, too, just like Howard, quick." Harry pointed toward the school, at the upstream end of the Village, and said Bessie taught Han there. Han is the language of the Hungwitchin. There are about thirty people in the world who speak it. A few are upriver, in the area of Dawson, but virtually all of them are in Eagle Indian Village. Han is one of the smallest subdivisions of the great Athapaskan language family, which reaches contiguously from Nulato and Koyukuk, in western Alaska, to southern Alberta and east to Hudson Bay—and makes a surprising jump, as well, across twelve hundred miles to the isolated Southwestern enclave of the Apache and the Navajo, which, among Athapaskans, are by far the most numerous. High on a pole outside the school we could see a small, dark movement—the flag of Alaska flying. The flag, as it happens, was designed by a native. It is lyrically simple, the most beautiful of all American flags. On its dark-blue field, gold stars form the constellation of the Great Bear. Above that is the North Star. Nothing else, as the designer explained, is needed to represent Alaska. It was the flag of the Territory for more than thirty years. Alaskans requested that it become the flag of the new state. The designer was a thirteen-year-old Aleut boy.

Michael went to high school in Tok, and he was "clever for anything," his father said. "With no trouble, he got into the Army. One day, he said, 'Dad, I'm going far to Anchorage with my friend.' He went far to Anchorage with his friend, and he got through the examination clean as a dollar. He went to California." Michael spent almost all of his two service years at the Presidio of San Francisco, where it never snowed, and he missed the winter. He also missed Sophie Biederman. She was a tall, slim, beautiful girl in brightly beaded moccasins. She had an outreaching smile, black hair, a complexion light and clear, notwithstanding that she went around with a can of soda pop almost constantly in her hand, and—eating virtually never —seemed to live on Coca-Cola alone. Harry told her she smoked too much marijuana. (Harry, for his part, does not even smoke tobacco.) Sophie's childhood had been roiled in her parents' troubles with alcohol. Nonetheless, she emerged with a joy in living, a fondness for excitement, a love of games. Her life and Michael's seemed to be spiralling upward through the summer of his return. Spilling Coke, she would dash into his arms. They planned a wedding, and he went to the North Slope to collect money to begin their married life. While he was there, she died of a gunshot wound, an apparent suicide. "Michael got broke down over her."

(Through the night, the rain becomes heavier—a long, unremitting spring rain—and in the morning it is a downpour. Michael and I and Minicup make no effort to get up—just lie half asleep under the big dripping spruce as if there were no today. In an important sense, there isn't, because Michael, coming up the river to fell trees for his new log cabin, discovered that while he brought a chain saw he forgot gasoline. The temperature is less than ten degrees above freezing. The brothers have only one sleeping bag and a lightweight blanket. Michael has spent the night in the blanket. Toward noon, the rain has somewhat diminished. Michael gets up and builds a fire. His first gesture of the day is to make a cup of Sanka and carry it to Minicup, who is awake but has remained in the sleeping bag. "Nights out in a wall tent at sixty below, you just get up in the morning, throw everything into the sled, and move," Michael remarks. "In two hours, you might be warm. When I trap, I still use dog teams—not snow machines. You can't find a gas station out there. I trapped two years ago at Champion Creek with Jacob Malcolm. Wolves. Wolverines. Martens mostly. Lynx. Mink. We got seventy martens. We tan moose and caribou hides. From the caribou hides we make babiche to make snowshoes." Of all the whites who have come into the country, he prefers by far the young ones who live out on the river. "They believe more like an Indian believes," he says. "They believe in living like an Indian. They have dog teams. They fish. They hunt. They live in the woods. They tan hides, make dog harnesses, trap, use animal furs. They get to know the forest. They make sleds of birch. They survive in the woods with nothing, hardly. They are a good thing, going back to Mother Earth—just as long as they don't build on Hungwit-chin lands."

With a cup of his own, he sits in the rain and makes an entry in a notebook. He tells me that he has been studying law, in a program offered by the Tanana Chiefs Land Claims College. A college education in earlier years was not possible for him, because he lacked the money, but now, as chief, he regards his present courses as imperative. "Other village corporations have gone bankrupt," he explains. "I would hate to see that happen to ours. The study of law is hard for me. It is hard for an Indian to understand contracts and corporations."

I ask if I may look at the notebook. He hands it to me, and I flip it open. "Judicial Department. Marbury v. Madison. Judges review, concept," says the first note I see. "Supreme Court don't make law but change them, and protect us from the government."

"The government wants to make a park down the river," Michael says. "Some of the best hunting grounds are down that way. It puts our native-land selections in a tight squeeze. I don't care very much for parks. I like to go into lands and check them out, not to be told what to do. But there is another side. If the government does not keep the land, someone will take over. I am against development in this country. Without the pipeline—without the Native Claims Act—I'd feel freer. The Alaska population is bigger now, because of the pipeline.

I don't like a lot of people. I like the lands. If the land-claim settlement did not exist, you could go anywhere and build a cabin. If we strike oil in this country, we'll all be very rich, because it's on our land. But I don't want to see that. With a lot of money, people get into trouble. Where money is, more people will come. There will be a new pipeline, through here. I don't think I want to be rich."

In the pre-white epoch, the Hungwitchin's Chief Charley led his people from the Charley River up the Yukon to Mission Creek, where they lived in houses of skin. In small increments thereafter, they moved their principal settlement on up the left bank of the Yukon. In the eighteen-eighties, they were about a mile from their present site, and lived in six log cabins with interdigitating roof poles that stuck up like sawbucks against the sky. Michael whimsically suggests that the Village should move once more. "Move it a few miles on up the river," he says. "Into Canada. Nice people there. They are different—more mellow. They don't have no pipeline."

From their log houses in the nineteenth century, the Hungwitchin went out for moose and mountain sheep, rabbits and caribou. Women sat on the bank and watched for salmon. When they saw the barely discernible ripples, they pointed them out to men by the water, who went after the fish in bark canoes. They had dip nets in their hands. They wrestled the big kings to land. They smoked them. They trapped wolverines for ruffs. They hunted game with bows and arrows. They used sheep-horn spoons, and made birch-bark pots, and cooked by dropping hot rocks into water-filled baskets woven of spruce roots. Family by family along the river, they had long-established fish camps, which were jealously defined, as were their hunting and trapping grounds. When people of another tribe happened into the country and killed game, they could eat the meat but they had to surrender the hide.

That was the general ambience that has since become encapsulated within the word "subsistence." They subsisted in the country, almost independent of the rest of the world. Even before the gold rushes, there were touches of the coming difference. They enjoyed the tea and the tobacco they got from white traders, the novelty of guns. When the miners came in great numbers, and the freight of white supplies, the dress and the diet of the Indians began to change. Subsistence from the country somewhat declined. It would decline more as a result of the job economy of the Second World War, and still more following the discovery of oil. Alaska's booms denature the natives. The Yukon River fish camps that were symbols of the working unity of Indian families have gradually been abandoned.

Meanwhile, to assist the natives in their adjustment to the new social order, federal programs administered by the Bureau of Indian Affairs have long provided support of various kinds, from food and clothing subsidies to social services—a tradition of plausible generosity that reached its supreme expression in the Alaska Native Claims Settlement Act of 1971, widely described as the most openhanded and enlightened piece of legislation that has ever dealt with aboriginal people. While giving them a tenth of Alaska and about seventeen thousand dollars for each man, woman, and child, the act created a dozen regional native corporations to hold and invest roughly half the money, and to distribute the rest, on established schedules, to individuals and to village corporations. Doyon, Ltd., is in area the largest of the regional corporations, covering the whole of the Athapaskan interior and including about nine thousand people in thirty-four native villages, among them the Hungwitchin, each of whom is a Doyon stockholder. Doyon's fine new headquarters in Fairbanks are spread out and spacious, and resemble the headquarters of almost any large Eastern company that has just moved to a meadow in Connecticut. It is Doyon that is drilling for oil in the upper-Yukon region—within a hundred miles of Eagle. Two wells have proved dry, at nine and eleven thousand feet, but Doyon is undissuaded.

The disposition of Native Claims Settlement land begins with
the villages, which get acreages related to population, and
village choices must start with the ground around them. Michael David is the land-selection agent for the Hungwitchin.
Because there are certain absentee stockholders, who belong to
the community but live elsewhere, Eagle Indian Village qual-
ifies for 92,160 acres. The selections will run from the Canadian border past Eagle and about thirty miles down the river,
stopping at the edge of the large area the National Park Service
hopes will become Yukon-Charley National Rivers (also as a
result of the Native Claims Settlement Act). Eagle City, on its
one square mile, and almost wholly white, has thus become an
island in the Indian ocean. People in the city believe that the
terms of the Settlement Act give Eagle the right to retain a
two-mile "buffer zone" on all its sides. While the Indian Village is three miles upriver from the white community, it is less
than two miles from the city line. Thus, the whites' buffer zone
would overlap most of the Indian Village. This situation, while
not the largest of the difficulties between the City and the
Village, has touched off an example of what Michael David
calls "modern-day Indian warfare." The Village would like to
own land right up to the city line and give the city compensat-
ing acreage somewhere else. The Department of the Interior
has rejected this. The Hungwitchin Corporation, with the help
of Doyon lawyers, has taken the matter to the Alaska Native
Claims Appeal Board and may take it to court. Michael calls
this "a pretty deep question," and goes on to say, "Sometimes
I wish the native land claims and the pipeline were not here.
I could do a lot of things I want to do. I don't even know why
they say 'own' land. You use land. You can't own land." As a
result of the Native Claims Settlement Act, his sense of land
—his people's sense of freedom of land—after ten thousand
years is archaic and obsolete. Michael is a stockholder now, a
landowner, a capitalist, a conscribed component of a distant

system. For all its overt benefits and generous presentations, the bluntest requirement of the Alaska Native Claims Settlement Act was that the natives turn white.

When the whites of Eagle talk about the Indians, almost nothing of what they say is flattering—and why would it be? For, as Michael puts it, "they are always knocking each other." Within the flow of general disdain, about all that seems interesting is the recurrent implication that the troubles and shortcomings of the Indians are based on their not adequately thinking or acting white.

"They live day to day out there, whereas the white philosophy is 'progress.' "

"Time means nothing to them. There is no future. Today is today is today."

No one—at least, no one I have heard—brings forth the remark that there is much to be envied in such an approach to one's day. No doubt it accounts for the easygoing grace, the humor, the companionability of the Hungwitchin, not to mention the lilting, unbusinesslike way they speak—a primal outlook, so durable that, for all its beauty, it is perhaps unfortunate that it has survived while superficial facts have changed. The Hungwitchin may look upon a wristwatch as "the sun's heart," but they know what time it is, and they work on the pipeline. They seem to hang suspended between a fast-fading then and a more than alien now. Meanwhile, their failures to adjust are much noted by the whites.

"They've been hitting the booze since the nineteen-thirties. They've pretty much hurt their heads. They don't care."

"They all wish they were something else. They have come to hate the fact they're an Indian. They have adopted cowboy boots, of all things. They put cowboy boots on their kids."

"They have difficulty coping with the regimented life style that the capitalist system imposes upon them."

"Boys do not develop ambition. They don't want to get married."

"The Indian man has been emasculated by the whites. Indian women want to marry whites."

"The people are soft. They have no discipline. They have a job, and if it's difficult, they say, 'It's too tough.' "

"The Village Council does not get things done."

"Now that Michael is the chief, nothing ever will get done."

"A settlement should be a settlement. They still get transportation, medical, dental, free snow machines, chain saws—anything they want. Handouts. If you make a settlement, that should be that. The Native Claims Act should have made the natives like everybody else."

"The sums that have so far come down through Doyon and into individuals' pockets have amounted to less than eighty dollars a year. There are many resources elsewhere for the natives. They work as firefighters. They work on the pipeline. They come home and collect unemployment compensation—two hundred and more a month. They work on local road maintenance and do miscellaneous labor. They join the crews of exploration geologists. Moreover, the Native Claims Settlement Act has not put the Bureau of Indian Affairs out of business in Alaska, and a native can still turn to the B.I.A. for many kinds of grants and relief. With other Indians of the upper Tanana, they belong to the United Crow Band, which, under contract, distributes money for the B.I.A. for everything from fishing boots to Indian welfare checks to Indian relief checks. Welfare and relief money is available from the state as well. Three hundred to six hundred dollars a month is available in Aid to Families with Dependent Children. Nearly all health costs are paid by the Alaska Native Health Service. People over sixty-five not only draw Social Security but also receive an Alaska Longevity Bonus—a hundred and twenty-five dollars a month for anyone who has been in Alaska twenty-five years. No wonder all they do out there is visit."

That anyone in the Indian community might regret the events of the past century is not an insight that floats about on the surface of white conversation, but now and again it does rise.

"Michael David is a fine chap, slightly confused. He is a completely acculturated Indian, now trying to find his way back into the wigwam—a classic example of the 'advances' made in educating the Indian. He has assessed the world around him. He is not enamored of technology. So he affects the long hair and the headband. Given a chance, Michael would be a real good Indian. He would be a hopeless failure as a white man. He is forthright. He does not speak out of both sides of his mouth. He is very honest."

I ask Michael, "What do you do as Village chief?"

He grins widely, and says, "What do I do as chief? Ha! Ask them in Eagle what I do. When I was elected chief, Louise Waller said, 'Now that Michael David is the chief, nothing is going to get done.' They are different people in Eagle. They don't understand us. We don't understand them. The town is Christians and bootleggers, and they fight between each other. They once had twenty preachers there. My people were happier before those people were ever here. The Indians did more things for themselves than they do now. I would like to have a post office in the Village, and a store of our own, run by Hungwitchin. I am working on the winterization program and improvements to the road around the Village. For Doyon, I am studying proposed easements to Doyon land. I am trying to get more jobs for Village people. Last year, the B.L.M. station-manager job went to a white who had been here six months. No one in the Village was given a chance even to apply. Oliver Lyman, of the Village, was fired as janitor of the school, and Charlie Ostrander was hired instead of a Village person."

"Who had the say?"

"I don't know who—but the town had the influence. Every year, it seems like the town's moving closer to the Village, and the town is half bootleggers. I hate the bootleggers. The constable makes twelve hundred dollars a month, and they bootleg right under his nose. The most important thing I try to do something about is the drinking in the Village. We get some help from the Alaska Native Commission on Alcoholism and Drug Abuse. Drinking is a sickness. I'm glad the town is dry. At this next meeting of the Village Council, there will be a big decision about alcohol. That is why the meeting is so important to me."

He speaks for a time of Tony Paul, who died recently of pneumonia complicated by cirrhosis of the liver. Admired for his intelligence, his energy, and his education, he was the brightest light of the Village. He was married and had a nine-year-old son, whom he often took camping. Tony was not yet thirty when he died. Larry Juneby, of Eagle, went out of a bar in Fairbanks and into the Chena River last week. Searchers are still dragging for the body. To drink, Michael says, Village people will sell their chain saws, their winter's wood—anything at all. On Easter, in bright sun by the white frozen river, they hold sawing contests, bag races, and tea races (make a fire from scratch, melt snow, and make tea), but such wholesome scenes are increasingly rare. Money was once collected for a Village well only to be spent on liquor. In various elections over the years, the white community has voted itself in and out of prohibition. It has been dry since 1967. Bootleggers get upward of two hundred dollars a case for blended whiskey—eighteen dollars a quart. "One of them did not like being wakened in the night," Michael tells me. "So he told the people just when to come around. He did that, really. He's bootlegging, and he's got hours."

I mention that I have asked Mayor Borg why the town did not stop the bootleg traffic, and Borg said, "Apathy. People don't want to become involved by signing a complaint. Reams of evidence would be needed before there could be an arrest. Meanwhile, the Village has been without any moral leadership for so long that there's very little sense of responsibility. It's each person for himself there, and alcoholism is widespread.

They give young children booze. No one is there to say they shouldn't. A strong Village Council would prevent that."

Michael makes no comment. He says that in Venetie and Arctic Village, Athapaskan communities to the north, mail-plane passengers and baggage and cargo are searched on arrival. Bottles are smashed. People actually drunk are returned to Fairbanks. "They get things done in those villages," he goes on. "They tan hides. They make babiche." By contrast, there are people of Eagle Indian Village who on arriving in Fairbanks are routinely detained and sent back to Eagle.

Last week, Michael went to see the most active bootlegger in the white community. He asked him to stop selling liquor to Village people, and mentioned that in his capacity as chief he might go to state authorities and seek their help in enforcing the local law. The bootlegger urged him not to do that but to put the matter before his own council instead. "If they vote that they want me to quit," said the bootlegger to the chief, "I'll quit."

❰ Outside my cabin window, on First Avenue, Eagle City, the afternoon's entertainment is Horace (Junior) Biederman, who ambles up and down with a beer can in his hand, inviting Eagle to care. He is muttering. I can hear him through the open door. "I don't know if this here town wants to live in the past, or what it's trying to do. It's the right of the people to drink—to do anything. I don't mind packing it up or down the street —a beer in my hand. I don't give a damn who sees me."

Horace (Sophie was his cousin) is three-quarters Indian and seems to hang suspended between the Village and the town. His father ran the store that his grandfather took over from the Northern Commercial Company, and Horace grew up in the white community, where he still lives. The whites regard him

as an Indian, the Indians regard him as white. "Junior Biederman has never been able to make up his mind which he would
rather be," says Jack Boone. "He is not faithful to either
community. He lives in the town like an Indian, in squalor. He
never has more than two days' wood supply. He never plans
ahead. That is the Indian way." Michael David's opinion is
even lower than Boone's. He refers to Biederman as "a half-
breed who is stuck in the middle, a bootlegger, and a husband
and father who provides no wood." Biederman's wife, Sara,
grew up a Juneby. Their marriage is a local dramatic series, one
of Eagle's preoccupying events. He is said to be an effective
hunter, knowledgeable in the ways of moose and caribou, but
of Horace in Eagle about the highest praise one hears is "We
sure did have a lot of hopes for Junior."

Odd, then, that he has been elected and reëlected to the
Common Council of the city of Eagle. Something deeper than
gossip makes a vote. Officially a white oligarch, he is a heavyset,
swarthy man with black curly hair. He may be called Junior,
but there is nothing of the child in his appearance. He looks
like a Mexican insurrectionist ten years after the coup. He
stops by occasionally to share a bit of time, and he comes in
now with his beer. His voice is a light one. It sounds like falling
sand. "I don't think the people in this town have grasped what
is happening," he says.

"What is happening?"

"The native people are coming into their own."

His mother, like Bessie David, was a Crow from Yukon
Territory. His grandfather carried mail with dogs on the river
—more than three hundred miles round trip to Circle—and
lost toes to frostbite, even pieces of his feet. Horace is a Cat
skinner. He has made $13.43 an hour when he has gone out
to work on the pipeline or at the drilling sites of Doyon. During
the king-salmon run when he was young, his family regularly
occupied a fish camp, abandoned now.

"I'd like to see everyone acknowledge that it is one town,

and get along," he remarks—an earnest, if lonely, wish. "I do care about my town." When he says that, he—uniquely—means all of Eagle, Village and City, white and Indian. He has taken a course in municipal government. He has been a vice-president of the Tanana Chiefs Conference, which is concerned with social welfare in the Doyon region. Even so, he confesses that he feels that the people of the Village do not wholly trust him. ("When Junior goes to the Tanana Chiefs, he is just there for the per diem and the trip," Michael has said to me.) "I'd like to see this Eagle become a stable town," Junior continues. "Not a modern city, with paved streets, but a growing town. I'd like to be able to live here and support my family without leaving. With the two communities together, there'd be opportunities for a utility company. I'd like to have lights."

"And running water."

"I don't really care about that. But we need a community center, a gym. The pipeline isn't going to go on and on, and without it people will need work. The town has got to grow, so somebody can support somebody. Right now, the major source of employment is firefighting for the B.L.M., because no one has figured out how to stop lightning. It's a hell of a note when your major part of your working force in your town is waiting for your country to burn up. In 1905, Amundsen came here to send a message to the world. Now you can't even call Tok. Something went haywire."

He falls silent and pensive, then suddenly changes direction. "My father was building the steeple for the church here in the city when he heard that I was born. My father was married in the church. He went through the door there on his last journey. Now the Bible group wants the church. The church belongs to all of us. I couldn't see trading it to a group that made me unwelcome. These people came here as missionaries for their own kind of Christianity, but they have not had much luck, particularly with me. As a group, they have not helped Eagle.

They keep the town dry. That is not the way to deal with the problem of alcohol. The only way is through regional school boards, through education—teaching in the classroom what alcohol does to you. If a town votes dry in Alaska, it applies for five miles around. The Village is three miles. The people there are outside the city limits and can't vote here in town. After the last vote, the boozers—we thought the votes got miscounted. We'd have still lost, but it would have looked a little better. I don't believe that everyone who comes here from now on is going to be a religious type. Eagle may become a wet town soon. Then I really think the amount of drinking might go down. You heard what happened today? There was going to be a vote on alcohol in the meeting of the Village Council, but the meeting had to be cancelled, because almost everyone but Michael David was drunk."

⟨[Mike Potts, who is white and from Iowa, lives in Eagle Indian Village and is married to Adeline Juneby. He first saw the country in 1971, when he was twenty. His father flew him in here in his Comanche 400. Approaching Eagle in early summer, they looked down on the headwaters terrain of the North Fork of the Fortymile, and Potts, impressed, asked his father to fly low. They crossed spruce forests and clear, dendritic streams—Happy New Year Creek, Eureka Creek, Bear Creek, Comet Creek, Champion Creek, Slate Creek, a great many more without names. All around were mountain summits. Without circling twice, Potts decided that he had at last found his own territory, the piece of the world he had dreamed of, and he laid claim, in his plans and in his imagination, to something over a million acres, over two thousand square miles of land, in which, from the air, he could see no evidence of humanity. In half a dozen years that followed, he would encounter only two people there—and they prospectors, passing through, not to return.

When Potts was seven, he saw a picture in an encyclopedia of a trapper on a trapline, and decided he wanted to be a trapper, too, and live off wild country. He grew up in West Des Moines—in a big, comfortable house on twenty acres of well-kept grounds—and went in summer to Vermilion Lake, in the Quetico-Superior. He became a hunter, a canoer. In his early teens, he put up on his bedroom walls sectional aeronautical charts that covered the north of North America from Labrador to Alaska. "I would sit there for hours and dream, thinking where I was going to go." His heroes by that time were the mountain men of the eighteen-twenties and thirties. He had begun to collect a small library on them—"Bill Sublette, Mountain Man," "The Fur Hunters of the Far West"—and the same books are now in his cabins. He has read them all four times. The day after his high-school commencement, he left West Des Moines for Alaska. He was scarcely seventeen. He had a pickup, given him for graduation. His driver's license was five days old. ("I was one scared kid.") He had six hundred dollars, five hundred of which his sister had paid him for a quarter horse he owned. He had a couple of guns, his books on the mountain men, and little more. ("I was not loaded up with supplies.") He stayed scared, he says, for one day. He spent a year in southeastern Alaska and two in the Wrangells, trapping, looking after horses, working for big-game guides. Eventually, he heard things that attracted him to the upper-Yukon country. His father, a real-estate appraiser, happened to come to Anchorage on a business trip and flew him north to see it.

In Eagle, Potts learned that the last trapper who had worked his utopian drainage had left it ten years before. He quickly made friends in Eagle Indian Village, and—not an easy thing for a white to do—found a place where he could stay there. The Junebys took to him—in a sense, adopted him. Soon he went into the mountains, to prepare for the trapping life. He

fixed up a cabin forty miles from Eagle. In the fall, he killed
a moose and cached it for the winter. It gave him a sense of
plenty. A bear took the moose. He killed rabbits, but there were
not enough. As the cold weather came on, he lived for weeks
on flour, rice, and beans. He set out traps, but nothing much
entered them. Three hundred and fifteen dollars would be his
income for the winter. All but one of his dogs died. "It took
me time to catch on to the country. It is always difficult when
you are learning. I was trying to learn to live like an Indian, and
do things better than most. My basic mountain education fell
in that year. Bob Stacy, one of the older men in the Village,
went out there with me for a while. I owe him a lot. A white
man thinks he's great in the woods—and he brings his snow
machine. Indians live with the woods instead of fighting it. The
white man thinks he has to pack everything in there. An Indian
will pack very little and use the woods. The old people in the
Village say, 'The driftwood sleeps at night.' They see everything as alive."

Potts saw himself as "in college." He almost took his final
exam one night that first winter. Making a trip alone across a
high divide, he overestimated the distance he could cover and
had to stop far short of a cabin in which he meant to stay. He
had shot a wolf and skinned it out. Considering himself to be
in no hurry, he used up the light of the day. The sun set at four.
The best route to the divide climbed two thousand feet in the
two and a half miles before him. Slowly, on snowshoes in the
dark, he attacked the steep ascent. His dogs had very little "go
power." They were "half sick and half starved." He was hungry, too. He had no food with him and had not eaten all day.
He was counting on the cache at the cabin. He decided, finally,
that he would have to stay where he was. He had no tent. The
temperature was twenty below zero. He saw a thick drift of
snow against a clump of stunted spruce. He dug a kind of grave
in the snow, almost down to the ground. He lined the bottom
with spruce boughs and placed over them the pelt of the wolf.

He took his lead dog in with him, leaving the others in harness. Across the top of his excavation he placed his snowshoes, which more than reached from side to side. Over the snowshoes he spread his tarp. He had a few candles. He lighted them, and melted some snow. The water was his dinner.

Potts, who is now established and successful, with cabins all over his trapping estate in addition to his principal home at the edge of the Village, told me that story in response to a question. I asked him if in all the seasons he had spent in that wilderness he had ever been afraid. "Yes—once," he said, and added at the end of the tale, "There was some uncertainty there. But I wasn't frightened to where I didn't have my head."

Potts is a big man, attractive, not wiry but hard. Now that he is twenty-five, his hair is disappearing on the top but hangs in long strings on either side. His eyes, bright and a rich blue, are so alert and dilated that they suggest anxiety until you hear the voice that calmly and confidently follows their gaze. His jacket is of fringed and beaded moosehide. His skin, where it shows, is as tan as his wife's. She is short and roundly soft in form. Her voice is light and slow.

Potts feels a world of difference between him and the whites of the river. While they are his good friends, his regard for them does not always stop shy of contempt. He will eat their boiled wolf and listen to their stories, but he is of the mountains and they are of the river, and "to get things to their cabin all they have to do is float them down." He continues, "In this day and age, few people would make the effort to go out where I go, to the North Fork. It is mountainous country. It isn't the Yukon, where you've got snow machines and a lot of people using the route. The mountain country is a lot tougher—and just myself breaking the trail. Long ago, when more people were out there in the mountains, it was a different type of man. There was no welfare and Social Security type stuff then. Nowadays, even on the river, people give up. They go hungry for a day and they quit. If it looks too hard, they can give it up and try something else: be a bum, like a lot of these people in Eagle."

⟨ Dick Cook, acknowledged high swami of the river people, does not share Potts' view of Potts. "He feels that he is living in the bush," Cook says. "But really he is living in town. All he has out there in the mountains is a few traps, and airdrop supplies." Cook is eating his breakfast, which begins with slices of moose sausage in bear casing, set in a bed of fried rice, prepared and served to him by Donna Kneeland. He sits in the larger of two chairs in his cabin, vaguely fifty miles into the wild from Eagle, and points out that we are as remote as we would be if the cabin were on Potts' trapline. We are nearly six miles from the Yukon as well.

The chairs are side by side, like thrones, against a windowless wall. I sat in Dick's chair once, and Donna warned me off it. Now I am in the other. With her plate in her lap, Donna is on the floor before us. Outside where Donna saws wood is a nine-pound maul, which she uses to split green spruce for her sheepherder's stove. In its tiny oven she bakes bread and pies.

"In this country, two people are necessary for each other," she says. "There is a purpose in what I do here. When Dick comes home, I have fixed his food."

"Out here, Donna is needed. Women in town are useless," says Cook.

"Women's lib, that's not me. Women's lib is women being like men. They are barking up the wrong tree. I'm helping Dick, not doing these things for the sake of being like a man. I can't be like a man. I couldn't haul a soaked moosehide out of the river. It's too heavy. But I haul fish. I cut and sew caribou socks. I train the puppies to pull a sled. Are we going to start planting the garden today?"

"I'll decide that this afternoon."

Clamped to a shelf is a hand-cranked grain mill, an import from Latin America, which carries in raised letters its own identification: "Molino Corona—Landers Mora & Cia., Ltda." Many people in the country have mills like this one. A young woman in Eagle said to me that because her mill came from Latin America she found the C.I.A. part "spooky." Making flour by stone friction is tough on the arm, a prizefighter's exercise, Donna's job. She seems amused when I take it over.

On the stove is a tin can full of simmering tea, under a sheet-metal lid that is a piece of a fuel can with a scorched clothespin clipped to it as a handle. Steam meanders upward past a slot window, low and wide, covered with clear soft plastic. The view is of segments of tree trunks. The cabin is on an island in a white rushing stream and stands in a grove of what for this country are specimen spruce. Some approach six feet in girth. For logs and lumber, Cook has selected the trees in a way that preserves the aesthetic of the grove. The cabin logs are not peeled—a practice he looks upon as repellently suburban.

The shanty that Dick and Donna use on stopovers in Eagle is only a little up from squalid. Old mattresses drape its roof, old wolf gristle lies on the cluttered floor, and many tons of junk are in profusion on the ground. Their fish camp down the Yukon can be discouraging, too—a dirty, fetid, lightless cabin astink in aging salmon. These more manifest habitations long ago earned Cook a reputation as a sloven—among people who have never been here. This secluded cabin (his home of homes) is neat and tidy—in fact, trig. For years, he was content with half of it, with ten by ten feet. Now, with Donna, he has added a second room, which is two steps lower—split-level. Down there is the bed, made of rough planks covered with the hide of a moose. They ate their Thanksgiving dinner sitting on the bed—roast of moose he had shot, with a sauce of cranberries she had picked, potatoes and rutabagas they had grown, alfalfa sprouts with vinegar and oil, "pumpkin" pie from Hubbard squash. Visitors sleep on the floor. The dogs, on their chains, are spaced among the spruce. They are usually quiet, but we hear them yelp, howl, or mutter from time to time. Curving overhead near the ridgepole is a curing pair of sled shoes, made from white birch. In very deep cold, steel runners stick to snow as if they were crossing sand. The cabin door is covered with a moosehide. Under the eave and the window, outside, is a workbench equipped with carpenter's tools and construction implements of high quality and extensive choice, all of them neatly, not to say meticulously, arranged. Around the cabin are Swede saws, a whipsaw, steel barrels, snowshoes, sleds, a shovel, a rake, a pickaxe, wedges, a crowbar, a hand sledge, axes, traps, the "Alaska Maytag" (basically a tub and plunger), a wall tent, a construction wheelbarrow with inflated tires, and any number of dozens of other things. We are as far down the Yukon from Eagle as New York City is down the Hudson from West Point, and the largest vehicle that can carry things the six miles up this tributary stream is a canoe. Dick means to bring a full-size cookstove soon, and an antique Singer sewing machine that belonged to his grandmother in Ohio. He says that half the work he has done, over the years, has been "hauling things in."

An amazing percentage of the cargo stands on the cabin shelves. Books everywhere. Books on carpentry, blacksmithing, metalcraft, guns, leather, taxidermy, trapping, woodcraft. "American Indian Medicine." "The Sacred Mushroom and the Cross." "A Room of One's Own." "A Field Guide to Animal Tracks." "The Harvard Brief Dictionary of Music." "Desert Solitaire."

I tell him I like that one very much.

"You have a right to your opinion. The author's mistake is that he tries to express the meaning of nature. When you are writing about nature, you are writing about God, and it cannot be put into words."

"Shooter's Bible." "The Holy Bible."

"Meat killed first three days after full moon said to keep better," says a note neatly written on a wall calendar. "Harvest roots and fruit in third to fourth quarter. Mushrooms best on full moon."

When Dick and Donna are away, the cabin door is always left standing wide open. Blankets are tacked across the windows. Breakable objects are put under the floorboards, in a small cellar. Roughly half the times they are gone, they return to evidence of the presence of bears. Donna picks up a can of Crisco that a bear examined on a recent visit. As the bear held the Crisco and studied the label, a claw punched through the side of the can. The hole is of the diameter that would be made by a .45-calibre bullet. "When you live with nature, you have to share with nature, whether you like it or not," says Cook. "The cabin is bear bait. Bears know when we're not here, because the dogs are gone. The damage bears do is part of living here." Since breaking and entering is their most expensive habit, the cost is lowered by masking the windows and opening the door, suggesting to a bear the best way in and out, so the bear will not demolish the cabin.

Bears are on my mind today, because tomorrow I have to walk out of here alone and I hope for no encounters on the way. I have arranged with Sarge Waller to come down the Yukon in his boat and meet me at Cook's fish camp. The six miles from here to there have been travelled enough to create a sporadic trail—segments of beaten thoroughfare that tend to disappear, now into sedge tussocks, now into knee-deep muskeg, now into heavy thickets. As Nessmuk said, "The trail . . . branched off to right and left, grew dimmer and slimmer, degenerated to a deer path, petered out to a squirrel track, ran up a tree, and ended in a knot hole." Getting lost will not be possible, though—not with a wall of hills on the right and the stream on the left and less than a mile of ground between. My apprehension is focussed wholly on bears, of which I am more wary than I was at one time. A while back, I confided this fear, in a general way, to Jim Scott in Eagle. I told him I had heard John Ostrander saying how bears are not long out of their dens these days and are walking around mean and vicious. "Don't listen to these terrorized people," said Scott. "Don't let them spoil your fun, you know what I mean? When you walk out from Cook's cabin, your chances, in effect, of encountering a bear will be roughly equivalent to your chances of encountering Jesus Christ."

Jack Greene strongly counselled me not to go into the woods without a gun, and offered me one of his. I thanked him but refused. Having never hunted, I have almost no knowledge of guns. Arriving here, I came in with Dick and Donna from the fish camp, backpacking, the sled dogs running circles around us in the woods—a noisy, armed safari. Snoopy—brother of Chipper, the lead dog—had a forty-pound pack on his back, too. When Dick put it on him, he at once walked into the Yukon. We had come perhaps three-quarters of a mile when we passed a big mound of scat. "Maybe we'll get a bear!" Donna said. "It can happen anytime." The thought seemed to quicken their appetites. Like a traveller checking his wallet, Cook instinctively felt for his rifle. He had left it at the fish camp. He dropped his pack and returned for the gun. Donna and I sat down by the spoor. "A woman needs a lot of confidence in the man she is living with out here," she said. "I have superconfidence in Dick. When I wanted to go out with a man and live in the bush, I wasn't about to go out with someone from a university. The trouble with some people living out here together is that neither of them knows a whole bunch." When Dick returned and we proceeded, we soon passed another pile of bear scat, fairly new—and, a half mile later, one that was even fresher. Now, on the morning before I leave, every bear story I know keeps running through my mind, every newspaper headline—"HIKERS DRIVE OFF BEAR SUSPECTED IN EARLIER DEATH," "RIFLE OFFERS PROTECTION FROM BEARS"—and every bearchew feature in *Alaska* magazine, with color pictures of discharge day at Anchorage hospitals, people's eyes awry, their faces like five-year-old baseballs. When I told Tom Scott of my own travels in the Brooks

Range, with unarmed but ecologically experienced companions (Sierra Club, Bureau of Outdoor Recreation, National Park Service types), he said, "Pardon my saying so, but those gentlemen are fools. Alaskans are thought of as being gun-happy, and maybe that is what they are, but nearly everyone carries a gun in the woods"—including his father, he went on to say, regardless of Whom he might expect to meet there. And here I am about to walk through the woods the distance merely from Times Square to LaGuardia Airport and I am ionized with anticipation—catastrophic anticipation. I may never resolve my question of bears—the extent to which I exaggerate the danger, the extent of the foolishness of those who go unarmed. The effect of it all, for the moment, is a slight but detectable migration of my internal affections from the sneaker toward the bazooka, from the National Wildlife Federation toward the National Rifle Association—an annoying touch of panic in a bright and blazing day.

I profoundly wish it were winter. The country has seemed more friendly to me then, all the bears staring up at the ceilings of their dens. The landscape is softened, in illusion less rough and severe—the frozen rivers flat and quiet where the waves of rapids had been. Dick goes out on the levelled stream and lays down harnesses on the snow. The sled is packed, the gear lashed under skins. Everything is ready for the dogs. They are barking, roaring, screaming with impatience for the run. One by one, Donna unchains them. Out of the trees they dash toward the sled. Chipper goes first and, standing in front, holds all the harnesses in a good taut line. Abie, Little Girl, Grandma, Ug—the others fast fill in. They jump in their traces, can't wait to go. If they jump too much, they get cuffed. Wait another minute and they'll have everything so twisted we'll be here another hour. Go! The whole team hits at once. The sled, which was at rest a moment before, is moving fast. Destination, Eagle; time, two days.

The bluff above the stream is pastel tan, the sky rich blue. "Great day!"

"The snow could be a little drier!" Cook shouts. "In this god-damned country, no matter what the conditions are you wish you had something else!"

With a bit of time behind them, the dogs steady down. Gradually, Little Girl's tail comes up, begins to wag. She is goldbricking. Richard O. Cook stops his team. He walks up and down the line. "All right, you all know what is happening. You know who I'm after. You all know who I mean. No, not you, Grandma. You're O.K., girl. You are doing your work. You have not yet started to fake. No, not you, Chipper. You, either, Ug." He comes to Little Girl. *"You* know who I mean. *You* know what is going on," he says, and whumps her very hard on both sides of her butt. Dick does not pull back when he hits his dogs. He really belts them. But he is never cruel, he would not gratuitously beat them down. They are all exuberant animals, not a chronic cringer among them, and the full warm context of his relationship with them is something wonderful to see. The sled moves again. Little Girl's tail is low and wagless, and her chest is on the leather.

"Females are temperamental, flighty, not nearly as steady as males," he says. "I have two. If I didn't need them for breeding purposes, I would have none in my team."

Dick has sometimes handed the sled over to me for two and three miles at a time, he and Donna walking far behind. On forest trails, with the ground uneven, the complexity of the guesswork is more than I'd have dreamed. We come to, say, a slight uphill grade. I have been riding, standing on the back of the sled. The dogs, working harder, begin throwing glances back at me. I jump off and run, giving them a hundred-and-fifty-pound bonus. The sled picks up speed in reply. Sooner or later, they stop—spontaneously quit—and rest. Let them rest too long and they'll dig holes in the snow and lie down. I have learned to wait about forty-five seconds, then rattle the sled, and off they go. I don't dare speak to them, because my voice is not Cook's. If I speak, they won't move at all. There are three main choices—to ride, to run behind, or to keep a foot on the sled and push with the other, like a kid propelling a scooter. The incline has to be taken into account, the weight of the sled, the firmness of the trail, the apparent energy of the dogs, the time since they last rested, one's own degree of fatigue. Up and down hill, over frozen lakes—now ride, now half ride, run. Ten below zero seems to be the fulcrum temperature at which the air is just right to keep exertion cool. You're tired. Ride. Outguess the dogs. Help with one foot. When they're just about to quit, step off and run. When things look promising, get on again, rest, look around at the big white country; its laden spruce on forest trails; its boulevard, the silent Yukon. On a cold, clear aurorean night with the moon and Sirius flooding the ground, the sound of the sled on the dry snow is like the rumbling cars of a long freight, well after the engine has passed. According to Harry David, dogs run faster in moon-light, because they are trying to get away from their shadows.

Now, at Cook and Kneeland's cabin, with the snow off the ground and the bears upon it, I am too abashed to confess my fright, although Cook, I have noticed, is rarely unarmed. Donna works at a muskrat skin. Dick assembles bee frames at his workbench. His hives look like cabinets and were made from the trees above. I examine his .22. "Is it loaded?"

He says, "Every gun here is loaded. A baseball bat is better than an unloaded gun."

And Donna says, "You may not get your meat if you're not ready."

Cook's bees gave him a heavy stinging last week, when he was already suffering from abscesses around his teeth. So, for the first time in twelve years, he prescribed for himself a course of penicillin. His first-aid supply also includes ammonia inhalers, a thermometer, tape, gauze, a scalpel, hemostats, sutures, Empirin Compound with Codeine No. 4, Darvon, paregoric, Pontocaine, and morphine.

One knee of his trousers has ripped out, possibly for the hundredth time. His long johns poke through. "We'd better learn to Indian tan or we're not going to have any clothes."

"I didn't even know how to split wood when I came out here," Donna says. "In this country, you can't afford the luxury of sitting around waiting for a man to cut firewood, of not being able to do it yourself. Someday he may be late."

"Someday he may not come back," Dick reminds her.

"I know. I think that every time you go out."

Donna hangs up some skins for airing—moose, caribou, two bearskins. One bear was shot by a stream near here, the other down at the fish camp. She hangs up the pelt of a wolverine. "The wolverine is the most verbally abused animal in the country," Dick says as he works on his bee frames. "And unjustly so. It's one of the finest animals out here. People say a wolverine is 'ornery,' 'mean,' 'vicious,' 'worthless.' They say it can't live with another wolverine. No animal is considered lower. My experience is entirely different. The wolverine is powerful. It hunts with its mate. If one is injured, the other will stick by it. Wolves are affectionate, too. They are really beautiful animals. I have come to know and love them. This year, I have a mating pair on my line. Two years ago, I had a whole pack. The nonbreeders pack up, so they won't get in the way of the sex game. Around the first of March, twenty-five of them went right by the cabin here. Wolves are easy to shoot in mating season. They're in love, I guess. They run in pairs. They don't pay attention to what they're doing. Indians call animals their brothers. You soon realize here that your life is no more important than the animals'. Animals give up their lives, and you will, too. You can't have life without death."

Through apertures in the tall spruce I can see far down the stream course, and even to the low hills on the opposite side of the Yukon. They are blue with distance. I wish I could jump that distance. It is the whole of the walk out of here, and then some. The hills appear to be on the outskirts of Mexico City.

Toward 6 P.M., Donna serves creamed squaw candy (smoked salmon) on whole-wheat biscuits. Resuming his work, Dick soon discovers that he is running out of foundations—the sheets of wax on which bees build their combs. He must have more foundations, he says, and the nearest supply is in Eagle.

"Come with me and Sarge tomorrow!" I tell him, the idea striking like sunlight. I can already see him on the trail before me, his rifle gently bobbing on its sling. Cook begins to think out loud. He must have the foundations. He must also plant his garden. He cannot go to Eagle and leave behind him an unplanted garden. This near the Arctic Circle, the margins of germination, growth, and harvest are extremely narrow. Even a couple of days can make a fatal difference. He and Donna live, in significant measure, on their crops. On the other hand, the bees have come all the way from Texas and are not easily replaced. He needs the honey. Possibly, enough of the more critical seeds and plants could be put into the soil tonight, and even early tomorrow morning, to free him to go with me and Sarge. "I want to do that if I possibly can," he says, and my heart soars like a hawk. "But we will have to work like bastards planting the garden tonight."

Cook's approach to high-latitude agriculture is detailed and scientific. His garden is twenty-five hundred square feet, and he has planned it to the half inch. He carries a thick notebook. The notes reflect research on the chances and characteristics of many hundreds of varieties of berries, vegetables, and flowers. A Norman monk would not have styled a neater arrangement. Asters, pansies, cress, nasturtiums, burdock, dill, sage, cabbage, savory. Some are this year's experiments, some are tried and sure. The soil is black silt. Oriental poppies, beets, marigolds, grass, broccoli, endive, kale. Strawberries. Four kinds of peas. Potatoes. Lettuce. Cook is a one-man experiment station. Instead of hunting him down and trying to kick him out of here, the federal government should come and farm his genius. Subsidize him. Not that he would accept. Parsnips, cabbage, parsley, beans, onions, horseradish, Jerusalem artichokes, corn, clover, alfalfa, rhubarb. The evening is extremely feverish. The garden is close by the rushing stream, above a steep and mucky bank. I scramble up and down filling buckets with water. A thousand gallons may do. Sunflowers, calendula,

radishes, rutabaga, shallots, turnips, tomatoes. Between buckets, I shovel compost, most of which is malamute-Siberian
mongrel turd. Cucumbers. There is a small plastic-covered
greenhouse, built by Donna, near the cabin. Cucumbers,
tomatoes, and peppers are greenhouse crops in Alaska, as is
Hubbard squash. Going away for a few days recently, Donna
hid flats of green shoots in the cellar, so bears would not knock
them over. Mice ate the young tomato plants and most of the
Hubbard squash—next winter's "pumpkin" pies. Ermine, frequently, will inhabit the cabin like mice. Cook once had a pet
weasel named Harriet that used to run on his table and knock
off dishes and look at him with a weaselly smile. Harriet acci-
dentally died in one of his traps.

Donna and I plant together, sliding opposite down the rows.
We must slow up and be careful, or Cook, with his notebook,
will find us at fault. Donna, in her generosity, seems as sensitive
to my goals as to his, to feel my desire to get the seeds into the
earth. Turnips form a four-inch grid. Radishes next. Beets.
There is a delaying search through the packet box for the right
succession of varietal carrots. Cook advances to the new strawberry bed, at the far end of the garden. Donna and I talk. She
mentions her honeymoon. When she married Bill Kneeland,
an architect in Fairbanks, they went off to a cabin in the bush
near Livengood that had been given her as a present. Her
employer soon flew in after them. He said he was desperate,
she had to come away and work. He ran an air-charter service
in Fairbanks, and he needed her as a stewardess on a big,
important job. What could she do, she wonders, giving a shrug,
dropping carrot seeds into the ground. Leaving Kneeland in
the cabin, she flew off with her boss.

After the honeymoon, she and the architect moved into a
big house in Fairbanks, where she "was supposed to look
pretty." She had nothing else to do. If she fulfilled the requirement by nature, she did not by predisposition. "That life was
just not my style. I like it more here. It's more worthwhile. The

satisfaction is in making your own living, as opposed to making money and buying your living—to have the garden all planted and a year's supply of salmon hanging on the racks. I get a lot of pleasure, too, out of having a nice piece of skin. When I tan it right, I feel good. I have sure learned a lot, stumbling around. In my first year, I broke two plates and several cups. I wouldn't do that now. I have a long way to go, though. I'm still not comfortable in boats."

To get over to their cabin when we arrived, we used Dick's canoe, which he had left in the mainland woods. First, we lined it up the shelf ice to a point opposite the island, where we would try to angle down the heavy rapids and get a purchase on the island side. The dogs, meanwhile, jumped in and swam. One was a seven-month-old pup, swimming a current for the first time in her life. The choppy torrent was sparkling with sun, and her head was hard to follow. She tried to swim straight upstream, and the river—thirty-three degrees—kept moving her backward. At best, she just held even. I thought she was going to die. Finally, a bit at a time, she ferried on the current, moved sidewise, and, after a very long baptismal swim, went shaking onto the bank. Now, in the canoe, we human beings shoved into the rapid. Dick had a pole and wanted no help. We bucked on into the haystacks. "That pup was really working," I said to Donna. "Quiet!" she replied. Her hands were wrapped around the center thwart, the knuckles white.

"I do worry a lot," Donna admits. "I worry about Dick. I worry about him and the river. I worry a whole hell of a lot when he is gone for weeks. I try to work on new skills. I'm learning to work with wood. I worked two months on a small wooden car for my son." The axles were of birch, the wheels of red alder, bound to the chassis with rawhide. The wheels had spokes of spruce. The body was cottonwood. The bumper was moose bone. The surface was finished with beeswax. Edward, Donna's son, is two. He lives in Oklahoma. His stepmother could not stand Alaska. Donna wrapped the finished car with extraordinary care and mailed it to Edward from Eagle, wondering to what extent he might sense that it had not come from a store.

It is 11 P.M. We have one section planted—roughly half a dozen to go. The strawberry bed is under way, and I help Dick there. It is his notion that strawberries in a depressed bed can survive a penarctic winter. So this bed will be six inches deep. A lot more than six inches has to be shovelled up and lugged away, though, because he has tons of compost for the bed.

By midnight, with half the excavation done, Dick straightens up and says he is ready to quit. He doubts he'll finish in the morning. So why not quit now? He enters a debate—with himself—aloud. Vegetables versus bees. Participation by others is not invited. He flings pros into the air like skeet, and one by one he shatters them with cons. He finally announces that he is not going to leave in the morning.

He has at least given me an evening off from my imagination. We go inside for a late dessert—cranberry shortcake with milk and sugar—and I pick at it while he reviews the sterner facts of nature. "In New York," he says, "people separate the concepts of life and death. In this country, their whole view of life and death would change. The woods are composed of who's killing whom. Life is forever building from death. Life and death are not a duality."

"These concepts aren't earthshaking," says Donna. "It's just that you can see it all here."

"You look at this country, it hits you in the face," Dick continues.

"What hits you in the face?"

"That life and death are not a duality. They're just simply here—life, death—in the all-pervading mesh that holds things together. Less than five minutes after a wolf stops chasing a moose, the moose is browsing. The wolf chases the moose again. Stops. Five minutes later, the moose is browsing. The moose does not go on thinking—worrying—about the wolf. Death is as much a part of life as breathing. People in cities seem to want life and death to remain at a standstill. Most people who are against killing are horribly afraid to die. They seem to think you can have life without death, and if so they have withdrawn from life. They seem to think the animals up here are smelling flowers. They use the word 'ecology' for everything but what it means. It means who's eating whom, and when."

I ask him what, if anything, makes him afraid.

"Uncontrolled fear and deep respect are two different things," he answers. "In one sense, there is nothing out here for me to fear. I'm going to die someday. I'll be food for somebody else. There are a lot of things up here that can kill you. You've got to have a healthy respect for the country."

I am supposed to meet Sarge at two in the afternoon. At ten-thirty in the morning, I ask Dick for a ride off the island. It took us four and a half hours to get up here, but I am sure I can get back in three, and I want some extra time in case I go astray. He poles me to shore. I jump out, thank him, and go up the bank. I go on up a rise, circle a swamp on a contour, and drop down among cottonwoods near the stream. I made notes coming in. "Go through sphagnum boggy open area after point of rock, hills to left, then into woods half a mile, then a quarter mile of tussocks, then by stream half a mile over gravel dry slough, then get up on bank and into willow." I attempt to follow this in reverse, and see nothing whatsoever that is mentioned in the notes. I am moving right along, though, finding here and there a bit of travelled path, here and there a sight of the stream. Animals use the same routes people do, especially where the way is narrow. The way is so narrow at times that the willow trunks simultaneously rub both ends of the rolled pad on the top of my pack.

Like an explosion in my face, a grouse starts up, two feet away, whirring. I break out in muskeg, back to heavy woods. I have a metal cup. I tap on it with a spoon. I pass bear scat, old and familiar. Tap. Now another mound. I have not seen that one before. Tap. Tap. In other words, never surprise a bear. One or two *must* be here somewhere. To make myself known, I deliver lectures to them in a voice designed to clear the hall. "Uncontrolled fear and deep respect are two different things," I explain to them. "You've got to have a healthy respect for what comes through the country."

An hour goes by, and more—fast-moving. I lose my way now, in dense alder. A path was clear before, but it is suddenly gone. With a couple of taps on the cup, I stand and wonder what to do. I go back, or what I think is back, but have lost where I have been. The brush is so dense I can't see the hills. I try moving laterally, toward and away from what I guess to be the direction of the stream. Now for some minutes I slowly walk in a rectangle, breaking branches to mark it, then build a larger one on that, and, while building a third one, come to beaten trail. In it is a mound of spoor. I recognize it as if it were a friend. It was the nearest defecation to the Yukon. Tap.

The trees finally end. I am pleased to see the big river. I make a bench of driftwood, eat cashews and apricots, and wait for Sarge. The walk took a little less than two hours. I don't feel elevated by that journey, nor am I shy to describe it—just happy that it is complete. I scarcely think I was crazy to do it, and I don't think I was crazy to fear it. Risk was low, but there was something to fear. Still, I am left awry. I embrace this wild country. But how can I be of it, how can I move within it? I can't accept anymore the rationale of the few who go unarmed —yet I am equally loath to use guns. If bears were no longer in the country, I would not have come. I am here, in a sense, because they survive. So I am sorry—truly rueful and perplexed —that without a means of killing them I cannot feel at ease. A punctual speck appears on the river. Staff Sergeant James Waller, United States Marine Corps, Retired. Tap.

◖ I have been hired as scribe to Mike Potts. My ancestors in Scotland were scribes to the likes of Potts, so I feel an atavistic rightness in accepting the position. I won't take pay. He feeds me instead—a meal here and there, a little bread and moose. I enjoy Potts. Like Dick Cook, he has a certain picture of himself and he paints it every day—another daub, another skill, becoming more and more of what he once only dreamed. With John Gaudio, he now wishes to offer two-week dog-team trips to anyone willing to travel this far and pay him enough, and he needs, in effect, a brochure. He is a skillful editor. "Verbal" is not the word that Potts first brings to mind, but he senses how language might be cut to fit him. Taking hold of the text, he roughs it up. "Day 10: Cross over the divide into the Seventymile River drainage and camp at the headwaters of Mogul Creek (tent)."

The stipend on Potts' table tonight was perhaps more than I had bargained for. What we consumed, in the main, was fresh shoulder of grizzly—giving a new, unexpected, and grimly ironic turn to my evolving approach to this creature. Potts and Gaudio took a canoe down the Fortymile a few days ago. The Fortymile goes into the Yukon thirty miles above Eagle, in Canada. Heading back from there, they got into their sleeping bags in the canoe and drifted through the night. One woke the other when he saw the bear. It was on the right bank and close to the water. The canoe moved silently upon it. The bear was walking upwind, downriver, looking the other way— just on the Canadian side of the border. The two raised their rifles, fired, and knocked it into the United States. Halved at the waist, it has been hanging in Potts' butchery, a few steps from his cabin. The butchery, merely a roof on poles, is also his fish cache, and the shelter for his dog pot—half a fifty-five-gallon drum that sits like a caldron above a fire and is a pot-au-feu for huskies. Fish parts, bear gut, the voluminous udder of a moose—what goes in there is "anything you got," lamb's-quarters, too ("for roughage"). I have once or twice helped him feed the dogs, carrying buckets to their stakes behind the cabin. They scream and leap in frenzy and plunge their noses into the buckets and swallow gobs of viscera at a gulp, then sit

down and pass the hours, bored at the ends of their chains.
Burgundy is the color of the grizzly's flesh. With the coat gone,
its body is an awesome show of muscular anatomy. The torso
hangs like an Eisenhower jacket, short in the middle, long in
the arms, muscles braided and bulging. The claws and cuffs are
still there. A great deal of fat is on the back. The legs, still
joined, suggest a middle linebacker, although the thought is
flattering to football. The bear was two years old.

  "Shar-cho," said Adeline Potts, means "big bear," means in
her language the brown—the grizzly—bear. "Why don't you
cook a bit?" said her husband. "I'm getting hungry." Across
the grain, he had sliced a pile of steaks, and she cooked them
in their own raging fat. The Potts' log cabin is fourteen feet
square, no more, but "big enough, and not too hard to heat."
A double bed, of planks, is in a corner, and above it the bunk
of Adeline's three-year-old son. There is a small chest of draw-
ers, a small cookstove, a half-drum heat stove, two benches, a
table in a corner. Four rifles ride the ridgepole. The logs were
cut in forests upstream, and yanked to the Yukon by Oddball
and Patches, huskies who fill in as horses. Oddball is Potts' lead
dog and is as white as a cue ball. The house in which Potts grew
up, in West Des Moines, looks out from big Naugahyde chairs
at handsome landscaping through picture windows. On the
wall is a painting of snow-capped mountains—a stag in the
foreground, its head held high. On the walls of Potts' cabin are
posters of chiefs. "Tah-Me-La-Pash-Me. Dull Knife. Chey-
enne. 1828–1879." "Oh-Cun-Ga-Che. Little Wolf. Chey-
enne. 1820–1904." Adeline would not eat the bear. She
cooked, in supplement, a platter of moose. She will eat lynx,
she said, which is "just like turkey," and wolf, which recalls
canned beef. But not this, never this meat. There might be
taste but there was terror in the bear. Mike ate happily and
hugely, fat and lean. "This is a fat-starved country," he said.
"The Lower Forty-eight has to have cottage cheese, skim milk,
and so on, because they have too much fat. The people there

are fat. Up here, this is a fat-starved country, and you take fat when you can get it. I got five pounds of lard from this bear." The moose was tough. I ate little of it. The grizzly was tender with youth and from a winter in the den. More flavorful than any wild meat I have eaten, it expanded my life list—muskrat, weasel, deer, moose, musk-ox, Dall sheep, whale, lion, coach whip, rattlesnake . . . grizzly. And now a difference overcame me with regard to bears. In strange communion, I had chewed the flag, consumed the symbol of the total wild, and, from that meal forward, if a bear should ever wish to reciprocate, it would only be what I deserve.

Potts makes two thousand dollars in a winter's trapping. He has worked on the pipeline three weeks for the same. He prefers trapping. For $11.27 an hour, he once operated a chain saw that helped to clear the pipeline's right-of-way. When he goes out into the mountains, he is often accompanied by Michael David, who now runs lines in adjacent terrain. In the eyes of some people in the Village, including older ones, such endeavors in the wild are retrogressive. Adeline's father, Willie Juneby, is just amused. "My dad thinks we're crazy sometimes." The Hungwitchin have historically been nervous about certain high ground in the area where Potts goes to trap. They call it the Devil's Chair, and fear for Adeline if she is there. Septembers, Potts puts out nets for the running chum salmon. He dries them and packs them, and eventually has a chartered plane drop hundreds of pounds of fish in the mountains, where he caches them for his dogs in winter. The plane, out of Tok and costing eighty dollars a trip, also drops flour, salt, sugar, matches, candles, tea, coffee, tobacco, milk, baking powder, rice, Mapleine, jello, and canned goods in heavy double bags. Potts does not otherwise seek assistance. With sled and gear, moving up and over his mountains, he has broken trail for as much as nineteen straight hours through deep blown drifts at sixty below.

In spring, he puts out a net for pike and grayling, in an eddy

up the Yukon where schools collect. His whole family gets into
his canoe—a lovely eighteen-foot Chestnut—and goes up to
discover the daily catch. Oddball pulls the canoe. He stands in
harness on the edge of the river, and a long rope runs from the
middle of his back over water to the bow quarter thwart. Potts
speaks. Oddball advances. The canoe—carrying, say, five hundred pounds—begins to slide upstream. Steering with a paddle,
Potts keeps the bow a few degrees off the grain of the current,
maintaining tension on the rope. The mighty Yukon drives one
way, mighty Oddball the other. Oddball defeats the river with
ease. He jumps logs, he swims around sweepers—responding to
remarks from Potts. The trip is not slow. The canoe fairly rips
along. Caught by the gills, pike and grayling are waiting. ("Stay
close to Potts," Jim Scott has urged me. "If for nothing else,
for the northern pike.")

We cleaned them, late one evening, under a rainbow that
vaulted from an orange northerly sky. Sonny Potts, half Eskimo, with wide soft eyes too deep to plumb, watched his
adoptive father scaling a fish. "Is that a mother?" he asked.
"Does it have beans in it?"

"We'll see," said Potts, a smile flapping the wings of his mustache. He slit the fish forward from the anus, spilling beans.

Sonny's father was Ray Foster, an Eskimo of Noorvik, who
left a wife and many children to marry Adeline, and who now
lives with the widow of Tony Paul. Potts was checking I.D.s
and stopping fights as a temporary bouncer in a bar in Fairbanks when Adeline happened in, divorced and depressed.
Mike talked her away from her troubles and the bar, and back
to Eagle Indian Village. He is said to have stabilized her life.
When he is in the Village, she is comforted and easy. He causes
her to feel at home. She is not a little bitter. Of the whites of
Eagle she has not much good to say. "They just want to cut
us down. They gossip behind our backs. They feel superior.
They give false grins." She is the first woman who has ever
served on the Eagle Village Council. She has tacked a
"Thanksgiving Prayer" to the rafters of her cabin. "Dear Lord,

we thank You for poverty, starvation, infant death, a 44-year lifespan, diseases like smallpox, tuberculosis, diphtheria, and v.d. We thank You for alcoholism and suicide. . . ." She and Potts feel as strongly as Michael David about the white bootleggers of Eagle. They once attempted to "turn them in." The response in Eagle was an instant story that Mike Potts was a habitual user of the hardest kinds of drugs. "The truth is," he says, "I've never even bought a lid of grass."

He is subject to worse gossip than that, as are the three or four other whites who live in the Village and are married to Indians. The essence of what is said is that in marrying into the tribe they knew what they wanted, and that was franchise. With the Bureau of Land Management chasing people away from all parts of the federal domain, the choices for the arriving settler, for the would-be modern pioneer, are to live in trespass in defiance of the government, to make an arrangement with the Indians, or to fold one's tent and try to rent in Eagle. The Hungwitchin are reluctant to enter into most arrangements. Marriage is one they have to accept.

"You get the husky-dusky maiden, you see, and then you spin off the benefits from the native claims—the Village land selections, the corporate profit-sharing, the direct payments coming down from the Alaska Native Fund."

"We call them land-claim bridegrooms."

"They are romantics, too, remember. Back to Mother Indian. They love sleeping in dry caribou skin and eating jerky."

Mike Potts appears to be only mildly disgusted by all this. He came into the country for what is here; others have come for what is not. While he has been turning into a seasoned performer—relaxed in the pleasure of his chosen life—these others have been turning into hecklers. He shrugs them off and hits the trail. He is teaching his young brother-in-law Benny Juneby the skills of the woods, including the handling of dogs. (There are six dog teams in the Village, of which three belong to whites.) He divides his game with the Village. He has often shot a moose and ended up with the least of it. He is good at getting meat. Once, in the mountains, he shot three moose in a day. Two wolves were on the first moose, about to pull it down. Everywhere he looked he saw wolves, like shadows flying through the trees. When he fired, the wolves vanished. The moose staggered into the North Fork of the Fortymile. Potts was downstream, and the current delivered the meat. In the same area, a grizzly chased Oddball not long ago and was within ten feet of destroying him when Potts fired true enough to stop the chase. There is game, at times, much closer to the Village. The long tall bluff across the Yukon is a natural fence, and unfortunate is the animal that walks beside it. There is no good direction for escape. A black bear once came out of the woods between Potts' cabin and the Village school, went down to the river, and swam across. Michael David, Potts, and Tony Paul crossed the river in Tony's boat with a .44 handgun and a .30-'06. They were waiting onshore under the bluff when the bear came out of the water. Grizzlies have died the same way, and moose, and caribou. Caribou have been low in the country, have been all but gone in recent years, and Potts is restless to find them. He talks more and more of the Porcupine drainage, a hundred miles north, where the herds in the mountains move like rivers, thirty miles long.

"Potts' only problem is that he's white. He has difficulty coping with that. He fancies himself a male Sacajawea. He's not looking for monetary gain."

"He brings a lot more meat into that Village than he eats."

"He is from Des Moines, Iowa, and he keeps the Village Indian."

❲ Now alone in mountains nearly a hundred miles west of Eagle and at least thirty from the nearest human being, I am puzzled by the hour of the day. I have no idea what it is. There has been no dark of night or visible sun. I don't wear a watch. I am like that Frenchman deep in the caves who hadn't a notion of the hour and slept and ate only according to need. I wonder: Could I have prepared and eaten three full meals in only two hours? In twelve? Fifteen? If I could see the sun, the sun would not help. I have neither a map nor a compass with which to assess its position, and now, at the summer solstice, it rides so low above the mountain ridges and dips so briefly behind them that 4 A.M. looks much like nine and noon. All of that is academic anyway. There is a leaden overcast, and the wind is driving a light, cold rain. Tracks are everywhere—wolf, grizzly, caribou. The mountainsides in surrounding view—sixteen doming tundra balds—are green and white, holding the winter and the summer in quilted fields of snow. In this remote landscape, as wild as any in the country—where not so much as a cabin stands in half a million acres around—my only companions are a backhoe and a bulldozer.

The nearest tree is a mile away. In fact, there is just one small colony of spruce in this otherwise treeless high terrain. The bowl the mountains form is a circumvallate world of what appear to be upsweeping lawns, and in fifteen or twenty square miles I can see—or, at least, I imagine I am capable of seeing—almost anything that moves. With my monocular I look around, scan the middle ground, glass the hills. "Schizomotive" is the word for this situation. I regularly check the landscape in hopes of seeing what I am reassuring myself is not there. Moving around from place to place, stopping to use the monocular, I am like a watchman with a Detex key. I would give a lot to see caribou, and more to see a wolf. I am content with the bears I have seen, and prefer that they keep their distance—notwithstanding this big fella on my shoulder, a Winchester .308.

At my request, Ed and Stanley Gelvin flew off and left me here in late afternoon, close to the confluence of two brooks in their gold-claims valley. They had things to do at home.

They said they would return soon after eight o'clock this morning. (I am assuming this is morning.) I began listening for them while I was making breakfast. I have recently finished lunch. Since Stanley and his father are as punctual as they are industrious—and are never unmindful of the high investment and short season here at the claims—I have about concluded that I ate breakfast in the night in the belief that it was morning and have since had lunch for breakfast; they should be here anytime.

They have been working twelve hours a day. When they chose the site for the airstrip, the longest and naturally flattest place was across meanders of a stream. With the D9, Stanley set the stream to one side, gave it a straight new bed, and spread its gravels beside it for the runway. I have since caught many grayling in the new version of the stream, which has fine pools and flows clear. Removing the tundra from a wide swath of ancient channels, Stanley dozed more gravel onto the strip, then packed it down—seventeen hundred feet. Welding steel —using twelve-foot H-beams and angle irons—Ed created something that weighed a couple of tons and resembled a carpenter's plane. He dragged that up and down with the backhoe, making the runway smooth. There was not a lot I could do. I threw small boulders off the field. When it was complete, the Cessna 206, their single-engine workhorse aircraft, could land. It can carry, among other things, three or four fifty-five-gallon drums full of diesel fuel. Because the airstrip consists of stream-bed gravels, it contains, in all likelihood, gold. Long-range plans include another airstrip, to be made from tailings. Then this first airstrip can be run through the sluice box and deposited in a bank. There is a poplin wind sock, flying east. Ed sewed it at home. Its color is camouflage green.

Strewn around the wanigan, which is in effect a plywood tent, are tools, Blazo cans, propane tanks, the welding equipment, the generator—items no more congruous in this wilderness than the backhoe or the D9. A piece at a time, Ed and Stanley have disassembled the rig that Stanley hauled up here on his April journey over alpine snow and ice. The sled he dragged has become the slick plate—a couple of hundred square feet of half-inch-thick sheet steel, at one end of which Ed has fashioned and welded a steel mouthpiece to guide gravel into the sluice box. To carry water to the plate and box, he welded nine fifty-five-gallon drums end to end, forming a thirty-foot pipe. He used welding rods acquired from the Trans-Alaska Pipeline. Using a circular drum top, he made a valve for the pipe, and he fitted it with a handle that can regulate the flow of water. After assembling the steel sluice box, which is thirty-six feet long and four feet wide, he began to fill it with "riffles." Riffles vary considerably, and are the signature of the miner. Their general purpose is to create in the box a confined simulacrum of stream rapids, to intrude upon the flow of water so that it will leap, dive, tumble in souse holes, reverse itself in mid-torrent, rage forward, stack up, back up, and eddy out—just what happens when God welds a river. Prospectors in search of gold would try the deep, quiet pockets of rapids. In like manner, gold will collect in the deep, quiet pockets of the box. Most riffles are lengths of steel set perpendicular to the flow and only a few inches apart, ladderlike. They are set at various angles and spacings according to the theories of the miner. Some miners make riffles with wooden poles, wooden blocks, boulders. They even use slices of rubber tires. After Ed and Stanley had lowered into place all of their seventy calculated riffles—mostly three-sixteenths-inch angle irons, with a channel iron every four feet—they were ready at last to set up their mine.

They had decided to make the first cut half a mile below the airstrip, dozing wholly into the left side of the valley. "Them old-timers in the old days, they covered this country more thoroughly than you can imagine," Ed explained. "Up here,

they worked only the left limit." Back from a hundred and fifty
feet of stream (the basic dimension of the cut), Stanley scraped
off the tundra in a swath that went out to "the width of pay"
—to the margin, near the rising slope of the hillside, where a
pan of gravel would no longer show colors of gold. His father
worked with the pan, which was of a type called a grizzly, fitted
with screens of varied mesh to simplify the job. Crouching in
pools, he swirled sands and gravels until the pan smiled. In
places it smiled wanly, in places not at all. He had found a few
rough nuggets, he said. Not worn flat, they could not have
travelled far. Adducing such evidence, he hoped to mine coarse
gold.

The size of the cut was unusually large, but so was the size
of the D9 Cat, with its fourteen feet of blade. For the sluicing
operation, a reservoir was needed. Stanley built one, damming
and diking the stream so that the reservoir stood beside the cut.
He embedded the water pipe in the wall of the reservoir. It
poked through to the low end of the cut. The idea was to
position the slick plate under the pipe (with the sluice box
adjoining), then doze heaps of placer onto the plate and turn
on the water. First, however, there was a problem of drainage.
The valley's natural gradient was slight, and the stream bed
itself would not have been adequate. So Stanley dug a deep
ditch and ran it out to contour, some four hundred feet downstream. There was a minor incident when he returned to the
cut. He crushed his father's grizzly.

The sluice box should have a slope of exactly ten degrees.
The D9—larger than most cabins, lurching over mounds of its
own rubble—seemed an unlikely instrument for so precise a
job. Stanley—in his high seat, hands and feet in rapid movement among the multiple controls—suggested a virtuoso on a
pipe organ even more than a skinner on a Cat. Gradually, a
smooth ramp appeared. He had wired a carpenter's level to the
deck of the machine and had shimmed one end of it so the
bubble would center when the Cat was on a slope of ten

degrees. As he finished, and drove his fifty-five tons of yellow iron up the ramp, from bottom to top the bubble scarcely moved. Clanking off to fetch the sluice box, he hitched it to the rear of the big bulldozer, and pushed it backward down the narrow top of the dike. The sluice box weighs a couple of tons. He gently eased it down the ramp. Then he went and got the slick plate, and backed that down the top of the dike, too. He was grouchy—had been crabby all through the day—because he had no snoose. He was trying to quit, and had been six days without a dip of Copenhagen. Repeatedly, he shook his head in apparent dismay and made despairing remarks about the way things were going—heard mainly by the roaring Cat. The mouthpiece on the slick plate is nearly four feet wide and was designed to fit into the sluice box with very little clearance. Stanley backed the slick plate down the ramp. It weighs three tons, and he moved it steadily—without hesitation, without a pause for adjustment (just ran it downhill backward)—until the mouthpiece entered the box. It had not so much as brushed either side. The clearance was five-quarters of an inch one way and three-eighths of an inch the other. The day's work finished, father and son flew home.

Still no sign of them. The light rain is long since gone and the clouds are breaking. Even so, there is no sound, no distant approaching drone. Perhaps I did not sleep at all. Perhaps I just lay down for an illusory minute, then got up and sprinkled salt in the iron pan for toast. Collecting the only available firewood —the dead stems of dwarf willows, thinner than straws—I make a little blaze for warmth. The temperature is under forty. Once more I scan the mountains, where nothing is passing but the day.

I have fished, cooked, thrown rocks off the airstrip. Now I write a letter home. ". . . When the Gelvins departed, I was cleaning some grayling, five in all. I caught one with my fishing rod. The Cat caught the others. When Stanley dammed the river, and diverted it into the pipe, he took it out of its bed for a couple of hundred yards. Pools remained there, like low tide, and as they slowly drained they revealed the graylings' dorsal fins. I walked from pool to pool, trapping the fish with my hands. This pretty little stream is being disassembled in the name of gold. The result of the summer season—of moving forty thousand cubic yards of material through a box, of baring two hundred thousand square feet of bedrock, of scraping off the tundra and stuffing it up a hill, of making a muck-and-gravel hash out of what are now streamside meadows of blue-bells and lupine, daisies and Arctic forget-me-nots, yellow pop-pies, and saxifrage—will be a peanut-butter jar filled with flaky gold. Probably no one will actually use it. Investors will draw it into their world and lock it in an armored cellar, while up here in these untravelled mountains a machine-made moon-scape will tell the tale. Am I disgusted? Manifestly not. Not from here, from now, from this perspective. I am too warmly, too subjectively caught up in what the Gelvins are doing. In the ecomilitia, bust me to private. This mine is a cork on the sea. Meanwhile (and, possibly, more seriously), the relationship between this father and son is as attractive as anything I have seen in Alaska—both of them self-reliant beyond the usual reach of the term, the characteristic formed by this country. Whatever they are doing, whether it is mining or something else, they do for themselves what no one else is here to do for them. Their kind is more endangered every year. Balance that against the nick they are making in this land. Only an easygo-ing extremist would preserve every bit of the country. And extremists alone would exploit it all. Everyone else has to think the matter through—choose a point of tolerance, however much the point might tend to one side. For myself, I am closer to the preserving side—that is, the side that would preserve the Gelvins. To be sure, I would preserve plenty of land as well. My own margin of tolerance would not include some faceless corporation 'responsible' to a hundred thousand stockholders, making a crater you could see from the moon. Nor would it

include visiting exploiters—here in the seventies, gone in the
eighties—with some pipe and some skyscrapers left behind.
But I, as noted, am out of sync with the day. Is it midnight?
Is it morning? Is it late afternoon? Where on earth could the
Gelvins be?"

The hum of Stanley's Aeronca Champion at last comes into
the sky. He goes overhead with the wind, turns, lands, and
when he cuts the engine I am under the wing. "I've been
wondering what time it is," I tell him.

"What time do you think it is?"

"You said you were coming soon after eight in the morning.
I suppose it is eight-fifteen."

Stanley smiles and withdraws his pocket watch. "The aircraft inspector showed up this morning. We didn't know he
was coming. The time is three in the afternoon. Not a whole
lot left of the day."

At the cut, Stanley shows disappointment with the velocity
of the water as it comes through the pipe, falls to the plate,
and races on through the box. It lacks power, he says, to
move the material at the rate it should be moved. If a guy
could expand the intake end of the pipe, where it sticks into
the reservoir, the pipe would deliver more water. "Without a
funnel effect, only so much will run in there. If a guy could
make something like a funnel . . ." What is needed, as is so
often the case, for thousands of purposes in Alaska, is a fifty-
five-gallon drum. There are several near the wanigan, and Ed
goes to get one while Stanley, with the Cat, opens the dam
and lowers the reservoir enough to expose the pipe. With his
torch, Ed cuts out the top and bottom of the drum and slits
it down the side. At one end of the slit he pries the walls of
the drum apart, making a V-shaped gap, which he fills in
with scraps of steel. Attached—welded to the pipe—the new
end flares like the bell of a trumpet, doubling the intake.
Funnel effect.

A fifty-five-gallon steel drum is thirty-four and three-quarters inches high and twenty-three inches in diameter, and is sometimes called the Alaska State Flower. Hundreds of them lie around wherever people have settled. I once considered them ugly. They seemed disappointing, somehow, and I wished they would go away. There is a change that affects what one sees here. Just as on a wilderness trip a change occurs after a time and you cross a line into another world, a change occurs with these drums. Gradually, they become tolerable, and then more and more attractive. Eventually, they almost bloom. Fifty-five-gallon drums are used as rain barrels, roof jacks, bathtubs, fish smokers, dog pots, doghouses. They are testing basins for outboard motors. They are the honeypots of biffies, the floats of rafts. A threat has been made to use one as a bomb. Dick Cook, who despises aircraft of all types, told a helicopter pilot he would shoot at him if he ever came near his home. The pilot has warned Cook that if he so much as points a rifle at the chopper the pilot will fill a fifty-five-gallon drum with water and drop it on the roof of Cook's cabin. Fifty-five-gallon drums make heat stoves, cookstoves, flower planters, bearproof caches, wood boxes, well casings, watering troughs, culverts, runway markers, water tanks, solar showers. They are used as rollers for moving cabins, rollers to smooth snow or dirt. Sliced on the diagonal, they are the bodies of wheelbarrows. Scavenged everywhere, they are looked upon as gold.

With the dam resealed and the reservoir again full, Stanley, in the D9, lowers the blade into the cut and moves onto the slick plate a dark, high pyramid of gravel and sand. Ed opens the valve. Water thunders from the pipe, crashes onto the plate, seemingly melts the material, and drives it through the box. The lighter gravels roar along. The boulders bounce like balls. Some are so big they stick, attracting piles of gravel behind them, deflecting curtains of water into the air. Ed, with a rock rake, sends them tumbling on their way. To make the rake, he welded a bent reinforcing rod to a strut from his damaged plane. Stanley shuttles the big Cat back and forth from the top to the bottom of the box, now adding material to the slick plate, now clanking down to the lower end to doze aside the growing heap of tailings. A year in preparation, they are finally mining gold. Stanley is all pessimism, pondering the economics of the Cat. "It's in motion five times as much as it should be," he shouts as he goes by. He likes even less the proximity of the bedrock ("That shallow ground ain't worth a damn"), and he is down on the volume of the stream ("Another two weeks and we won't have enough water").

Ed, on the other hand, is obviously pleased. He grins as he works with his strut. "It's an odd way to make a living," he comments. "Just as it was for the old-timers. In winter, they'd go down in a frozen drift and shovel up gravel in the dark. They'd sluice in the summer, and then head into town with their poke, and some slick would come along and take it away. The same sort of thing happens now—to people coming off the North Slope."

At the end of the day, Stanley scoops a dark concentrate from the box. He puts it in a pan, partly submerges it, and swirls away the sand. Gradually, the pan's bottom begins to sparkle like a river under sun—flashing pinpoints, flickerings of yellow. Counting thirty-eight, thirty-nine, forty flecks of gold.

"Gold is like farming to me," Ed remarks. "One year, you don't have enough water. Another year, the Cat breaks down. You put more money in the ground than you ever take out. But I like the creeks. I like being out here in the country."

Stanley looks up from the pan. He says, "It cost fifty thousand dollars to get to this point. I'm sure glad to see that gold."

❲ The last time I went through the country was in the winter, 1977, and a speakeasy had risen in Eagle. A large building by regional standards, it had blank walls on three sides and, around

back, a single window that was the size of a hand mirror. A
naked light bulb was outside the window, and, close by, there
was a complicated foyer, wherein arrivals were processed
through a double set of heavily hardwared doors. Stools and
benches, rough spruce floor. A hundred-dollar bill had been
inlaid in the bar. The first high school in Eagle's history had
also been established, but the two teachers who had been sent
to do the job had discovered an unusual P.-T.A., and had
already announced their resignations, explaining privately that
"picking on people" seemed to be Eagle's "winter sport." I saw
a sled being pulled by an Irish setter, another by a mongrel
collie, a third by a pedigreed scottie. Daniel Boone's descendant Jack Boone had at last set foot in the wild, taking a daughter down the river in summer and hiking in to Kneeland and
Cook's. A geologist, about then, had been killed by a black bear
up in Potts' trapping land between Eagle and the Charley
River. He was using a magnetometer and could therefore carry
no additional metal. A partner heard his distant screams and
hurried to help him, but found him dead and partly eaten. Fur
prices were up—up, for example, to four hundred and fifty for
a top-grade lynx. Sarge Waller went out and got himself a
top-grade lynx. A good marten was bringing a hundred and ten
dollars. It was something of a trapping-world bonanza. When
Jimmy Carter was elected, Horace (Junior) Biederman stepped
out of his cabin into the snow with his Remington 12-gauge
pump shotgun and blasted three holes in the air. He had been
listening to KFAR. He wished there were some way to let the
new President know that the Indians of Eagle were for him—
all the Hungwitchin, the whole Village, en bloc. The white
City, with few exceptions, went the opposite way. Some
months earlier, at a community fête, Junior attacked Mike
Potts with a club, and was himself subdued by Constable
Whitaker, who was wearing a lead-filled glove. Now Junior had
circulated a petition to the effect that Eagle did not require and
therefore could ill afford a constable, and Whitaker was leaving

town. Potts had been belatedly arrested by Alaska Fish and Game for failing to travel a hundred and fifty miles to submit, as the law requires, the skin of the grizzly that came close to killing Oddball. No one knew, for sure, who had turned Potts in. Viola Goggans was gone. Jim Dungan, after an at last successful operation on his leg, was away, working again for G.S.I. Michael David was on the North Slope.

The Hungwitchin had written to the Episcopal Diocese of Alaska asking for a minister, and the church had sent John Four Bear and his wife, Sandi. He is a ruggedly handsome man with a wide, strong build, and is only twenty-eight. He holds his services in the small drafty church in the Village, with its wooden benches and its rusted barrel stove, and he turns it into a cathedral. Danny David, Edward David, Isaac Juneby, Archie Juneby, Benny Juneby, Adeline Potts, Sonny Potts, Sara Biederman read together from the Book of Common Prayer. Firelight shows through a hole in the stove. In a congregation of thirty, perhaps a third are white—a fresh counterbalance for the Eagle Bible Chapel. John Four Bear has some regrets for the Indians of Alaska. He wishes that in their history they had chosen to resist the invader. He wishes they had a more compelling affection for their own culture and would not allow themselves to be bought white. John is a full-blooded Hunkpapa Sioux, who comes from Standing Rock, South Dakota. It is said of him in the Village, "He is the smartest Indian in Eagle, and he has to be a Sioux."

"I did not come here like a white missionary to rescue the heathen from the clutches of the Devil," he told me. "I came here to tell the word of God, and if they don't want to hear it that is up to them. It took some time, but the Village people have at last put a claim on me. They have said, 'This is our preacher.' When they said it a third time, I knew they meant it. I think I can help them some in the city. At least, I can deal with the white man on his own terms—which is not difficult in Eagle."

In a small cabin on the Seventymile River, I had a long talk
with Brad Snow—nothing much to do, with time on our
hands, but work out the fate of Alaska. He agreed that it is
sheer foolishness to approach Alaska in terms of the patterned
traditions of the Lower Forty-eight, and that this basic consideration—Alaska seen as a largely different country—should be
Square One, should be the beginning of any plan made for
Alaska by the federal government. Where this is not the case
at present, the government should be urged to go back to
Square One. In the society as a whole, there is an elemental
need for a frontier outlet, for a pioneer place to go—important
even to those who do not go there. People are mentioning
outer space as, in this respect, all we have left. All we have left
is Alaska, which, on the individual level, and by virtue of its
climate, will always screen its own, and will not be overrun. If
I were writing the ticket, I would say that anyone at all is free
to build a cabin on any federal land in the United States that
is at least a hundred miles from the nearest town of ten thousand or more—the sole restriction being that you can't carry
in materials for walls or roofs or floors. Brad said he appreciated
the thought but that specific numbers and written restrictions
—however few or well-intentioned they might be—were
anathema to him.

Mike and Adeline Potts were expecting a baby. Jack Boone's
neighbor Jack Greene, worrying about the possible collapse of
the economy, was investing his savings in gold. The Gelvins'
D9 Cat, meanwhile, was collecting snow in the mountains.
They planned to bring it out. It had made two cuts, and when
the hundreds of tons of gravel had passed through the box the
cleanup both times was disappointing. They had hoped for
coarse gold, but were getting only fine. Mining money, they
were not quite making it. They had no intention of quitting
the claims. They would keep them, and bide their time, and
watch the price of gold. Meanwhile, taking into account the
current price, the cost of equipment and fuel, the amount of

water, the quantity of ground to be moved, they folded their mountain show. A helicopter, taking off in Circle, tilted crazily and flew sidewise into Frank Warren's Citabria. The Gelvins —opportunistic—bought it from the insurance company for seven thousand dollars. They were fixing it to sell for fourteen. On an ice-fishing trip, Ed and Ginny, in their own repaired Citabria, were forced down by weather and, in "a squirrelly wind," smashed into a stand of trees. Well over a hundred miles north of home, they camped for three days and nights, wreckbound. When they did not come back, Frank Warren went out and found them. They meant to salvage that plane, too.

Of the people I had seen coming into the country—particularly the young ones arriving in summer to seek the mountains and the river—the one I remembered best was an immense young man in a blue parka and blue rain pants and a wide-brimmed black hat, who walked up to me, total stranger, and said he had heard I had maps. Sure, I told him, and I took him into my cabin to a topographical stack. His beard was about a foot deep and his eyes were diamond blue. He was from southern California, he said, and he had "overwintered" down in southeastern Alaska—a preliminary and orientational kind of shakedown experience—and now he was ready for the Yukon. No one much remembered him in the winter. Not even John Borg had an idea where he might be. He was just one of the annual dozens who come into town preparing to try the country. He had been to the Eagle General Store, where he bought a standard gold pan and a length of gold nylon rope, which was coiled around his shoulder. He told me he had talked with someone named Cook and found him prickly. He took a close long look at the maps. He was as amiable as he seemed determined, and his manner suggested momentum—suggested that this was his time and his place and, from Doyon, Ltd., to the federal government, whoever didn't like it could step out of the way. Stuck in the band of his big black hat were a tall eagle feather and the dogtooth jaw of a salmon. I asked him where he meant to go.

"Down the river," he said. "I'll be living on the Yukon and getting my skills together."

I wished him heartfelt luck and felt in my heart he would need it. I said my name, and shook his hand, and he said his. He said, "My name is River Wind."

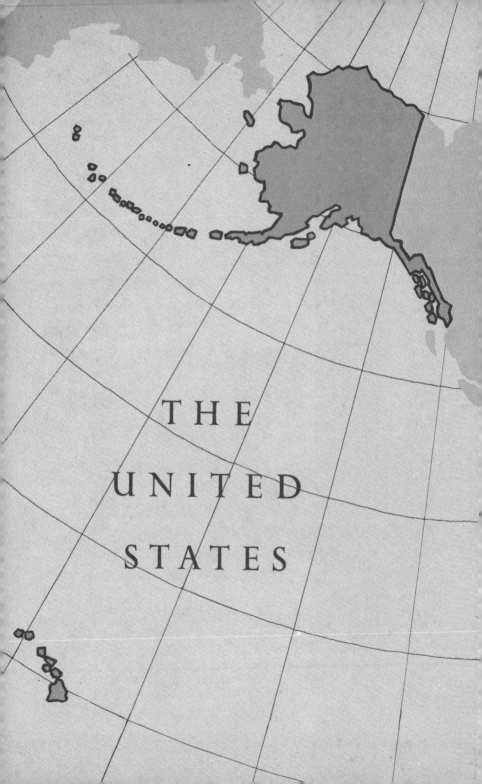

THE

UNITED

STATES